STEVEN MOORE
DIE FAKTEN HINTER
DER FÄLSCHUNG

STEVEN MOORE
DIE FAKTEN HINTER DER FÄLSCHUNG

EIN FÜHRER DURCH WILLIAM GADDIS' ROMAN
»DIE FÄLSCHUNG DER WELT«

Deutsch von Klaus Modick

ZWEITAUSENDEINS

Deutsche Erstausgabe.
1. Auflage, November 1998.
Die Originalausgabe erschien 1982 unter dem Titel
»A Reader's Guide to William Gaddis's The Recognitions«
bei der University of Nebraska Press
und wurde für die vorliegende deutsche Ausgabe
neu durchgesehen und aktualisiert.
Copyright © 1998 für die deutsche Übersetzung
bei Zweitausendeins, Postfach, D-60381 Frankfurt am Main.

Alle Rechte vorbehalten, insbesondere das Recht der mechanischen,
elektronischen oder fotografischen Vervielfältigung, der Einspeicherung
und Verarbeitung in elektronischen Systemen, des Nachdrucks
in Zeitschriften oder Zeitungen, des öffentlichen Vortrags, der Verfilmung
oder Dramatisierung, der Übertragung durch Rundfunk, Fernsehen oder Video,
auch einzelner Text- und Bildteile. Der gewerbliche Weiterverkauf
und der gewerbliche Verleih von Büchern, Platten, Videos oder anderen Sachen
aus der Zweitausendeins-Produktion bedürfen in jedem Fall
der schriftlichen Genehmigung durch die Geschäftsleitung
vom Zweitausendeins Versand in Frankfurt.

Redaktion Marcus Ingendaay.
Einbandgestaltung Bernd Leberfinger, Möttingen.
Satz und Herstellung Dieter Kohler GmbH, Nördlingen.
Druck Buch- und Offsetdruckerei Wagner GmbH, Nördlingen.
Gebunden bei G. Lachenmaier, Reutlingen.
Printed in Germany.

Dieses Buch gibt es nur bei Zweitausendeins im Versand, Postfach,
D-60381 Frankfurt am Main, Telefon 01805-23 2001 oder 069-420 8000,
Fax 01805-24 2001 oder 069-417089. Internet www.zweitausendeins.de,
E-Mail info@zweitausendeins.de. Oder in den Zweitausendeins-Läden
in Berlin, Düsseldorf, Essen, Frankfurt, Freiburg, 2x in Hamburg,
in Köln, Mannheim, München, Nürnberg, Saarbrücken, Stuttgart.

In der Schweiz über buch 2000,
Postfach 89, CH-8910 Affoltern a. A.

ISBN 3-86150-281-X

Inhalt

Vorwort
7
Einführung
9
Inhaltsübersicht
35
Kurzer Hinweis zu den Anmerkungen
57

A Reader's Guide to William Gaddis's »The Recognitions«
61
Preface to Revised Edition
63
Annotations
65
Abbreviated Sources and References
285

Vorwort

Schon beim ersten Blick in Gaddis' *Fälschung der Welt* wußte ich, daß ich eine literarische Herausforderung jener Art gefunden hatte, die in den letzten Jahren immer seltener geworden ist. Wie jedesmal, wenn ich auf anregende Literatur stoße, fragte ich mich, wie Literaturkritik und Wissenschaft das Werk aufgenommen hatten, rechnete mit Bergen an Material und wunderte mich insgeheim, wie mir ein solches Riesenwerk hatte entgehen können. Zu meiner Bestürzung stieß ich allerdings nicht auf Berge, sondern auf Maulwurfshügel – und das 1975, immerhin zwanzig Jahre nach Erscheinen des Buchs. Offenbar hatte der Roman wie eine Insel im Strom der amerikanischen Literatur gelegen, war wohl einige wenige Male umschifft worden, aber letztlich ein weißer Fleck auf der Landkarte geblieben. Da ich mich von der akademischen Forschung im Stich gelassen fühlte, begann ich, durchaus zu meinem eigenen Vergnügen, mit der Niederschrift jenes Buchs, das schon längst hätte geschrieben werden müssen.
Der erste Schritt im Umgang mit einem Werk, das offensichtlich von hochgelehrten Bezügen nur so strotzt, bestand meiner Meinung nach logischerweise darin, es zu kommentieren – die Insel sozusagen zu kartieren. Dieser Kommentar begann als eine Art Hobby und entwickelte sich nach und nach zu einer regelrechten Obsession, welche ich (schon meiner Gesundheit zuliebe) allein durch die Lektüre von P. G. Wodehouse halbwegs in Grenzen halten konnte. Erst die Entdeckung, welche Bücher William Gaddis persönlich als Quellen benutzt hatte, brachte die Anmerkungen auf ihren gegenwärtigen Stand. Lediglich drei oder vier Quellen sperrten sich trotz intensiver Recherche der Identifikation. (Eine ähnliche Erfahrung machte Robert Minkoff mit Ganssenios *Vita Dominicii Ordinis Praedicatorum Fundatoris* – das Buch war und blieb ein unlösbares Rätsel.) Peter W. Koenig, der für seine Dissertation beneidenswerterweise die Möglichkeit hatte, Gaddis' Notizen und Manuskripte auszuwerten, förderte die Bücher von Graves, Lang, Lethaby, Phythian-Adams, Smith und de Rougemont *(The Devil's Share)* zutage. Minkoff, der während der Recherche für seine Dissertation direkten Kontakt zu William Gaddis hatte, brachte de Rougemonts *Love in*

the Western World ein; die übrigen Quellen, abgesehen von denen, die in der *Fälschung der Welt* direkt genannt werden, entdeckte ich im Verlauf meiner Nachforschungen, manche durch schlichtes Kombinieren, andere durch pure Fügung. (Die Leser werden deshalb herzlich gebeten, Ergänzungen oder Korrekturen zu den Anmerkungen über die Verlagsanschrift an mich zu schicken.)

Diese Untersuchung legt womöglich allzu großen Nachdruck auf das humanistische Erbe in der *Fälschung der Welt*, und das zu Lasten seiner übergeordneten Themen und Motive. Tatsächlich könnte man den Eindruck gewinnen, es sei meine Absicht gewesen, das Buch lediglich auseinanderzunehmen, um seine wahren Geheimnisses dann unbeachtet links liegen zu lassen. Tatsächlich bot sich mir im Rahmen der vorliegenden Untersuchung einfach nicht der Raum für die weit wichtigere Aufgabe, den Roman im Licht der durch die Detailuntersuchungen gewonnenen Informationen zu rekonstituieren. In der Einleitung werden zwar einige grundlegende Erkenntnisse angerissen, doch eine umfassende Darstellung der *Fälschung* wäre am Ende kaum kürzer geworden als der Roman selbst. Entsprechend verstehe ich das vorliegende Buch weniger als vollständige Analyse denn als Materialsammlung für eine solche Analyse.

Mr. Gaddis hat es höflich abgelehnt, mich bei meinen Nachforschungen zu unterstützen. Ihn interessiert die kritische Aufnahme seines Werks nur am Rande, lieber konzentriert er sich auf seine eigentliche Arbeit. Trotzdem gebührt ihm unter allen, denen ich Dank schulde, der erste Platz, denn er hat einen Roman geschrieben, der mich bis heute mehr fasziniert als jedes andere literarische Werk unserer Zeit.

Danken möchte ich auch Mr. Mory Cloud und Mrs. Judy Newall, die parallel zur *Fälschung* eine frühe Fassung der Anmerkungen gelesen und Verbesserungsvorschläge gemacht haben; meinen Übersetzern, die am Ende des Quellenverzeichnisses aufgelistet sind; Professor Frank Baldanza, der mir ein Exemplar von Leverences »Gaddis Anagnorisis« beschafft hat; Mr. Richard Flowers vom Museum of Modern Art für Informationen zu Picassos Gemälde *Nächtlicher Fischzug in Antibes*; Miss Victoria Utemark, die relevante Teile von Eudels *Trucs et truqueurs* übersetzt hat; Mr. Heidi Yamamoto für die Übersetzung von Yokichi Miuamotos Artikel über Gaddis; Dr. Robert Brownson für ein informatives Kamingespräch über *Die Fälschung der Welt*, dem ich unschätzbare Hinweise zur Entschlüsselung problematischer Bezüge verdanke; und nicht zuletzt meinem Vater, ohne dessen finanzielle Unterstützung ich diese Arbeit kaum in vertretbarer Zeit hätte abschließen können.

Einführung

Gleich zu Anfang eines Trivialromans aus den späten fünfziger Jahren (Titel: *Epitaph for a Tramp*), durchsucht ein Detektiv die Wohnung eines College-Studenten in Greenwich Village. In der Schreibmaschine steckt eine Seite eines Literaturreferats. Der neugierige Detektiv nimmt das Blatt heraus und liest:
»Und somit komme ich zu dem Schluß, daß *Die Fälschung der Welt* von William Gaddis nicht nur der beste amerikanische Roman unserer Epoche ist, sondern vielleicht sogar die bedeutendste Einzelpublikation innerhalb der amerikanischen Belletristik seit *Moby Dick*, handelt es sich doch um ein Buch, dessen weitgespannter Blickwinkel, dessen Komik und tiefsinniger Beziehungsreichtum derart ...«[1]
Dieses Zitat aus einem Trivial-Thriller mag als merkwürdiger Auftakt in der Auseinandersetzung mit dem vielleicht bedeutendsten amerikanischen Roman seit *Moby Dick* erscheinen, doch es markiert einen kuriosen Punkt hinsichtlich der literarischen Reputation der *Fälschung der Welt*: daß nämlich das stärkste Echo fast immer aus dem literarischen Abseits kam – wie dem eben erwähnten Groschenroman oder jener mysteriösen Rezension eines gewissen Jack Green in einem handvervielfältigten *newspaper*. Insgesamt sind es nicht mehr als eine Handvoll Artikel in zumeist obskuren Zeitschriften sowie einige Bücher fernab des akademischen Bereichs. Es gab sogar einmal einen kleinen Club in Cleveland, der sich ausschließlich zu dem Zweck versammelte, die *Fälschung der Welt* zu analysieren. Skandalöserweise wird der Roman von vielen immer noch als »Kultbuch« abqualifiziert, als ob seine Bedeutung sich lediglich einer kleinen Gruppe literarischer Exzentriker mit ausgefallenem Geschmack erschlösse, obwohl er doch jedem, der sich ernsthaft für amerikanische Literatur interessiert, etwas zu sagen hat. Bleibt also die Frage: Handelt es sich bei der *Fälschung der Welt* tatsächlich um »die bedeutendste Einzelpublikation innerhalb der amerikanischen Belletristik seit *Moby Dick*?« Wenn nicht, warum sind dann derart extravagante Zuordnungen erfolgt? Und wenn doch, warum hat das Buch nicht die akademische Aufmerksamkeit erregt, die einem solchen Meisterwerk angemessen gewesen wäre? Diese Studie versucht das

Rätsel zu lösen, indem sie darstellt, daß *Die Fälschung der Welt* all das (und noch viel mehr) ist, was der oben erwähnte Literaturstudent über das Buch sagt, und daß nur die enormen Schwierigkeiten, die die Lektüre aufwirft, eine weitergehende Wertschätzung des Romans verhindert haben. Doch erst nach Analyse dieses raffinierten Bezugssystems erweist sich die dem Roman zugewiesene Bedeutung als wirklich gerechtfertigt, und die *Fälschung der Welt* kann endlich als einer der großen Wendepunkte der amerikanischen Literatur etabliert werden, als Resümee der Vergangenheit ebenso wie als neues Erzählmodell, an dem alles Folgende gemessen werden müßte.

Das Ausmaß, in dem der Stammbaum amerikanischer Literatur in der *Fälschung der Welt* verwurzelt ist, zeigt sich bereits in der Vielzahl der Autoren, deren Einfluß auf Gaddis' Roman von Kritikern angemerkt worden ist: Washington Irving, Poe, Emerson, Hawthorne, Melville, James, Frank Norris, T. S. Eliot, H. P. Lovecraft[2], Thoreau, Dos Passos, Nathanael West, Thomas Wolfe, Faulkner, Hemingway und Henry Miller finden Erwähnung.[3] Und die Stellung des Buchs innerhalb der Entwicklung der zeitgenössischen amerikanischen Literatur ist von John Aldridge hinlänglich zusammengefaßt worden:

> Wie bei allem, was grundsätzlich neu ist, dauerte es eine ganze Weile, bis das Publikum soweit war, die *Fälschung der Welt* zu akzeptieren. Das Problem bestand nicht nur in der Länge des Romans, der verwickelten Handlung, sondern auch in der Tatsache, daß selbst das gebildete Lesepublikum der fünfziger Jahre mit der ungewöhnlichen Fiktionsform, des Buches noch nicht vertraut war. Obwohl die Großschriftsteller der klassischen Moderne mittlerweile Anerkennung gefunden hatten, gab es kurioserweise immer noch Widerstand gegen literarische Experimente, ganz besonders, wenn diese von lebenden Autoren unternommen wurden. Die bestimmende Schreibweise in der seriösen Belletristik der fünfziger Jahre war in erster Linie realistisch ausgerichtet, während der fabulierende, von Schwarzem Humor geprägte Roman – dem *Die Fälschung der Welt* später als herausragendes Beispiel zugerechnet wurde – sich noch nicht durchsetzen konnte. Tatsächlich waren die Schriftsteller, die zu den führenden Repräsentanten des Schwarzen Humors wurden, um 1955 entweder völlig unbekannt oder blieben unentdeckt. John Barth veröffentlichte erst 1956 seinen ersten Roman, und Thomas Pynchon, dessen *V.* offenbar zutiefst von Gaddis beeinflußt war, betrat erst 1963 die Szene. Auch John Hawkes, der bereits einige brillante, experimentelle Romane verfaßt hatte, war 1955 noch genau so unbekannt wie William Gaddis, und Hawkes hat bis heute noch nicht die Aufmerksamkeit erlangt, die ihm gebührt. Aber *Die Fälschung der Welt* nahm das Interesse vorweg, das diese und andere Autoren später den parodistischen Tendenzen entgegen-

bringen sollten, dem Einsatz von Fiktionen innerhalb der Fiktion zur Erzeugung von Komik und insbesondere dem Themenkomplex Fälschung und Fabel. Im Verlauf der letzten zwanzig Jahre haben diese Werke einen Kontext geschaffen, der Gaddis' Roman überhaupt erst als Pionierleistung erkennbar macht. Nur mit dieser Leseerfahrung im Kopf läßt sich ermessen, welcher Stellenwert der *Fälschung der Welt* innerhalb der zeitgenössischen Literatur zukommt.[4]

Insofern ist *Die Fälschung der Welt* keine exzentrische Verirrung, keine »grandiose Kuriosität«[5] jenseits der akzeptierten Grenzen der literarischen Tradition Amerikas, sondern ein Vorläufer dessen, was man in späteren Jahren als eine der kreativsten Perioden der amerikanischen Literatur begreifen sollte. Dabei ist der Roman alles andere als ein nationales Produkt. Wie vor ihm Henry James, verfügt Gaddis über eine weltbürgerliche Offenheit, die gesamte westliche Kultur ist seine Domäne. Wie erfolgreich er in dieser Hinsicht gearbeitet hat, wird nicht zuletzt in der Zustimmung sichtbar, welche *Die Fälschung der Welt* in italienischer, spanischer und französischer Übersetzung erfahren hat.
Gleichwohl wird diese Meinung nur von denen geteilt, die sich eine Zeitlang mit dem Roman auseinandergesetzt haben. Tatsächlich wird *Die Fälschung der Welt* immer noch mehr gelobt als gelesen, mehr bestaunt als studiert. Gefragt, ob er die *Fälschung der Welt* kenne, antwortete der Autor John Barth: »Ich kenne das Buch nur von außen. 950 Seiten: länger als *The Sot-Weed Factor*. Man bat mich, die neue Ausgabe zu rezensieren, aber ich lehnte ab, weil ich mir nicht vorstellen kann, daß es in der Literatur etwas gibt, was zugleich der Rede wert ist und mehr als 806 Seiten beansprucht.«[6] Abgesehen von ihrer Schnoddrigkeit dürfte diese Antwort auch für viele Akademiker typisch sein. Insbesondere der Umfang wird häufig als abschreckend bezeichnet.[7] Allerdings hat George Stade schon recht, wenn er bemerkt: »Das Buch scheint doppelt so lang wie seine tausend Seiten, aber nicht, weil es etwa langweilig wäre, was es durchaus nicht ist, sondern weil hier in jedem Satz mehr als sonst mitgeteilt wird.«[8] Auch die zahlreichen Anspielungen haben die Rezeption sicher nicht erleichtert. Vielen Kritikern ist wahrscheinlich klar geworden, daß man nur dann kompetent und verbindlich über den Roman reden kann, wenn man zuvor die große Menge an Quellen, all die literarischen Verweise, Buchtitel, die obskuren historische Bezüge, die religiösen und mythologischen Anspielungen sowie die fremdsprachigen Wendungen verstanden hat – mit einem Wort: wenn man den Roman kommentiert. Hinzu kommt die Tatsache, daß *Die Fälschung der Welt*

nicht immer lieferbar war, was die meisten Kritiker wohl darin bestärkt hat, den Roman zu ignorieren.

Aber diesen Ausflüchten ist längst der Boden entzogen: Das Buch ist zumindest seit 1970 in den USA ständig erhältlich gewesen, und die vorliegende Studie identifiziert und kodifiziert das umfangreiche Quellen- und Referenzmaterial auf leicht zugängliche Weise. Dennoch bleibt *Die Fälschung der Welt* ein schwieriger Text, weshalb sich dieser einführende Essay im folgenden einigen dieser Schwierigkeiten widmen wird.

»Man kann sich des Eindrucks nicht erwehren, daß die Menschen gemeinhin mit falschen Maßstäben messen, Macht, Erfolg und Reichtum für sich anstreben und bei anderen bewundern, die wahren Werte des Lebens aber unterschätzen.« So beginnt Freuds *Das Unbehagen in der Kultur*. *Die Fälschung der Welt* erzählt die Geschichte einer Reihe von Personen, die dieses Unbehagen empfinden, deshalb nach den »wahren Werten des Lebens« suchen (oder auch nicht) und am Ende feststellen müssen, wie schwer es ist, in einer verlogenen Welt zu echten Erkenntnissen (engl. *recognitions*) zu gelangen. Als Sucher erscheint zunächst Wyatt Gwyon, der uns als extrem verunsichert vorgestellt wird, auf andere jedoch wie die ideale Verkörperung eines entwicklungsfähigen Individuums wirkt, dessen Einfluß sich kaum jemand entziehen kann: »Denn er ist ja da, die ganze Zeit über ist er da. Niemand kann etwas tun, ohne daß es auf vertrackte Weise nicht auch mit ihm zu tun hätte, niemand ... reagiert, ohne nicht zugleich mit ihm oder auf ihn zu reagieren ...« (S. 354) Obwohl sich der Roman in erster Linie mit Wyatts Suche nach Authentizität in Kunst und Leben befaßt, präsentiert uns Gaddis etliche Kontrastfiguren, denen Wyatt wie eine unnahbare Lichtgestalt vorkommt, nicht unähnlich dem Engel in Rilkes *Duineser Elegien*. (Zitate aus diesem Werk finden sich überall in der *Fälschung* verstreut.) J. B. Leishman bemerkt darüber:

> Der Engel könnte als Hypostasierung der Idee eines vollkommenen Bewußtseins umschrieben werden – ein Wesen, in dem die Beschränkungen und Widersprüche der menschlichen Natur transzendiert sind, ein Wesen, in dem Geist und Tat, Innerlichkeit und Engagement, Wille und Fähigkeit, Ideal und Wirklichkeit zur Deckung kommen. Er ist sowohl eine Inspiration als auch ein wandelnder Vorwurf, eine Quelle des Trostes, aber auch ein Hort des Schreckens; indem er nämlich auf der Gültigkeit der höchsten Ideale besteht, erinnert er den Menschen ständig daran, wie weit er sich von seiner Bestimmung entfernt hat.[9]

Die eigene Wirkung auf andere mag Wyatt gleichgültig sein, die unendliche Entfernung von seiner eigentlichen Bestimmung aber ist ihm ständig und quälend völlig bewußt. Seine Bemühungen, diese Bestimmung zu verstehen und zu erreichen, gleichen denen des Lesers, der sich entsprechend durch den Text mühen muß. Sowohl Wyatt als auch der Leser sind gezwungen, durch »Berge von Schmutz, Perversion, Falschheit und Langeweile« zu waten,[10] aus denen Gaddis zufolge die Welt besteht. Tony Tanner bringt es auf den Punkt: »Wenn wir uns durch den komplizierten Bau des Romans bewegen und uns dabei gelegentlich verloren, fehl am Platze und desorientiert vorkommen, machen wir lediglich dieselbe Erfahrung wie die Figuren in diesem Buch.«[11] Die Effektivität dieser bewußt eingesetzten, künstlerischen Technik wird jeder Leser nachvollziehen können, der sich bei der ersten Lektüre wie vor dem Kopf gestoßen fühlt. Auktoriale Zurückhaltung trägt gleichfalls zur Verwirrung bei. Gaddis erklärt nichts von dem, was passiert, im Gegenteil, in entscheidenden Momenten verläßt er den Leser sogar, um ihn mit den Unsicherheiten, den bewußten Lügen und der getäuschten Wahrnehmung der Figuren allein zu lassen. Der Leser soll selbst sehen, wie er zurechtkommt, vom Autor ist keine Hilfe zu erwarten. (Gaddis hat diese Technik in seinen folgenden Romanen zur Perfektion entwickelt.)

Am abschreckendsten dürfte schließlich der labyrinthische Plot der *Fälschung* sein. Es bedarf mehrerer intensiver Lektüren, um überhaupt zu begreifen, *was* geschieht (vom Warum ganz zu schweigen). Insofern ist es verständlich, daß bislang den meisten Kommentatoren des Romans im Hinblick auf die Handlungsführung Fehler unterlaufen sind. Der Leser kann sich an die Inhaltsübersicht im folgenden Kapitel halten, doch die Meisterschaft, mit der Gaddis die bizarren Handlungsstränge miteinander verknüpft, läßt sich unmöglich auf knappem Raum darstellen. Wie in allen großen Romanen haucht auch hier das einzigartige Figurenensemble der Erzählung erst Leben und Bedeutung ein. Obwohl alle Charaktere Verkörperungen bestimmter psychologischer oder künstlerischer Haltungen darstellen, meistens in scharfem Kontrast zu Wyatt, sind sie doch alle so lebendig, wie Literatur überhaupt etwas lebendig machen kann. Sie zählen zu den denkwürdigsten Charakteren der modernen Literatur, aber nicht, weil sie etwa besonders bewundernswürdig wären, sondern wegen der Tiefe und Intensität, die Gaddis ihnen verleiht, und wegen seines ausgeprägten Sinns für dramatische Situationen, in denen sich der wahre Charakter der Figuren am besten entfalten kann. Gleichermaßen beeindruckend und effektiv ist die Sprache des Romans, eine Prosa, die an Sir James George Frazers eleganten, belesenen Stil erinnert (und diesen gelegentlich ironisiert), aber auch an seine anthropologisch motivierte Unvoreingenommenheit bei der Katalogisierung der Erscheinungsformen des Irrsinns innerhalb der Moderne – als wären unser Verhalten und unsere Sorgen, allem Fortschritt zum Trotz, immer noch genauso irrational und abergläubisch wie bei unseren primitiven Vorfahren. Mit seiner streckenweise geradezu barocken Erzähltechnik[12] findet Gaddis den angemessenen Ton für seine Reise durch Das Wüste Land; und mit seiner Dialogführung (die später in seinem zweiten dritten Roman *JR* zum fast völligen Verzicht auf narrative Elemente führen sollte) erweist er sich als der größte Dialogschriftsteller in der Geschichte des Romans überhaupt. Sein Humor, ob man ihn nun als »schwarz« oder sonstwie bezeichnen will, kommt überall in dieser erbarmungslosen Gesellschaftssatire zum Vorschein. Trotzdem bleibt ihm, so nochmals Aldridge, »bei aller Kritik darüber, wie sehr wir uns von den Maßgaben der Humanität und Vernunft entfernt haben, das Gefühl für das rein Menschliche erhalten.«[13] Am eindrucksvollsten hingegen ist immer noch die Handlungskonstruktion des Romans und das breitgefächerte, symbolische Netzwerk, das nicht nur den gesamten Plot grundiert, sondern auch den umfangreichen Gebrauch von Quellenmaterial erst rechtfertigt und die verschlungene Handlung zu einem strategisch organisierten Ganzen werden läßt.

Es ist vielleicht eher verwirrend als erhellend, von der Symbolwelt als dem Unbewußten eines Romans zu sprechen, doch im Hinblick auf die *Fälschung der Welt* erweist sich diese These als besonders zutreffend, da die zahlreichen Symbole des Romans eine Projektion von Wyatts Unbewußtem darstellen.[14] Diese Gehalte sind allgegenwärtig, aber verschüttet und wirken als heimliche Motive für Wyatts ungewöhnliche Ansichten und Verhaltensweisen (von seinen exzentrischen Lektüren zu schweigen). »Alles, was ich beobachtet habe«, schrieb Gaddis in seinen Notizen, »habe ich nur wegen seines symbolischen (gleichnishaften) Werts beobachtet. Alles wird meinem Bezugsrahmen eingepaßt: also das genaue Gegenteil von Hemingway. Ich wollte die Situation usw. immer als gleichnishaft auffassen, und ich wollte sie auf eine Weise niederschreiben, daß sich später die notwendige Wirklichkeitstreue wie von selbst ergibt. [...] Im Grunde ist nichts wirklich stichhaltig; jede (Szene) existiert lediglich in ihrer symbolischen Funktion.«[15] Wie in einigen der alchemistischen Traktate, die Wyatt liest und in denen jeder Satz symbolisch interpretiert werden muß, ist vieles, was in der *Fälschung der*

Welt geschieht (und viele der scheinbar willkürlichen Quellen) dem Roman »nur wegen seines symbolischen (gleichnishaften) Werts« eingefügt. Die Identifizierung dieses Bezugssystems macht infolgedessen eine der zentralen Probleme der Romananalyse aus.

Die Identifizierung der von Gaddis benutzten Quellen erleichtert uns diese Aufgabe jedoch ungemein. Diese Quellen zerfallen in zwei Kategorien: 1. Sammlungen ungewöhnlichen, doch für die Struktur und topische Bezüglichkeit relevanten Materials (vgl. Quellenverzeichnis am Ende der Anmerkungen). 2. Untersuchungen, denen zwar auch aussagekräftige Details und anekdotisches Material entnommen wurde, die aber im wesentlichen zum »Unbewußten« beitragen (es, genauer gesagt, erst konstituieren). Graves *Weiße Göttin* und Jungs *Integration der Persönlichkeit*, weniger de Rougemonts Bücher, sind die entscheidenden Bücher, aus denen Gaddis den Schluß zog, daß der moderne Mensch die spirituellen Antriebskräfte für ein sinnvolles Leben verloren hat, ein Schluß, den er mit T. S. Eliot teilt. Um es ganz einfach, wenn nicht gar etwas oberflächlich auszudrücken: Wyatts Bestimmung ist die Integration der Persönlichkeit, die sich nur aus einer Anerkennung *(recognition)* der überlegenen Weißen Göttin ergeben kann.

»Für das Kind«, wußte Gaddis aus C. G. Jungs Studie über Alchemie, »liegt die Anima in der Überlegenheit der Mutter verborgen, die manchmal eine lebenslange, sentimentale Bindung erzeugt und die männliche Entwicklung ernsthaft behindern kann.«[16] Letztlich bedeutet die Konfrontation mit der Anima (der weiblichen Komponente der männlichen Psyche) eine Anerkennung des Emotionalen, Intuitiven, ja sogar des Irrationalen. Robert Graves würde den Zusammenhang so fassen, daß der Mann in einem durch und durch weiblichen Universum existieren muß und deshalb dem Ewig-Weiblichen huldigen sollte, statt mit sterilem, männlichen Intellektualismus dagegen aufzubegehren. Eine detailliertere Untersuchung der Metaphorik des Romans ergäbe ein breitgefächertes Netzwerk weiblicher Symbole, die alle um die psychische Verstörung nach dem frühen Verlust der Mutter kreisen. Die Überwindung des nach Graves sinnenorientierten Matriarchats durch patriarchalische Prinzipien jedenfalls endet für Wyatt in hartnäckigen Schuldgefühlen bezüglich seiner Fälschungen, die in seinen Augen die weibliche Schöpferkraft entehren.

Nacht, Mond, Ozean sind nicht nur zentrale Symbole des Romans, sondern stehen in sowohl in Mythologie als auch Psychologie meist mit dem Unbewußten und Weiblichen in Verbindung. So sind die Nachtszenen in der *Fälschung der Welt* einerseits mit den traditionellen Assoziationen besetzt (Tod, Sünde, Schuld, Schrecken, Verbrechen), jedoch auch, weniger traditionell, mit künstlerischer Arbeit. Wyatt malt nachts, weil ein blauer Sommerhimmel mit künstlerischer Arbeit nicht vereinbar ist. »Das Licht ist viel zu grell, und es ist überall. Gegen dieses Licht kann man nicht anmalen, und man kann es auch nicht neu verteilen, dazu ist es einfach zuviel. Aber genau darauf kommt es beim Malen an, die selektive Illumination einer Fläche ...« (S. 321)

Daß das Licht aus der Dunkelheit kommt, ist ein zentrales Thema in Religion, Mystik und Alchemie, und um dieses Konzept zu verstärken, spielt Gaddis auf eine große Anzahl literarischer Werke an, welche die Nachtseite der Seele oder entsprechende mythologische Verarbeitungen wie den Abstieg in de Hölle thematisieren – letztlich allesamt Metaphern für die Konfrontation mit der Anima, dem Unbewußten. Wie in der folgenden Grafik dargestellt, gibt es zwischen »Nacht« und »Erlösung« zwei Verbindungen. Der eine Weg führt über die künstlerische Schöpfung, der andere über Anima und Hölle.

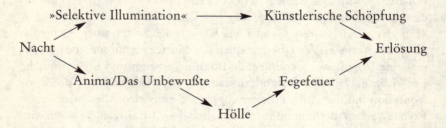

Erleuchtung (Illumination) sucht Wyatt vornehmlich in der Nacht, wo er Erlösung durch authentische Kunst zu finden hofft. Jedoch verwickelt ihn diese Vorliebe in einen Konflikt mit seinem Unbewußten, der nur durch eine Versöhnung mit seiner Mutter gelöst werden kann. Erst nach einer Höllenfahrt (in II. 8) kann er im Fegefeuer Buße tun und so zu einer Art Erlösung gelangen.

Wyatts innere Konflikte werden in der *Fälschung der Welt* in eine konsequente Bildsprache umgesetzt, vornehmlich durch die symbolische Parallelisierung von Reverend Gwyon mit der Sonne und Camilla mit dem Mond. In der ersten Hälfte des Romans glaubt Wyatt, den Konflikt dadurch lösen zu können, daß er zu seinem Vater zurückkehrt und sein Theologiestudium wieder aufnimmt, weil er sich nicht bewußt ist, daß er nicht zu seinem Vater, sondern zu seiner Mutter zurückkehren muß, nicht zu den Sonnenreligionen (des Christentums wie auch des Mithraskultes), die den apollinischen Intellekt repräsentieren, sondern zur dionysischen Gottheit des Mondes, der Weißen Göttin Graves'. Und immer wartet auf ihn der Mond »wie ein Memento kalter Wachsamkeit«. (S. 85) Während das unvollendete Porträt und die byzantinischen Ohrringe als bewußte, unmittelbare Erinnerungen an Camillas Macht über ihren Sohn fungieren (oder vielleicht auch an seine Schuld ihr gegenüber), bilden die umfangreichen Bildprojektionen des lunaren Elements eine unbewußte, symbolische Erinnerung ihrer Anwesenheit.

Im mythologischen Denken wurde die Mondbewegung am Himmel oft mit einer Seereise verglichen. Der dritte große Bildkomplex in der *Fälschung der Welt*, das Meer, schließt bruchlos daran an. Die aus vielen Mythen bekannte nächtliche Seefahrt repräsentiert noch eine weitere Konfrontation mit dem Unbewußten oder der Anima, insofern das Meer ein gängiges Symbol des Weiblichen ist. Gaddis gründet auf diesen archetypischen Symbolismus eines der Hauptthemen des Romans. »Ich glaube, dieses Buch sollte von Seereisen handeln, ihr ganzer Mythos und ihre Metaphorik in moderner Zeit«,[17] vermerkt Gaddis in seinen Notizen, und entsprechend schwer hat Wyatt auf seiner Reise an Mythos und Metaphorik zu tragen. Diese *pelagianische* Atmosphäre wird im gesamten Roman durchgehalten, nicht nur durch die submarine Metaphorik, sondern auch in Dutzenden von Vergleichen zwischen Land und Meer, Tätigkeiten an Land und Tätigkeiten auf dem (in, unter) dem Meer. Indem er absichtlich Land- und Himmels- und Meeressymbolik vermischt, verleiht Gaddis fast allen Aktionen Wyatts (und vieler anderer Charaktere ebenfalls) die Attribute einer Seereise. Obwohl er dreimal den Atlantik überquert, werden interessanterweise die wirklichen Reisen Wyatts nie beschrieben, sondern nur die der anderen Figuren. Auf diese Weise wird der Roman zur Geschichte eines Psychotrips – wie bei Peer Gynt, Odysseus, dem Fliegenden Holländer oder dem Ewigen Juden. Faust steigt ins »Reich der Mütter« hinab wie Dante, Christus und Orpheus in die Hölle – zum unbewußten, aber alles dominierenden Mittelpunkt der Psyche.

Die symbolischen Entsprechungen des Nacht-Mond-Ozean-Komplexes gruppieren sich alle um die Auseinandersetzung mit der Großen Mutter.[18] Doch handelt es sich in der *Fälschung der Welt* nicht nur um die Geschichte einer Figur mit Mutterkomplex. Dieser Konflikt und seine Lösung bilden vielmehr das eigentliche Hindernis in einer grundsätzlichen

Auseinandersetzung um die Integration der Persönlichkeit. Und hier stoßen wir auf die Grundmetapher des gesamten Romans, nämlich der des *opus alchymicum*.

Nach einer ersten Lektüre der *Fälschung* wird man das Thema Alchemie wohl dem breiten Spektrum der Geheimwissenschaften zurechnen, das den gesamten Roman durchzieht, und womöglich rasch wieder vergessen. An die lange Passage über Alchemie auf den Seiten 177–79 mag man sich vage erinnern, aber den wenigstens Lesern würde daran etwas Besonderes auffallen. Wenn man jedoch das innertextliche Bezugssystem aufgedeckt und Gaddis' Quellen entschlüsselt hat, wird sogleich offenbar, daß Alchemie in diesem schwierigen Werk eine zentrale Funktion zukommt, sowohl für die Zusammenführung der symbolischen Elemente und des referentiellen Materials als auch für die Herstellung eines spirituellen Subtexts, der die äußere Handlung ergänzt und plausibilisiert.

Daß sich die Alchemisten mit Wichtigerem beschäftigten als nur mit der Suche nach dem Stein der Weisen, der einfache Materie in Gold verwandelt, ist mittlerweile gesicherte Erkenntnis, vor allem durch die umfangreichen Forschungen des Schweizer Tiefenpsychologen Carl G. Jung.[19] Natürlich hat es eine große Anzahl verwirrter Geister gegeben, die ihr Leben und ihr Vermögen im Laboratorium damit verschwendeten, genau dies zu tun, aber mit seinen Analysen der alchemistischen Texte hat Jung nachgewiesen, daß Alchemie tatsächlich eher eine Art (häretischer) christlicher Mystik war. Wie die *Geistlichen Übungen* Loyolas (S. 448), waren auch die alchemistischen Verfahren weniger chemischer als meditativer Natur, welche oftmals die Grenzen des nach christlicher Vorstellung Erlaubten weit hinter sich ließen. Aus diesem Grund zeigt Gaddis auch wenig Respekt vor der modernen Naturwissenschaft, hat sie sich doch von ihrer Herkunft, der religiösen und philosophischen Spekulationen, längst losgesagt. Die Alchemisten glaubten noch, daß Christus zwar die Menschheit, nicht jedoch die Natur erlöst habe. Und auf ihre demütige Art (und der echte Alchemist war stets demütig), trachteten sie danach, das Werk Christi durch der Erlösung der Natur zu vervollständigen. Die moderne Naturwissenschaft verwarf später diese Anstrengungen als irrelevant für eine »exakte« Wissenschaft, konnte sie jedoch nie durch neue Werte oder Moralvorstellungen ersetzen, was zu den bekannten »geistfernen« Experimenten führte, die Gaddis immer wieder als abschreckende Beispiele erwähnt.

Jung entdeckte eine Parallele zwischen alchemistischen Verfahren und dem, was er den »Prozeß der Individuation« nennt (S. 147), und genau unter diesem Blickwinkel bringt Gaddis die alchemistische Tradition ins Spiel. »Was die Symbole der Alchemie ausdrücken, ist nichts anderes als das gesamte Problem der Persönlichkeitsentwicklung [...] der sogenannte Individuations-Prozeß«, schreibt Jung in *Psychologie und Alchemie*, und Gaddis entdeckte in der Alchemie eine nützliche (wenn auch verborgene) Metapher für Wyatts persönliche Entwicklung. Letztlich ist *Die Fälschung der Welt* der Bericht über eine persönliche Integration inmitten kollektiver Desintegration, über das Zu-sich-selbst-Kommen eines Individuums in einer sich auflösenden Gesellschaft. Und genauso, wie Gaddis die apokalyptische Tradition[20] nutzte, um den allgemeinen Zerfall zu beschreiben, wählte er die Alchemie als engste Parallele zur persönlichen Integration.

Das Motiv der Alchemie wird bereits auf der ersten Seite des Romans angeschlagen.[21] Die Verse aus dem zweiten Teil von Goethes *Faust* stammen aus der Laboratoriums-Szene, in der Wagner einen Homunculus erschafft. Dieser erste von vielen Bezügen auf den Fauststoff ist aus mancherlei Gründen bedeutsam, nicht zuletzt wegen Jungs Interpretation des *Faust* als »letztes und größtes Werk der Alchemie«.[22] In seiner Studie *Goethe the Alchemist* stimmt Ronald D. Gray nur teilweise mit Jung überein, daß es sich bei *Faust II* um eine »poetische Darstellung alchemistischer Tätigkeit« handele,[23] doch kam Gaddis diese Konzeption offenbar entgegen, um Wyatt als faustischen Menschen anlegen zu können.

Auf den ersten hundert Seiten des Romans tauchen noch eine ganze Anzahl weiterer Bezüge zur Alchemie auf. Alchemie gehört zu den vielen Themen, mit denen Reverend Gwyon seinen Sohn vertraut macht (S. 41). Auch einige der Bücher auf dem Schreibtisch des Reverends sind entweder alchemistische Traktate oder solche Werke, die Jung im Zusammenhang mit Alchemie zitiert. I.2 schließt mit einer Andeutung, daß Wyatt auf den Spuren des Alchemisten Raymond Lully wandern wird.[24] (S. 107) Die wichtigsten Bezugspunkte zur Alchemie finden sich jedoch in I.3. Mit Wyatts Teufelspakt beginnt auch seine Karriere als Alchemist.

Daß Wyatt sich während dieses Kapitels intensiv mit Alchemie beschäftigt, läßt sich aus seiner Lektüre schließen. Unter den alchemistischen Werken in seiner Bibliothek befinden sich Boyles Streitschrift *The Sceptical Chemist*, *La Chimie au moyen âge*, die *Turba Philosophorum*, *The Secret of the Golden Flower*, *Problems of Mysticism and Its Symbolism*,

Prometheus und Epimetheus, und die *Cantilena Riplaei.* Daß er das Thema auch mit Otto (dem »Wagner« des faustischen Wyatt) diskutiert hat, wird deutlich, wenn Otto Wyatts Bemerkungen nachredet:

> —Ja aber, ich meine, zum Beispiel heute haben wir uns über Alchemie unterhalten und all die Geheimnisse, hinter denen man immer schon, also die Erlösung der Materie, daß es nicht einfach nur Goldmacherei ist, also einfach um echtes Gold herzustellen, sondern daß die Materie ... Die Materie, sagte er, die Materie war gewissermaßen der einzige große Luxus, den sich der Mensch erlaubt hat, und daß die Materie insofern, ich meine die Erlösung von der ... (S. 175)[25]

Zwei Seiten später folgt sogar eine Liste der alchemistischen Pioniere, obwohl sogleich deutlich wird, daß Otto vom spirituellen Wesen der Alchemie praktisch keine Ahnung hat. Ein kurzer Bericht über den Untergang der Alchemie in der modernen, materialistischen Welt schließt mit den Worten: »Sobald sich die Chemie einmal als ihr rechtmäßiger Sohn und Erbe etabliert hatte, war es um die Alchemie geschehen. Vor die Tür gesetzt wie ein trunksüchtiger Vater, erreichten seine gellalten Phantasien immer weniger und immer abgerissenere Fahrende der Einsamkeit.« (S. 179)

Einer dieser Fahrenden ist Wyatt. Daß er seine herkömmlichen Studien zugunsten von Alchemie und Schwarzkunst aufgibt, ähnelt der Haltung Fausts im Eröffnungsmonolog des Dramas. Nach gescheiterter Ehe, in einem unbefriedigenden Beruf, künstlerisch blockiert, von Schuldgefühlen, Depressionen, Alpträumen und Einsamkeit geplagt, befindet sich Wyatt in einem Zustand, der von der Alchemie als *nigredo* bezeichnet wurde. Jung führt aus: »Das *nigredo* oder die Schwärze ist das Anfangsstadium, das entweder schon von Anfang an als Zustand der *prima materia* vorherrscht, des *chaos* oder der *massa confusa*, oder durch die Trennung *(solutio, separatio, divisio, putrefactio)* der Elemente entsteht«. An anderer Stelle vergleicht Jung diesen Zustand mit dem Moment, da der Mensch zum erstenmal seinem eigenen »Schatten« gegenübersteht[26], also den dunklen Elementen des Unbewußten.

> Die Begegnung mit dem Schatten führt zuerst zu einer Totenstarre, einem Stillstand, der moralischen Entscheidungen im Weg steht und Überzeugungen unbrauchbar oder sogar unmöglich macht. Alles erscheint zweifelhaft, weshalb die Alchemisten diesen Zustand *nigredo, tenebrositas, chaos, melancholia* nannten. Es trifft zu, daß das *magnum opus* an diesem Punkt beginnen sollte, da es in der Tat eine nahezu unbeantwortbare Frage ist, wie man in diesem zerrissenen und geteilten Zustand der Wirklichkeit entgegentreten soll.

Diesen Zustand erreicht Wyatt in I.3 – »Verzweiflung als Ausgangspunkt«. (S. 173) Spätestens hier aber beginnt auch der Prozeß der psychischen Selbstreinigung.

Nach I.3 finden sich im weiteren Verlauf des Romans nur noch gelegentliche Anspielungen auf das Thema. Beispielsweise kolportiert Herschel auf Max' Party das Gerücht, Wyatt habe sich mit einem internationalen Fälscherring eingelassen: »In seinem Versteck macht er Gold für seine Auftraggeber, aus abgeschnittenen Fingernägeln und ...« (S. 231) – eine humoristische Anspielung auf die ungewöhnlichen Zutaten, die man in manchen alchemistischen Rezepturen findet. Als Wyatt zum erstenmal auf Basil Valentine trifft, meint er nur: »Irgendwie kommt mir Ihr Name bekannt vor. Ich weiß nur noch nicht woher.« (S. 351) Erst später kann er den Namen einordnen.

> —*Der antimonische Triumphwagen.* Jetzt weiß ich auch, weswegen mir Ihr Name so bekannt vorkam. Basil Valentine, so hieß der Alchemist, der entdeckte, daß sich stibiumhaltiges Futter hervorragend zur Schweinemast eignet. Die Tiere wurden sehr viel fetter dabei. Also lag der Gedanke nahe, das Zeug auch einmal an fastenden Mönchen auszuprobieren. Leider hat keiner von ihnen das Experiment überlebt. (S. 519)

Bereits zwei Seiten zuvor hatte Wyatt sich und Valentine als einen Alchemisten und einen Priester bezeichnet. Eine letzte, direkte Anspielung auf Alchemie findet man in der Partyszene auf Seite 849, wo sich Musik und Zigarettenrauch zu einem »Brodem aus der Giftküche des Alchemisten« verbinden.

Die Funktion der Alchemie im Roman wird in seinen Notizen von Gaddis genau umrissen:

> Zuerst gibt es das Ideal. In diese Ideal bricht die Realität ein, Chaos und Tod im Gefolge. Durch Verschmelzung von Ideal und Realität kommt es zur Wiederauferstehung. *Ergo: Wyatt ist Alchemist,* es gibt keine engere Parallele.[27]

Große Kunst war das Ideal des jungen Wyatt, Recktall Brown verkörpert den Einbruch der Realität. Im »Chaos« vollzieht sich Wyatts Aufstieg als Fälscher, ein Aufstieg, der mit seinem symbolischen Tod auf See in III.4 endet.[28] Wenn wir Wyatt/Stephen zum letztenmal begegnen, wird angedeutet, daß er endlich die richtige Balance zwischen dem »Ideal« und der »Realität« gefunden hat. Die Versöhnung der Extreme, die ihm gelingt, treffen allerdings später in der Gestalt des Schriftstellers Ludy erneut und verstörend aufeinander. Die weißen Vögel, die Ludy von fern als »ideale« Wesen bewundert, machen ihm aus der Nähe angst. (S. 1026; 1076)[29]

Erinnern wir uns noch einmal daran, daß der gemeinsame Nenner sämtlicher Symbole des Romans in der psychomythologischen Auseinandersetzung mit dem Archetypus der Großen Mutter besteht, das heißt mit der Anima. »Während das *nigredo* der Beerdigung andauert, herrscht die Frau«, heißt es in einem anonymen alchemistischen Traktat. Den Alchemisten ging es um die Verbindung des Gegensätzlichen, was oft mit der Verbindung des Weiblichen und Männlichen verglichen worden ist und zu einigen recht schlüpfrigen Bildern geführt hat. Auch die Idee der spirituellen Wiedergeburt war ohne das Bild einer Urmutter nicht zu denken. Ein erhellendes Beispiel findet sich in einem Werk, das auch in der *Fälschung der Welt* zitiert wird, nämlich die *Cantilena Riplaei*. Jung hat das allegorische Gedicht in *Psychologie und Alchemie* folgendermaßen paraphrasiert:

> Es war einmal ein edler König [das *caput corporum*], der keine Nachkommen hatte. Er beklagte seine Unfruchtbarkeit und kam zu dem Schluß, daß ihn ein *defectus originalis* ergriffen habe, obwohl er »unter den Schwingen der Sonne« ohne körperliche Defekte aufgewachsen war. Er sagt mit seinen eigenen Worten: »Ach, ich fürchte und weiß mit Gewißheit, daß ich niemals ein Kind zeugen werde, wenn mir nicht sogleich die Hilfe meiner Art teilhaftig wird. Doch habe ich mit großem Erstaunen durch den Mund Christi vernommen, daß ich aufs neue geboren werden soll.« Er wünscht sich dann, in den Schoß seiner Mutter zurückzukehren und sich dort in *prima materia* aufzulösen. Seine Mutter bestärkt ihn in dieser Absicht und hält ihn von da an unter ihren Röcken verborgen, bis sie ihn in sich wiedergeboren hat. Dann wurde sie schwanger. Während der Schwangerschaft aß sie Pfauenfleisch und trank das Blut des grünen Löwen. Schließlich gebar sie das Kind, das dem Monde glich und sich dann in den Glanz der Sonne verwandelte. Der Sohn wurde wieder König. Der Text sagt: Gott hat Euch die glänzende, gleißende Rüstung der vier Elemente gegeben, und in deren Mitte war die Gekrönte Jungfrau [*Virgo redimita*].« Aus ihr entsprang ein wunderbarer Balsam und ihr Gesicht war von Strahlen umgeben und mit dem Edelstein gekrönt. In ihrem Schoß aber lag der grüne Löwe[30], aus dessen Seite Blut floß. Sie wurde mit einem Diadem gekrönt und als Stern an den höchsten Himmel erhoben. Der König wurde ein großer Triumphator, ein Heiler der Kranken und der Erlöser [*reformator*] aller Sünden.

Das *Rosarium Philosophorum* (S. 61) arbeitet mit einer ganz ähnlichen Allegorie wie die *Cantilena* und die *Turba Philosophorum*. Tatsächlich bieten die meisten der in der *Fälschung der Welt* aufgelisteten alchemistischen Werke in der einen oder anderen Form diese Allegorie oder spielen mit ihrer symbolischen Sprache darauf an. Die Ähnlichkeit zwischen dem alchemistischen Konzept der Wiedergeburt und dem des Christentums ist ebenso offensichtlich wie absichtsvoll.[31] Jung schreibt zum Beispiel über Sir John Ripley (den Autor der *Cantilena*): »Wenn wir uns klarmachen, daß der Autor kein Laie war, sondern ein hochgelehrter Kanonikus, dürfen wir ihm kaum unterstellen, daß er sich nicht der Parallelen mit bestimmten Grundideen des christlichen Dogmas bewußt gewesen sei.« In der Tat finden sich die meisten neutestamentarischen Passagen über die Bedeutung einer spirituellen Wiedergeburt, die in der *Fälschung der Welt* zitiert werden (vor allem diejenigen mit Bezug auf Nikodemus und die Pflicht, »den alten Menschen auszuziehen«[32]) bereits in den alchemistischen Traktaten. Wieder und wieder, ob in Alchemie, Religion, Mythologie oder moderner Psychologie, erkennen wir die Notwendigkeit, zur Mutter zurückzukehren, uns mit dem Weiblichen zu konfrontieren. Gaddis hat zu dieser Konzeption derart viele Bezüge aus den unterschiedlichsten Bereichen aufgetürmt, daß wir bald merken, daß Herschels hingeworfene Bemerkung, bei Wyatts Problemen dürfte es sich »eher um einen Vaterkomplex oder einen Mutterkomplex handeln oder etwas vergleichbar Unanständiges« (S. 231), mehr Wahrheit enthält, als man auf den ersten Blick vermuten würde. Und es ist typisch für Gaddis, daß er diesen Schlüssel zu Wyatts Persönlichkeit unter seitenlangem, törichtem Gerede versteckt, so daß er dem Leser ebenso leicht entgehen kann wie der Juwel, der in Spittelers *Prometheus und Epimetheus* unbeachtet auf der Straße liegt.[33]

Faktisch haben alle Motive, die im Zusammenhang mit der Auseinandersetzung mit der Anima stehen – Nacht, Höllenfahrt, der Mond, das Meer, Seereisen – ihre Entsprechungen in der Symbolsprache der Alchemie. Der Zusammenhang zwischen Nacht und dem *nigredo*-Zustand liegt allein schon aufgrund des Wortes nahe, und es ist nun auch keine Überraschung mehr, daß die *nigredo* (oder *mortificatio*) in den alchemistischen Schriften manchmal mit dem Abstieg in die Hölle verglichen wurde. »Besuche die inneren Erdteile; durchs Destillieren wirst du den verborgenen Stein finden«, lautete ein bekanntes Alchemisten-Motto.[34]

Nach dem männlichen und weiblichen Prinzip waren für die Gegensätze, aus deren Verbindung spirituelles Gold entstehen sollte, die Sonne und der Mond die bekanntesten Symbole. Gaddis führt als Beispiel den Alchemisten Michael Majer an, »der im Golde kleine Sonnenteilchen erblickte, die im Verlauf von Myriaden Umdrehungen der Sonne auf die

Erde geschleudert worden waren, damals, als die Sonne noch fast das Ebenbild Gottes war.« (S. 178) John Leverence weist darauf hin, »daß das grundlegende Versprechen der Alchemie darin besteht, sogar in unedlen Metallen ein goldähnliches Potential zu entdecken«[35] – eine weitere Metapher für den Prozeß allmählicher Vervollkommnung, der ins Königreich Gottes führt, den Aufstieg durch die sieben Himmel der Gnosis,[36] die aristotelische Entelechie, das in Rilkes Engel verkörperte Ideal oder, wie in Jungs Psychologie, den Prozeß der Individuation bzw. die Integration der Persönlichkeit. Entsprechende Eigenschaften wiesen die Alchemisten dem Mond zu; Jung stellt dem männlich-solaren Bewußtsein das weiblich-lunare gegenüber, und es fällt nicht weiter schwer, Wyatts Mond-Sucht zu verstehen:

> Sein Licht ist das milde Licht des Mondes, das die Dinge eher miteinander verschmilzt als sie voneinander zu trennen. Es zeigt die Gegenstände nicht in ihrer erbarmungslosen Härte und Vereinzelung, wie das gleißende Tageslicht, sondern überzieht sie mit einem täuschenden Schimmer von Nähe und Ferne, verwandelt auf wunderbare Weise Kleines in Großes, Hohes in Niedriges, läßt alle Farbe zu einem blassen Dunst verschwimmen und zieht die nächtliche Landschaft zu einer ungeahnten Einheit zusammen. (*MC* 179)

»Aufteilung, Trennung, Desintegration sind die Ursachen der ganzen Misere«, gesteht Wyatt gegen Ende des Romans, nachdem er das lunare Bewußtsein erreicht hat. »Daß jedes Detail immer nur für sich existieren soll, ist das Grundmuster …« (S. 1045 f.) Wyatts Ziel wie auch das der Alchemisten ist die Verschmelzung psychischer Gegensätze, und Gaddis folgt den alchemistischen Autoren, indem er immer wieder auf lunare respektive solare Symbole zurückgreift, aus denen sich Dutzende von Gegensatzpaare ableiten lassen. Sie alle wirken als psychische Kräfte in Wyatt: Reverend Gwyon/Camilla; Sonne/Mond; Sol (Gold)/Luna (Silber); Logos/Eros; Christentum/Heidentum; Bewußtsein (Rationalität)/Unbewußtes (Irrationalität); Trennung/Einheit; Aktivität/Passivität; Gott (König)/Jungfrau (Königin); Tag/Nacht[37] und so weiter. Wyatts Geschichte erzählt von dem Versuch, diese Gegensätze in Einklang zu bringen, und *Die Fälschung der Welt* könnte im Untertitel durchaus heißen: *Mysterium Coniunctionis*.

Ein weiteres, bekanntes Symbol alchemistischer Literatur ist das Meer, das manchmal die *prima materia*[38] symbolisiert, manchmal das *nigredo*, aber stets »das Symbol des kollektiven Unterbewußten darstellt, weil unerforschte Tiefen unter seiner spiegelnden Oberfläche verborgen liegen.«[39] Arisleus, einer der Personen in der dialogischen *Turba Philosophorum*, spricht an anderer Stelle »von seinen Abenteuern mit dem *Rex marinus*, in dessen Königreich nichts gedeiht und nichts hervorgebracht wird, schon gar keine Philosophen, nur Gleiche unter Gleichen, und deshalb gibt es dort auch keine Zeugung.« *(Philosophie und Alchemie)* Dieses Wüste Land des Meeres taucht in alchemistischen Schriften immer wieder auf. In der *Fälschung der Welt* verströmen Künstler- und Intellektuellenkreise, egal ob arriviert oder nicht, jene »pelagische Atmosphäre«. (Es sei daran erinnert, daß auch Faust der Herrscher eines unterseeischen Königreichs ist.) Gleichwohl steht das Meer auch für Reinigung und Erneuerung. Im *Faust* wählt Homunculus das Meer, das die Verbindung zwischen männlich und weiblich repräsentiert, als sein Reich und beendet so seine Suche nach »Substantialität«, wie auch Wyatt, der Homunculus in Gaddis' »aktueller Version« des *Faust*-Stoffs (S. 877), sein Ziel erreicht, indem er bei seiner Konfrontation mit dem Weiblichen symbolisch im Meer ertrinkt.[40]

Schließlich dürfte es nunmehr auch nicht mehr überraschen, daß die Alchemisten, immer auf der Suche nach geeigneten Metaphern, das *opus alchymicum* als Seereise allegorisierten. Dieser Aspekt des Werks wurde als die *peregrinatio* bezeichnet und steht in enger Beziehung zu den Schriften Michael Majers, der sich das *opus* als Wanderung oder Odyssee vorstellte, etwa so wie die Seereise der Argonauten auf der Suche nach dem *aureum vellus* (dem Goldenen Vlies), ein von den Alchemisten sehr geschätztes Motiv, das in den Titeln mancher ihrer Traktate auftaucht.[41] Für Majer wie für Wyatt liegt das Ziel ihrer Reise in der Erlangung psychischer Ganzheit; merkwürdigerweise repräsentiert ausgerechnet Afrika das vierte und letzte Stadium von Majers Reise – jenes Stadium, das Jung dem Unbewußten zuordnet – wie auch Nordafrika der letzte Kontinent ist, den Wyatt besucht.

Wie schon oben erwähnt, zielte das Hauptinteresse der Alchemisten auf Erlösung. Daß sich Gaddis' Helden auf die Alchemie verlegen statt auf das traditionelle Christentum (das ja wesentlich vom Erlösungsgedanken geprägt ist), erscheint auf den ersten Blick vielleicht unnötig obskur. Die zahlreichen kirchenkritischen Bemerkungen, die den Roman wie ein rotes Band durchziehen, lassen allerdings keinen Zweifel an Gaddis' grundsätzlicher Einschätzung, daß die Kirche den Bezug zu ihrer ursprünglichen Bestimmung verloren hat und zu einer Art organisiertem Aberglauben verkommen ist (S. 1099). Insofern ist das Christentum für den religiösen Geist etwa das, was die Chemie für die Alchemie ist, eine moderne Entwicklung ohne jeden spirituellen Wert. Jack Green weist darauf hin, daß in der *Fälschung der Welt* »Naturreligion und Alchemie nicht umsonst dem modernen Christenglauben und der Chemie überlegen sind, verfügen sie doch über einen unvergleichlich dichteren *emotionalen* Gehalt«.[42] Deshalb orientiert sich Wyatt auf der Suche nach Erlösung an der Alchemie und nicht am Christentum.

Ein wichtiger Unterschied zwischen dem christlichen und dem alchemistischen Erlösungsbegriff besteht darin, daß in letzterem »*der Mensch sowohl erlöst werden muß als auch selbst Erlöser ist*«. Jung weiter: »Die erste Formulierung ist christlich, die zweite alchemistisch. Im ersten Fall beansprucht der Mensch für sich die Notwendigkeit, erlöst zu werden, überläßt die Erlösung jedoch ... der autonomen, göttlichen Instanz; im zweiten Fall nimmt der Mensch die Pflicht auf sich, das erlösende *opus* selbst zu vollbringen.« (*Psychologie und Alchemie*) Das erinnert sowohl an die Forderung des Pelagius, die eigene Erlösung selbst in die Hand zu nehmen, als auch an Emersons und Thoreaus Prinzip der Eigenverantwortung, das von Wyatt verkörpert wird (und das Esther als Egoismus mißversteht).[43]

Deshalb auch läßt Basil Valentine einer Figur namens Willie (Gaddis' Alter ego) ausrichten, »daß die Erlösung vom Übel heutzutage so viel von ihrem konkreten Ansatz verloren hat, daß sie als Daseinszweck praktisch ausgedient hat. Was? ... Nein, ich wollte damit nur sagen, der mittelalterliche Mensch war eben noch grundsätzlich von der Existenz einer Seele überzeugt, und nicht nur einer Seele, sondern auch der Notwendigkeit ihrer Erlösung.« (S. 504) Knapper kann man das Thema des Romans nicht zusammenfassen,[44] und in der Alchemie fand er die engste Parallele zum Erlösungswerk. Die säkularisierte Erlösung in der *Fälschung der Welt* nimmt höchst erfolgreich die Form der erlösenden Kraft der Kunst an. Die Liebe einer (oder zu einer) Frau wird bestenfalls als ambivalenter Weg zur Erlösung gesehen, doch die Schaffung authentischer Kunst scheint von solcher Ambivalenz frei zu sein. »Der kreative Akt ist Arbeit des Künstlers an seiner Selbsterlösung«, bemerkt Gaddis in seinen Notizen,[45] und aus diesem Grund erstrahlt die Kunst in der *Fälschung der Welt* auch in einer quasireligiösen Aura.

Jung schreibt, daß die »wahre Alchemie nie ein Geschäft oder eine Karriere darstellte, sondern ein echtes *opus*, das durch beharrliche, aufopferungsvolle Arbeit erreicht wurde«, und die Haltung der Alchemisten zu ihrem Werk entspricht Gaddis zufolge der Haltung des wahren Künstlers zu seiner Kunst. Echte Alchemisten »wurden nicht müde, den

Novizen der Kunst einzuschärfen, daß der Glaube, das Studium der Heiligen Schrift und Rechtschaffenheit die wichtigsten Bestandteile des alchemistischen Prozesses waren«,[46] und Wyatt selbst zitiert das Diktum »Amor perfectissimus«, womit laut Jung der Alchemist Morienus einst seine Adepten auf die richtige Einstellung zu ihrem Werk einschwor. Unter den Künstlern in der *Fälschung der Welt* nehmen außer Wyatt nur noch Stanley und der Meisterfälscher Frank Sinisterra diese Haltung zu ihrer Arbeit ein. Allerdings muß Wyatts Haltung noch genauer differenziert werden. Er ist so sehr davon besessen, den richtigen Geist gegenüber seiner Schöpfung zu entwickeln, daß er zu vergessen scheint, lediglich Fälschungen zu produzieren. In einer vielzitierten Passage prahlt Wyatt damit, wie sehr er zu einem Maler des fünfzehnten Jahrhunderts geworden sei.

> —Das geht so weit, daß ich … es klopft an der Tür, und ich denke, das sind die Goldinspektoren der Gilde, die wissen wollen, ob ich anständiges Material verwende … denn ich … ich bin ein Maler in der flandrischen Gilde, verstehen Sie? Und wenn sie feststellen, daß ich nicht absolutes reines Gold verwende, sondern … dann vernichten sie das betreffende Material, und ich muß Strafe zahlen, weil … alles ist genau vorgeschrieben … dieses Ultramarin etwa, ich muß ihnen dieses venezianische Ultramarin zeigen oder dieses rote Pigment, dieses Ziegelrot aus Flandern … denn ich habe den Gildeeid geleistet, aber nicht für die Kritiker oder die Experten, auch nicht für euch, denn ihr kommt ja nach mir. Dieser Eid hat überhaupt nichts mit euch zu tun, sondern allein mit der Gilde … nur der Gilde bin ich verpflichtet, zu arbeiten mit reinen Materialien und unter den Augen Gottes …[47]

Wyatt betont, welche Bedeutung dem Ausgangsmaterial zukommt, die Verwendung von reinem Gold ist obligatorisch. Auch die Alchemisten hatten vor schlechtem Material gewarnt. »In der Kunst entstehen alle Irrtümer daraus, daß der Mensch nicht mit der rechten Substanz beginnt,« schreibt der Autor des *Rosarium Philosophorum*, und Jung erwähnt den Alchemisten Richardus Anglicus (Todesjahr etwa 1242), der »den ganzen Schmutz, mit dem die Alchemisten arbeiteten, verwarf, als da sind Eierschalen, Haare, das Blut eines rothaarigen Mannes, Eidechsen, Würmer, Kräuter und menschliche Fäkalien. ›Was immer der Mensch säet, das wird er auch ernten. Deshalb wird er Schmutz ernten, wenn er Schmutz säet.‹« Im Licht der alchemistischen Studien besitzt Gold also eine einzigartige Bedeutung, und im Roman wird es oft als Symbol für Authentizität benutzt. Als er das gefälschte Tafelbild von Hieronymus Bosch entdeckt (Valentine hat das Original wieder nach Europa geschickt), verzweifelt

Wyatt: »Mit der Kopie einer Kopie, so fing alles an. Ist das nicht komisch […] Angenommen, das Gold, das ich machen wollte, gibt es gar nicht. Wenn also das, was ich fälschen wollte, nie existiert hat. Wenn ich folglich immer nur … immer nur … (S. 516)
Seine einzige Rechtfertigung, sich auf Fälschungen einzulassen, bestand in der »rechten« Haltung zu seinem Werk und in einer Art »mystischer Einfühlung« in die Maler der von ihm kopierten Bilder, was natürlich seine Magie verliert, wenn er nur noch eine Kopie kopiert. Verständlich seine Erleichterung, als sich herausstellt, daß er doch echte Bosch-Gemälde kopiert hat, denn »Gold macht man immer noch aus Gold«.[48]
In einem seltenen Moment der Selbsterkenntnis sieht sogar Otto im Gold ein Symbol der Echtheit:

> —[…] Und dieses ganze Chaos, die eigenen Gefühle zum Beispiel. Man will Gefühle investieren, aber man kriegt sie einfach nicht mehr hin. Sie sind zwar da, sie kommen sogar an die Oberfläche, aber man erkennt sie nicht wieder, weil sie alle schon anderswo verbraucht wurden, in den Dreck getreten, ausgebeutet, vertan, was weiß ich. Alle Welt verlangt Gefühle von dir, und du bezahlst so gut du kannst. Aber irgendwann kommt jemand, der möchte, daß du in Gold bezahlst, und das kannst du nicht. Du kannst es nicht, du stehst da mit leeren Händen und kannst nicht. (S. 828)

»Wer verlangt denn von dir, daß du mit Gold bezahlst«, fragt Esther zurück, ohne etwas von seiner Beziehung zu Esme zu wissen. Die »Erkenntnis« oder »Anerkenntnis« *(recognition)*, die der amerikanischen Ausgabe seinerzeit den Titel gegeben hat, bezieht sich also auch auf die goldenen Originale, die unter gefälschter Kunst, falscher Religion und, besonders in Ottos Fall, unter falschen Gefühlen verschüttet liegen.
Trotz seines guten Materials, seiner »rechten« Haltung und seinem Streben nach dem Gold der Authentizität, bleibt Wyatt doch ein Fälscher. Alchemisten und Fälscher finden sich in Dantes Hölle in der gleichen *bolgia* wieder, und Wyatts Rationalisierungen schwinden schließlich allesamt unter der seltsamen Macht dahin, die vom Porträt seiner Mutter ausgeht. Als er ihren Tod enthert, wird ihm schließlich klar, daß er seine Fälschungen offenlegen muß, aber als Valentines List ihm diesen Ausweg versperrt und die Gemälde ein Raub der Flammen werden, reist Wyatt nach Spanien, wo er seinen Frieden findet und Stück für Stück seine Ästhetik revidiert.
Die meisten Kommentatoren der *Fälschung der Welt* haben sich über die Funktion der Kunst innerhalb des Romans geäußert; die beste, ausführliche Analyse ist Joseph S. Salemis *To Soar in Atonement: Art as Expiation*

in Gaddis's »The Recognitions«,⁴⁹ und seine Ergebnisse müssen an dieser Stelle nicht wiederholt werden. Aber selbst Professor Salemi hat keine Erklärung für die merkwürdige Tatsache, daß neben Wyatt und Stanley ausgerechnet Frank Sinisterra zu den hochbewußten Künstlerfiguren des Romans zählt, was gleich mehrere Fragen über Gaddis' Glauben an die erlösende Kraft der Kunst aufwirft. Ist Kunst wirklich der Königsweg zur Erlösung, wenn zwei der drei vorgestellten Künstler in Wahrheit Fälscher sind und der dritte ein neurotischer Katholik, der sein Werk schließlich mit dem Leben bezahlt?⁵⁰ Ist der merkwürdige Zustand, in dem sich Wyatt/Stephen am Ende des Romans befindet, wirklich die vielversprechende Erlösung, die den echten Künstler erwartet? William Gaddis' eigenes Künstlerleben spricht da eine ganz andere Sprache. Sein Erstling *Die Fälschung der Welt* jedenfalls, obschon eines der größten Werke des 20. Jahrhunderts, blieb lange Jahre nahezu unbeachtet, so daß er gezwungen war, sich als Lehrer, Werbetexter und Skriptschreiber für Army-Lehrfilme durchzuschlagen – von Erlösung keine Spur.⁵¹

Viel besser sieht genau gesehen im Roman auch nicht aus. Wyatt verabschiedet sich in eine ungewisse Zukunft, Stanley und Sinisterra sterben einen sinnlosen Tod. Eine letzte Parallele aus der Alchemie könnte uns zumindest den Ansatz einer Erklärung liefern. Und zwar berichtet Jung über den Alchemisten Michael Majer, daß dieser sich am Ende seiner *peregrinatio* eingestehen mußte, weder auf Mercurius [den Stein der Weisen] noch den Phoenix [der Unsterblichkeit] gestoßen zu sein, sondern nur auf eine Feder – seine eigene Schreibfeder! Fazit: Die ganze Mühe hat zu nichts weiter geführt als einem Haufen Literatur. (*P&A* 431) Doch anders als die Alchemisten, die in großen Mengen fast unlesbare Schriften hinterließen, die heute selbst als bildhafte Umschreibungen psychischer Vorgänge nur noch geringen Wert haben, bereichert Gaddis mit seinem faszinierenden Riesenwerk, einer *peregrinatio* durch die kulturelle Wüsten der Neuzeit, die Welt beträchtlich. Mehr kann niemand leisten.

Anmerkungen

[1] David Markson, *Epitaph for a Tramp* (New York: Dell 1959), zitiert nach Jack Green, »Fire the Bastards« (Normal, Il: Dalkey Archive Press, 1992) p. 77–78.

[2] Diese neun Autoren, allen voran Lovecraft, werden erwähnt und analysiert in Monique Bouchouk: »Un long voyage sur la Terre Vaine: *Les Reconnaissances* de William Gaddis«. *Caliban* XII (1975), p. 3–15.

[3] Britische und andere europäische Autoren eingeschlossen, kommt Jack Green auf insgesamt »112 Nennungen von 53 verschiedenen Autoren« allein in den Rezensionen

(obwohl davon, man muß es nicht extra betonen, nur ein Bruchteil von Interesse ist); vgl. »Fire the Bastards«, p. 4ff.

4 »The Ongoing Situation« (Rezension über Gaddis' Roman *JR*), *Saturday Review*, 4.10.1975, p. 27. Aldridge war einer der ersten, die darauf hinwiesen, daß *Die Fälschung der Welt* bei Erscheinen von der Kritik falsch bewertet worden war. Schon 1956 schrieb er im Hinblick auf Gaddis' Roman und Alan Harringtons *The Revelations of Doctor Modesto* (gleichfalls 1955 erschienen): »Diese beiden Romane besitzen Qualitäten, die innerhalb der Literaturkritik eigentlich eine stürmische Kontroverse hätten auslösen müssen. Wären sie zehn oder fünfzehn Jahre früher erschienen, als noch ein Edmund Wilson für sie hätte eintreten können, wie er das für den jüngeren Hemingway oder wie es ein Malcolm Cowley für den unterschätzten späten Faulkner tat, hätten diese Romane auch ein angemessenes Publikum erreicht. Stattdessen rutschten sie gleich nach Erscheinen ins Abseits, und nichts konnte diesen Prozeß aufhalten.« »The Function of the Book Critic«, wiederabgedruckt in Aldridges *In Search of Heresy* (New York: McGraw-Hill, 1956) als auch in *The Devil in the Fire* (New York: Harper's Magazine Press, 1972).

5 Milton Rugoffs Bewertung in seiner Rezension über die *Fälschung der Welt* (*New York Herald Tribune Book Review*, 13.3.1955, p. 6). In *JR* mutiert Rugoff übrigens zu einem Rezensenten namens »Milton R. Goth« (*JR*, S. 728) Die dort vorgestellte Liste von Neuerscheinungen besteht ausschließlich aus anagrammatischen Versionen des Originaltitels der *Fälschung der Welt (The Recognitions)* sowie den verballhornten Namen einiger Rezensenten, die den Roman seinerzeit verrisssen haben.

6 »John Barth: An Interview«. *Wisconsin Studies in Contemporary Literature* 6 (winter/spring 1965). Die Erstausgabe von John Barths *Der Tabakhändler* (engl. *The Sot-Weed Factor*) hat einen Umfang von 806 Seiten.

7 Gaddis schreibt »nicht mit Absicht« derart umfangreiche Romane. Während der Arbeit an *JR* bemerkte er einmal: »Ich wollte eigentlich kein langes Buch schreiben, wie ich auch beim ersten Mal kein langes Buch schreiben wollte. Es ist nur so, daß ich es nicht beenden kann, solange es noch nicht stimmt.« (Zitiert nach Israel Shenker: »2d Heller Book Due 13 Years after First«, *New York Times*, 18.2.1974, p. 30.) Als Gaddis die erste Fassung der *Fälschung* beim Verlag Harcourt/Brace einreichte, war der Roman noch sehr viel länger und enthielt sogar Fußnoten.

8 Rezension von *JR*, *New York Times Book Review*, 9.11.1975, p. 1.

9 Rainer Maria Rilke, *Duino Elegies*, with an English translation, introduction, and commentary by J. B. Leishman and Stephen Spender (New York: Norton, 1939) p. 87f.

10 Robert Graves, den Gaddis 1948 in Spanien kennengelernt hatte, schrieb folgenden Klappentext (den Harcourt/Brace auch für die einzige Werbeanzeige nutzte, die der Verlag für den Roman plazierte): »Die Präzision des Stils von William Gaddis ist innerhalb seiner Schriftstellergeneration höchst ungewöhnlich. Und ich bin beeindruckt, daß jemand, der so vertraut ist mit den Bergen von Schmutz, Perversion, Falschheit und Langeweile, doch die Kraft aufgebracht hat, seinen Kopf klar, sein Herz warm und seinen Bericht lesbar zu halten.« Möglicherweise hat Graves Gaddis auch mit Frazers *Der goldene Zweig (The Golden Bough)* und den *Recognitiones* des Clemens Romanus bekanntgemacht. Umgekehrt war Gaddis von Graves' *Weißer Göttin (The White Goddess)* stark beeinflußt und bezieht sich auch im Roman auf einige andere Werke Graves'.

11 Rezension über die *Fälschung der Welt* im *New York Times Book Review*, 14.7.1974, p. 27.

12 In seinem ausgezeichneten Essay »Gaddis Anagnorisis« zitiert John Leverence aus Morris W. Crolls Standardwerk *The Baroque Style in Prose* (1929): »Der sogenannte lockere Barocksatz beginnt ohne Umschweife und präsentiert seine Idee in der naheliegendsten Form; der folgende Satz wird durch die Situation bestimmt, in der sich das Bewußtsein

befindet, nachdem der erste ausgesprochen wurde, und so weiter durch den gesamten Absatz hindurch, wobei jedes Glied nur eine direkte Folge der vorausgehenden Situation ist. Der Text wird, jedenfalls in der Theorie, nicht gemacht, er entsteht. Er vollendet sich selbst und ist ein Spiegel des Bewußtseins, das ihn ausdrückt.« (*Itinerary*, no. 3/1977, p. 49)

[13] »The Ongoing Situation«, op. cit., p. 30. Dieser Punkt wird von Gaddis' Kritikern gern übersehen und hat beispielsweise John Gardner zu der absurden Vorhersage verleitet, Gaddis' Werke »würden allein aufgrund ihrer puren Herzlosigkeit schnell verschwinden.« (*On Moral Fiction*, New York: Basic, 1978. p. 94).

[14] Die psychologische Ausrichtung basiert im wesentlichen auf Jung. Aufschlußreich ein Zitat Jungs *Psychologie und Alchemie*, das Gaddis (in einer früheren Fassung mit dem Titel *Die Integration der Persönlichkeit*) für nahezu alle alchemistischen Bezüge nutzte: »Es ist natürlich unmöglich, sich ohne eifriges Bemühen aus der eigenen Kindheit zu befreien, wie die Forschungen Freuds schon seit langem gezeigt haben. Auch durch rein intellektuelles Wissen kann dies nicht gelingen; erfolgversprechend ist einzig eine Erinnerung, die zugleich ein Wieder-Erleben ist. Das Dahineilen der Jahre und der überwältigende Eindruck der neu entdeckten Welt lassen eine Unmenge an Material zurück, das nie bewältigt wird. Wir schütteln dies jedoch nicht ab; wir bewegen uns höchstens davon weg. So daß wir in späteren Jahren, wenn wir zu den Erinnerungen unserer Kindheit zurückkehren, Bruchstücke unserer Persönlichkeit immer noch lebendig vorfinden; sie umgeben und durchdringen uns mit dem Gefühl früherer Zeiten. Da diese Bruchstücke sich noch im Stadium der Kindheit befinden, ist ihre Wirkung sehr mächtig. Sie können jedoch nur dann ihren infantilen Charakter verlieren und korrigiert werden, wenn sie mit dem erwachsenen Bewußtsein vereint werden. Um dies ›persönliche Unbewußte‹ muß stets gerungen werden, das heißt, es muß bewußt gemacht werden, weil sich sonst das Tor zum kollektiven Unbewußten nicht öffnen läßt.« – Jungs »eine Erinnerung die zugleich ein Wieder-Erleben ist«, ähnelt Gaddis' Konzeption von *recognition*.
Gaddis Haltung zur Psychoanalyse ist ambivalent; sie wird im Roman dauernd ins Lächerliche gezogen, doch bezieht der Autor sich häufig auf psychoanalytische Theorien. Man fühlt sich an Joyces Haltung gegenüber Vico erinnert: »Ich würde diesen Theorien nicht allzu viel Aufmerksamkeit zukommen lassen, abgesehen von dem Nutzen, den sie für mein Buch gehabt haben.« (*Letters 1*, ed. Stuart Gilbert. New York: Viking, 1966. p. 241).

[15] Zitiert nach Peter W. Koenig, »Splinters from the Yew Tree: A Critical Study of William Gaddis' *The Recognitions*« (Ph. D. diss., New York University, 1971), p. 80. Koenigs Dissertation, für die er die Möglichkeit hatte, Gaddis' Notizen und Manuskripte auszuwerten, ist wegen vieler solcher Zitate von unschätzbarem Wert.

[16] *Die Integration der Persönlichkeit* (aus einem Abschnitt, der in *Psychologie und Alchemie* nicht mehr aufgenommen worden ist).

[17] Zitiert nach Koenig, p. 33.

[18] Diese notwendigerweise kursorischen Bemerkungen über den Symbolismus in der *Fälschung der Welt* habe ich in meiner Monographie *William Gaddis* (Boston: Twayne, 1989) erweitert.

[19] Wie schon oben erwähnt, war Jungs erstes Buch über Alchemie, *Die Integration der Persönlichkeit*, Gaddis' Hauptquelle für alchemistische Hintergrundinformationen. (Daneben entnahm er einige Details auch dem Artikel »Alchemy« aus der 14. Auflage der *Encyclopaedia Britannica*.) Jungs Buch wurde später überarbeitet und erweitert und erschien als Vol. 12 der *Collected Works*; Seitenverweise beziehen sich in aller Regel auf diese Augabe (Abk. P&A), gelegentlich auch auf Jungs Meisterwerk über Alchemie, *Mysterium Coniunctionis* (Abk. MC), und auf Jungs Kommentar der symbolischen Illu-

strationen des »Rosarium Philosophorum« unter dem Titel *Die Psychologie der Übertragung*.
20 In seinem Nachwort zur Signet-Ausgabe von *The Confidence-Man (Der Hochstapler)* stellt R. W. B. Lewis die *Fälschung der Welt* in die Reihe der von Melville beeinflußten Romane und merkt dazu an: »Melvilles Erbe ist in allen diesen Büchern spürbar, die Vision einer Apokalypse, die schrecklich, aber auch äußerst komisch ist, die Selbstauslöschung einer durch Täuschung, Hochstapelei und allerlei Maskeraden geprägten Welt sowie die Figur des Großen Versuchers (des ›super-promiser‹, wie West ihn in *The Day of the Locust* nennt). Diese und andere Bücher bilden das dauerhafte Gegengewicht zum amerikanischen Traum.« (New York: New American Library, 1964, p. 263)
21 Im Grunde erscheint die erste Anspielung auf die Alchemie bereits auf dem Buchumschlag und der Vorsatzseite: Das älteste und bekannteste Emblem des *opus alchymicum* war der *uroborus*, der Drachen, der sich in den eigenen Schwanz beißt.
22 »Psychologie der Übertragung«, para. 407. Diese Lesart des *Faust* ist typisch für alle Schriften Jungs zur Alchemie.
23 Cambridge: Cambridge University Press, 1952. p. 219.
24 Daß die frühere Fassung dieses Kapitels, unter dem Titel »Le Chemin des Anes« veröffentlicht, nicht mit einer Anspielung auf Lully, sondern auf den Heiligen Franziskus endet, legt die Vermutung nahe, daß die alchemistischen Motive erst später in den Text eingearbeitet wurden, möglicherweise zwischen 1952 und 1953, als Gaddis den Roman völlig überarbeitete.
25 Deshalb sagt Wyatt über Brown: »Gott, welche Fülle, welche Fülle!« (S. 914 et al.) Auf der symbolischen Ebene entspricht Brown der Materie, wie auch schon der Name andeutet.
26 In der *Fälschung der Welt* gibt es eine Menge Schattensymbole, die zweifellos dieser Konzeption und/oder ihren folkloristischen Entsprechungen entspringen.
27 Zitiert nach Koenig, p. 87 (Hervorhebung von Gaddis).
28 Diese Stufen haben ihre Entsprechungen im *opus alchymicum*, und aus diesem Grund kommt Leverence zu dem Schluß: »Gaddis' Roman ist explizit wie implizit alchemistisch, sowohl thematisch als auch strukturell als auch motivisch.« Demnach wäre das *opus alchymicum* für *Die Fälschung der Welt* das, was Homers *Odyssee* für Joyces *Ulysses* war: eine beherrschende, strukturelle Metapher, die allerdings nie so streng gehandhabt wird, daß sie den Handlungsrahmen einengt.
29 Im Roman ist Ludy der letzte, der eine beunruhigende Erfahrung mit weißen Vögeln macht. Ein plötzlich niederschießender, weißer Vogel ist bereits für Ottos Unfall verantwortlich, und Ottos Freund Ed Feasley stürzt mit dem Flugzeug ab, nachdem er mit einem Schwarm weißer Vögel kollidiert ist. Bis in einzelne Bilder hinein stoßen wir auf dieses Wappentier der Desintegration. Die Fetzen des Briefs, den Reverend Gwyon am Schluß von I.1 von Wyatt erhält »flatterten, aufgeschreckt wie ein Schwarm weißer Vögel, davon.« (S. 87) Aber es geht auch umgekehrt: »Die weißen Vögel, die umsonst das Wasser abgesucht hatten, flatterten, aufgeschreckt durch den Donnerschlag, im Schwarm empor und zerstoben wie die Schnipsel eines zerrissenen Briefs.« (S. 1011)
30 Der grüne Löwe ist sonst mit dem Einhorn identisch, das nur von einer Jungfrau gezähmt werden kann und dann seinen Kopf in ihren Schoß legt.
31 »Paracelus schreibt, daß der, ›welcher das Reich Gottes erlangt, erst mit seinem Körper in seine Mutter eingegangen und dort gestorben sein muß‹, und daß die Seele ›in Gott eingeht wie in ihre Mutter‹. Seiner Ansicht nach mußte sich die ganze Welt diesem Gesetz unterwerfen und in ihre ›Mutter‹ eingehen …, ihre *primam materium, massam confusam* und *abyssum*, um die Ewigkeit zu erlangen.« (Gray, p. 31) Diese Vermischung alchemistischer mit theologischen Begriffen ist für das alchemistische Schrifttum typisch.

[32] Zu Nicodemus vgl. S. 453; 523 ff. Otto, Valentine und Sinisterra betonen alle die Notwendigkeit, »den alten Menschen auszuziehen mit seinen Werken« (S. 642). Selbst in Wyatts/Stephens letzten Worten im Roman klingt das Thema Wiedergeburt an: »Die Glocken des Alten. Er schickt mich zurück in die Welt.« (S. 1080) Natürlich erscheint die Vorstellung, sterben zu müssen, um wiedergeboren zu werden, sowohl in der Alchemie als auch im Christentum. Sie ist eine Grundidee in den meisten Religionen und Mythen der Welt, was Gaddis wohl ebenfalls dem *Goldenen Zweig* entnommen haben dürfte.

[33] Wenn Jung Spitteler zitiert, bezieht er sich stets auf diese Anekdote.

[34] In seiner lateinisches Form ergibt dies berühmte Motto eine akrostische Schreibweise von VITRIOL (d. h. Schwefelsäure oder eine vergleichbar schimmernde, kristalline Substanz), Bestandteil in vielen alchemistischen Rezepturen.

[35] »Gaddis Anagnorisis«, p. 57.

[36] »Die Gnostik weist überzeugende Parallelen zum Symbolismus des Individuationsprozesses auf.« (Jung)

[37] »Von Indien bis zu den Küsten des Atlantik wird überall, wenn auch auf unterschiedlichste Weise, das Mysterium von Tag und Nacht mit dem Mysterium jenes tödlichen Kampfs gleichgesetzt, der sich im Innern des Menschen abspielt.« (Denis de Rougemont, »Love in the Western World«. New York: Harcourt, Brace, 1940, p. 58.)

[38] Die symbolische Entsprechung zwischen Meer/Himmel/Land, von der oben schon die Rede war, findet eine Parallele in der Alchemie, wo die einzelnen Begriffe mit der *prima materia* in Verbindung gebracht werden, »der Grundlage für die Herstellung des philosophischen Goldes«. (P&A)

[39] P&A. Die entfaltete Spiegel-Symbolik in der *Fälschung der Welt* läßt sich auf diese Weise vielleicht am besten begreifen: »Der Weg der Seele auf der Suche nach ihrem verlorenen Vater führt somit zum Wasser, zum dunklen Spiegel, der auf seinem Grunde ruht.« In *Die Integration der Persönlichkeit* schrieb Jung: »Der Mann, der in den dunklen Spiegel des Wassers blickt, sieht natürlich vor allem sein eigenes Gesicht. Wer zu sich selbst geht, riskiert stets eine Auseinandrsetzung mit sich selbst. Der Spiegel schmeichelt nicht, sondern zeigt getreu den, der hineinschaut; besonders das Gesicht, das wir der Welt nie zeigen, weil wir es mit der *persona* verdecken, der Maske des Handelnden. Doch der Spiegel liegt hinter der Maske und zeigt das wahre Gesicht.«

[40] In Teil III verwechselt Esme Wyatt sowohl mit dem schiffbrüchigen Seemann, der während der Überfahrt entdeckt wird, als auch mit dem ertrunkenen Seemann aus der Erzählung von Gervasius von Tilbury. Die erste Assoziation ist von großer Bedeutung, weil sie Wyatts symbolischen Tod im Meer darstellt, der schon mehrmals zuvor im Roman seine Schatten vorauswirft. (S. 82; 356; 579) Im Bellevue Hospital lächelt Esme Stanley an, »als habe sie ihm soeben den Tod prophezeit: entweder durch stürzende Säulen oder auf See«, (S. 903) wodurch Stanleys tatsächlicher und Wyatts symbolischer Tod vorweggenommen wird.

[41] Eine Anspielung auf das Goldene Vlies erscheint schon auf Seite 11 des Romans.

[42] »Fire the Bastards!« p. 32.

[43] Koenig (p. 88 f.) weist darauf hin, daß »Wyatt, das Selbst, das mehr tun könnte, paradoxerweise der egoistischste und zugleich potentiell der selbstloseste Charakter des Romans ist. Gaddis schreibt dazu in seinen Notizen: ›Dieser Egoismus ist eine sehr gefährliche Sache. Und Esther hat allen Grund, zornig zu werden, wenn auch aus den falschen Gründen. Denn selbst sie als Intellektuelle kann ihrer weiblichen Beschränkung nicht entfliehen: nämlich Stifterin einer Erlösung zu sein, an der sie selbst keinen Anteil hat. Es ergeht ihr wie Senta im *Fliegenden Holländer* und Solveig in *Peer Gynt*, ein romantisches Trugbild, das sehr mächtig ist.‹«

44 Als wolle er Valentine widerlegen, zitiert Gaddis andere Werke des 20. Jahrhunderts, die sich ebenfalls mit dem Erlösungsthema befassen: Maughams *Auf Messers Schneide* (S. 849), Aldous Huxleys *Geblendet in Gaza* (S. 856), Masefields *The Everlasting Mercy* (S. 1015) und Fairbanks witzige Parodie mit dem Titel *Die Exzentrizitäten des Kardinals Pirelli betreffend* (S. 1112)

45 Zitiert nach Koenig, p. 90.

46 Herbert Silberer: *Problems of Mysticism and Its Symbolism*, New York: Moffat, Yard, 1917. p. 146 f. Das Buch wird in der *Fälschung der Welt* erwähnt (S. 134), doch hat es Gaddis wahrscheinlich nicht gelesen, sondern nur den Titel aus Jungs *Integration* übernommen. Das ist auch mit vielen anderen Titeln im Roman der Fall.

47 S. 336 f. Daß es wichtig sei, gutes Material zu verwenden, wird in dem Abschnitt aus Cenninis *Libro dell' Arte* betont, aus dem Otto auf Seite 198 laut liest. Otto benutzt für sein Stück in der Tat gutes Material, allerdings nicht sein eigenes!

48 Vgl. Grace Eckleys »Exorcising the Demon Forgery, or the Forging of Pure Gold in Gaddis's *Recognitions*« (in: *Literature and the Occult*, ed. Luanne Frank, p. 125 ff. Arlington: University of Texas, 1977.) Mit Bezug auf den Satz »Gold macht man immer noch aus Gold« zitiert Eckley einen Brief von Gaddis an Miss Howes (8. 3. 1972), in dem der Autor die Stelle als »den Schlüssel zum ganzen Buch« bezeichnet, »falls es denn einen gibt«.

49 *Novel* 10 (winter 1977): p. 127–36.

50 Was Johan Thielemans über die Künstler in *JR* geschrieben hat, trifft wohl auch auf die Künstler in Gaddis' erstem Roman zu: »Bis zu einem bestimmten Punkt sind sie alle menschliche Versager, aber in unvorhersehbaren Momenten schaffen sie einzigartige, künstlerische Werke, und diese Werke scheinen sich dem allgemeinen Betrug zu entziehen. Kunst ist keine erfreuliche Antwort auf den erbärmlichen Zustand der Welt, aber sie ist die einzige Antwort, die uns bleibt.« (»Gaddis and the Novel of Entropy«, *TREMA*, no. 2, 1977. p. 9.)

51 Über seine Zeit als Lohnschreiber wird Gaddis folgendermaßen zitiert: »Diese Texte schrieb ich nicht unter meinem eigenen Namen. Es war mir egal, weil ich nur an der Bezahlung interessiert war. Ich mochte diese Arbeit sogar lieber als das Verfassen von Essays oder Zeitungsartikeln, weil sie für mich eine größere Herausforderung darstellten.« Yokichi Miuamoto, »Rainichi shita William Gaddis: Yomu Tanoshisha to Kaku Tanoshisha«, *Eigo Seinem* 122 (1. Dezember 1976), p. 404–5.

Inhaltsübersicht

Die vorgeschlagenen Datierungen basieren auf den Ergebnissen, zu denen ich in meiner Untersuchung »Chronological Difficulties in the Novels of William Gaddis« (*Critique* 22, No. 1 [1980]: p. 79–91) gekommen bin, auf die der interessierte Leser bei Detailfragen zurückgreifen kann.

I.1
7–87 [3–62] Etwa 1919 – etwa 1935

Kurz nach Ende des Ersten Weltkriegs treten Reverend Gwyon und seine Frau Camilla von Boston aus eine Seereise nach Spanien an, wo sie Urlaub machen wollen. Der Geldfälscher Frank Sinisterra, auf der Flucht vor seinem Prozeß, gibt sich als Bordarzt aus. »Am siebten Tag nun, es war Allerheiligen, und die Hälfte der Reise lag hinter ihnen, ging Gott an Bord der *Purdue Victory* und fügte: und Camilla war geprüft mit einer akuten Appendizitis.« (S. 8) Unter seinen inkompetenten Händen stirbt Camilla noch am gleichen Abend. (Camillas Geist wird später jedesmal zu Allerheiligen ihrem Sohn Wyatt erscheinen.) Reverend Gwyon sorgt dafür, daß seine Frau auf dem Friedhof von San Zwingli beerdigt wird. Sie wird in einer weißen Leichenkutsche, die eigentlich nur für Kinder und Jungfrauen bestimmt ist, zur letzten Ruhe geleitet und direkt neben »einem kleinen, schieläugigen Mädchen« (S. 12f.) begraben, das zwölf Jahre zuvor einer Vergewaltigung zum Opfer gefallen ist.
Der untröstliche Gwyon begibt sich in ein spanisches Franziskanerkloster namens *Real Monasterio de Nuestra Señora de la Otra Vez*. Kurz nach Weihnachten fällt er in ein Delirium, wo ihm im Mondlicht seine verstorbene Frau entgegentritt. Am nächsten Tag bringen ihn die besorgten Mönche auf einem Maultier nach Madrid, wo er sich schließlich erholt.
Im Frühling des folgenden Jahres kehrt er nach Neuengland zurück, zum Entsetzen der calvinistischen Gemeinde ohne Camillas sterbliche Überreste, dafür jedoch mit einem Berberäffchen und einer Sammlung

katholischer Heiligenbilder und Reliquien, mit denen er das düstere Pfarrhaus vollstopft. Sein Sohn Wyatt ist zu diesem Zeitpunkt vier Jahre alt. Da er keine Mutter mehr hat, gerät er, ohne sich dagegen wehren zu können, unter die Obhut seiner strengen Tante May. Als Wyatt älter wird, legt er ein ausgeprägtes Maltalent an den Tag; seine Erziehung wird jedoch bestimmt von der Erbauungsliteratur der Tante und den okkulten Studien des Reverend sowie den bunten Abenteuergeschichten, die ihm sein Großvater, der Stadtzimmermann, erzählt.

Tante May verurteilt Wyatts künstlerisches Talent und hält ihn statt dessen dazu an, sich auf eine geistliche Laufbahn vorzubereiten. Obwohl sie stirbt, als Wyatt erst zwölf Jahre alt ist, hat ihn ihr Einfluß und der Mangel an mütterlicher Liebe für immer geprägt. Schuldgefühle peinigen den angehenden Maler, und seine Bilder vergräbt er deshalb stets unter dem Komposthaufen hinter der Küche. Obwohl ihn zu dieser Zeit nichts mehr mit dem Christentum verbindet, tritt er, als er volljährig wird, dennoch ins Priesterseminar ein. Zuvor wäre er fast einer rätselhaften Krankheit erlegen, von der ihn aber nicht die ärztliche Kunst heilt, sondern sein Vater – und zwar mit einem jahrhundertealten Ritual der Dämonenaustreibung samt Opferung des Berberäffchens.

Malend verbringt Wyatt seine Rekonvaleszenz, und zwei Bilder aus dieser Periode bestimmen maßgeblich die weitere Handlung. Das erste ist eine Kopie von Boschs Altarbild *Die sieben Todsünden*, das Reverend Gwyon aus Europa mitgebracht hat, das zweite ein Porträt seiner Mutter, das er nach einer Fotografie anfertigt. Als Wyatt später aus dem Priesterseminar nach Hause zurückkehrt, sind beide Bilder noch unvollendet. Da sein Vater ihn keineswegs zum Pfarrberuf drängt, beschließt Wyatt, die Theologie aufzugeben und statt dessen in Europa Kunst zu studieren. Um die Reise zu finanzieren, vollendet er seine Bosch-Kopie und vertauscht sie mit dem Original, das er, wie er später erklärt, heimlich und zu einem Spottpreis an Recktall Brown verkauft, seinen zukünftigen Auftraggeber. Von der Abreise nach Europa erfährt Reverend Gwyon erst, als er einen Brief aus München erhält. Er begreift: »Aufgrund von Schuld kann mein Sohn leider sein Studium für das Pfarramt nicht fortsetzen«, was jedoch seine eigene Verachtung für das tradierte Christentum mit »seinen Schreckgespenstern der Wankelmütigen« (S. 85) nur noch verstärkt. Abgesehen von dem geistig zurückgebliebenen Dienstmädchen Janet lebt er jetzt allein im Pfarrhaus und vergräbt sich in seine heidnischen Studien, vor allem in den Mithraskult, der ihm »in späteren Jahren noch zugute kommen sollte«. (S. 14)

I.2
88–107 [63–77] Etwa 1938

Drei Jahre später begegnen wir Wyatt im Paris der Dreißigerjahre wieder. Zuvor hatte er in München bei einem Herrn Koppel Kunst studiert, der Wyatt nicht nur gute Ratschläge gegeben hatte (»Formen werden auch nicht neu erfunden, man hat sie, hier, im Herzen, man kennt sie auswendig, verstehen Sie ...« (S. 122f.), sondern auch eins von Wyatts Gemälden in betrügerischer Absicht als einen wiederentdeckten Memling verkauft. Später wird es noch Hinweise auf Wyatts Gefährten in jener Zeit geben, einen Kunststudenten namens Han. (In einem Abschnitt, den Gaddis aus der endgültigen Fassung des Romans eliminiert hat, wurde Han als brutaler Homosexueller dargestellt. Während einer Bergtour zur Jungfrau in der Schweizer Alpen versucht Han, Wyatt zu verführen, der sich daraufhin nach Paris absetzt.)
Mit der Touristenkunst auf dem Montmartre hat Wyatt indes nichts zu tun. Er arbeitet allein, zumeist nachts, und benutzt manchmal ein Modell namens Christiane. Kurz vor der Eröffnung einer Ausstellung seiner Gemälde, wird Wyatt von einem Kunstkritiker namens Crémer besucht, der ihm günstige Kritiken seines Werks anbietet, dafür jedoch zehn Prozent vom Verkaufserlös verlangt. Natürlich lehnt Wyatt ab, was dazu führt, daß er keine einzige Arbeit verkaufen kann. Als er erfährt, daß seine Memling-Imitation als Original »wiederentdeckt« worden ist, entscheidet er sich zum Bruch mit der Kunstwelt und verläßt Paris in der gleichen Stimmung, in der sieben Jahrhunderte zuvor der Alchemist Raymond Lully das schöne, aber verpestete Ambrosia de Castello hinter sich ließ.

I.3
108–206 [78–153] Etwa 1946 – Frühjahr 1949

Etwa sieben bis acht Jahre später lebt Wyatt in New York, wo er eine Frau namens Esther geheiratet hat, eine aufstrebende Schriftstellerin mit promisker »Village-Vergangenheit«. Er arbeitet als technischer Zeichner, entwirft aber auch gelegentlich Brücken, die sein Vorgesetzter Benny als eigene Leistung ausgibt. Nebenbei restauriert er Gemälde, hat aber seit seiner Pariser Zeit keine eigenen Werke mehr geschaffen. Die Beziehung zwischen Wyatt und Esther ist ein Trauerspiel; die Spannungen zwischen den beiden nehmen noch zu, als Esther die Bekanntschaft Otto Pivners macht, eines angehenden Theaterautors, der gerade sein Studium in Harvard abgeschlossen hat. Wyatt, der schließlich sowohl von seiner Arbeit als auch von seiner Frau frustriert ist (deren Affäre mit Otto er zumindest ahnt), verläßt beide, um im Auftrag des Kunsthändlers Recktall Brown, der sich auf Wyatts Teufelsbeschwörung hin einstellt, Bilder zu fälschen. Otto und Esther ziehen zusammen. Benny gelingt es nicht, Wyatt zu überreden, in seinen alten Job zurückzukehren. Nach etwa einem Jahr wird Esther auch von Otto verlassen, dessen Stelle schnell vom zynischen Werbefachmann Ellery eingenommen wird. Wyatt ist von diesem Kapitel an namenlos.

I.4
207–225 [154–168] Sommer – Herbst 1949

Während der zweiten Jahreshälfte arbeitet Otto im Büro einer Bananenplantage in Mittelamerika und schreibt zugleich an seinem Stück *Die Eitelkeit der Zeit*. (Der Titel stammt aus Reverend Gwyons Grabrede für Tante May, welche Otto unter Wyatts Sachen entdeckt. Reverend Gwyon wiederum hatte sich das Wort von William Law ausgeliehen.) Otto muß die unerwünschte Gesellschaft des tätowierten Jesse Franks ertragen und freut sich darauf, bald wieder nach New York zurückkehren zu können – braungebrannt, sein Stück vollendet, und trotz bester Gesundheit angetan mit einer dramatischen Armschlinge, wovon er sich die Bewunderung der Daheimgebliebenen verspricht.

I.5.
226–269 [169–201] Dezember 1949

Otto kehrt Anfang Dezember nach New York zurück und wird dort zu einer Party in Greenwich Village eingeladen, auf der ein neues Gemälde von Max enthüllt werden soll (das nichts anderes als das in einen Rahmen gespannte Hemd eines Arbeiters ist). Obwohl einige der auf dieser Party versammelten Figuren bereits vorher schon kurz aufgetreten sind – Agnes Deigh (S. 136), Anselm (S. 141) – wird hier fast das gesamte Figurenensemble des Romans vorgestellt: Arny und Maude Munk, ein kinderloses Ehepaar, das vergeblich versucht, ein Kind zu adoptieren; Herschel, ein witziger Homosexueller, der unter anderem für einen Senator und einen General als Ghostwriter arbeitet; Agnes Deigh, Literaturagentin und ehemalige Katholikin, die sich in der Gesellschaft von Schwulen am wohlsten fühlt; Hannah, eine pummelige Village-Künstlerin und Amateurpsychologin, die von der Sozialhilfe und ihrem

Mutterwitz lebt und sich ebenso für Bier wie für Stanley interessiert, einen überzeugten Katholiken und Komponisten von Orgelwerken, der sich wiederum Sorgen ums Seelenheil von Agnes und Anselm (eigentlich Arthur) macht, einem akneqeplagten, innerlich zerrissene Religionsfanatiker und Dichter; dazu allerlei Village-Volk (der selbstmordgefährdete Charles Dickens, der von Schuldgefühlen verfolgt wird, weil er zur Besatzung eines Atombombers gehörte; der onanistische Kritiker im grünen Wollhemd; Buster Brown; Sonny Byron; Adeline Thing); Ed Feasley, hauptamtlicher Witzbold und ehemaliger Studienkamerad von Otto, der nicht weiß, was er mit seinem Leben anfangen soll; Big Anna, ein schriller Schwuler aus Schweden; Mr. Feddle, ein trotteliger, alter Mann, der Gedichte schreibt und auf eigene Kosten verlegt; und schließlich Esme, ein manisch-depressives Junkie-Mädchen, das ebenfalls Gedichte schreibt und für Wyatt Modell sitzt. Die Party endet in einem Fiasko, als Herschel Hannah schlägt und Anselm sich mit der gesamten Partygesellschaft anlegt. Otto begleitet Esme nach Hause.

I.6
270–296 [202–221] Dezember 1949

Zu den Klängen von Verdis *Aida* erwacht Otto am nächsten Morgen in Esmes Wohnung und geht für ein paar Stunden aus. Als er zurückkommt, ist Esme soeben aufgewacht, und Otto geht in einen Drugstore, um einen Kaffee zu trinken. Als er schließlich wiederkommt, wird er gleich zweimal enttäuscht: Esme kann sich nicht mehr daran erinnern, daß er sie nach Haus gebracht hat, und zugleich muß er feststellen, daß er einen Rivalen hat, in Gestalt des heruntergekommenen Chaby Sinisterra, Frank Sinisterras Sohn. Die drei frühstücken zusammen und begegnen Stanley. Am Nachmittag wandert Otto zunächst ziellos durch die Straßen, kehrt aber dann zu Esme zurück und schläft mit ihr. Anschließend träumen beide von Wyatt, und als Esme erwacht, verläßt sie die Wohnung, um Wyatt zu besuchen.

I.7
297–373 [222–277] Dezember 1949

Zur selben Zeit führt Fuller, Recktall Browns schwarzer Diener, den Hund aus und kauft sich, in einem weiteren Versuch, Browns Herrschaft zu entfliehen, eine Bahnfahrkarte. Als er nach Haus zurückkehrt, fordert

Brown ihn auf, die Fahrkarte herauszugeben (Fuller hatte sich zuvor verraten, als er von Brown hatten wissen wollen, »ob US-Währung auch gültig an ein Ort wie Utica«? (S. 303) Brown wendet seine Aufmerksamkeit nun Basil Valentine zu, einem Kunstkritiker, der mit Brown kollaboriert, indem er zuerst die Echtheit der in Browns Auftrag gefälschten Werke öffentlich anzweifelt, dann jedoch ihre Echtheit bestätigt. (Brown hat soeben Wyatts alte Memling-Kopie erworben, hält sie allerdings für echt.) Valentine will sich mit Wyatt treffen, um ihm weitere Fälschungen vorzuschlagen. Als Wyatt eintrifft, merkt er schnell, daß Valentine im Hinblick auf die Schwierigkeiten des Fälscherhandwerks weitaus sensibler reagiert als Brown. Valentine ist von Wyatt gleichfalls fasziniert, und zwischen den beiden entwickelt sich allmählich eine vorsichtige Beziehung. Im Verlauf der Unterhaltung zieht Valentine die Echtheit des Bosch-Gemäldes in Zweifel, das sich in Browns Besitz befindet, um diesen dazu zu bringen, das Bild begutachten zu lassen. Später wird Valentine den Bosch durch eine Kopie austauschen und das Original wieder nach Europa schicken, »wo er auch hingehört«. (S. 907) Offenbar ist er bereits mit anderen Werken Browns so verfahren.

Valentines Plan sieht vor, daß Wyatt ein Werk Hubert Van Eycks fälschen soll, angeblich Jan Van Eycks älterem Bruder. Es geht um eine *Verkündigung*, die Wyatt jedoch nie realisiert. Nach dem Treffen teilen sich Valentine und Wyatt ein Taxi (das beinah Mr. Pivner überfährt, Ottos Vater, der im nächsten Kapitel vorgestellt wird). Sie trennen sich, und Wyatt trifft überraschend mit John zusammen, einem Kommilitonen aus dem Priesterseminar. Damit laufen sich die beiden bereits zum zweitenmal über den Weg, fast zwei Jahre zuvor sind sie sich schon einmal zufällig begegnet. (S. 156) Die beiden hocken sich in eine Bar, wo John von Wyatts Vater berichtet, der seine Gemeinde mit seltsam heidnischen Predigten erbaut.

Später erscheint Esme in Wyatts Atelier in der Horatio Street, um ihm Modell zu sitzen, wird jedoch nicht gebraucht. Nachdem sie (auf deutsch) aus den Märchen der Gebrüder Grimm gelesen hat, entdeckt Wyatt in ihrem Gesicht jene Linien, die ihm zur Vollendung des Porträts seiner Mutter fehlten, als er es fünfzehn Jahre zuvor begonnen hatte. Er faßt den Entschluß, das Gesicht in seinem nächsten Gemälde zu benutzen. Zwischen Esme und Wyatt kommt es zu einem intimen Moment. Sie legt die Arme um seine Schultern, aber er richtet sich plötzlich auf und schüttelt sie ab. Esme geht nach Hause, setzt sich einen Schuß und versucht, ein Gedicht zu schreiben. Als ihr das nicht gelingt, beginnt sie damit, Rilkes *Erste Duineser Elegie* niederzuschreiben, wird dabei jedoch von einem geheimnisvollen Klopfen an der Tür unterbrochen.

II.1
377–462 [281–342]
Montag, 19. Dezember – Mittwoch, 21. Dezember 1949

Am Ende seines Arbeitstags verläßt Mr. Pivner das Büro und geht in seine einsame Wohnung. Nachdem er sich Insulin gespritzt hat, hört er Radio und liest pflichtbewußt die Zeitung, aus der er unter anderem erfährt, »daß in einem Pfandhaus in Hell's Kitchen zwei Bilder von Dierick Bouts aufgetaucht« seien (S. 387) – Fälschungen von Wyatt. Mr. Pivner freut sich, weil Otto ihm geschrieben hat, daß er ihn anrufen wolle, um ein Treffen zu verabreden – Otto und sein Vater haben sich noch nie im Leben gesehen – und wartet nun geduldig auf den Anruf seines Sohns.

Am nächsten Nachmittag lehnt Agnes Deigh in ihrem Büro Ottos Manuskript ab. »Also, wissen Sie, was mich angeht, *mir* hat es gefallen«, sagt sie diplomatisch, obwohl sie es überhaupt nicht gelesen hat. (S. 398) Als er fort ist, beobachtet sie aus ihrem Fenster, wie der Zahnarzt in der gegenüberliegenden Praxis ein Mädchen schlägt und meldet den Vorfall (»Grobe Mißhandlung. Oder besser Sadismus. Ja, Sadismus.«) bei der Polizei (S. 400), erfährt jedoch später, daß es sich »nicht um einen Fall von schwerer Mißhandlung im Sinne einer strafbaren Handlung, sondern um eine elterliche Erziehungsmaßnahme« gehandelt hat (S. 741) und daß der beschuldigte Dr. Weisgall sie möglicherweise wegen übler Nachrede verklagen wird. Zur gleichen Zeit sitzt Esme in ihrem Zimmer, liest Stevensons *Olalla* und grübelt über Wyatt nach. Wieder wird sie von einem Klopfen an der Tür gestört; diesmal ist es Chaby Sinisterra.

Deprimiert verläßt Otto das Büro der Literaturagentin Agnes Deigh, begegnet Fuller und geht zu Esme, wo er Chaby antrifft, der sich gerade die Hose zuknöpft. Chaby geht, und Otto lädt Esme zum Essen ins *Viareggio* ein, »eine kleine italienische Bar, in der man früher einmal bedient wurde wie bei Mama, bevor die Schickeria den heimeligen Ort für sich entdeckt hatte«. (S. 411) Dort treffen sie Max, Anselm, Ed Feasley und einige andere Szenegänger, die bereits auf der Party waren (dazu einen Ernest-Hemingway-Lookalike, der aus dieser Ähnlichkeit Kapital schlägt). Otto ruft seinen Vater wegen des geplanten Treffens an und begleitet Esme und Feasley auf einen Tuntenball nach Harlem.

Am Ende dieser »Saturnalien« (S. 445) machen Ed Feasley und Otto eine

Spritztour. Aus einer plötzlichen Laune Feasleys heraus dringen sie in die Leichenkammer eines Krankenhauses ein und stehlen dort ein amputiertes Bein (das Stanleys Mutter gehört hat). Otto hat die gemeine Idee, es Edna Mims zu schenken, eine College-Schönheit, die jetzt für Brown arbeitet und, wie Otto vorher an diesem Abend erfahren hat, mit Max geschlafen hat (der wiederum auch mit Esther und Esme geschlafen hat). Aber Otto überlegt es sich anders, und sie beschließen, das Bein bei Stanley abzuliefern.

Als der Morgen graut, ist Stanley noch wach. Hannah, auf der Suche nach einem Schlafplatz, kommt vorbei, und Stanley läßt sie bei sich übernachten. Er geht zur Frühmesse, wo er überraschend auf Agnes Deigh trifft, die nach dem Tuntenball dorthin geflohen ist. Ed und Otto fahren bei Stanley vorbei, sehen Hannah durchs Fenster und nehmen an, daß Stanley mit ihr geschlafen hat. Inzwischen hat Agnes den arglosen Stanley mit zu sich nach Haus genommen, wo sie ihn zu verführen versucht. Er flieht vor ihr wie Joseph vor Potiphars Frau, läßt aber nicht sein Gewand, sondern seine Brille zurück.

Der von Schlaflosigkeit geplagte Basil Valentine ist im Morgengrauen gleichfalls noch wach und beschließt, Wyatt zu besuchen. Unterwegs wird er von dem Betrunkenen belästigt, der auch auf Johns und Wyatts letztem Treffen anwesend war. Wyatt, der die Nacht über gearbeitet hat, zeigt Valentine das beschädigte Bild vom Tod der Jungfrau Maria und deutet an, daß er am liebsten mit der Fälscherei Schluß machen würde. Am Abend zuvor hat Wyatt das Beweismaterial, Leinwandreste von seinen früheren Fälschungen, in der Wohnung seiner Frau versteckt, willigt jedoch in Valentines Vorschlag ein, dieses künftig bei ihm zu deponieren.

Als Stanley von Agnes Deigh zurückkehrt, trifft er in der U-Bahn auf Valentine, der gerade von Wyatt zurückkehrt. Nachdem sich vor den beiden eine Frau entblößt hat, begegnet er ebenfalls dem Betrunkenen. Schließlich wirft er sich erschöpft auf sein Bett, denn Hannah ist mittlerweile verschwunden. Der Betrunkene erbricht sich durchs geöffnete Fenster von Stanleys Kellerwohnung.

II.2
463–526 [343–389] Mittwoch, 21. Dezember 1949

Noch am selben Tag bringt Wyatt das aus Gründen der Authentizität schwer beschädigte Gemälde zu Brown. Vor Browns Ankunft nutzt Fuller die Abwesenheit seines Arbeitgebers, um seine Ansichten über das

Böse, die Frauen und den Glauben darzulegen – Themen, die für Wyatt nicht unwichtig sind.

Inzwischen hat Brown in seinem Büro ein spöttisches Gedicht von Esme mit dem Titel *Effluvium* erhalten. Seine Lektüre wird von Otto unterbrochen, der das Manuskript seines Stücks offenbar auf dem Tuntenball verloren hat und hofft, daß Brown noch eine der Kopie hat, was aber nicht der Fall ist. Brown rät Otto, die verletzenden Plagiatsvorwürfe einfach zu ignorieren und komplimentiert ihn hinaus. Seine Lektüre des Gedichts wird jedoch ein zweites Mal durch Basil Valentine unterbrochen. Valentine verrät ihm, daß Wyatt die Absicht hat, seine Fälschungen offenzulegen.

Brown geht nach Hause, wo er Wyatt betrunken vorfindet. Wyatt will aus dem Geschäft aussteigen, und Brown versucht ihn davon abzuhalten. Nur mit Mühe widersteht Wyatt dem plötzlichen Wunsch, seinen alten Zwingherrn umzubringen.

Wyatt begibt sich anschließend zu Esther, um sein Beweismaterial abzuholen, das er in der Nacht zuvor dort deponiert hatte. Zu diesem Zeitpunkt glaubt Esther, schwanger zu sein (eine »hysterische« Schwangerschaft, wie sich später zeigen soll), und Ellery macht sich auf die Suche nach einem Arzt, der eine Abtreibung vornehmen würde. Ellery unterbreitet Wyatt ein absurdes Jobangebot und fragt ihn, ob er sich Wyatts Exemplar von Foxes *Buch der Märtyrer* ausleihen könne. Er plant nämlich eine protestantische Version seiner Erfolgsendung *Leben unterm Heiligenschein*. Wyatt verläßt angewidert die Wohnung.

Wyatt bringt das Beweismaterial zu Valentine, der am Telefon soeben einige Hintergrundinformationen zu den *Recognitiones* des Clemens Romanus durchgibt – und zwar für einen Bekannten des Anrufers, einen Schriftsteller namens »Willie« (alias William Gaddis). Zu dieser Zeit steht Wyatt kurz davor, verrückt zu werden, ganz wie sein Bruder im Geiste van der Goes (wie Valentine bereits angedeutet hat). Schwer betrunken, orientierungslos und verwirrt stolpert er herum, stiehlt hinter Valentines Rücken dessen Goldenen Stier und geht zum Bahnhof, in der Absicht, zu seinem Vater zurückzukehren und sein Theologiestudium wieder aufzunehmen. Dort begegnet er zum dritten und letzten Mal seinem ehemaligen Kommilitonen John. Wyatts Heimfahrt wird mit dem Weg der Sonne bei Nacht verglichen, die (zumindest in der Mythologie) über unterirdische Kanäle an ihren Ausgangspunkt im Osten zurückkehrt, um in der Morgendämmerung als der triumphierende Sonnengott Baal wieder zu erscheinen.

II.3
527–595 [390–445] Donnerstag, 22. Dezember 1949

Wyatts Heimkehr im Morgengrauen vollzieht sich in einem komplexen, inneren Monolog. Schließlich trifft er seinen Vater vor dem Pfarrhaus, wo dieser auf den Sonnenaufgang wartet. Der Reverend wie auch alle anderen Bewohner des Pfarrhauses scheinen über den Besucher nur verzerrte Vorstellungen zu haben. Gwyon glaubt nämlich, sein Sohn sei zurückgekehrt, um Mithras-Priester zu werden. Der Großvater, der Stadtzimmermann, hingegen hält ihn für Prester John, und Janet, das Hausmädchen verwechselt ihn gar mit Jesus Christus. Auch die Damen der »Use-Me«-Gesellschaft erkennen ihn nicht, sehen in ihm vielmehr jenen mysteriösen Reverend Gilbert Sullivan, dessen Name bereits verschiedentlich in den Gesprächen aufgetaucht ist. Wyatt selber empfindet sich als Reinkarnation von Johan Hus.
Janet, die über Vers 24.24 des Matthäus-Evangeliums gebrütet hat, kommt schließlich zu dem Schluß, daß es sich bei Wyatt um den falschen Christus handelt. Sie wirft ihre Druckpresse um (auf der sie etwas druckt, was später für Dick, den Nachfolger von Reverend Gwyon weder Hand noch Fuß hat), läuft zum Kutschenhaus und gibt sich (wie einst Pasiphaë) dem Stier hin. Als Wyatt ihr nachläuft, begegnet er dort auch seinem Vater, der im Gewitter nach dem Stier sehen will, und in der dramatischsten Szene des ganzen Romans fragt Wyatt seinen Vater: »Vater ... Bin ich der, für den Christus gestorben ist?« (S. 589) Im selben Moment schlägt der Blitz ins Kutschenhaus ein. Da Wyatt von seinem Vater keine Antwort erhält und ihm allmählich klar wird, daß seine Rückkehr ein schwerer Fehler war, nimmt er noch am gleichen Abend den Zug zurück nach New York, nicht ohne vorher in der *Depot Tavern* noch das »Ei eines Greifen« gekauft zu haben.
Als er um elf Uhr abends in New York ankommt, geht Wyatt zuerst zu Brown. Brown ist allerdings auf Geschäftsreise, und Wyatt stellt fest, daß sich Fuller der Weißen Magie bedient (à la Frazer), um seinen Herren zu vernichten.

II.4
596–648 [446–486] Donnerstag oder Freitag, 22. oder 23. Dezember 1949

Am nächsten (vielleicht auch noch am gleichen) Tag, an dem Wyatt seinen Vater besucht (an diesem Punkt gerät das Zeitschema des Romans durcheinander), trifft Otto Esme in einem Drugstore, wo sie gerade mit einem Pornoproduzenten frühstückt, der sich verabschiedet, als Stanley und Max eintreffen. Otto bezahlt die Zeche für alle und macht auf dem anschließenden Spaziergang Esme einen Heiratsantrag, doch ihre Reaktion ist kühl. Sie nimmt den Antrag nicht ernst und läßt ihn stehen. Otto trifft bald darauf Max und Stanley wieder, aber auch Anselm, der sich als Babysitter um Don Bildows Tochter kümmert.

Esme ist zu Wyatts Unterkunft in der Horatio Street gegangen, doch Wyatt scheint zu schlafen (vielleicht ist er auch gar nicht anwesend). Sie geht auf und ab, redet mit sich selbst, stößt mit dem Fuß gegen das Ei des Greifen, das Wyatt mitgebracht hat, legt schließlich Camillas Ohrringe an, schminkt sich grell mit Wyatts Farben und schreibt ihm einen Brief. Da sie davon ausgeht, daß sie für ihn nur als Gemälde existiert, schließt sie ihren Brief mit den Worten: »Umgehen läßt sich die Malerei nur durch den absoluten Tod.« (S. 631) Anschließend kehrte sie in ihre Wohnung zurück und unternimmt einen Selbstmordversuch.

Am nächsten Tag kommt Otto aus einer Bar, um ins *Viareggio* zu gehen, wo er von Esmes Selbstmordversuch hört. In seiner Eitelkeit nimmt er an, er sei der Grund dafür gewesen, eilt in ihre Wohnung, um ihr zu verzeihen und sie zu trösten, und steht dort wiederum vor Chaby (der Esme gerettet hat). Esme verfällt wieder in Schizophrenie und spricht von da an nur noch in der dritten Person von sich. Otto erfährt, daß sie Wyatt Modell gesessen hat, und nachdem er ihr einmal mehr seiner Liebe versichert hat (wie auch seiner Abscheu vor Chaby) macht er sich auf den Weg, seinen Vater zu treffen.

II.5
649–723 [487–541] Freitag, 23. Dezember 1949

Frank Sinisterra haßt seinen mißratenen Sohn Chaby ebenfalls, wie wir gleich zu Beginn des Kapitels im Rahmen einer häuslichen Szene erfahren. Er bereitet sich auf ein Treffen mit einem Kontaktmann vor, dem er fünftausend Dollar in frisch gefälschten Zwanziger-Scheinen übergeben will, auf die er besonders stolz ist. Beim Verlassen der Wohnung wickelt er sich einen grünen Schal um den Hals, den Otto bei Esme liegengelassen und den Chaby später mitgenommen hat.

Auch Mr. Privner begibt sich in das Hotel, wo Vater und Sohn sich verabredet haben – ebenfalls mit einem grünen Schal, dem vereinbarten Erkennungszeichen. Versehentlich zerbricht er seine letzte Insulin-

Ampulle, nimmt sich jedoch vor, unterwegs eine neue zu kaufen und sie sich auf der Toilette des Hotels zu injizieren. Leider fällt er beim Betreten der Eingangshalle aufgrund einer akuten Unterzuckerung in Ohnmacht, wird vom Hotelpersonal für einen Betrunkenen gehalten und durch einen Seitenausgang auf die Straße befördert.

Otto wartet derweil in der Hotelbar; seine Gedanken kreisen zugleich um seinen Vater wie um eine Blondine namens Jean, die neben ihm an der Theke sitzt. Als Sinisterra eintrifft, kommt es zur schönsten Verwechslungsszene des ganzen Romans. Sinisterra hält Otto für den Abnehmer der Blüten und übergibt ihm das Falschgeld. Otto dagegen hält die fünftausend Dollar für ein außergewöhnlich großzügiges Weihnachtsgeschenk. Kurz darauf trifft der echte Kontaktmann ein, und gemeinsam nimmt man die Verfolgung von Otto auf. Sie fahren ihm ins *Viareggio* nach, wo Otto so tut, als rühre die plötzliche Liquidität aus dem Verkauf seines Theaterstücks. Großzügig leiht er sowohl Anselm als auch Stanley Geld. Dann kehrt er ins Hotel zurück, wo ihm Nacktfotos von Esme angeboten werden. Sinisterra und der Kontaktmann sind ihm immer noch dicht auf den Fersen. Doch ehe sie zuschlagen können, fällt Otto auf einen Lockvogel der Sittenpolizei herein und wird verhaftet.

Mister Pivner hat inzwischen das Mißverständnis mit der Polizei klären können und ist ins Hotel zurückgekehrt. Vergeblich wartet er auf seinen Sohn, geht schließlich nach Hause und nimmt sich vor, am nächsten Abend wiederzukommen.

II.6
724–758 [542–567] Samstag, 24. Dezember 1949

Wyatt und Valentine haben sich am Weihnachtsmorgen im Zoo verabredet. Wyatt ist wieder völlig durcheinander, weiß nicht, wie es weitergehen soll, und Valentine (wie auch der Leser) hat Schwierigkeiten, seinen zusammenhanglosen Bemerkungen zu folgen. Wir erfahren, daß Wyatt vor seiner Abreise die letzten Bilder im Kamin verbrannt hat und beabsichtigt, auf Browns Weihnachtsparty den Schwindel auffliegen zu lassen. Als Valentine ihn bittet, ihm das *Stabat Mater* als Geschenk zu überlassen, macht ihm Wyatt weis, daß auch dieses Bild verbrannt sei. In der nachfolgenden Unterhaltung über das Bild fällt Valentine schnell auf, daß Wyatts Entscheidung, einen Schlußstrich zu ziehen, vor allem von dem Wunsch geleitet ist, Buße zu tun für seine Mutter und »Himmels-

königin« Camilla. (S. 736) Valentine macht sich über dieses Motiv lustig und bringt es (offenbar korrekt) in Beziehung zu Wyatts neuerwachten Gefühlen für Esme.
Am gleichen Nachmittag kommt Agnes in ihre Wohnung zurück, wo sie Big Anna, den schwulen Schweden, vorfindet, der unter der Höhensonne eingeschlafen ist und sich schwere Verbrennungen zugezogen hat. Im Briefkasten liegt ein Schreiben der Polizei, in dem Agnes juristische Konsequenzen wegen ihrer ungerechtfertigten Anschuldigungen gegen Dr. Weisgall angekündigt werden. Ihre Schuldgefühle lassen sie bis zum Schluß des Romans nicht mehr los.
Der Rest des Personals macht sich bereit für die große Weihnachtsparty. Stanleys Mutter begeht Selbstmord, indem sie aus dem Fenster des Krankenhauses springt.
Mr. Pivner erhält per Kurier einen Morgenmantel – Ottos Weihnachtsgeschenk. Abermals begibt er sich in das besagte Hotel, in der Hoffnung, seinen Sohn endlich dort vorzufinden (Tatsächlich stehen sie, ohne einander zu erkennen, einen Moment lang nebeneinander am Pissoir des Hotels.) Mr. Pivner wartet an der Bar, flankiert von Frank Sinisterra und Jean, die mit einem von Ottos falschen Zwanzigern zahlt.

II.7
759–858 [568–646] Samstag, 24. Dezember 1949

Die Weihnachtsparty in ihrer eigenen Wohnung bietet Esther die willkommene Gelegenheit, zwanglos einen ihrer Lieblingsschriftsteller kennenzulernen. Die meisten anderen Gäste sind alte Bekannte von einer früheren Festivität (I.5). Während Esthers geistesgestörte Schwester Rose Schallplatten mit Händel-Musik abspielt, tauschen die Gäste pseudointellektuellen Klatsch und Tratsch aus. Anwesend sind auch Edna Mims sowie der Leiter der argentinischen Handelsmission (wie immer auf der falschen Party) und Benny, Wyatts ehemaliger Vorgesetzter, der jetzt mit Ellery in der Werbebranche arbeitet.
Überraschend taucht Wyatt auf, um ein paar seiner alten Sachen abzuholen. Esther, die anfangs noch hofft, er wolle zu ihr zurück, merkt nach einem sinnlosen Streit, daß er sich nicht verändert hat. Als Wyatt geht, wird er auch von Benny bemerkt. Benny erinnert sich an ihre frühere Zusammenarbeit, und ihm wird bewußt, wie sehr er ohne Wyatt heruntergekommen ist. Die Party geht weiter. In unregelmäßigen Abständen steht ein kleines Nachbarsmädchen vor der Tür und bittet die

Gäste um Schlaftabletten für ihre Mutter. Zwischen den Füßen der Gäste krabbeln eine Katze und ein Baby herum. Stanley verdoppelt seine Anstrengungen, die vom katholischen Glauben abgefallene Agnes wieder auf den rechten Pfad zurückzuführen. Der schwarze Kritiker mit dem grünen Wollhemd (offenbar alles, was er an Garderobe besitzt), erfährt, daß Benny fürs Fernsehen arbeitet und bricht einen Streit über die Nichtswürdigkeit dieses Mediums vom Zaun. Doch Benny weiß sich zu wehren und gibt den Kritiker als pseudointellektuelle Drohne der Lächerlichkeit preis. Inzwischen ist auch der Ehrengast eingetroffen, dem kurze Zeit später auch der völlig durchnäßte Otto folgt. Er und Esther geraten in eine Auseinandersetzung, die der vorangegangenen zwischen Wyatt und Esther bis in die Formulierung hinein ähnelt. Anselm, der bis dato schweigend das Geschehen beobachtet hat, fängt an, die Gäste zu beleidigen und entlarvt Max als Plagiator von Rilkes *Duineser Elegien*. Erst die Nachricht, daß Charles versucht hat, sich im Badezimmer umzubringen, beendet seine haßerfüllte Hochstimmung. Er nimmt Charles das Rasiermesser ab und steckt es ein, dasselbe Rasiermesser, das Wyatt einst seinem Vater gestohlen hat. Mit sanftem Druck versucht der Kritiker, Anselm zum Verlassen der Party zu bewegen, doch Anselm beschimpft ihn als »Mister Handbetrieb« (S. 846), woraufhin ihn der Kritiker niederschlägt. Stanley kümmert sich um den am Boden liegenden Anselm, allerdings fordert auch Agnes seine Aufmerksamkeit. Stanley versucht ihr zu erklären, daß er Anselm nicht im Stich lassen könne, aber während er noch redet, schleicht sich Anselm aus der Wohnung.
Die Party endet in einem gewaltigen Chaos. Die Katze wird getötet, als sich Agnes aus Versehen auf sie setzt (und das Tier dann einfach in ihre Handtasche stopft). Maude Munk stiehlt das anonyme Baby, während ihr Mann mit Sonny Byron homosexuellen Verkehr hat. Mr. Feddle zitiert Tolstoi und bringt damit unbeabsichtigt Benny auf Selbstmordgedanken. Esther stellt fest, daß Ellery im Verlauf der Party mit Adelaide geschlafen hat. Und Ed Feasley verpatzt die einmalige Chance, das Kriegsschiff seines Vaters an den Argentinier zu verkaufen. Esther zieht sich mit dem schwarzen Kritiker in ihr Schlafzimmer zurück, der sie auffordert, ihn beim Masturbieren zuzugucken.
Inzwischen kriecht Anselm die Treppe zur U-Bahn hinunter und begegnet dort seiner Mutter; er flieht vor ihr in eine öffentliche Toilette und kastriert sich mit Reverend Gwyons Rasiermesser.
Auf dem Heimweg mit Stanley wird Agnes Deigh von einem Straßen-

räuber die Handtasche entrissen. Stanley versucht, sie in eine Kirche zu ziehen, aber sie macht sich von ihm los und flüchtet statt dessen in eine Bar. Dort reift der Gedanke, sich ein Hotelzimmer zu nehmen und Dr. Weisgall einen Brief zu schreiben. Stanley will ihren Drink mit einem von Ottos falschen Zwanzigern bezahlen, wird aber vom Barkeeper festgehalten und der Polizei übergeben.

II.8
859–921 [647–699] 24. Dezember 1949

Die Handlung dieses Kapitels verläuft zeitgleich zu II.7. Es beginnt mit einem Gespräch zwischen Mr. Inononu, einem ungarischen Geheimagenten, und Valentine, der in Spionageaktionen sowohl der katholischen Kirche als auch des ungarischen Regimes verwickelt ist. Inononu hat den Auftrag, einen rumänischen Ägyptologen namens Yák zu ermorden, und hofft, ihn dadurch aufspüren zu können, daß er sich (unter dem Namen Kuvetli) als wissenschaftlicher Kollege ausgibt. Im Verlauf des Gesprächs erscheint Wyatt und hämmert gegen Valentines Wohnungstür. Wyatt will seine Beweisstücke abholen, die er auf Browns Party dem versammelten Fachpublikum präsentieren will. Er ist bereits auf der Party gewesen, allerdings ohne irgend jemanden von seiner Geschichte überzeugen zu können, wie Fuller später berichtet. »Er gekommen vor eine kleine Weile und wandelt konvenabel zu jeder Mann, sehr liebenswürdig, ich aber habe grüne Augen gesehen [...]« (S. 868) Valentine und Inononu schleichen sich durch die Hintertür aus dem Haus und fahren zu Brown.

Unter den Anwesenden auf Browns Weihnachtsparty, die im wesentlichen von neuen Romanfiguren bevölkert wird, ist auch Crémer, der Kunstkritiker aus Wyatts Pariser Zeit. Brown hat einige Kunstsammler eingeladen, die sich Wyatts letzte Fälschung ansehen sollen, einen *Tod der Jungfrau Maria* des flämischen Malers van der Goes. (Valentine hat eigenhändig versucht, den zerstörten Kopf der Jungfrau zu restaurieren.) Nachdem er das Gemälde gezeigt hat, steigt der betrunkene und nervöse Brown in eine Ritterrüstung, eines seiner Sammlerstücke, und stürzt in diesem Ding, als Wyatt dazukommt, tödlich die Treppe hinab. Wyatt hat inzwischen entdeckt, daß Valentine das gesamte Beweismaterial verbrannt hat – keine Chance mehr für ihn, den Betrug aufzudecken. Schockiert über den Unfall, verlassen die Gäste die Party. Nun ist der Weg frei für Valentine, der Wyatt ganz für sich und seine Zwecke einsetzen sill, doch Wyatt sticht ihn mit Browns Taschenmesser nieder. Er läßt den Schwerverletzten liegen und beschließt, das Land zu verlassen. Auch Fuller, der Browns verwöhnten Pudel getötet hat, will nach dem Tod seines Herrn in seine Heimat zurückkehren. Wyatt begibt sich auf die Suche nach Esme, als ihm klar wird, daß seine *Stabat Mater* ein Raub der Flammen geworden ist.

Otto sucht Esme ebenfalls. Da er sie jedoch nicht mitten in der Nacht im Bellevue Hospital besuchen kann, geht er in die Horatio Street, um wenigstens Wyatt zu sprechen. (Agnes Deigh wird in einem Hotel gezeigt, wo sie wieder und wieder einen Brief an Dr. Weisgall zu schreiben versucht.) Kurz bevor er Wyatt findet, wird Otto von Stanley angesprochen, der nach dem Vorfall mit dem gefälschten Zwanzigdollarschein längere Zeit im Polizeigewahrsam verbracht hat. Doch Stanley, wie es seine Art ist, verzeiht Otto. (Eine weitere Vignette zeigt Mr. Pivner, wie er im Büroboten Eddie Zefnic den Sohn findet, der Otto ihm nie war.) Otto und Wyatt begegnen sich vor Esmes Wohnung, doch Otto verschweigt ihm Esmes Aufenthaltsort. Wyatt wendet sich ab und läßt Otto in seiner kalten Hölle allein.

II.9
922–945 [700–720]
25. Dezember 1949 – Anfang 1950

Am Morgen des ersten Weihnachtstags vollzieht der mittlerweile wahnsinnige Reverend Gwyon mit seiner Gemeinde den Mithras-Kult. Er wird in ein Irrenhaus eingeliefert, wo er von einem Mitpatienten namens Farisy gekreuzigt wird. »Dick«, der junge Nachfolger des Reverends, schickt seine Asche ans Kloster *Real Monasterio de Nuestra Señora de la Otra Vez*.

III.1
949–961 [723–732] Januar 1950

In diesem, dem kürzesten Kapitel des Romans, flieht Otto mit seinem Falschgeld nach Mittelamerika. Nachdem er in New York immer nur mit Revolutionsgeschichten angegeben hat, wird er endlich Augenzeuge eines Aufstands. Er wird von einem stürzenden Pferd zu Boden gerissen und verletzt. Mit einem gebrochenen Arm und der Ménièrschen Krankheit erwacht er aus der Bewußtlosigkeit. Letztere Diagnose ist reichlich ungesichert, denn der behandelnde Arzt, ein gewisser Dr. Fell, entpuppt sich als derselbe, der auch schon bei Wyatt versagt hat. Otto ist desorientiert, trägt den jetzt tatsächlich gebrochenen Arm in einer Schlinge und nennt sich Gordon (nach der Byronschen Heldenfigur aus seinem Stück).

III.2
962–1008 [733–768] Januar 1950

In einem Fernsehsender in New York besprechen Ellery, Morgie Darling und ein nicht weiter spezifizierter Typ »von einer Busch-Uni in Alabama« ihre geschmacklosen Werbekampagnen, als sie plötzlich auf einem der Bildschirme mit ansehen müssen, wie sich Benny von einem Kirchturm stürzt. In einem anderen Teil der Stadt versucht auch Agnes Deigh, sich das Leben zu nehmen. Sie hält sich seit etwa einer Woche in einem Hotelzimmer verschanzt, um ihren Brief an Dr. Weisgall zu Ende zu bringen. Schließlich springt sie aus dem Fenster und überlebt nur deshalb, weil sie auf einen vorbeikommenden Briefträger fällt. Wir erfahren auch, daß Señor Hermoso Hermoso (aus Kapitel I.1) eine Zeitung wegen Verleumdung verklagt, weil über dem Namen des Mannes, der vierzig Jahre zuvor das schieläugige Mädchen, die künftige Heilige, vergewaltigt hat, irrtümlich sein Bild abgedruckt wurde. (Señor Hermoso Hermoso hat die Absicht, die Entschädigungssumme in die Finanzierung ihrer Heiligsprechung einzubringen.) Mr. Pivners Beziehung zu Eddie Zefnic hat sich bestens entwickelt, aber als Eddie ihn eines Abends besucht, um sich gemeinsam mit diesem Händels *Messias* im Radio anzuhören, wird Pivner von Beamten des Schatzamts als Geldfälscher verhaftet.

Ansonsten bereitet man sich allerseits auf den nächsten Europa-Trip vor. Stanley will nach Italien, um in der Kathedrale von Fenestrula sein Orgelkonzert zu spielen. Max und Hannah zieht es nach Paris. Don Bildow freut sich auf erotische Abenteuer, hat nur ein schlechtes Gewissen wegen seiner merkwürdig aufgequollenen Tochter, die wahrscheinlich von ihrem ehemaligen Babysitter Anselm geschwängert wurde. Anselm hat sich unterdessen in den Westen abgesetzt, um in ein Kloster einzutreten und dort seine Bekenntnisse niederzuschreiben. Arny Munk (mittlerweile voll in der Coming-out-Phase) sowie die meisten anderen schwulen Romanfiguren wollen in Paris die Hochzeit von Rudy und Frank feiern. Frank Sinisterra will zurück nach Spanien. Stanley besucht sowohl Agnes als auch Esme im Bellevue Hospital und schmuggelt daraufhin Esme als blinden Passagier an Bord. Mit von der Partie sind auch Basil Valentine, Father Martin, die »Silberlocke« von Browns Weihnachtsfeier sowie verschiedene andere Nebenfiguren. Diejenigen, die in New York bleiben wie Ed Feasley (dessen Vater einen Schlaganfall erlitten hat), Maude Monk (die ihr gestohlenes Baby mißhandelt), und Ellery (der von dem kleinen Mädchen aus der unteren Etage zu dessen toter Mutter geführt wird), sie alle versinken in Depressionen. Die Abfahrt des Schiffs erinnert in vielerlei Hinsicht an die unheilvolle *Purdue Victory* vom Anfang des Romans.

III.3
1009–1072 [769–823] Anfang 1950

Unter dem Falschnamen Yák (wahrscheinlich hat er in New York dessen Paß gekauft) quartiert sich Sinisterra in einer Madrider Pension ein und sinnt auf neue Taten. Daß er damit ins Visier des Killers Inononu (alias Kuvetli) gerät, ahnt er nicht. Er studiert die lokalen Zeitungen, »auf der Suche nach neuen Herausforderungen […], um die jüngste Scharte auszuwetzen«, (S. 1014) und hat plötzlich die Idee, eine Mumie für den bekannte Ägyptologen »Señor Kuvetli« zu fälschen.
Sinisterra reist zu dem Friedhof bei San Zwingli, um die Möglichkeiten einer diskreten Leichenbeschaffung zu eruieren. Dort trifft er zufällig auf Wyatt, der das Grab seiner Mutter sucht. Als Sinisterra erfährt, daß Wyatt der Sohn derselben Frau ist, die er vor dreißig Jahren unabsichtlich getötet hat, nimmt er ihn unter seinen Fittiche, teils um seine Schuldgefühle loszuwerden, teils weil er bei dem Mumien-Projekt auf Wyatts Hilfe angewiesen ist. Er verschafft Wyatt einen schweizer Paß, ausgestellt auf den Namen »Stephan Asche«. (Man erinnere sich, daß Camilla ihren Sohn ursprünglich »Stephen« nennen wollte.) Wyatt/Stephan läßt sich zwar zur Mitarbeit überreden, interessiert sich zu diesem Zeitpunkt allerdings mehr für Alkohol und Prostituierte. Da ist zunächst die attraktive Blondine Marga, die sich in Sinisterras Pension aufhält, dann ein schlichtes Zigeunermädchen namens Pastora, die sich von ihm ein Kind wünscht. Sinisterra und Stephan exhumieren die Leiche und zwar die des »schieläugigen Mädchens«. Camillas Leiche, die zuvor mit der des kleinen Mädchens verwechselt worden ist, befindet sich auf dem Weg nach Rom, wo sie als Reliquie heiliggesprochen werden soll. Auf dem Rückweg nach Madrid erfahren sie, daß die

Polizei nach einem amerikanischen »falsificador« fahndet. Stephen verläßt schleunigst die Stadt, und Sinisterra macht sich allein ans Werk.

III.4
1073–1111 [824–855] Anfang 1950

In der Enge der Kabine entwickelt sich Stanleys Seereise mit seinem blinden Passagier Esme schnell zum Alptraum. Esme hat überdies zu Valentine Kontakt aufgenommen (den sie den »Kalten Mann« nennt). Einmal dreht das Schiff bei, um die Überlebenden eines gesunkenen Frachters aufzunehmen (die *Purdue Victory* aus Kapitel I.1). Einer der Schiffbrüchigen, der Wyatt sehr ähnlich sieht, stirbt später, und Esme fällt in Ohnmacht. Stanley bringt sie in ihre Kabine zurück, aber sie besteht darauf, den toten Matrosen ein letztes Mal zu sehen. Stanley hält sie mit Gewalt zurück (und bekommt während der Rangelei einen Orgasmus).

Später hört Esme mit an, wie Father Martin dem Sterbenden die Letzte Ölung gibt. Anschließend geraten Esme und Stanley in ihrer Kabine erneut aneinander, allerdings gibt es Hinweise darauf, daß Stanley die Szene nur halluziniert und in Wahrheit allein ist. Am nächsten Morgen wird die sterbliche Hülle des Matrosen dem Meer übergeben. Esme, die immer noch davon überzeugt ist, daß es sich bei dem Toten um Wyatt handelt, will über Bord springen, was Stanley gerade noch verhindern kann. Stanley unternimmt später einen ähnlichen Versuch. (Überhaupt ist bei Gaddis der Sprung in den Tod die mit Abstand beliebteste Selbstmordmethode.)

An Bord befindet sich ein »renommierter Autor« namens Ludy, der nach Spanien unterwegs ist, wo er für ein kitschiges Buch über Religion recherchieren will. Seine Lektüre von Masefields *The Everlasting Mercy* (zur Einstimmung) wird jedoch von einem angetrunkenen Journalisten unterbrochen. Dieser gehört derselben Zeitung an, die von Señor Hermoso Hermoso verklagt worden ist, und erfreut Ludy mit falsch zitierten Zeilen aus Joaquin Millers *Columbus* und einigen zynisch-witzigen Informationen über die Entdeckung Amerikas.

Stanley erwacht auf der Krankenstation des Schiffs, nachdem ein italienischer Stewart ihn daran gehindert hat, über Bord zu springen. Er liegt dort offenbar in demselben Bett, in dem der Seemann gestorben ist. Ein anderer Patient hat mit angehört, was Stanley in seinem Delirium gesagt hat und macht sich über seine Ängste lustig. Stanley behauptet jedoch, er könne sich an alles genau erinnern. Tatsächlich ist die Grenze zwischen Realität und Halluzination an diesem Punkt völlig verschwommen. Esme geht zusammen mit Valentine in Neapel von Bord, Stanley bleibt auf der Krankenstation zurück. Das Kapitel endet mit einer Variante des Satzes »Neapel sehen und sterben« – ein böses Omen für Stanley.

III.5
1112–1168 [856–900] Frühjahr 1950

Wyatt hat sich wie einst sein Vater ins Kloster *Real Monasterio de Nuestra Señora de la Otra Vez* zurückgezogen, wo er Gemälde restauriert. (Inwieweit sein Wahnsinn echt oder nur gespielt ist, bleibt unklar.) Ludy, der »renommierte Autor«, zählt ebenfalls zu den Gästen des Klosters und müht sich vergebens, den religiösen Geist des Hauses in Worte zu fassen. Es kommt zum Gespräch zwischen Ludy und Stephen, aus dem hervorgeht, daß es Wyatt zunächst nach Nordafrika verschlagen hat, wo er Han, seinen Kumpan aus der Münchener Zeit wiedergetroffen hat. Han ist mittlerweile in der Fremdenlegion und glaubt, Stephen wolle ebenfalls Legionär werden. Später erschießt ihn Wyatt im Streit und flieht zurück nach Spanien und in das besagte Kloster, um für seine Schuld Buße zu tun und wie Thoreau sein Leben radikal zu vereinfachen. Die letzte Szene zeigt ihn, wie er das Kloster verläßt, möglicherweise auf der Suche nach seiner und Pastoras Tochter. (Jedenfalls hatte Gaddis in einer frühen Fassung der *Fälschung der Welt* diese Wendung vorgesehen.) Im Gegensatz zu Stephen, der schließlich doch so etwas wie einen Ausweg aus seinem Dilemma findet, wehrt sich Ludy bis zum Schluß gegen jede unmittelbare religiöse Erfahrung.

Epilog
1169–1241 [901–956] Frühjahr 1950

Wyatts Geschichte ist beendet; das abschließende Kapitel widmet sich ausschließlich dem weiteren Schicksal der Nebenfiguren. Stanley, endlich in Rom, begibt sich zu Agnes Deighs Mutter in der Via Flaminia. Über ihre guten Beziehungen hofft er die Genehmigung zu erhalten, seine Orgelkomposition in der Kathedrale von Fenestula aufzuführen. Während seines Aufenthalts in Rom begegnet er zahlreichen anderen Figuren aus der New Yorker *Village*-Boheme. Einmal spioniert er Esme nach, wird aber von Don Bildow gestört (der von ihm das italienische

Wort für Verhütungsmittel wissen will). Er fragt Big Anna nach Esmes Verbleib und erfährt, daß Esme die Absicht hat, Nonne zu werden. Ellery erzählt Stanley, daß er Esme als Jungfrau Maria für einen geplanten Bibelfilm verpflichten will. Esme selbst ist nach Assisi gepilgert, um Ablässe für Wyatt zu sammeln (den sie im Fegefeuer wähnt).

Inzwischen hat Anselm seine Bekenntnisse veröffentlicht, in denen er über seine ehemaligen Freunde herzieht. Wir erfahren auch, daß Inononu den falschen Yák (nämlich Sinisterra) aufgestöbert und erschossen hat. Der nächste Kandidat auf seiner Liste ist Father Martin – die entscheidenden Hinweise kommen von Valentine, der damit seinen ehemaligen Schulfreund ein letztes Mal verrät. Stanley am Nebentisch bekommt nicht nur diese Verschwörung mit, er muß nach Inononus Weggang sogar erleben, wie Esme dem »Kalten Mann« Valentine einen Heiratsantrag macht, der natürlich ablehnt.

Der verwirrte Stanley erzählt Mrs. Deigh später, Esme hätte *ihm* einen Antrag gemacht. Kurz darauf der nächste Schock, als ihn Mrs. Deigh nackt in ihre Privatkapelle entführen will (der Tick geht auf ein Kindheitserlebnis im Zusammenhang mit dem Wunder von Fátima zurück). Stanley flüchtet auf die Straße und wird beinahe von einem Fiat überfahren.

Es folgen noch einige kurze Vignetten. In Barbados arbeitet Otto (alias Gordon) als eine Art Assistent für Dr. Fell. Den Eingeborenen hat er die Namen seiner ehemaligen Freunde gegeben. Ed Feasley hat auf dem Anwesen seines Vaters am Hudson River alle Hände voll zu tun, seine geisteskranken Patienten zu betreuen (für die in der nahegelegenen Klinik kein Platz mehr war). Auch Feasley hat ihnen die Namen seiner alten Bekannten gegeben.

Eddie Zefnic hat Mr. Pivner einen Brief geschrieben, in dem er ihn noch einmal von der Richtigkeit der Gehirnoperation überzeugen will, der sich Mr. Pivner auf Eddies Betreiben hin unterzogen hat. (Ziel der Lobotomie ist es, Mr. Pivner von seinen angeblich kriminellen Neigungen als Geldfälscher zu heilen.) In aller Unschuld berichtet Eddie von bedenkenlosen wissenschaftlichen Experimenten und erwähnt auch einen Zeitungsartikel über Sinisterras »Selbstmord« in Spanien. Der Artikel wird später, auf Plastik verewigt, von einer obskuren Firma namens *Memento Associates* der Witwe zum Kauf angeboten.

In New York benutzt der trottelige Mr. Feddle Rezensionen über Anselms Buch, von denen er die Überschriften abgetrennt hat, um damit seinen eigenen, unlängst erschienenen Gedichtband aufzuwerten. Das Buch, das er als seines ausgibt, ist in Wahrheit Dostojewskijs *Idiot*, versehen mit einem selbstgemachten Schutzumschlag, der seinen Namen trägt. Der Kritiker im grünen Wollhemd allerdings läßt sich nicht täuschen. Er schleppt seinerseits ein dickes Buch mit sich herum – allem Anschein nach eine Ausgabe der *Fälschung der Welt*, die er zu rezensieren gedenkt. Entsprechend fallen die Kommentare aus.

In Paris, wo sich nicht viel verändert hat, seit Wyatt in den 30er Jahren dort war, machen Hannah, Max und die anderen so weiter wie immer. Crémer hat Max den gleichen Vorschlag unterbreitet, den er seinerzeit Wyatt gemacht hat. Max, wie könnte es anders sein, stimmt begeistert zu, denn »ein guter Agent nimmt auch zehn Prozent«. (S. 1220) Rudy und Frank haben unterdessen geheiratet. Arny Munk schreibt Maude einen Brief, in dem er ihr sein Coming-out mitteilen will, kommt aber beim Einsturz seines Hotels ums Leben.

Meldungen aus aller Welt von Selbstmord, Dummheit und Korruption runden das Bild ab. (Wenn II.8 die Höllenfahrt war, dann schildert das letzte Kapitel die Apokalypse.) In einem Krankenhaus in Budapest geht Valentine derweil an Schlaflosigkeit ein. Noch auf dem Sterbebett erfährt er vom Attentat auf Father Martin und fällt in ein Delirium, ehe der Priester ihm die Absolution erteilen kann. Auf Barbados, wo Fuller inzwischen lebt, erfährt Otto/Gordon, daß Jesse sein Falschgeld gestohlen hat, und Dr. Fell rät ihm, wieder ganz von vorn anzufangen.

Unterdessen schlägt für Stanley in Rom das Schicksal gleich mehrmals zu. Father Martin wird erschossen, Esme ist tot, und das Empfehlungsschreiben entpuppt sich als schnöde Einkaufsliste. Auf dem Bahnhof begegnet er ein letztes Mal Don Bildow, der mit seinem neuen, maßgeschneiderten Anzug als einzigem Gepäck nach Paris reist. (Später auf der Zugtoilette stopft er seine alte Garderobe ins Klo, muß dann aber feststellen, daß sich in der Pappschachtel des Schneiders nur ein Matrosenanzug für kleine Jungen befindet.)

Ostersonntag in der Kathedrale von Fenestrula: Der Tag der Uraufführung ist da, auch wenn Stanley das Stück zunächst nur für sich spielen will. Leider versteht er kein Italienisch und bekommt daher nicht mit, wie ihn der Priester eindringlich vor der Verwendung von starken Bässen und Dissonanzen warnt. Er zieht sämtliche Register (»sein Werk verlangte es«), und die Vibrationen lassen die alte Kirche einstürzen. Stanley stirbt unter den Trümmern. Seine Werk aber ist »bis heute nicht in Vergessenheit geraten, wird von Eingeweihten hochgeschätzt, aber selten aufgeführt.« (S. 1241)

Kurzer Hinweis zu den Anmerkungen

Wie die *Cantos* von Ezra Pound, die späteren Werke Joyces, die langen Gedichte David Jones' und selbst noch (wie Alfred Appel gezeigt hat) Nabokovs *Lolita*, ist *Die Fälschung der Welt* ein moderner Text, der geradezu nach Anmerkungen schreit – was nicht nur dem eher pedantischen Akademiker auffällt, sondern jedem Leser, der sich mit der enormen Menge versteckter Informationen konfrontiert sieht. Wer lieber weiterblättert, sobald er etwas nicht versteht, muß nicht nur kräftig blättern, ihm entgeht auch viel. Zweifellos hat nicht einmal William Gaddis damit gerechnet, daß der Leser alle Anspielungen und Bezüge versteht. Liest man also den Roman unter Zuhilfenahme der folgenden Anmerkungen, wird der von Gaddis ursprünglich intendierte Lektüreeindruck durchaus abgeschwächt (dementsprechend empfehlen sich diese Anmerkungen auch weniger für die erste als vielmehr für eine zweite Lektüre. Aber eine vernünftige Würdigung des Romans setzt nun einmal ein umfassendes Verständnis aller seiner Aspekte voraus, und zu diesem Zweck sind die Anmerkungen entstanden.
Absicht der folgenden Kommentare ist der Nachweis des gesamten, dem Roman zugrunde liegenden Quellenmaterials, weniger dessen Interpretation. Da ich natürlich nicht weiß, was beim Leser als bekannt vorausgesetzt werden darf, habe ich mich zu größtmöglicher Vollständigkeit entschlossen und alles nachgewiesen, was sich nicht in einem normalen Handlexikon findet. Ähnlich sind auch Don Gifford und Robert Seideman in ihrem verdienstvollen *Notes for Joyce: An Annotation of James Joyce's »Ulysses«* (1974) verfahren, das für diese Untersuchung Vorbildcharakter hatte. Es kann sein, daß dem einen oder anderen (etwa bei Reverend Gwyons Predigten) soviel Genauigkeit überflüssig erscheint, doch wollte ich lieber zuviel als zuwenig erklären.
Jede Erläuterung folgt unmittelbar auf die erste Nennung des Stichworts, es sei denn, das Verständnis ergibt sich aus dem Zusammenhang. Der Umfang der Anmerkungen hängt im allgemeinen vom Bekanntheitsgrad der Quelle ab und weniger von ihrer Wichtigkeit; deshalb beansprucht ein Stichwort wie »exhomologesis by Calixtus I« eine halbe Seite, während eine Anspielung auf ein Shakespeare-Drama lediglich zitatweise

nachgewiesen wird. Die Anmerkungen entsprechen somit weitgehend einer Quellenanalyse. Gaddis' Umgang mit dem Quellenmaterial ist gelegentlich etwas exzentrisch, aber stets interessant, weshalb ich so oft wie möglich aus den Originalwerken zitiere. Gleichwohl sollte man sich von Anfang an bewußt sein, daß viele dieser Quellen aus heutiger Sicht problematisch sind. Zum Beispiel hat Frazers *Der goldene Zweig (The Golden Bough)* großen Einfluß auf die Literatur- und Geistesgeschichte des 20. Jahrhunderts ausgeübt, wie John Vickery nachgewiesen hat (*Literary Impact of »The Golden Bough«*, Princeton: Princeton University Press, 1973, p. 155), und das, obwohl viele von Frazers Informationsquellen unzuverlässig waren, zum Teil auf Vorurteilen, zum Teil sogar schlicht auf Falschinformationen beruhten, so daß sie praktisch von Anfang an der Kritik ausgesetzt waren. Andrew Langs *Magic and Religion* etwa verfährt so, und die Tatsache, daß Langs Studie auch von Gaddis als Quelle benutzt wurde, deutet darauf hin, daß Gaddis sich zumindest der Fragwürdigkeit von Frazers Ansatz bewußt war. Graves' *Weiße Göttin*, ein faszinierendes Werk und als mythologische »Grammatik« noch heute brauchbar, hat die meisten Spezialisten, auf deren Terrain Graves gewildert hat, zu harscher Ablehnung veranlaßt. Und über *Architecture, Mysticism and Myth* schrieb Lethaby rückblickend: »Mein kleines Buch war höchst ungenügend und stand in vielerlei Hinsicht auf wackligen Beinen. Zweitklassige Autoritäten und solche, die ich nur ungenügend kannte, vermischten sich mit Originalquellen, so daß das Ganze ziemlich unkritisch ausfiel.« De Rougemonts Bücher sind meiner Meinung nach ebenso tiefschürfend wie naiv, von der einseitigen Parteinahme für die katholische Kirche ganz zu schweigen. Und im Hinblick auf Gaddis' wichtigste Quellen zum Thema Heiligenlegenden – Foxes (protestantisches) *Book of Martyrs* und Reverend Montague Summers (katholisches) *Physical Phenomena of Mysticism* – lassen sowohl Foxe als auch Summers jede wissenschaftliche Distanz vermissen. (Über das letztere urteilt sogar Summers getreuer Biograph, daß »es darin zwar von interessanten und entlegenen Details nur so wimmelt, aber kaum zu Summers besten Büchern zu zählen ist.«) Phytian-Adams' *Mithraism* und Smiths *Counterfeiting* zählen in Fachkreisen kaum zu den Standardwerken, und auch Jungs psychologische Interpretation alchemistischer Literatur ist nicht unwidersprochen geblieben. Sowohl Marshs *Mediaeval and Modern Saints and Miracles* als auch Conybeares *Magic, Myth and Morals* sind in ihrer bilderstürmerischen Konsequenz leicht veraltet, allerdings als Gegengewicht zu den naiven Studien von Foxe und Summers nützlich. Über den *Malleus Maleficiarum* (mit den treuherzigen Anmerkungen des Reverend Summers), Carnegies *Wie man Freunde gewinnt (How to Win Friends and Influence People)* sowie die Apokryphen des Neuen Testaments muß nichts weiter gesagt werden. Natürlich sind alle diese Bücher auf ihre jeweilige Art noch nützlich, doch sollte man hier die Spreu vom Weizen trennen – ein Selektionsprozeß, den Gaddis nicht immer vorgenommen hat. Gleichwohl muß man sich vergegenwärtigen, daß Gaddis' Anleihen lediglich künstlerischen Zwecken dienten, und daß er keine Enzyklopädie, sondern einen Roman schreiben wollte.

Schließlich wird schnell deutlich werden, daß ich nicht alles kommentieren konnte und daß ich auch nicht alles, was ich kommentiert habe, restlos verstanden habe. Weitere Quellen des Autors, vielleicht auch eine Reihe versteckter Anspielungen im Text, die anderen ins Auge springen, mögen mir entgangen sein. Manchem wird sogar der Sinn dieses teilweise recht langwierigen Unternehmens zweifelhaft erscheinen. In diesem Fall möchte ich mich mit den Worten von Denis de Rougemonts vorsorglich entschuldigen: »Ich darf nur damit rechnen, denjenigen zu genügen, denen es genügt, mehr über einen bestimmten Gegenstand in Erfahrung zu bringen.«

A Readers Guide to William Gaddis's »The Recognitions«

Anmerkungsteil
der Originalausgabe

Preface to Revised Edition

Sixteen years have passed since the first edition of this book was published (University of Nebraska Press, 1982), and during those years I have been gathering materials for what I hoped would be a second edition. The discovery of several more of Gaddis's source books – especially Haggard's *Devils, Drugs and Doctors* and Saltus's *Anatomy of Negation* – enabled me to plug many gaps and clarify other references, as did my realization that Gaddis used the *Encyclopædia Britannica,* Baedeker's *Spain and Portugal,* and the *Oxford Dictionary of Quotations* much more extensively than I first imagined. I have also benefitted from a few Gaddis critics who wrote to offer suggestions and corrections – specifically Marc Chénetier, Rodger Cunningham, and Joseph Tabbi – though I had hoped to hear from more. (Gaddis himself wrote me a long letter clarifying many points, though his remarks, he said, were "not exhaustive.") At any rate, the annotations are much fuller and more precise than the previous edition, though a few untraced references remain to bedevil me.

For this edition, I have focused solely on the annotations. Gone are the introduction and appendices to the first edition, and the plot synopsis has been broken up and scattered to introduce each chapter. (The synopses retain the dating I first arrived at in my "Chronological Difficulties in the Novels of William Gaddis," though I now feel it is too literal-minded to accommodate Gaddis's more flexible temporal structures.) Many of the sources I originally cited were later, revised editions *(Love in the Western World, Psychology and Alchemy, The White Goddess),* which I thought would be more accessible to Gaddis scholars, but I have changed those to refer to the editions Gaddis actually used. Gone too are the cross-references to the Avon edition of *The Recognitions,* which in 1982 was the only edition available. Thankfully, a corrected Penguin edition seems to be here to stay, so all references are to that edition. (The Penguin edition has the same pagination as the first edition, as does the Meridian and British editions of 1962 and the Harvest edition of 1970, so my page/line references correspond to every edition of *The Recognitions* except for the Avon, a textually corrupt edition that should be ignored by Gaddis scholars.) The original edition's bibliography of Gaddis criticism, which listed everything that had been written on *The Recognitions* at that time, has been confined to those works actually cited in the annotations. I have also altered the method of indicating ellipses; since Gaddis uses them so extensively, it is necessary to distinguish his from mine, so bracketed, unspaced ellipses like this [...] indicate mine, while his are left spaced, as in the text, like this ... For consistency, this practice has been followed in other works cited.

Annotations

[title] *The Recognitions*: the title of a third-century "theological romance" attributed to Clement of Rome (see 373.1 ff.). In his working notes for the novel Gaddis wrote: "*The Recognitions* as title I like perfectly because it implies the impossibility of escape from a (the) pattern"; and elsewhere: "THE RECOGNITIONS is I think in the first place a simple lable [sic], deceptively simple perhaps, and all the better" (quoted in Koenig's "'Splinters from the Yew Tree,'" 13, 85). One form or another of the word *recognition* appears in the following places: 22.21, 51.31, 68.13, 78.epigraph, 84.24, 88.15, 91.42, 92.6, 98.6, 107.36, 123.9, 139.37, 152.12, 206.10, 207.20, 220.27, 232.43, 250.17, 269.19, 275.44, 285.4, 288.38, 292.21, 303.7, 303.18, 306.20, 306.40, 322.14, 325.30, 332.15, 335.19, 343.epigraph, 373.1, 384.24, 405.35, 414.6, 414.9, 417.21, 451.41, 453.28, 458.35, 472.29, 477.8, 487.epigraph, 490.6, 501.42, 507.39, 508.16, 516.21, 517.34, 535.2, 543.31, 552.9, 552.15, 552.18, 563.3, 564.6, 616.34, 621.43, 644.16, 744.8, 758.7, 758.11, 759.14, 759.43, 761.17, 762.6, 762.22, 762.23, 767.44, 771.42, 782.6, 859.26, 863.23, 865.35, 901.epigraph.
The dragon eating its tail on the title page is the alchemical uroborus, symbol of the *opus alchymicum* in "that the *opus* proceeds from one thing and leads back again to the One" (*IP* 227).

2 [epigraph] Nihil cavum sine signo apud Deum. – Irenaeus, *Adversus haereses*: "In God nothing is empty of sense: *nihil vacuum neque sine signo apud Deum,* said Saint Irenaeus. So the conviction of a transcendental meaning in all things seeks to formulate itself. About the figure of the Divinity a majestic system of correlated figures crystallizes, which all have reference to Him, because all things derive their meaning from Him" (*WMA* 183–84; the source of Gaddis's variant is unknown). Irenaeus (fl. 130–200), bishop of Lyons, is considered the first great ecclesiastical writer; Foxe relates the story of his martyrdom (*BM* 13). His *Against Heresies* (187?) is a long and tedious refutation of Gnosticism (and other current heresies) and an exposition of primitive Catholicism.

4 [dedication] *For Sarah | The awakened, lips parted, the hope, the new ships*: not added until the 1993 Penguin edition – Sarah Gaddis is the author's only daughter, and the quotation is from the conclusion of T. S. Eliot's 1930 poem "Marina."

I.1

7 Die erste Drehung der Schraube [3] THE FIRST TURN OF THE SCREW: see 5.19; only this chapter and III.3 ("The Last Turn of the Screw") have titles. Grace Eckley finds a parallel between *R*'s twenty-two chapters and the twenty-two tarot cards ("Exorcising the Demon Forgery," 131).

More relevant, perhaps, is Graves's comment that "The secret sense of 22 – sacred numbers were never chosen haphazardly – is that it is the measure of the circumference of the circle when the diameter is 7," another sacred number (*WG* 191). Gaddis later commented drolly: "while the 7s were intentional, the 22 = 22 tarot cards is the kind of scholarly ingenuity I find fascinating (since it never occurred to me) (but am willing to remain silent & take full credit: perhaps there *is* a guiding hand, a 'grand design'?)" (WG/SM).

7 MEPHISTOPHELES [...], – Goethe, *Faust* II [3.epigraph]: "Mephistopheles (*more softly*): What's going on? / Wagner (*more softly*): A man is being made" (ll. 6834–35). Wagner, Faust's pedantic associate, is in an alchemical laboratory creating Homunculus (cf. 262.17–20), who later leads Faust and Mephistopheles to the Classical Walpurgisnacht.

Camilla [3.1]: the virgin queen of the Volscians who helped Turnus against Aeneas (cf. *Inferno* 1:101, 4:124), and of whom Vergil says, "over the mid sea, hung upon the swelling billow, she would keep on her way, nor wet her nimble soles on the surface of the water" (*Aeneid* 7, trans. Lonsdale and Lee), as indeed Camilla does here. Camilla was a devotee of Diana (in her capacity as goddess of the moon) and is the first woman mentioned in Dante's *Inferno*. (Gaddis put this on the same level of "scholarly ingenuity" as Eckley's tarot reading, implying there was no particular referent for Camilla's name [WG/SM].)

den zypressenbestandenen Hügel [3.3] cypress trees: a funeral tree, dedicated by the Romans to Pluto, by the Greeks to Artemis (Diana). "Cypress is still the prime resurrection symbol in Mediterranean church-yards" (*WG* 222).

an den vierzehn Stationen des Kreuzwegs [3.5] fourteen stations of the cross: fourteen incidents in Christ's passage from the judgment hall to Calvary; in a funeral service, prayers are offered at each station (listed at 778.18).

[3.8] her soul, if it had been discernible: cf. "The soul, doubtless, is immortal – where a soul can be discerned," from stanza 12 of Robert Browning's "A Toccata of Galuppi's," a poem quoted elsewhere in *R* (191.34–36, 193.12–14, 797.36).

Reverend Gwyon [3.9]: according to de Rougemont, Gwyon was a Celtic divinity whose name "(whence 'guyon' meaning 'guide' in Old French) means the *Führer* who has in his custody the secret of initiation into the way of divinization" (*LWW* 210 n.1). Also relevant are Gawain from the Grail romances (see *FRR*) and Gwion, a semilegendary bard whose poetry hides "an ancient religious mystery – a blasphemous one from the Church's point of view – under the cloak of buffoonery" (*WG* 55);

one of Gwion's poems is quoted at 467.5. (Asked once how to pronounce Gwyon, Gaddis said he didn't know; he had never said it aloud. It probably should be pronounced as one syllable, like "Gwynne," its more common form.)

8 *Purdue Victory* [4.10] *Purdue Victory*: cf. *perdu* (French: lost, ruined).

[4.14] ad hominem: in rhetoric, an attack on the speaker instead of on the ideas expressed by the speaker.

10 mit nichts weniger als der Rembrandtschen Formel [5.13] Rembrandt's formula: given in a footnote in *CCP* (144 n.3).

Die erste Drehung der Schraube begleicht alle Schulden [5.19] *The first turn of the screw pays all debts*: that is, one's debts on shore can be dismissed with the first turn of the ship's screw – a sentiment, says Eric Partridge in his *Dictionary of Catch Phrases*, "so optimistic as to verge upon the mythical."

Dantes Augenzeugenbericht [5.28] Dante's eye-witness account [...] florin: see *Inferno* 30:49–129. Malebolge (literally "Evil Pouches") is that part of hell in which cantos 18–30 take place. Adamo da Bescia (d. 1281) is also mentioned in *GAF* (67).

Alfonso Liguori [5.37]: Saint Alphonsus Liguori (1696–1787), Italian prelate and author of many theological works, including *The Glories of Mary* (see 23.34) and *Theologia Moralis*, which Sinisterra owns (see 489.4).

Pope Pius IX vgl. S. 651 [5.37]: see 488. 37–42.

11 **National Counterfeit Detector Monthly** [5.44] *The National Counterfeit Detector Monthly*: subtitled "Recognized Authority for the Detection of Counterfeit Currency" (began publication in 1908).

Plejaden [6.14] Pleiades [...] Mordad, and the angel of death: the Greek sailing season extended from the rising of the Pleiades in May (cf. 892.36–38) to their setting in early November. The many customs and legends associated with these stars are recorded in Olcott's *Star Lore of All Ages* (411–13), the relevant portions from which read:

Memorial services to the dead at the season of the year when the Pleiades occupied a conspicuous position in the heavens are found to have taken place, and to have been a feature in the history of almost every nation of the earth, from remote antiquity to the present day. [...]

Among the Aztecs of South America we find the Pleiades the cynosure of all eyes, a nation trembling at their feet. At the end of every period of fifty-two years, in the month of November when the Pleiades would culminate at midnight, these rude people imagined the world would end. Human sacrifices were offered, while the entire population passed the night upon their knees awaiting their doom.

Far removed from the Aztecs we find the people of Japan in their great national festival, the Feast of Lanterns, a feast that is alive to-day. [...]

The Persians formerly called the month of November "Mordad," meaning "the angel of death," and that month marked the date of their festival of the dead. [...] [J. F.] Blake tell us [in his *Astronomical Myths*] that the first of November was with the ancient Druids of Britain a night full of mystery, in which they annually celebrated the reconstruction of the world. Although Druidism is now extinct the relics of it remain to this day, for in our calendar we still find Nov. 1st marked as "All Saints' Day," and in the pre-Reformation calendar the last day of October was marked "All Hallow Eve," and the 2nd of November as "All Souls'," indicating clearly a three days' festival of the dead, commencing in the evening, and originally regulated by the Pleiades.

11 Argo [6.25]: the southern constellation (the Ship) into which Athena transformed the Argonauts after the failure of their quest for the Golden Fleece (6.34)(*SL* 431–32).

Vom Bugspriet bis zum Mast ein düsteres Gefährt [6.29] "Obscure in parts [...] other portions blaze with light": the description of the constellation Argo in Frothingham's translation (see 597.10) of the poetic *Phenomena* (or "Appearances of the Stars") of Greek scholar and poet Aratos (ca. 315–240 B.C.), as quoted by Olcott (*SL* 431):
Against the tail of the Great Dog [Sirius] is dragged
Sternward the Argo, with no usual course
But motion contrary, [...]
So sternward labours the Jasonian Argo
Obscure in parts and starless, as from prow
To mast, but other portions blaze with light.

Algeciras [6.31]: city and port in southwestern Spain, five miles west of Gibraltar.

12 Vela, die Segel, Carina, den Kiel? [6.32] Vela, the sails? Carina, the keel?: the ancient constellation Argo Navis, the Ship, was divided by later astronomers into four groups: Puppis, the Stern; Carina, the Keel; Vela, the Sails; and Pyxis, the Compass.

"Importación ilegal de carnes dañadas" [6.39]: "Illegal importation of spoiled meats."

San Zwingli [7.2]: "an open parody on Escorial" (Gaddis's notes [Koenig, "The Writing of *The Recognitions*," 23]), the huge granite structure near Madrid enclosing a palace, church, and monastery, originally built by Philip II in the sixteenth century. In this century it has become a summer resort and a great tourist attraction. Ulrich Zwingli (1484–1531), founder of the Reformation in Switzerland, was of course not a saint but a Catholic heretic.

bóveda [7.9]: Spanish: vault, burial place.

in einem Land, in dem sogar Leprakranke verbrannt [...] wurden [7.11] a land where even lepers [...] communicate their disease to the dead around them: a bookseller of

Compostella told George Borrow (see 892.11) that those who die of elephantine leprosy "should, according to law, be burnt, and their ashes scattered to the winds: for if the body of such a leper be interred in the field of the dead, the disorder is forthwith communicated to all the corses [sic] even below the earth" (BS 253).

13 **Menander** [7.40] Menander [...] with languid step and slow ...": Greek comic poet and dramatist (341–290 B.C.). "Phaedrus, Fab[les] v. 1, tells how Demetrius [governor of Athens] was fawned upon not merely by prominent politicians but also by retired lovers of ease: 'among whom Menander, famous for his comedies – whom Demetrius had not known personally though he had read him and admired his genius – came, perfumed and in flowing robe, with languid step and slow. Seeing him at the end of the line the tyrant asked "What effeminate is that who dares to enter my presence?" Those nearest replied "This is Menander, the writer!" (EB 15:237).

Thomas von Aquin [7.42] Thomas Aquinas: (1225–74), Italian theologian, considered one of the greatest philosophers of the Middle Ages.

Roger Bacon [7.42] Roger Bacon, formidable geometric proofs of God: (ca. 1214–94), English philosopher and scientist. His geometrical "proofs" of God – more contrived than formidable – can be found in his *Opus Majus*, book 4, trans. Robert Bell Burke (Philadelphia: University of Pennsylvania Press, 1928), 1:234–42.

15 **mit der »unerbittlichen Pünktlichkeit des Zufalls«** [9.5] "unswerving punctuality of chance": source unknown. Gaddis told me a fellow student at Harvard had used this line and it had always stuck with him. In fact, it appears in all four of his novels.

Málaga [9.9]: city and port sixty-five miles northeast of Gibraltar.

Abd-er-Rahman [9.14]: (1778–1859), sultan of Fez and Morocco (1822–59).

Kartäuserkloster [9.15] Carthusian: a contemplative order of monks founded by Saint Bruno of Cologne in 1084. They are vegetarians and observe almost perpetual silence.

Real Monasterio de Nuestra Señora de la Otra Vez [9.19]: "Royal Monastery of Our Lady of Another (or Second) Time," fictitious name for the Real Monasterio de Guadalupe (formerly the Convento de los Jerónimos) in Guadalupe, a small town in Estremadura, where Gaddis stayed for ten days in March 1949. It was founded in 1389 by Alfonso XI; see Baedeker 461 for a history and description. (On Gaddis's name for the monastery, critic Rodger Cunningham comments: "Gaddis seems to think that *otra vez* means the same as the French *autrefois*, which it doesn't. Gaddis's Spanish, evidently learned orally, is frequently ungrammatical and Frenchified" [letter to me, 25 January 1991].)

16 *Homousianisch* oder *homoiusianisch* [9.30] *Homoiousian*, or *Homoousian*, that was the question [...] hung on a dipthong: Gaddis glosses this well enough; the substance under question, of course, is God/Jesus. (The sentence structure echoes Hamlet's famous dilemma.) In its article on Athanasius the Great, *EB* warns: "The popular idea that the controversy between Catholics and Arians was simply 'over a dipthong' ignores the complexity of the problem and the variety of shades of opinion" (2:598).

Konzil von Nicäa [9.32] Nicæa [...] Nicæan Creed: Nicaea (in Bithynia, Asia Minor) was the meeting place of a council (325) that, aided and developed by the Council of Constantinople (381), formulated the Nicene Creed, designed to combat the doctrinal errors of Arianism (among others) and emphasizing the trinitarian aspect of God. It has been in liturgical use since the eighth century.

Arius [9.36]: a presbyter of the church of Alexandria in the fourth century who proposed, among other things, that Jesus was of *like* substance but not equal to God. Conybeare believes that "with the defeat of Arianism, the last gleam of good sense and reason in Christian theology was extinguished" (*MMM* 185).

der heilige Antonius [9.42] Saint Anthony: (ca. 251–ca. 354), Egyptian hermit and patriarch of all monks, a supporter of Saint Athanasius in his struggle against Arianism. The "pornographic" temptations of Saint Anthony in the desert have been treated often in art and literature, perhaps most memorably in Flaubert's *La Tentation de Saint-Antoine* (1874; cited by Jung, *IP* 104).

Bruder Ambrosio [...] Abt Shekinah [...] Fr. Eulalio [10.9] Brother Ambrosio [...] Abbot Shekinah [...] Fr. Eulalio: all fictitious. *Shekinah* is a Hebrew word denoting "the visible glory of the Lord" (*PPM* 37).

17 Inhaber der dreigeschossigen Tiara [10.27] triple-tiered Italian in the Vatican: the three "crowns" of the pope's headdress symbolize sovereignty over Rome, earth, and heaven. The majority of popes have been Italian.

18 caudillos [11.2]: Sp.: chiefs, leaders.

Fr. Manomuerta [11.2]: a bilingual pun on Spanish "dead hand" and *mort main*, the French legal term for property (usually ecclesiastical) in perpetual possession (and cf. 359.34).

der Beichtvater des jungen Königs [11.4] confessor to the young king: the young king would be Alfonso XIII, age sixteen when he ascended the Spanish throne in 1902.

[11.6] vitando: Sp.: to be shunned; the distinction between *toleratus* and *vitandus* is pointed out at 916.16–23.

18 Teufelsanbetung s. S. 503 [11.14] Black Mass: see 372.31 ff.

19 der Pfarrer von Ars [11.30] Saint Jean Vianney, the Curé d'Ars: according to Rev. Summers (*PPM* 70),

The Curé d'Ars, St. Jean Vianney [1786–1859], was sensibly persecuted by devils. At night the infernal enemy would rouse him from his few hours' sleep by thundering blows upon the doors and walls of the presbytery. [...] An awful silence followed for a few moments, and there were heard yells of maddened laughter which froze the very blood of the listeners. [...] This persecution of the demon – the *grappin* as St. Jean Vianney called him – continued for a period of no less than 30 years, and the phenomena are attested by dozens of impeccable witnesses. Thus the infernal enemy would drum incessantly upon the table or chimney-piece, would imitate the clearing of wood, planing boards, hammering nails, just as if a carpenter were noisily at work in the house; would overthrow platters and smash a water-jug to smithereens. M. Monnin, who was actually present, relates how one night the evil one set fire to the heavy serge curtains of the Saint's bed. "Ah, this is a good sign," mildly observed the Curé, "the demon is very angry with us."

eine Zeit [...], in der der Tod noch nicht in die Welt getreten war [11.44] a time before death entered the world, before accident: as Koenig points out ("'Splinters,'" 77), this is from Lang's *Magic and Religion* (85): "Early men, contrary to Mr. Frazer's account, suppose themselves to be *naturally* immortal. The myths of perhaps all races tell of a time when death had not yet entered the world. Man was born deathless. Death came in by an accident, or in consequence of an error, or an infraction of a divine command."

vor der Magie und der Verzweiflung daran, der Religion [12.1] before magic despaired, to become religion: Lang summarizes Frazer's thesis of the evolution of religion thus: "But as men advanced from almost the lowest savagery, they gradually attained to higher material culture, developing the hitherto unknown arts of agriculture, developing also religion, in the despair of magic, developing gods, and evolving social and political rank, with kings at the head of society. [...] But though it was in the despair of magic that men invented gods and religion, yet, as men will, they continue to exercise the magic of which they despaired" (*M&R* 83). Lang, however, disagrees and cautions: "This question cannot be historically determined. If we find a race which has magic but no religion, we cannot be certain that it did not once possess a religion of which it has despaired" (*M&R* 47).

21 eine goldenen Stunde, besetzt mit sechzig diamantenen Sekunden [13.38] Lost: one golden hour, set with sixty diamond minutes: from American educator Horace Mann's (1796–1859) "Lost, Two Golden Hours": "Lost, yesterday,

somewhere between Sunrise and Sunset, two golden hours, each set with sixty diamond minutes. No reward is offered, for they are gone forever" (*ODQ*).

22 der Zimmermann [14.14] Town Carpenter: an analogy with the profession of Joseph or Jesus or both is perhaps implied.

23 jene wiederverwertbare Göttin, die alljährlich mit stets sich erneuernder Unschuld [14.44] remontant goddess [...] with her virginity renewed: probably Artemis (Diana): according to Graves, Actaeon witnessed "her *anodos,* or yearly reappearance, when she refreshed her virginity by bathing naked in a sacred fountain" (*WG* 181).

Don Felipe V. [15.10]: first Bourbon king of Spain (ruled 1700–24), a mediocre, irresolute, and pious ruler.

El aire de Madrid [15.13] El aire de Madrid [...] un candil: "The air is so keen and so subtle that, according to a popular couplet, it will kill a man, while it will not blow out a candle ('*el aire de Madrid es tan sútil, que mata á un hombre y no apaya á un candil*')" (Baedeker 59); cf. 772.18–19).

24 Die Zeit würde kommen [15.25] There would be time: an often-repeated echo of the phrase "there will be time" in T. S. Eliot's "Love Song of J. Alfred Prufrock."

Bedeutung in der Form [15.44] significant form: Clive Bell (1881–1962) outlined his theory of "significant form" in his 1914 book *Art* (rev. ed. 1949), a book WG has referred to elsewhere. Although not quoted hereafter in *R*, Bell's book deeply informs Wyatt's aesthetic and his view of the artist's place in the world.

die ausgeweidete Moschee zu Córdoba [16.1] the disemboweled mosque at Córdoba, the mighty pile at Granada, and that frantic demonstration at Burgos: a cathedral sits awkwardly in the middle of the Mezquita, an eighth-century mosque in Córdoba; "the mighty pile at Granada" would be the Alhambra, a thirteenth-century Moorish palace; Burgos features a grand cathedral also dating from the thirteenth century, the exterior of which is Gothic at its most flamboyant.

eine aus Kabeljau und einem Äffchen gefertigte Meerjungfrau [16.5] mermaid composed from a monkey and a codfish: several hoaxes such as this were perpetrated in the past, such as P. T. Barnum's "Feejee Mermaid" (made in Japan).

25 ein elfjähriges Mädchen [16.12] eleven-year-old girl: based closely on the life of Saint Maria Goretti (1890–1902), canonized on 24 June 1950. Gaddis picked up "a cheap Spanish paperbound on the Goretti girl" while in

Spain in 1948–49 (WG/SM), perhaps Alexander Gits's *A Modern Virgin Martyr: Saint Maria Goretti* (831.35). The canonization of the eleven-year-old girl will be referred to often in the course of the novel.

25 Señor Hermoso Hermoso [16.35]: *hermoso* (Sp.: beautiful, handsome).

26 que fervorosa [...] esposa de Jésus! [17.32]: "what a passionate honeymoon for that little bride of Christ!"

27 sicher vor allfälligem Mißbrauch in düsteren Ritualen [18.7] holy oils, holy water [...] stolen and used in sorcery: cf. *MM* 113–14, 117.

28 Wyatt [18.31]: it might be noticed Wyatt Gwyon and William Gaddis share the same initials; in response to a query made by his editor at Harcourt, Brace, Gaddis wrote: "I am Wyatt, & Anselm, & Otto, & Stanley: and I have my Basil Valentine moments" (Koenig, "'Splinters,'" 10). Later Gaddis wrote to me: "no specific reason for the name Wyatt (though I'll tell you, the physical person I envisioned in Wyatt was a man I'd met around 1947 & had very high regard for, the photographer Walker Evans – not to say that the character of Wyatt was based on him beyond that)" (WG/SM).

30 kurz nach Halloween [20.7] right after Hallowe'en [...] she came in. She was dressed in white: Frazer notes that "not only among the Celts but throughout Europe, Hallowe'en, the night which marks the transition from autumn to winter, seems to have been of old the time of year when the souls of the departed were supposed to revisit their old homes" (*GB* 634). White is widely associated with death and apparitions; cf. Graves's White Goddess, especially in her capacity as "the White Lady of Death and Inspiration" (*WG* 50).

32 alles, was wir haben, alle unsre Gaben sind, o Gott, von Dir [21.26] All things come [...] from Whom all blessings flow: from two hymns in *PH*: #541, "All Things Come of Thee, O Lord," a choral response adapted from Beethoven (text from 1 Chron. 29:14), and #518, "For Thanksgiving," an introit by Louis Bourgeois (1551).

34 Daß eine Hexe mit dem Leben davonkommen sollte [23.2] to suffer a witch to live [...] and Wesley: "To spare a witch was considered an insult to the almighty," writes Saltus. "Luther was particularly vehement on this point; so, too, was Calvin; and Wesley was as great a fanatic as any" (*AN* 91). Gaddis altered Saltus's "spare" to "suffer" to echo Exod. 22:18: "Thou shalt not suffer a witch to live" (cited in many of his source books: *DDD* 312, *EPD* 463, *MM* xi, etc.).

den Rekord der heiligen Inquisition [23.4] Holy Inquisition [...] burned in half a century: Saltus notes that attendance at a black mass was punishable by burning:

"The first punishment for this offence occurred in Toulouse in 1275. During the next fifty years over four hundred people were burned in the neighborhood" (*AN* 91).

34 **Alles andere ging sie nichts an.** [23.10] The rest was not their business: from Eliot's "East Coker," part V: "For us, there is only the trying. The rest is not our business." "East Coker" is the second of *Four Quartets*; at an early stage, Gaddis planned to weave in every one of its lines into his novel.

Zuñi, Mojave, Plains-Indianern und Kwakiutl [23.20] Zuñi and Mojave, the Plains Indians and the Kwakiutl: native American tribes. The Zuñi of New Mexico and the Kwakiutl of British Columbia are discussed at length in Benedict's *Patterns of Culture*.

Euripides [23.24]: (ca. 484–406? B.C.), Greek dramatist. "There was not an article of Hellenic faith that he did not scoff at," Saltus notes with approval (*AN* 35).

hl. Teresa von Avila [23.24] Saint Teresa of Avila: (1515–82), Spanish nun whose mystical experiences are recounted in many books, e.g., *The Interior Castle* (see 600.40). De Rougemont refers to her often in *LWW*.

Denys dem Kartäuser [23.25] Denys the Carthusian: Flemish mystical writer (1402–71), given the title *Doctor Ecstaticus* by the church. "His hours were spent in raptures and the fruition of heavenly apparitions," Summers writes (*PPM* 35), but he found time to compose a large body of writings, many of which are discussed in *WMA*.

Plutarch [23.25]: Greek biographer and essayist (ca. 46–ca. 127); held a priesthood at Delphi. Plutarch's religious essays (collected in *Moralia* and cited by Frazer [*GB* 291]), rather than his more famous biographical studies, would interest Rev. Gwyon.

Clemens Romanus [23.25] Clement of Rome: Clement I, the third pope after Peter, is considered the first of the apostolic fathers. Little is known of his life, and the traditional story of his martyrdom (see 44.3–6) is without historical foundation. *The Recognitions* (see 373.1) was traditionally ascribed to him, though internal evidence makes his authorship impossible.

Apokryphen des Neuen Testaments [23.26] Apocryphal New Testament: a few books have had this title, but the reference here is to M. R. James's edition (1924), a collection of the large body of religious writings that were excluded when the final canon of the New Testament was established. Many of the excluded writings are of a mystical nature and became the bases of heretical beliefs as well as popular Christian folklore.

34 *Osservatore Romano* [23.26]: official newspaper of the Vatican.

einem Traktat der Gesellschaft zum Schutz vor Beerdigung Scheintoter [23.27] a tract from the Society for the Prevention of Premature Burial: perhaps *Premature Burial* (1909) by the Society for the Prevention of Premature Encoffinment, Burial or Cremation.

De Contemptu Mundi [23.27]: Summers cites two works of this name (On the Worthlessness of the World): a study of mysticism by Denys the Carthusian (above, 23.25; *PPM* 35), and a tractate by Saint Bonaventura (below, 38.37; *PPM* 149). Petrarch also wrote a book with this title (*WMA* 299), as did Erasmus. The close proximity of Denys's name suggests his is intended.

Historia di tutte l'Heresie [23.28]: Summers cites a 1717 edition of this book by Domenico Bernino (*PPM* 49 n.64) in his discussion of the heresy of Quietism (a kind of radical mysticism).

Christ and the Powers of Darkness [23.28]: twice Summers quotes with approval (*PPM* 82 n.51, 91) this Catholic work by the "famous psychic investigator, the late J. Godfrey Raupert, K.S.G.," published in 1914. Apparently it concerns the ways evil forces can invade religious thought.

De Locis Infestis, Libellus de Terrificationibus Nocturnisque Tumultibus [23.29]: concluding his discussion of "demonic molestations," Summers writes: "Such phenomena are well known. They have, indeed, been described and classified by the learned Peter Thyraeus, S. J., of Nuys (Cologne) in his great work *De Locis Infestis* and the *Libellus de Terrificationibus Nocturnisque Tumultibus* (*On Haunted Places*, and also a *Treatise on The Terrors of Darkness and Midnight Noises*)" (*PPM* 70). The two works date from the end of the sixteenth century.

Malay Magic [23.20]: a study of the folklore and popular religion of the Malay Peninsula by Walter W. Skeat (1900), frequently quoted by Frazer.

Religions des Peuples Noncivilisés [23.30]: an 1883 study by French Protestant clergyman Albert Réville (1826–1906).

Le Culte de Dionysos en Attique [23.31]: a study in comparative religion by French writer Paul R. Foucart (1904); he maintains (with Herodotus) that "the Greek Dionysus was nothing but a slightly disguised form of the Egyptian Osiris" (quoted in the unabridged, 12–vol. edition of *GB* [London: Macmillan, 1911–15], 6:113 n.2).

Philosophumena [23.31]: lost until 1842, this work by Hippolytus (170–236) is a refutation of the Gnostic heresy. His work differs from that of Saint Irenaeus, his mentor, in deriving Gnostic beliefs from pagan sources rather than from the Gnostics' own vivid imaginations, as Irenaeus supposes. Weston devotes half a dozen pages to it (*FRR* 151–57). Francis Legge's English translation, *Philosophumena; or, The Refutation of All Heresies*, appeared in 1921.

34 *Lexikon der Mythologie* [23.31]: W. H. Röscher's once-standard *Lexikon der griechischen und romischen Mythologie* (1886–90), often quoted by Frazer and Weston.

Sir James Frazer [...] »Die Opferung des Königssohns« [23.32] Sir James Frazer [...] Sacrifice of the King's Son: Frazer's (1854–1941) monumental *Golden Bough* is an encyclopedic survey of religion, myth, and magic, with an emphasis on vestiges of pagan beliefs still present at the beginning of the twentieth century, especially in institutional Christianity and popular holidays and superstitions. "Sacrifice of the King's Son" (289–93) concerns the ancient practice of killing the king's son rather than the king himself at the end of his fixed term. (Frazer hints that the crucifixion of the Son of God reflects this practice.)

35 **Die Herrlichkeit Mariens** [23.34] *The Glories of Mary* [...] – There is no mysticism without Mary: a theological treatise by Saint Alphonsus Liguori (see 5.37). This classic of Mariology, first published in 1750, is a compilation of "all that the holy Fathers and the most celebrated writers have said on this subject" (Introduction). Summers, himself a translator of one of the English versions, writes: "There is no mysticism without Mary. So St. Alphonsus teaches" (*PPM* 37). Gaddis apparently assumed the dictum was a direct quotation from the *Glories* (cited elsewhere in *PPM*); however, nowhere in its 670 pious pages could I find those exact words. The book is often slighted in *MMSM* (78, 130ff.).

Taxus [23.36] yew trees: "the death-tree in all European countries, sacred to Hecate in Greece and Italy" (*WG* 160).

Geschichte des Pilatus [23.38] acts of Pilate: a conflated version of the Passion, followed by the Harrowing of Hell; also known as the Gospel of Nicodemus (in *ANT* 94–146). The original *Acts of Pilate*, a pagan attack on Christianity utilizing arguments of Porphyry (see 436.24), has not survived. The extant work bearing that name is a Christian forgery, probably written to combat the influence of the original. It is occasionally cited in *MMM*.

koptische Legenden [23.38] Coptic narratives: under the heading "Coptic Narratives of the Ministry and the Passion," James summarizes thirteen fragments, all dating from no earlier than the fifth century (*ANT* 147–52). "The Copts were tireless in producing embroideries upon the Biblical stories," James comments, "and perhaps in rewriting older documents to suit their own taste."

35 *Pistis Sophia* [23.38]: "A manuscript, probably of the fifth century, in the British Museum, called Codex Askewianus from a former owner Askew, contains a bulky work, or works (for not all the treatises of which it is composed are of one date) known as the *Pistis Sophia* (Faith[ful] Wisdom) from the spiritual being of that name with whose progress through the universe it is largely concerned. This is also in the form of revelations given to the apostles and holy women after the resurrection. It is of the third century, has been more than once edited, and has been translated into English" (*ANT* xxiii).

aquinische Schilderung [23.38] Thomas's account of the child Jesus turning his playmates into goats: recorded by James as an appendix to the apocryphal Gospel of Thomas:

And it came to pass that Jesus went out one day and saw a company of children playing together, and went after them, but they fled before him and went into a furnace (*al.* cellar). And Jesus came after them and stood by the door and said unto the women who were sitting there: Where are the children who came in here before me? And the women said unto Jesus: No children came here. Then Jesus said unto them: Then what are the beings that are inside the house? And the women said unto him: They are goats. And Jesus said unto them: Let the goats which are in the furnace go out to their shepherds. And there came forth from the furnace goats which leaped round about Jesus and skipped joyfully. And when the women had seen what had taken place, they wondered, and great fear laid hold upon them.

After some moralizing, the young Jesus restores the children to their original form (*ANT* 68).

Obras Completas [...] Dunkle Nacht der Seele [23.40] *Obras Completas* [...] *Dark Night of the Soul*: Saint John of the Cross (1542–91) is Spain's most celebrated mystic. His writings usually take the form of a poem (often in the erotic style of the Song of Solomon) followed by long explanations of its theological significance. His *Dark Night of the Soul* describes the necessary "dark night" of purgation that precedes ecstatic union with God. Gaddis would have known of Saint John's work from *PPM* (passim) if from nowhere else.

unbeschnittenes Otterngezücht [24.11] generation of vipers: a phrase used by both John the Baptist and Jesus to describe their contemporaries (Matt. 3:7, 12:34, 23:33).

trink nicht mehr Wasser [24.15] Drink no longer [...] infirmities: 1 Tim. 5:23, traditionally ascribed to Paul but now considered pseudonymous.

Sankt Edmund [24.20] Saint Edmund: saint and king of East Anglia (855–70). Conway makes passing reference to what he calls Saint Edmund's "valde eminentem" in *VEF* (19).

36 jenseits des sechzigsten Breitengrads [24.22] the sixtieth parallel: i.e., south of Lapland (Oslo and Saint Petersburg are on the sixtieth parallel).

Janet [24.25]: takes her name from the possessed woman in Robert Louis Stevenson's short story "Thrawn Janet" (see 392.34).

Bergpredigt [25.4] Sermon on the Mount (Matt. 7:1): "Judge not, that ye be not judged."

37 Watts Bild von Sir Galahad [25.17] Watts's painting of Sir Galahad: George Frederick Watts (1817–1904), English historical painter. *Sir Galahad* dates from 1862.

Olalla [25.24]: the Spanish form of Saint Eulalia of Mérida, one of the most celebrated virgin martyrs of Spain; she died ca. 304 at the age of thirteen (see *BM* 28 for the fanciful story of her martyrdom). Stevenson's short story "Olalla" is quoted at 298.12ff.

ein älterer Breughel [25.26] elder Breughel: Pieter Breughel (ca. 1525–69), Netherlandish painter, influenced by Bosch (see below). This painting is later said to represent some "horror" (35.20), which could be any one of a number of his paintings.

Wahnsinn des heiligen Antonius in der Wüste [25.26] Saint Anthony's insanity manifest in the desert: subject of numerous paintings, including one by Bosch.

Hieronymus Bosch [...] die sieben Todsünden [25.36] Hieronymus Bosch [...] Seven Deadly Sins: Bosch (ca. 1450–1516), called the greatest master of fantasy who ever lived, painted many allegorical, satirical works depicting the excesses of the medieval world. (It has been suggested that the obscure symbolism in his works expresses alchemical concepts.) The authenticity of *The Seven Deadly Sins* (ca. 1475, Prado) was questioned in the sixteenth century, though it is now considered genuine; the authenticity of Rev. Gwyon's painting is likewise disputed many times in the course of the novel, likewise emerging as genuine (see 59.36ff., 246.8ff., 688–89).

38 *Cave, Cave, D^s videt* [25.40]: Lat.: "Careful, careful, God is watching."

Spieglein am Kreuz kundtat [25.42] mirrors in the arms of the cross [...] their purpose: apparently they heighten the identification of the supplicant with the sufferings of Christ, sometimes leading to the bestowal of stigmata.

Al-Shira-al-jamânija [...] heller Stern des Jemen [26.22] Al-Shira-al-jamânija [...] the bright star of Yemen: the Arab name for Sirius, the Dog Star (see 27.18), which sets in the direction of Yemen.

39 Foxes *Buch der Märtyrer* [26.28] Foxe's *Book of Martyrs*: John Foxe (or Fox) (1515–87), English religious writer, whose *Acts and Monuments of the Church* (1563, popularly known as the *Book of Martyrs*: see 35.31 for its subtitle) was second only to the Bible as a force in British puritanism, not to mention anti-Catholicism. It is a vivid, detailed (but historically naive as concerns the early martyrs), and very partisan account of persecutions and sufferings, primarily of those who suffered in the name of Protestantism. It runs to eight volumes in its complete form; Aunt May (and Gaddis) apparently uses a one-volume abridgment.

39 Müßiggang ist aller Laster Anfang [27. 2] the devil finds work for idle hands: a popularized version of Isaac Watts's (1674–1748) couplet "For Satan finds some mischief still / For idle hands to do" (*ODQ*).

Adam hat genascht verbotne Bissen [27.3] In Adam's fall / We sinned all: an illustrative quote for the letter A in the *New England Primer* (earliest extant copy dated 1727), a popular Puritan schoolbook.

40 Ossian [27.18]: *The Works of Ossian* (1765) were alleged translations from ancient Gaelic poetry by Scottish poet James Macpherson (1736–96). The authenticity of the poems was soon discredited, but that did not prevent the works from influencing (if not initiating) the Romantic movement and expanding interest in ancient Gaelic literature.

Theophrastus [27.18]: (372?–288? B.C.), Greek Peripatetic philosopher, a disciple of Aristotle; see 28.28.

der Hundsstern [...] Al-Shira-al-jamânija [27.18] Dog Star [...] Al-Shira-al-jamânija: both Arab names for Sirius, as noted in *SL* (101), where the many attributes of this distant sun (such as heralding the inundation of the Nile, adding its heat to the "dog days" of summer, etc.) are discussed at length (*SL* 95–105).

Stephen [27.25]: although this name led early critics to see resemblances between Wyatt and Joyce's Stephen Dedalus, Gaddis states: "I'm quite certain that the Stephen name was chosen simply because he was the first Christian martyr [see 909.4] & I saw Wyatt as the last one; nothing to do with Joyce" (WG/SM).

[27.39] the present, unredeemed though it may be: adapted from Eliot: see 160.30.

41 Das mit den sieben Himmeln [28.10] seven havens, made out of different kinds of metal: an ancient Islamic belief: see 265.8.

daß die Sterne die Seelen der Menschen wären [28.12] stars were people's souls [...] sorcerers could tell the good from the bad: source unknown.

41 **Hexen, die den Mond vom Himmel holen** [28.15] witches drawing the moon down from the heavens [...] Thessalonian witches: this practice, which has to do with channeling the alleged occult powers of the moon (still done by witches today), is recorded in Lucan's *Pharsalia* (book 6), in Vergil's *Bucolics* (see next entry), and elsewhere in classical literature. Goethe refers to the practice in the second part of *Faust* (l. 6977).

Vergil [...] **the eighth** *Bucolic* [...] **Carmina vel caelo** [28.22]: "Carmina vel caelo possunt deducere lunam" ("Charms can even bring the moon down from heaven" – Basil Valentine's translation [236.23]). The *Bucolics* are ten pastoral poems by the Roman poet Vergil, written between 47 and 37 B.C.; the eighth contains two love elegies, in both of which the singers use magic refrains – for this reason the poem is sometimes called *Pharmaceutria* ("Sorcery"). The quoted line is cited by Conybeare in illustration of the belief that ancient witches had "a power of binding and loosing inanimate nature through their incantations" (*MMM* 246), a power (he points out) conferred by Jesus on Simon Peter and the rest of the apostles (Matt. 16:19, 18:18).

daß Sonnenstrahlen im Wasser zu Perlen werden [28.24] pearls are the precipitate of sunlight: "Pearls were supposed to be generated by rays of sunlight striking down through the sea, on the floor of which they coagulated and took a material consistency in the oyster shell. They are thus a precipitate of sunlight. Jesus, engendered by rays of divine light or fire striking down through the Virgin's ears and consolidated within her, was by analogy and metaphor termed the Pearl, not, of course, without reference to the parable (Matthew xiii.46) of the pearl of great price" (*MMM* 232).

Milchstraße [...] **Theophrast** [28.28] Milky Way [...] Theophrastus: Lethaby records Theophrastus's opinion that "the milky way was the junction of the two halves of the solid dome [of the firmament] so badly joined that the light came through" (*AMM* 19). Cf. *SL* 392.

42 **Gervasius von Tilbury** [28.32] tale about the sky being a sea [...] Gervase of Tilbury: "There is an amusing story of this celestial sea as late as Gervase of Tilbury [thirteenth century]. Some people coming out of a church were surprised to see an anchor dangling by a rope from the sky, which caught in the tombstones, presently a man was seen descending with the object of detaching it, but as he reached the earth he died as we should if drowned in water" (*AMM* 15). See 257.1–10.

Lügenmärchen von den bösen Geistern [28.44] evil spirits who keep the path to Paradise dirty [...] the Wathiwathi: this belief, held by the Australian aboriginal tribe Wathi Wathi, is recorded by Lang (*M&R* 72–73).

[29.10] the man who jumps into the bramble bush and scratches out both eyes: a popular Mother Goose rhyme reads:

There was a Man so Wise
He jumped into
A Bramble Bush,
And scratcht out both his Eyes.
And when he saw,
His eyes were out
And reason to Complain,
He jumpt into a Quickset Hedge,
And Scratcht them in again.

(#28 in *The Annotated Mother Goose*, ed. William S. and Ceil Baring-Gould [New York: Bramhall House, 1962], 40; cf. the actions of Saint Francis of Assisi at 830.20ff.)

[29.13] The man of double deed: another Mother Goose rhyme: see 98.39ff.

43 **Buffons *Naturgeschichte*** [29.32] Buffon's *Natural History*: Comte G. L. L. de Buffon (1707–88), French naturalist, wrote with others an *Histoire naturelle* (44 vols., 1749–1804), completed after his death. Various editions and abridgements in English have appeared since the nineteenth century.

44 **Cave, cave, Dominus videt s. S. 38** [30.10]: see 25.40.

Skandalgeschichte des päpstlichen Hofes zu Avignon s. S. 411 f. [30.25] Papal court at Avignon: 1309–77, a time of simony, papal extravagance, and clerical immorality. See Petrarch's comments at 305.43ff.

Doktor Youngs Der letzte Tag [30.27] Doctor Young's *The Last Day*: (1713) a long poem on the Second Coming by English poet and divine Edward Young (1683–1765).

***Das Grab* von Blair** [30.28] *The Grave* of Blair: another long, didactic poem (1743), stylistically reminiscent of Jacobean drama, by Scottish poet Robert Blair (1699–1746).

***Tod* von Bischof Beilby Porteus** [30.29] Bishop Beilby Porteus, *Death*: a "poetical essay" in the same vein as the two preceding works; Porteus (1731–1808) was bishop of London as well as a poet. Given Gaddis's reliance on other books by Montague Summers, he probably took the above three titles from a sentence in Rev. Summers's introduction to his popular *Supernatural Omnibus* (1931; rpt. London: Gollancz, 1949): surveying the Victorian interest in funereal matters, he writes: "We must not forget, too, those expressions of elegant piety such as Blair's *The Grave*, Young's *The Last Day*, Samuel Boyse's *A Deity*, and *Death* by Bishop Beilby Porteus, which for a century and a half exercised an almost universal influence in the spheres of such theology as loved to ponder upon the skull, the hour-glass, crossbones, hatchments, mournful and sorrowing cherubim" (32).

45 das Gelege des Vogel Greif s. S. 511 [30.43] griffins' eggs: see 378.5.

Frau mit dem Stier [30.44] the woman and the bull: the well-known legend of King Minos's wife Pasiphaë (Graves calls her a Cretan moon goddess), who fell in love with a white bull and asked Daedalus to construct a hollow wooden cow in which she could hide to mate with the bull. The result of their coupling was the Minotaur.

Kubla Khan, Tamerlan oder Prester John [31.2] Kublai Khan, Tamerlane, and Prester John: Kublai Khan was a Mongol emperor of China (1260–94); Tamerlane (or Timur) was a Mongol leader who ruled Persia (1369–1405); Prester John was a legendary king of East Africa (or India in other accounts). The exploits of all three rulers, especially those of Prester John (see II.3), have been highly romanticized and spun into legends.

Herakles [31.13] Heracles [...] Hercules: "Heracles" is the Greek ("glory of Hera") and "Hercules" the Roman form of the name of this famous mythical hero, the subject of countless legends. See 40.23.

46 die Weißdornbüsche [31.40] hawthorn tree: generally considered unlucky, it is also known as the may tree, after the month with which it was associated; see Graves for the many mythical properties of the hawthorn/may (*WG* 144–46).

47 Johann Hus [32.20] John Huss [...] that "pale thin man in mean attire": all the details here and elsewhere (pp. 47, 407–8, 412, 545, 651) – including the descriptive phrase "pale thin man in mean attire," which will later be used for Wyatt (220.26, 407.41) – are from *EB*'s article on Huss (11:942–43). See 545.18 for details of "his betrayal by the Emperor Sigismund" (which is discussed at length by Marsh as well: *MMSM* 26 ff). Wenceslaus IV of Bohemia was not the same as the "good King Wenceslaus" of the carol, a tenth-century duke of Bohemia who was assassinated by his brother for trying to convert his subjects to Christianity.

Kyrie eleison [32.28]: "Lord, have mercy": opening words of a short petition used in Roman and Orthodox churches, especially at the beginning of Mass. See 545.18 for Huss's death.

Die Synode von Dordrecht [32.43] Synod of Dort: an assembly held by the Reformed churches in 1618–19 at Dort (i.e., Dordrecht, the Netherlands); the five doctrinal points agreed upon were "unconditional election, limited atonement, total depravity, irresistibility of grace, final perseverance of the saints" (*EB* 7:545).

48 **John H. Gwyon** [33.27] John H.: John H. Gwyon (see 22.41), apparently named after John Huss.

49 **Jesus, laß den Namen Dein** [33.40] Jesus permit thy gracious name [...] upon her heart: "this is simply from a sampler in the family many years & I don't know the girl's source" (WG/SM).

OHNE KREUZ KEINE KRONE [34.7] NO CROSS NO CROWN: Quaker founder William Penn wrote a pamphlet with this name (1669), taking his title from English poet Francis Quarles's *Esther*: "The way to bliss lies not on beds of down, / And he that has no cross deserves no crown" (*ODQ*).

Rotkehlchen [34.10] robin: "in British folklore," Graves notes, "the Robin Red Breast as the Spirit of the New Year sets out with a birch-rod to kill his predecessor the Gold Crest Wren, the spirit of the Old Year. [...] The robin is said to 'murder its father,' which accounts for its red breast" (*WG* 154). Wyatt has killed a wren (31–32) and later associates himself with Welsh hero Llew Llaw Gyffes (545.32), whom Graves associates with the robin (*WG* 261).

50 **ein Feuer zu entzünden** [34.17] Lucifer is the morning star: i.e., the planet Venus. "Lucifer" (Lat.: light-bringer) was the Authorized Version translation of "Day Star, son of Dawn," an epithet (based on the names of Canaanite deities) applied to boastful Nebuchadnezzar derided in Isaiah 14. Saint Jerome and other early church fathers applied the name, by analogy, to Satan.

denn er verstieß gegen die göttliche Ordnung [34.20] To sin is to falsify something in the Divine Order: a paraphrase of de Rougemont's belief that "It is through freedom, because of it, and in it, that we have the power to sin. For to sin is to cheat with order, to oppose our egoistic derogations, errors of calculation and interested false views to the divine law. To sin is to falsify something in the arrangement of the cosmos. It is always in some manner telling a lie or effecting one" (*DS* 38).

sein eigenes Reich hat er ja jetzt [34.22] Bringer of Light [...] to bear his own light!: identifying Lucifer as "the Bearer of Light," de Rougemont writes: "Satan rebelled, he refused to serve, he refused to transmit his divine message, he wished to become original, the author of his own destiny, the bearer of his own light" (*DS* 29).

der junge Lorbeerbaum [34.39] bay tree: sacred to Apollo and thus a safeguard against thunder and lightning.

Zaunkönig [35.2] wren: see 34.10 above as well as 47.33 ff.

51 *Geschichte der protestantischen Märtyrer* [35.31] Lives, Sufferings [...] Persecutions: subtitle of Foxe's *Book of Martyrs*.

51 **Prophezeiungen des Malachi** [35.36] Malachi prophecy: the so-called *Prophecies of Malachi*, once attributed to Saint Malachi O'More (1095–1148), is a forgery believed to date from around 1590. It consists of 111 Latin phrases that are supposed to apply to the popes from Celestine II (made pope in 1143) to the final pope, to be called Peter II, who will rule at the end of the world. Cf. 944.25 ff.

Penetralia von Andrew Jackson Davis [35.40] *Penetralia* of Andrew Jackson Davis: American author (1826–1910) of works on spiritualism. *The Penetralia; Being Harmonial Answers to Important Questions* (1856) seems to have been the most popular of his many books.

das Werk von William Miller [35.41] William Miller [...] Behold the Saviour comes!": American sectarian leader (1782–1849), author of *Evidence from Scripture and History of the Second Coming of Christ, about the Year 1843* (1842), from which presumably the quote is taken. Stood up by Christ, Miller eventually organized the Adventists.

52 **Scopes-Prozeß im fernen Tennessee** [36.30] Scopes trial in distant Tennessee: John T. Scopes was tried in July 1925 in a highly publicized trial for teaching evolution in defiance of a state law (William Jennings Bryan prosecuting, Clarence Darrow for the defense).

53 **ich *bin* die Auferstehung und das Leben** [36.42] I *am* the Resurrection and the Life: John 11:25.

Mode aus den Bumslokalen [37.5] bawdy houses, where all fashions originate: from *DDD* 266; see note to 938.41.

54 **Breve Guida della Basilica di San Clemente** [37.27]: "Compact Guide to the Basilica of Saint Clement" – see note to 906.6.

La Basilica [...] **Nostra Signora col Gesù Bambino** [37.35]: "The Subterranean Basilica Dedicated to the Memory of Saint Clement, Pope and Martyr" [...] "Our Lady with the Child Jesus."

Il Tempio di Mitra [38.2]: "The Temple of Mithra." A photograph like the one Aunt May beholds can be seen in Maria Luisa Ambrosini's *The Secret Archives of the Vatican* (Boston: Little, Brown, 1969), following p. 178.

55 **vom heiligen Bonaventura** [38.37] Saint Bonaventura [...] of the righteous": the Italian bishop and theologian (1221–74) was the author of many influential books on philosophy, theology, and mysticism; source of quote unknown.

57 **aus dem Werk von John Wesley** [40.6] John Wesley [...] dead body compare: Wesley (1703–91), English theologian, evangelist, and founder of Methodism,

published many collections of hymns; source of this particular one unknown.

57 **Nachfolge der heiligen Teresa** [40.7] Saint Teresa, "to die of not being able to die": the refrain of a poem that has been translated "The Life Above, the Life on High." De Rougemont cites the exclamation often: "'I die of not being able to die,' Saint Teresa says; but she means that she is not able to die to the old life enough to become alive in the new, and thus to obey without anguish" (*LWW* 124). Elsewhere, he comments in a note: "This famous exclamation of Saint Teresa's was inspired by the Franciscan Angela di Foligno, who said: 'I die of a desire to die!'" (*LWW* 133 n.2). The complaint is quoted again at 300.39.

Herakles war [...] ausgebrochen [40.23] Heracles [...] tree was dead: "It is obvious" to Charles Leslie Banning ("The Time of Our Time," 151 n.9) "that the scene of Heracles uprooting Aunt May's hawthorn bush [sic] and her subsequent demise that Gaddis is working from J. G. Frazer's telling of Hercules slaying Syleus and then digging up his vines, which Syleus had compelled passers-by to cultivate for him" (*GB* 442).

58 **War es auch besser freien, denn Brunst leiden** [40.31] better to marry than to burn: 1 Cor. 7:9.

die heilige Umiliana [41.6] Blessed Umiliana: Blessed Humiliana de' Cerchi (1220–46), Florentine nun.

mit den Worten von William Law [41.11] lines of William Law [...] reaped in eternity": (1686–1761), English theologian and mystic. The quoted passage is from *An Appeal to All Who Doubt or Disbelieve the Truths of the Gospel* (1740), a summary of his beliefs and considered by many to be the most important of his many writings. Source uncertain: the passage is quoted in Aldous Huxley's *The Perennial Philosophy* (New York: Harper and Row, 1945), 174–75, as well as in *The Selected Mystical Writings of William Law*, ed. Stephen Hobhouse (New York: Harper & Bros., 1948), 44–45.

60 **Dr. Fell** [42.19] Doctor Fell: no doubt named after John Fell (1625–86), English scholar and prelate, subject of this well-known quatrain by English hack writer Thomas Brown (1663–1704):

I do not love thee, Dr. Fell
The reason why I cannot tell;
But this I know, and know full well,
I do not love thee, Dr. Fell.

(Robert Graves included it in *Less Familiar Nursery Rhymes* [1926]; it also appears in *ODQ* and *A&H* 17–18.)

61 **der grausame April** [42.38] cruel April and depraved May: from Eliot's "The Waste Land" and "Gerontion," respectively.

61 *erythema grave* [43.3]: a tropical illness that Gaddis himself suffered from during high school; symptoms include a reddening of the skin, weight-loss, and high fever.

Doughtys *Reisen in die arabische Wüste* [43.13] Doughty's *Travels in Arabia Deserta*: Charles M. Doughty (1843–1926), English explorer, travel writer, and poet. His famous *Travels* (1888) recounts his wanderings in North Africa, Syria, and especially Arabia in an unusual style made up of archaisms and arabisms, elevating the travelogue to a kind of metaphysical quest. It was greatly admired by T. E. Lawrence, who wrote an introduction for the 1921 edition (see 405.31ff.).

Eine koptische Abhandlung aus dem Codex Brucianus [43.14] *A Coptic Treatise Contained in the Codex Brucianus*: an anonymous Gnostic work (second century?), consisting of the "Two Books of Jeû." Jung found it worth citing (*IP* 133–35), but James had no patience for it: "The revelations they contain are conveyed in mystic diagrams, and numbers, and meaningless collections of letters, and it requires a vast deal of historical imagination and sympathy to put oneself in the place of anybody who could tolerate, let alone reverence, the dreary stuff" (*ANT* xxiii). Charlotte A. Baynes's English version appeared in 1933.

Rosarium Philosophorum [43.14]: The Rose Garden of the Philosophers (or The Philosophers' Rosary) was one of the more popular alchemical tracts and emphasized the spiritual, rather than the chemical, aspects of alchemy. It dates from the middle of the fifteenth century and is frequently cited in Jung's *IP*.

zwei Bücher aus Dantes *Göttlicher Komödie* [43.15] two books of Dante's *Divine Comedy*: probably the first two, for Wyatt's career parallels that of Dante only through hell and purgatory.

Wyer's *De Præstigiis Dæmonum* [43.15]: Johan Weyer (or Wier, Wierus, etc.) (1515–88), Belgian physician. This book (On the Wiles of the Devil, 1563) made one of the first attempts to challenge and ridicule the superstitious belief in witchcraft. A long work, it is in a sense a Protestant rebuttal to the Catholic *Malleus Maleficarum* (49.14). (In the first edition of *R*, this title was spelled *De Prestigiis Dæmonum* – the spelling used in the brief bibliography to Michelet's *S&W*, which is where Gaddis undoubtedly found it and the next title.)

Llorentes *Inquisition d'Espagne* [43.16] Llorente's *Inquisition d'Espagne*: Juan Antonio Llorente (1756–1823), Spanish priest and historian. His multivolume Inquisition of Spain (Paris, 1817–18), commissioned by Joseph Bonaparte after the Inquisition was abolished in 1808, is an official study valuable for its use of original sources no longer extant. It is cited in *S&W*'s bibliography and in *PPM* (213 n.59).

62 **Monogramm von Clemens, dem Märtyrer** [44.3] Clement's monogram […] gettato a mare con un'ancora […] threw him into the Black Sea: traditionally, Clement was sentenced to hard labor in the Crimea and later lashed to an anchor and thrown into the sea. Since then (or rather, since the fabrication of this legend) an anchor has been Saint Clement's emblem. The Italian phrase ("was cast into the sea with an anchor") is repeated by Wyatt at 382.17.

64 **die heilige Orsola Benincasa** [44.41] Venerable Orsola Benincasa: from Summers (*PPM* 106):

The Ecstasies of the Venerable Orsola Benincasa, Foundress of the Theatine Nuns (1547–1618), were so frequent as to be almost uninterrupted. Directly the trance came on she at once became entirely insensible to any exterior happenings. When she was a child these Ecstasies were not understood, and rough methods were employed to arouse her. She was pricked with needles and even cut with sharp lancets; her hair was pulled; bystanders nipped and pinched her black and blue; they bruised her with their blows; they even went so far as to burn her with a naked flame, but all these injuries affected her not in the slightest, although when she returned to herself she keenly felt the result of such ill-judged, and indeed cruel, maltreatment.

am Abend des Gründonnerstag [45.3] eight o'clock on Thursday evening […] following afternoon at three: in a discussion of the rapturous Saint Gemma Galgani of Lucca (1878–1903), Summers notes: "The Rapture, or Extraordinary Ecstasy, frequently accompanied by mystical phenomena, used (as it was observed) to entrance her every Thursday evening about eight o'clock (the hour of the Last Supper) and on Friday afternoon about three (the hour of Calvary)" (*PPM* 110).

Zuñi-Priester [45.14] Zuñi priests planting prayer sticks: made from willow shoots and painted and adorned with feathers, these prayer sticks (referred to again at 885.3) are mentioned throughout chapter 4 of Benedict's *PC* (especially pp. 62 and 97).

65 **zum Fest des heiligen Johannis** [45.32] Saint John's […] Midsummer's Day […] sprigs of oak trees: Frazer shows that the festivities of Saint John's Day are superimposed on the pagan customs of Midsummer Day (*GB* 622) and discusses the oak's association with that day (620, 661–62), as does Graves (*WG* 146–47).

bei den Mojave-Indianern [45.43] Mojave Indians […] in the next life: Benedict notes that the medicine man in some primitive tribes was held in suspicion because "He had the power to harm more particularly than he had the power to help. […] The Mojave, a non-Pueblo tribe of the Southwest, carried this attitude to great lengths. 'It is the nature of doctors to kill people in this way just as it is in the nature of hawks to kill little birds for a living,' they say. All those whom a medicine man killed were in his power in the after life" (*PC* 121).

66 den Heiligen Laurentius [46.15] Saint Lawrence: one of the most celebrated of the early Roman martyrs. According to unreliable legends, he was roasted alive on a gridiron three days after the martyrdom of Pope Sixtus II in 258 (*BM* 19–20).

Heilige Katharina [46.16] Saint Catherine: of Alexandria (d. ca. 310 according to some sources). She survived torture on a spiked wheel only to be beheaded. There are doubts she ever lived and conflicting reports of her career if she did.

Tyndale [46.17]: William Tyndale (ca. 1494–1536), English translator and theologian, whose own translation of the Bible influenced the King James Version. He was strangled and burned as a heretic at Vilvorde, his last words being: "Lord! open the king of England's eyes" (*BM* 176–84).

Johann Hus, der seinen Mördern [...] verzieh [46.18] words of forgiveness on the lips of John Huss [...] O Sancta simplicitas!: Huss is said to have repeated the last words of Christ ("Forgive them, father, for they know not what they do," etc.) and finally "O holy simplicity!"

Äskulap [46.24] Asclepius [...] Zeus slew him with a thunderbolt: "The death of Æsculapius [Gaddis uses this spelling at 393.25–26] came about as the result of an occurrence which has been attributed to no physician since his time. Pluto complained to Zeus that the prolongation of life on the earth, due to the ministrations of Æsculapius, was keeping down the population of Hades. Zeus, to restore the balance of population, slew Æsculapius with a thunderbolt" (*DDD* 16).

zu Zeiten des böhmischen Königs Johann [46.27] John of Bohemia [...] Hungarian king five centuries ago: "The attitude toward men practicing surgery in the Middle Ages and Renaissance was such that the surgeons were continually in jeopardy of life. [...] In 1337 a surgeon was thrown into the river Oder because he failed to cure John of Bohemia of blindness, and in 1464 the king of Hungary [Matthias I] proclaimed that he would reward the surgeon who cured him of an arrow wound, but would put him to death if he failed" (*DDD* 135).

wie die des heiligen Kyrill [46.33] Saint Cyril: commenting on the connection between faith-healing and diet, Dr. Haggard writes: "a Greek monk of the eleventh century records the fact that the physician who performed the autopsy on the divine Cyril cut out and ate his liver. He thus obtained the virtues of the subject he was dissecting" (*DDD* 318). Saint Cyril was a deacon of Heliopolis, martyred by the pagan population there during the reign of Julian the Apostate (ca. 362).

Papst Innozenz VIII. [46.34] Pope Innocent VIII [...] three small children: "It is said that a sorcerer and itinerant physician sought to cure a nervous disease of

Pope Innocent VIII [pope 1482–92] by having him drink the blood of three small children" (*DDD* 318).

66 **Kardinal Richelieu** [46.36] Cardinal Richelieu: "The physicians of the sixteenth and seventeenth centuries apparently tried to make the deaths of their patients as unpleasant as possible; when Cardinal Richelieu was on his death-bed a female charlatan prescribed for him a mixture of horse dung in white wine, and the cardinal drank it" (*DDD* 328). The duc de Richelieu (1585–1642) was Louis XIII's chief minister (1624–42) but virtually ruled France until his death. Wyatt repeats the anecdote at 376.44.

caduceus [46.40] caduceus [...] conducted souls to Hell: "The *caduceus* of Hermes, his wand of office while conducting souls to Hell, was in the form of coupling snakes" (*WG* 208).

67 **der Gebrauch der Guillotine** [47.6] guillotine: Joseph Ignace Guillotin (1738–1814) urged the adoption of the instrument that now bears his name (invented centuries earlier) to prevent unnecessary pain.

Rock of Ages s. JRS. 449 [47.9]: *PH* #149, the well-known hymn composed by Augustus Montague Toplady (1740–78) and first published in *Gospel Magazine* (1775). For a ribald account of the song's genesis, see *JR* 318–19.

[47.17] When the seed began to blow: from "There Was a Man of Double Deed" (see 98–99, where "grow" takes the place of "blow").

Freies Geleit durch Kaiser Sigismund s. S. 47; S. 728 [47.19] safe-conduct from Emperor Sigismund: see 32.20, 545.18.

Pfad zum Paradies s. S. 42 [47.20] Keeping the road to Paradise littered with filth: see 28.44.

Unausweichlichkeit der Gnade [47.21] Limited atonement [...] irresistibility of grace: the conclusions reached at the Synod of Dort (see 32.43).

[47.25] The power of God to guide me [...] Christ in height: the source of Janet's litany, extending over 47–48, is the Faed Fiada, or Deer's Cry, attributed to Saint Patrick.

68 **mit den Zaunkönigen ist das so eine Sache** [47.33] a wren [...] around Christmas: Frazer identifies the British custom of killing a wren on Saint Stephen's Day (December 26) as a throwback to pagan scapegoat ceremonies. He points out that by many European peoples "the wren has been designated the king, the little king, the king of birds, the hedge king, and so forth, and has been reckoned amongst those birds which it is extremely unlucky to kill" (*GB* 536). Graves too notes the custom (*WG* 76, 153–55). Commenting on a nursery rhyme that reflects this custom, the editors of *The Annotated Mother Goose* note: "There is an old tradition

that the first Christian missionaries to Britain were offended because the pagan druids showed great respect for the wren, 'the king of all birds.' The missionaries ordered that the wren be hunted and killed on the morning of Christmas Day. The custom was later transferred to the morning of the following day, December 26th" (42 n.64).

68 **Von da an gehörte der Tag Johannes dem Täufer** [48.10] Midsummer Day magic of bonfires [...] raised splendid harvests: from *GB* 622–32.

die russischen Frauen [48.15] rain in Russia: "Bathing is practised as a rain-charm in some parts of Southern and Western Russia. [...] Sometimes it is the women who, without stripping off their clothes, bathe in crowds on the day of St. John the Baptist" (*GB* 70).

ein frischverstorbener Trunkenbold [48.14] corpse of a villager: "In Russia, if common report may be believed, it is not long since the peasants of any district that chanced to be afflicted with drought used to dig up the corpse of some one who had drunk himself to death and sink it in the nearest swamp or lake, fully persuaded that this would ensure the fall of the needed rain" (*GB* 71).

[48.41] an Arabian camel [...] Bactrian: see 409.44 ff.

70 **auf dem *Ägyptischen Totenbuch*** [49.13] Egyptian *Book of the Dead*: generic name for collections of funeral texts composed by ancient Egyptian scribes to assist the dead in the afterlife. They are a major source of knowledge for Egyptian mythology and religious practices. The best-known version is E. A. Wallis Budge's 1913 edition of the papyrus of Ani, a Theban recension.

Hexenhammers [49.14] *Malleus Maleficarum*: the Hammer of Witches (1488) was written by two Dominican inquisitors, Heinrich Kramer and Jakob Sprenger, to alert the public to the dangers and varieties of witchcraft, and to set guidelines for judges in the prosecution of witches. Exerting a morbid fascination, the *Malleus* (in Montague Summers's 1928 English translation) is a source for many arcane references in *R* (and reappears in both *JR* and *Carpenter's Gothic*).

Index [49.18]: *Index Librorum Prohibitorum*, the Index of Prohibited Books that Catholics were forbidden to read, except with permission in special circumstances. The first Index was issued by the Inquisition in 1557, and was updated by the Holy Office until it was finally abolished in 1966. A number of the world's greatest writers (but never an American) were placed on the *Index*; Jung notes that even the Bible was on the *Index* (*IP* 188).

tu das Werk eines evangelischen Predigers [49.18] Make full proof of thy ministry: 2 Tim. 4:5b, traditionally attributed to Paul.

70 Ensemble von Steinen [49.21] "Close to the outskirts [...] a hulock may not be used": from Major A. Playfair's study *The Garos* (1909), as quoted by Frazer (*GB* 568–69). It concerns the annual expulsion of evils in an animal scapegoat by the Garos of Assam (India).

71 Sor Patrocino [50.12]: María Rafaela Quiroga (1809?–91); Summers recounts the stigmatic's life and influence on Spanish politics (*PPM* 240–44) but says nothing of the cruz-con-espejos, mittens, or the sobriquet "the Bleeding Nun," indicating a different source. (Summers does feature a portrait of Sor Patrocino – grim and with hands hidden – facing p. 97.)

mesa de los pecados mortales [50.15]: Sp.: "table of the deadly sins" – Bosch's painting.

Abscondam faciem [...] novissima eorum [50.16]: this inscription on the bottom of Bosch's table painting is from Deut. 32:20: "I will hide my face from them, I will see what their end shall be."

die Worte jenes Bibelübersetzers aus dem vierzehnten Jahrhundert [50.18] that fourteenth-century translator [...] – In this world God must serve the devil: John Wycliffe (1320?–84), English religious reformer. Posthumously condemned by the Council of Constance (1415, the same that condemned his disciple Huss), his body was disinterred, burned, and thrown into the river Swift (*BM* 135–39). Source of quotation unknown.

einen großen Spiegel mit einem Tischtuch zu verhängen [50.27] cover a large mirror with a tablecloth: it was once believed that one's reflection in a mirror (or water) was the soul: "in time of sickness, when the soul might take flight so easily, it is particularly dangerous to project it out of the body by means of the reflection in a mirror" – hence the custom of covering up mirrors in time of sickness or after death, when the soul of a bystander, "projected out of the person in the shape of his reflection in the mirror, may be carried off by the ghost of the departed" (*GB* 192).

72 Joseph von Copertino [51.18] "With regard to Saint Joseph of Copertino Rapture was accompanied by Levitation": quoted from *PPM* (105). The Italian ecstatic (1603–63) is said to have been subjected to many ecstasies and while deep in prayer involuntarily levitated. Cf. 910.41.

Janets heisere Schreie s.S.52 [51.21] had he chased her [...] black man: from Stevenson's "Thrawn Janet": see 392.34.

74 Odyssee [52.43] *Odyssey* [...] Chapman's translation [...] Ogygia: Renaissance in spirit, George Chapman's 1616 translation of Homer's epic inspired Keats's equally famous sonnet (see 290.30). Ogygia is Calypso's isle (as Graves often notes); for Prester John, see 31.2 and the annotation at 408.14.

75 **Tissandiers *Histoire des ballons*** [53.8] Tissandier's *Histoire des ballons*: Gaston Tissandier (1843–99), French aeronaut and writer. *Histoire des ballons et des aéronautes célèbres* was published in a two-volume edition in Paris in 1887–90.

Morgenrot von den Rosen des Garten Eden [53.14] roses of Eden [...] the Talmud [...] fires of Hell: Lethaby (*AMM* 110) records this belief in connection with ancient speculations on the geographical location of Paradise.

77 **denn er war sehr groß** [54.42] A large stone [...] for it was very great: a parody of Christ's burial; the phrase "for it was very great" is from Mark 16:4.

78 **die sieben Todsünden** [55.18] Seven Deadly Sins [...] Invidia: Lat.: Pride, Wrath, Lust, Avarice, Envy (not given are Gula [Gluttony] and Accidia [Sloth]).

Saturnalien [55.25] Like Pliny [...] Saturnalia: "This festival (in late times held in December, 16–23) so closely resembled our Christmas in jollity, that Pliny (like some of us) used to withdraw to the most retired room in his Laurentine villa to escape the noise" (*M&R* 108). Pliny the Elder (23–79) is best known for his *Natural History* (see 334–21); he also wrote about the druids (next entry).

Druiden [55.31] druidical reverence [...] lightning: from *GB* 709. Druids were an ancient Gaulish and British order of priests; little is known about their religion aside from its emphasis on magic, astrology, and the transmigration of souls, and that they held the oak and mistletoe sacred.

Aurora Borealis [55.33] Aurora Borealis [...] Second Advent: such celestial phenomena have always been taken by the superstitious as signs of divine intervention; Gaddis's source unknown.

Moses im Koran der Hexerei bezichtigt [55.40] Moses had been accused of witchcraft in the Koran: suras 20 and 28 retell the encounter between Moses and Pharaoh's sorcerers (Exodus 7) and attribute Moses' magical powers to divinely inspired sorcery.

Sklaven und ehrloses Gelichter [55.42] "slaves and disreputable people [...] god-dedicated virgins": source unknown.

unter Karl dem Großen [56.1] Charlemagne: king of the Franks (768–814); subjugated the Saxons by 785.

79 **der Heilige Olaf** [56.3] Saint Olaf: king of Norway (1016–28), noted for his harsh measures for converting his subjects to Christianity.

Bacchus [56.12]: Roman god of wine and fertility (counterpart to the Greek Dionysus). He sprang from the thigh of Zeus (a kind of virgin birth) after being prematurely born from Semele. The wine of the Eucharist has been traced to Bacchic rites.

79 **Osiris** [56.12]: Egyptian god of the underworld, brother/husband of Isis, who reassembled his parts after he was dismembered by his brother Set (see 258.30–31). The Greeks identified Osiris with Dionysus as a symbol of fertility and life (cf. annotation to *Le Culte de Dionysos en Attique*, 23.31).

Krishna [56.12]: Hindu deity, the greatest of the incarnations of Vishnu (56.17). His uncle, King Kamsa, having been warned that one of his nephews would kill him, murdered Devaki's children at birth; Krishna was smuggled away and lived to kill him. The obvious parallels are Oedipus, Zeus (see 212.38), Moses, Jesus, et al.

Buddha [56.12]: title given to Prince Siddhartha (or Gautama, ca. 623–543 B.C.), founder of Buddhism; see 877.2 for his "immaculate conception."

Adonis [56.12]: hero of the Greek vegetation myth, annually reborn amid great celebrations on the part of his followers. He plays a central role in Frazer's *GB* and Weston's *FRR*.

Marduk [56.12]: chief deity of the ancient Babylonian religion, avatar of many other Babylonian gods.

Balder [56.12]: Scandinavian god of light; the final hundred pages of Frazer's *GB* focus on "Balder the Beautiful."

Attis [56.12]: a fertility god whose cult began in Asia Minor and spread to Greece. Annual death and rebirth link him to the worship of Adonis and his mutilation to Osiris (links explored in detail by Frazer and Weston).

Amphion [56.12]: son of Zeus by Antiope (see 385.1) who, according to Greek legend, built Thebes by the music from his lute. At his birth, Amphion, like Oedipus, was left exposed to die on a hillside but was rescued by a passing herdsmen. He was finally slain by Apollo.

Quetzalcoatl [56.12]: Aztec deity who, after instructing his people in agriculture, metallurgy, and other arts, left promising one day to return. (When the first Spaniards arrived in Mexico, some Aztecs thought Quetzalcoatl had finally returned.) All the foregoing gods (except Amphion) are discussed by Frazer.

Schicksalstag, an dem die Sonne ihr Antlitz verborgen hatte [56.13] sad day the sun was darkened [...] Julius Caesar: as Conybeare points out (*MMM* 284–85), the tradition of the sun's darkening at Jesus' crucifixion was based on the earlier tradition of its doing likewise at the assassination of Caesar (44 B.C.), which in turn was borrowed from earlier stories.

Brahma, Vishnu, und Shiva [56.17]: the Hindu trinity: "From man to Brahmâ, a series of higher forms are traceable in an ascending scale till three principal divinities are reached. These, the highest manifestations of the First

Cause, Brahmā the Creator, Vishnu the Preserver, and Siva the Destroyer, constitute the Tri-murti, the Trinity, typified in the magically mystic syllable Om" (*AN* 7).

79 **Unbefleckte Empfängnis [...] Romulus und Remus** [56.18] Immaculate Conception [...] Romulus and Remus: the legendary and eponymous founders of Rome were, traditionally, sons of Mars and Rhea Sylvia, a vestal virgin. She was put to death and the twins were suckled by a wolf. (Virgin birth and/or immaculate conception is a common attribute of gods and heroes; see Conybeare's long chapter "Birth Legends" in *MMM* 186–234).

andere Räume, andere Stimmen [56.23] other voices and other rooms: *Other Voices, Other Rooms* (1948) is the title of Truman Capote's (1924–84) first novel, a Southern Gothic about a boy's coming of age. (Gaddis knew Capote in the late 1940s: both worked for a while at the *New Yorker*.)

vom Letzten Abendmahl in den Eleusinischen Mysterien [56.26] Last Supper at the Eleusinian Mysteries: Frazer (*GB* 394–95), Weston (*FRR* 146–48), and Summers (*PPM* 22) speak of the rites performed at Eleusis (Attica, Greece) in ways that indicate parallels to the Last Supper.

Schlange im Garten Eden s. S. 457 [56.27] snake in the Garden of Eden: either the "snake of consciousness" (338.27) or a phallic symbol representing sexual awakening.

›Hüfte‹ [56.28] the word 'thigh': stands for testicles.

den ursprünglichen Sinn des triunischen Dreiecks [56.30] Triune triangle: the female generative organs.

seines symbolischen Gegenstücks im Reproduktionsprozeß, des Kreuzes nämlich s. S. 42f. [56.31] origin of the Cross: see 312.11–15.

80 **Praxiteles s. S. 168** [57.20]: Greek sculptor of the fourth century B.C.; see 124.7.

81 **Mithraismus** [57.36] Mithras [...] Mithraism [...] failed because it was so near good: this ancient Persian religion, suppressed by Zoroastrianism, became very popular with Roman soldiers and traders of the first century A.D. and soon became Rome's state religion. The cult centered on Mithras, a deity of sun and light, who later became a mediator between the forces of evil and the spirit of heavenly light. What little is known of the mystery religion has been deduced from surviving inscriptions and icons. Under the Roman Empire the religion spread throughout Europe (altars have been found as far north as England) and was the principal rival of Christianity until the time of Constantine. It finally disappeared with the advent of Islam.

On the oft-noted resemblances between Christianity and Mithraism,

W. J. Phythian-Adams, whose *Mithraism* was Gaddis's principal source, writes: "To the outward eye the two religions of Mithras and Christ appeared to differ in accidental details only; at many important points they presented the most startling resemblances, which Christian apologists admitted with horror, but could not explain except by a charge of diabolical agency" (*M* 3; cf. 535.43, 536.16 ff., 719.13). At the end of his short study, Phythian-Adams concludes – as does Rev. Gwyon – "It fell at the last, not because it was entirely bad, but *because it was so nearly good*" (*M* 94). Frazer and Weston also comment on the parallels between the two religions (*GB* 358, *FRR* 164–74).

81 **Pelagianismus** [57.43] Pelagianism: the British monk Pelagius (360?–420?) rejected the doctrine of original sin and insisted that one is free to do good or evil and is personally responsible for his or her own salvation, as opposed to the Augustinian doctrine (which became dogma) that mankind, as a result of Adam's fall, suffers from "innate depravity" and can attain salvation only by the grace of God (and his church). One of the great heresiarchs, Pelagius is the author of *On the Trinity, On Free Will*, and other tracts.

Der freie Wille [58.7] Free will: the existence and necessity of free will is a major theme in the Clementine *Recognitions*.

82 **bei einer Doktrin angelangt, die er die aristotelische nannte** [58.16] the doctrine, which he called Aristotelian [...] shock His worshipers: from Conybeare's discussion of the development of the Eucharist (*MMM* 266–67):

The Aristotelian distinction of substance and accident was also called in to explain its nature. The substance of the bread, it was argued, becomes the substance of the flesh, even though the accidents of the bread – *e. g.*, colour, size, hardness, taste, weight, smell, etc. – remain; as if, forsooth, a bit of bread had any substance apart from the entire complex of its attributes. However, the substance of the body and blood having, on this view, replaced in the act of consecration that of the bread and wine, the recipient is declared to masticate, with teeth and tongue, the real flesh and blood. It is only by the merciful providence of a God unwilling to shock and stupefy his worshippers, that the attributes or accidents are allowed to remain, and the holy bread or victim, as it is called, prevented from appearing on the altar as a bleeding mass of raw human flesh.

Erlösung der stofflichen Welt s. S. 175 [58.19] redemption of matter: the primary concern of alchemy; see 129.30–34.

83 **Conte di Brescia** [59.36]: apparently fictitious (a descendant of Adamo da Brescia [5.30]? related to Seraphina di Brescia [314.32]?); see 246.8 ff. for details of "the brave deceit." The *Conte di Brescia* is also the name of the ship on which Stanley and Esme cross the Atlantic in part III.

84 **o Flut von Blut** [60.1] O Blood ineffable [...] with my Beloved: source unknown.

85 München [60.40]: when *R* was first submitted to Harcourt, Brace in 1953 it contained a whole section concerning Wyatt's stay in Munich. Though cut from the final version, vestiges of this section appear in the next two chapters.

an jenem gelben Tag [60.43] yellow day in Boston [...] Krakatao: on 27 August 1883 the volcano Krakatao (also Krakatoa, Krakatau) exploded, killing 35 000 with its tidal waves and sending smoke and ashes around the world. The volcanic island is between Java and Sumatra.

Manto [61.2]: Greek prophetess, daughter of Tiresias. She was Apollo's "pythoness" at Delphi and is mentioned in Dante's *Inferno* (20:50).

sein Amt redlich auszurichten [61.2] make full proof of his ministry: see 49.18.

Allerseelen, wo man auf den französischen Friedhöfen Picknicks veranstaltete [61.5] All Saints' [...] in France there would be picnics in the cemeteries: a practice mentioned by Olcott (*SL* 413) in his discussion of the Pleiades' influence on ceremonies for the dead (see annotation to 6.14).

86 mit dem Rigorismus einer heiligen Clara [61.34] transformation [...] Blessed Clara: a transformation is a wig; Blessed Clara may be Blessed Clare Agolanti of Rimini (1282–1346), who, after a dissipated life, founded a nunnery and practiced rigorous penances.

Worte von William Rufus [62.4] words of William Rufus [...] *upon me!*: King William (II) Rufus of England (ruled 1087–1100) made this famous oath after recovering from an illness in 1093, blaming his maker for his sickness and vowing revenge. Bishop Gundulf (or Gundulph) was a family friend as well as the guardian of Saint Anselm (see 103.34). Swearing by the Holy Face of Lucca – an ancient wooden image of Christ (cf. *Inferno* 21:51) – was a habit of William's (as noted in Margaret A. Murray's *The God of the Witches* [New York: Oxford University Press, 1952], 163–64, where it is suggested Lucca is a corruption of Loki, the Scandinavian god of trickery).

I.2

88 Très curieux [...] *Trucs et truqueurs* [63.epigraph]: Fakes and Fakers (1907) is one of many books on art forgery by French writer Paul Eudel (1837–1911). The quotation is from a chapter entitled "Tableaux Anciens," in which a bitter critic remarks to a financier: "Very curious, your old masters. Only the most beautiful are forged" (Paris: Librairie Molière, n.d., 445).

Dôme [63.1] the Dôme: I have felt it unnecessary to annotate the many Parisian places mentioned in this chapter unless they have special literary or historical significance. Gaddis's knowledge of Paris was based on his stay there in 1950–51.

88 **George Washington** [63.2] George Washington [...] Ohio Territory: 1753, when Washington was twenty-one; cf. 312.25 and 938.11.

Voilà ma propre Sainte Chapelle [63.7]: "Here is my own Sainte Chapelle" (famous Parisian church dating from the thirteenth century).

transition [63.11]: an avant-garde review – subtitled *An International Quarterly for Creative Experiment* – founded in Paris in 1927 by Eugene and Maria Jolas; it ran until 1938.

J'vous en prie [63.13]: "If you please."

Nicht kann sie altern, hinwelken, [...] Stumpfsinn [63.17] age had not withered her [...] infinite vulgarity: praising Cleopatra, Shakespeare's Enobarbus says: "Age cannot wither her, nor custom stale / Her infinite variety" (*Antony and Cleopatra* 2.2.240–41). Cf. 938.16 ff.

The Teddy Bears' Picnic [63.21]: written for solo piano by John Walter Bratton in 1908; lyrics added by Jimmy Kennedy in 1933. The song became famous first as a hit for Bing Crosby and later as the theme for *The Big John and Sparky Show,* a radio program of the 1950s.

89 **Highgate** [63.25]: cemetery in London where many notables (like Marx) are buried.

corde du roi [63.27]: Fr.: the king's cord – corduroy, originally made of silk, was worn by the kings of France while hunting.

Er stirbt. Da kann ich ihn schlecht auf die Straße setzen [63.28] I've got to show these pictures [...] dying like that: taken from an episode in Henry Miller's *Tropic of Cancer* (1934), in which Miller is ill on the day an artist friend named Kruger plans to give a private exhibition (New York: Ballantine, 1973, 176–77).

enkonnü, [...] Zehnfrangpurboah [64.8] ankonoo [...] poorbwar: Fr. *inconnu* (unknown) and *pourboire* (tip, gratuity).

90 **A mon très aimé frère Lazarus** [64.31] "A mon très aimé [...] M. Chasles [...] collection of autographs: as an example of "how a man can be great in his own specialty, yet likely to be taken in under peculiar and rather astonishing circumstances," Nobili (*GAF* 200–201) instances a collection of autographs sold to French mathematician Michel Chasles (1793–1880) by a forger named Vrain-Lucas:

Among other things there was included: a private letter of Alexander the Great addressed to Aristotle; a letter of Cleopatra to Julius Cæsar, informing the Roman Dictator that their son "Cesarion" was getting on very well; a missive of

Lazarus to St. Peter; also a lengthy epistle addressed to Lazarus by Mary Magdalen. It should be added that the letters were written in French and in what might be styled an eighteenth-century jargon, that Alexander addressed Aristotle as *Mon Ami* and Cleopatra scribbled to Cæsar: *Notre fils Cesarion va bien.* Lazarus, no less a scholar in the Gallic idiom, and to whom, maybe, a miraculous resurrection had prompted a new personality, writes to St. Peter in the spirit of a rhetorician and a prig, speaking of Cicero's oratory and Cæsar's writings, getting excited and anathematic on Druidic rites and their cruel habit *de sacrifier des hommes saulxvaiges.*

Mary Magdalen, who begins her letter with a *mon très aimé frère Lazarus, ce que me mandez de Petrus l'apostre de notre doux Jesus,* is supposed to be writing from Marseilles and thus would appear to be the only one out of the many who can logically indulge in French, the *jargon-bouillabaisse* that Vrain-Lucas lent to the gallant array of his personages.

After such a practical joke played on the excellent good faith of M. Chasles, some of the other autographs seem tame. The package, however, also contained scraps jotted down by Alcibiades and Pericles, a full confession of Judas Iscariot's crime written by himself to Mary Magdalen before passing the rope round his neck; a letter of Pontius Pilate addressed to Tiberius expressing his sorrow for the death of Christ. Other astounding pieces of this now famous collection were: a passport signed by Vercingetorix, a poem of Abelard and some love-letters addressed by Laura to Petrarch, as well as many other historical documents down to a manuscript of Pascal and an exchange of letters between the French scientist and Newton on the laws of gravitation, the Frenchman claiming the discovery as his own. [...] Among other historical blunders is the supposition that Newton could have exchanged letters with Pascal on the laws of gravitation. The former being but nine years old when Pascal died, he had certainly not yet given his mind to the observations bringing about his marvellous discovery.

(Gaddis followed Nobili's own blunder regarding Newton's age in the first edition, but corrected "nine" to "nineteen" for later editions.)

90 **damals in La Salette [...] auf französisch kundgetan** [64.42] Virgin appeared to Maximin and Mélanie at La Salette: Mary allegedly appeared as a sorrowful, weeping figure to these two peasant children at La Salette in southern France on 19 September 1846. The message she confided to them (the necessity of penance) was communicated to Pope Pius IX in 1851 and has since been known as the "secret" of La Salette. *MMSM* 154–61 gives full details.

Académie Française [65.8]: founded in 1635, the French Academy is restricted to forty members at a time ("The Immortals") chosen from distinguished men of letters (women were ineligible until 1980), formed to perfect and preserve the purity of the French language.

91 **keine Meerjungfrau (nicht einmal die in Dschibuti)** [65.32] Siren of Djibouti: Djibouti is a tiny area in east Africa at the point where the Red Sea and the Gulf of Aden meet. Apparently, the Siren of Djibouti is a faked mermaid similar to those described by Gwen Benwell and Arthur Waugh in their *Sea*

Enchantress: The Tale of the Mermaid and Her Kin: "It was for long – and until recently – the practice to exhibit a faked mermaid in Aden, and many travellers have told of the posters advertising the wonder which waited – at a moderate price – to gratify the curious" (New York: Citadel, 1965, 126).

91 **Voice votre Perrier [...] pas d'eau Perrier** [65.33]: "Here is your Perrier, sir." "But I said café au lait, not Perrier water."

Son putas, y nada mas [65.34]: Sp.: "They're whores, and nothing more."

Kafka [65.36]: in the 1930s Austrian writer Franz Kafka (1883–1924) was still largely unknown.

Très amusant [...] très original [65.39]: "Very amusing, gay, very very original."

Quelquefois [...] un tableau [65.43]: "Sometimes I'll spend an entire night finishing a painting."

Witz von Kavallerist Carruthers [66.1] the joke about Carruthers and his horse: two stuffy British majors are discussing the latest scandal: "Heard about Carruthers?" "No, what?" "Been drummed out of the army." "God, what for?" "Caught in the act with a horse." "Ghastly! Mare or stallion?" "Mare, of course – nothing queer about Carruthers!" The joke is referred to throughout the novel, with the punch line finally coming at 941.22.

92 **Banlieu** [66.6]: not a proper name but a word meaning "suburb, outskirts." Cf. 944.15.

Sacré Cœur [66.8]: "Sacred Heart," the national church of France. Situated at the top of Montmartre, it was begun in 1876 as an expression of hope and contrition after the disastrous Commune and Franco-Prussian War (1870).

Voulez vous voir [...] Deux femmes [66.11]: "Do you want to watch something dirty? Two women... ."

das sichtbare Eingeständnis der Niederlage gegen die Jesuiten [66.19] Jesuit victory over France: most of the following details concerning Jesuit activity in France are from Marsh's anti-Jesuitical *MMSM* (98ff.).

Ignatius of Loyola [66.20]: (1491–1556), Spanish soldier and ecclesiastic, founded the Society of Jesus (Jesuits) in 1534.

Jansenisten [66.26] Jansenists: followers of the doctrine formulated by Cornelius Jansen (1585–1638), which adopted the teachings of Saint Augustine along Calvinist lines. Louis XIV opposed them, and they were finally put down by Pope Clement XI in 1713.

92 **Pascals Beiträge** [66.26] Pascal: Blaise Pascal (1623–62), French mathematician and philosopher, a student (if not an adherent) of Jansenism. He attacked the Jesuits in his *Lettres provinciales* (1656–57), which earned it a place on the *Index*.

das Wunder vom heiligen Dorn [66.27] *Miracle of the Holy Thorn*: "Marguerite Périer, Pascal's niece, was cured of a fistula lachrymalis on 24 March, 1656, after her eye was touched with this sacred relic, supposed to be a thorn from the crown of Christ. This miracle made a great impression upon Pascal" (from the notes in the Everyman's edition of Pascal's *Pensées*, introduction by T. S. Eliot, who discusses Pascal's interest in Jansenism; the spelling of "lachrymalis" – instead of "lacrymalis" as in *EB*'s account of the miracle [17:350] – along with Gaddis's interest in Eliot, suggests the Everyman's edition as his source).

eine eigene kleine Marguerite [66.29] its own Marguerite: Marguerite Marie Alacoque (1647–90), French nun whose famous vision in 1673 led to the founding of the devotion of the Sacred Heart, which was opposed by the Jansenists. See Marsh (*MMSM* 104–6) for a sarcastic summary of her "searing narrative."

Père La Colombière [66.30]: Claud La Colombière (1641–82), beatified in 1929. His role in Marguerite's case is described by Marsh (*MMSM* 99–103).

Papst Pius IX. [66.36] 1864, Pope Pius IX: "Pius IX., ever 'good at need,' on the 23rd of August, 1846, declared by solemn decree that the nun had practiced the 'heroic' virtues ascribed to her; on the 24th of May, 1864, by another decree, affirmed the truth and reality of the miracles attributed to her intercession; and on the 19th of August, 1864, pronounced her beatification" (*MMSM* 107–8). Marguerite was canonized in 1920.

93 **das Wunder strahlte gar auf die Akte Marguerite selber ab** [66.38] the petition itself participated in the miraculous [...] unable to write their names: from Marsh (*MMSM* 108 and note).

Kaum zehn Jahre später [66.41] a decade after: on 22 April 1875, "thus making the acceptance of this devotion a cardinal feature of the religion of Rome" (*MMSM* 108–9).

ewiger Rosenkranz [67.2] Devotion of the Perpetual Rosary: one of many devotions that sprang up in France in the nineteenth century. Marsh explains (*MMSM* 161):

> The splendid success of La Salette soon led to new attempts to get up analogous manifestations elsewhere, but, as we have hinted, they were often smothered by the local jealousies of the clergy. A late movement in favor of the Perpetual Rosary of Mary was formidable enough to threaten not only La Salette and

Lourdes, but even the Sacré Cœur, and it was defeated only by a solemn resolution of the General Congress of the French Catholic Committees at Paris. At this congress, as appears by recent journals, Père Edouard, a Dominican, urged, as an infallible means to save France and the Church, the Devotion of the Perpetual Rosary, while Père Ramière, a Jesuit, stoutly defended the Devotion of the Sacred Heart as more efficacious. Monseigneur de Ségur said that the Holy Virgin shows *very good taste* by choosing France for the theatre of her apparitions, and that Gallicism in France is dead and buried since the 19th of July, 1870 [when France declared war on Prussia]. He declared himself in favor of the Sacred Heart, which was finally sustained against the Perpetual Rosary.

93 **Jungfrau von Lourdes** [67.3] Virgin of Lourdes: in 1858, a peasant girl named Bernadette Soubirous (1844–79) claimed that the Virgin Mary – identifying herself as the Immaculate Conception – had appeared to her on eighteen occasions. A spring with miraculous healing powers supposedly appeared at the same time, and after Bernadette's visions were legitimized, the pilgrimage to Lourdes received ecclesiastical recognition in 1862 (*MMSM* 163–74; the details on "85 liters per minute" and taxation difficulties are from a footnote on pp. 170–71). Bernadette was canonized in 1933.

der heilige Denis [67.8] Saint Denis: (fl. third century) first bishop of Paris. He was beheaded along with two companions during the persecution of Decius, but, as the legend goes, "at once the body of Dionysius [the Greek form of Denis] stood erect, and took his head in its hands; and with an angel guiding it and a great light going before, it walked for two miles, from the place called Montmartre to the place where by its own choice and by the providence of God, it now reposes" (Jacobus de Voragine's *Golden Legend*). See 938.26 for Madame du Deffand's captious comment on this feat.

»öffentliche Einrichtung« [67.9] "public utility": "France professes to recognize the legal equality of Protestant and Catholic churches," Marsh writes, "and has no national, no State religion; but the recent action of the Legislative Assembly, prompted by Jesuit influence, in declaring the construction of a church dedicated to the Sacred Heart, on the heights of Montmartre, to be a work of 'public utility,' is very nearly the equivalent to a formal recognition of that devotion as the religion of the State" (*MMSM* 112 n.).

Kardinal Erzbischof Guibert [67.10] Cardinal Archbishop Guibert: Joseph Hippolyte Guibert (1802–86), archbishop of Paris at the time (*MMSM* 109).

William Godwin [67.12]: (1756–1836), English philosopher and novelist. Marsh investigates the charge that the Jesuit Devotion of the Sacred Heart was plagiarized from Godwin's tract *The Heart of Christ in Heaven towards Sinners on Earth* (*MMSM* 100–103).

93 **Monsignore Ségur** [67.14]: Louis Gaston de Ségur (1820–81), French priest and author of some sixty religious works; see note to 67.2 above.

[67.16] **Bourse**: Paris's stock exchange.

des touristes [...] type là [67.16]: "Tourists, yes, but filthy English, ... there, look at that one there."

94 **Surrealismus** [67.36] surréalisme: surrealism (the French word was taken from Apollinaire) was at its height in the 1930s.

Jean-Jacques Henner [68.3] Henner [...] the only way of being original: Jean-Jacques Henner (1829–1905), French painter. Henner's precept is noted in Eudel's *Trucs et truqueurs* (449) in a passage that can be translated: "One could even see, o decadence! in one of the most frequented quarters of Paris, an old improvident art student in a stall. On a platform, he executed his paintings by the minute, always the same view, following the precept of Henner, the only way of being original."

95 **die Fabel vom Streit zwischen Sonne und Wind** [68.19] fabled argument between the sun and wind: one of Aesop's fables, in which the sun and wind, each claiming to be stronger than the other, attempt to strip a traveler of his coat. The wind's furious attack fails, but the sun's gentle warmth causes the traveler to gladly remove his coat. (Moral: persuasion is better than force.) The fable is related in *HWF* 3.4 in illustration of a sales technique.

[68.26] **Bitte?**: Ger: pardon?

[68.30] Allerheiligen-Hofkirche's [...] Frauenkirche: two noted Munich cathedrals.

[68.35] déracinés: those uprooted from their native land.

96 **der von den Toten auferweckt worden war?** [69.15] (what became of the man who was raised?): upon being raised from the dead (John 11:44), Lazarus is regarded by the Jewish chief priests as a contributing factor in Jesus' popularity and consequently they decide to do away with him (12:10–11). Whether this was carried out is left unsaid. Huizinga comments: "Nothing betrays more clearly the excessive fear of death felt in the Middle Ages than the popular belief, then widely spread, according to which Lazarus, after his resurrection, lived in a continual misery and horror at the thought that he should have again to pass through the gate of death" (*WMA* 131–32).

[69.34] melancholia of things completed: see 599.5.

97 **Où allez-vous donc?** [...] **vous savez** [69.37]: "Where are you going then?" "Home." "Your papers, please." "My passport? I don't have it on me, it's at home." "Where do you live?" "Twenty-four rue de la Bourse."

"What do you do?" "I'm a painter." "Where?" "At home." "Where do you live?" "But ..." "Do you have means?" "Yes ..." "OK, you should always have some on you, money, you know... ."

97 **Crémer** [70.4]: although there was a minor alchemist named John Cremer (said to have lived in the fourteenth century) – WG expressed surprise at this (WG/SM) – Rodger Cunningham is probably correct in suggesting Crémer is a Frenchified version of German *Kramer*, merchant, specifically a shifty, petty shopkeeper.

La Macule [70.14]: Fr.: the stain, blot, blemish; also, blind spot.

98 **Van Eyck** [70.29]: the brothers Van Eyck, Hubert and Jan (fl. fifteenth century), will be noted later (249 ff.).

Roger de la Pasture [...] Van der Weyden [70.31]: (1400–64), one of the major artists of the fifteenth century in Flanders and one of the few equals of Jan Van Eyck. Conway notes: "Being a French-speaking person, he would not have called himself 'Van der Weyden,' but 'de la Pasture'" (*VEF* 129; chap. 11 of Conway's study concerns him).

Memling [70.35]: Hans Memling (or Memlinc, d. 1494), Flemish painter, a student of Van der Weyden. His calm and pious pictures and his excellent portraits are in the style of his teacher and Dirk Bouts and show little originality. See chap. 17 of *VEF*.

Gerard Davids Gemälde *Die Schindung des Kambyses* [70.37] Gheerardt David's painting *The Flaying of the Unjust Judge*: Flemish painter (d. 1523), last master of the Bruges school. *The Flaying of the Unjust Judge* is the second half of a diptych called *The Story of Sisamnes*, in which King Cambyses (sixth century B.C.) punishes Sisamnes the judge for his corruption.

99 **Degas** [71.11] Degas [...] his remark [...] criminal commits his deed: Edgar Degas (1834–1917), French painter; source of quotation unknown.

Ich garantiere Ihnen dafür eine hervorragende Presse [71.34] I could guarantee you excellent reviews: a similar offer was made to Han Van Meegeren (1889–1947), a forger much in the news when *R* was being written, and whose career Gaddis used as a model for Wyatt's. Frustrated at the critical neglect of his own work, Van Meegeren over a period of ten years in the 1930s and 1940s forged several Vermeers (supposedly dating from a gap in Vermeer's life) that completely fooled the critics and were sold at prices befitting rediscovered old masters. When for political reasons Van Meegeren finally confessed, the red-faced critics denied he had the talent to forge such works; materials were brought to his prison cell, and there he forged another for the benefit of these critics. Van Meegeren died in jail shortly thereafter. Both his technical accomplishments – especially reproducing chemically the aging process a seventeenth-century painting would have undergone – and his "spiritual" identification with Vermeer were adapted by Gaddis as components in Wyatt's approach to his own forgeries. For a fuller discussion, see Tom Sawyer's "False Gold to Forge: The Forger behind Wyatt Gwyon," *Review of Contemporary Fiction* 2.2 (Summer 1982): 50–54.

100 **Il faut [...] savez** [72.14]: "You should always have some on you, money, you know" – repeated from 69.40–41.

J. L. David [72.25]: Jacques Louis David (1748–1825), French painter. An ardent Bonapartist, he painted *Napoleon Crossing the Alps* as well as the famous *Coronation* (72.28). On the Romanization of Napoleon's Paris, Nobili notes with scorn: "Yet faking passes from the field of art to that of real life, the new Republic apes Roman customs. David the artist is faked into a Tribune while busy painting Romans that seem to have been brought out of a hot-house and he sketches semi-Roman costumes for the new officials of the Republic, garments that with all the foppishness of the 'old regime' had Roman Consular swords, Imperial chlamys (mantle), faked buskins or ornamented cothurnus (boots worn by tragedians)" (*GAF* 133).

Kaiserin Josephine [72.28] Josephine doing her very best [...] to look above suspicion: cf. Nobili: "One of the late Rothschilds [...] used to say that all the objects of his collection were, like Cæsar's wife, above suspicion" (*GAF* 152).

die Vision vom Rom des Kaiser Konstantin [72.32] Constantine's Rome [...] gods in ivory and gold: the Rome of Constantinople I the Great (ruled 306–37); the municipal details are from *GAF* 44–45.

101 **Papst Urban VIII.** [72.37] Pope Urban VIII had declared the Coliseum a public quarry: though there were laws prohibiting the export of Roman art objects out of the city, "the best buildings in Rome were allowed to fall into utter ruin without a protest. This state of things reached the climax of absurdity in the seventeenth century when Urban VIII, of the Barberini family, declared the Coliseum a public quarry, where the citizens might go for the stones they needed for new constructions – an act still commemorated in the protest of all lovers of art with the proverbial pun, *Quod non fecerunt barbari fecerunt Barberini* (What barbarians did not do, the Barberini did)" (*GAF* 105).

Kardinal Mazarin [72.41] Cardinal Mazarin [...] et qui m'ont tante couté: Nobili devotes a chapter to the unique collection of French statesman Jules Mazarin (1602–61); during his final illness, he said farewell to his precious collection: "'Good-bye, dear paintings that I have loved so much, that have cost me so high a price!'" (*GAF* 121; the French original is given in a succeeding paragraph).

101 **der römische Connaisseur** [72.43] Roman connoisseur could distinguish [...] sardonyx from cheap colored jasper: details noted by Pliny, recorded by Nobili (*GAF* 51, 58).

»**Un client [...] Fabriquons-en**« [73.3]: "A customer wants Corots? There's a shortage on the market? Make some." The hypothetical remark is made in Eudel's *Trucs et truqueurs* (451), where greed for unobtainable art objects is held responsible for the practice of forgery. (Both Eudel and Nobili censure avaricious, ill-educated art collectors; but for them, there would be no market for fakes.) Jean Baptiste Camille Corot (1796–1875): French landscape painter.

Coulanges zu Madame de Sévigné [73.8] As Coulanges said to Madame de Sévigné, – Pictures are bullion: "'Pictures are bullion,' writes the fat Coulanges to his cold-blooded and well-behaved cousin, Mme. de Sévigné, 'you can sell them at twice their price whenever you like'" (*GAF* 124). Mme. de Sévigné (1626–96), famous for her own letters, corresponded with several members of the illustrious Coulanges family.

fünfzig Millionen Franzosen konnten doch nicht irren [73.13] fifty million Frenchmen couldn't be wrong: a remark attributed (in *ODQ*) to American nightclub hostess Texas Guinan (1884–1933).

Lutetia [73.17]: ancient name for Paris, which in Roman times was a collection of mud hovels (Lat. *lutum*, mud). Caesar called it Lutetia Parisiorum ("mud-town of the Parisii," the tribe that inhabited the area), which was finally shortened to Paris. Cf. 938.36.

Mnesarete (vulgo »Phryne«, die Kröte) [73.19] Mnesarete, "Phryne": Mnesarete, nicknamed (and more popularly known as) Phryne ("Toad"), was a famous Athenian courtesan of the fourth century B.C. One of the more famous incidents from her life is recounted below (73.40–41: she was acquitted).

102 *Millet* [73.26]: Jean François Millet (1814–75), French painter, best known of the Barbizon school.

Künstlerghettos [73.32] their own squalid bohemias [...] handing the original over to their hungry neighbor: Bohemia (Czechoslovakia) was "handed over" to Germany via the Munich Pact (29–30 September 1938), signed by France, Great Britain, Germany, and Italy.

Maginot-Linie [73.33] Maginot Line: a zone of fortifications built along the eastern frontier of France between 1929 and 1934. With this line the French believed they were secure from any threat of German invasion.

102 **Versailler Vertrag** [73.34] Versailles treaty: signed 28 June 1919; the treaty was punitively harsh on Germany, and on 16 March 1935 Germany formally renounced the clauses concerning disarmament and began building up its forces.

Attentat auf einen deutschen Gesandten in Paris [73.35] a German envoy [...] shot in Paris: Ernst vom Rath, third secretary of the German Embassy in Paris, was shot and killed on 7 November 1938 by a young Polish Jew named Herschel Grynszpan in retaliation for the mistreatment of Jews in Nazi Germany. The assassination led to the notorious *Kristallnacht* a few days later. (In *JR*, Gibbs and Eigen use "Grynszpan" as a cover name at their 96th Street apartment.)

Abkommen [...] neue Ausgabe des großen Völkerschlachtens [73.36] peace pact signed: between France and Germany, that is, on 6 December 1938.

»Il y a tant [...] jamais« [73.38]: "There are so many saints that they form a bulwark around Paris, through which the zeppelins never pass" – source unknown.

Tag des heiligen Bartholomäus [73.44] Saint Bartholomew's Day: 24 August (cf. 75.9–10 below). In light of the subject of the forgery below (74.40), it's worth noting Saint Bartholomew was likewise flayed alive.

103 **Sainte Madeleine** [74.16] the Madeleine's peripteral imposture: the Madeleine is the popular name for the church of Saint Mary Magdalene, which is built in the style of a Roman temple and surrounded by a majestic Corinthian colonnade ("peripteral" means surrounded by columns).

Fleischflaute [74.22]: that is, "flesh flute."

Archaïque [...] Résurrection [74.25]: "Archaic, hard as rock, derivitive, without heart, without sympathy, without life, finally, a spirit of death without the hope of the Resurrection" (Jack Green's translation). A dozen years later Crémer will say the same thing about Wyatt's final forgery (see 665.38).

einen echten Memling wiederentdeckt [74.30] an original painting by Hans Memling: not an original but Wyatt's student imitation (see 70.35–40; 95.15–18; 421.26–27).

in der Alten Pinakothek [74.38] Old Pinakothek: art gallery and museum, destroyed in the Second World War.

Kaiser Valerian [74.40] Valerian [...] Sapor: from Foxe (*BM* 21–22):

It is here proper to take notice of the singular but miserable fate of the [Roman] emperor Valerian, who had so long and so terribly persecuted the Christians. This tyrant, by a stratagem, was taken prisoner by Sapor, emperor of Persia, who carried him into his own country, and there treated him with the most unexampled indignity, making him kneel down as the meanest slave, and treading upon him as a footstool when he mounted his horse. After having kept him for the space of seven years in this abject state of slavery, he caused his eyes to be put out, though he was then eighty-three years of age. This not satiating his desire of revenge, he soon after ordered his body to be flayed alive, and rubbed with salt, under which torments he expired [A.D. 267]; and thus fell one of the most tyrannical emperors of Rome, and one of the greatest persecutors of the Christians.

Wyatt associates Valerian with his father (405.6–10, 421.18); Brown later acquires this painting – thinking it genuine (231.32) – from which Wyatt will cut out the figure of Valerian when he leaves for Spain; Valerian is later associated by Ludy (and perhaps by Wyatt as well) with the porter at the Real Monasterio (896.1ff.). The description of Wyatt's Memling closely matches David's painting (see 70.37), even to the red cloak in the foreground.

104 **Bouts** [75.6]: Dierick (or Dirk) Bouts (1415?–75), Flemish painter, treated in chap. 12 of *VEF*. (*Die Fleischflaute*'s rating of Memling over "the minor talents of the Van Eycks, Bouts, Van der Weyden" is an example of uncritical nationalism.)

Papst Gregor XIII. [75.9] Gregory XII [...] heretics: Gregory (pope 1572–85) was a vigorous opponent of Protestantism (from a Catholic viewpoint synonymous with heresy at that time); the Saint Bartholomew's Day Massacre, beginning in Paris on 24 August 1572, was ordered by Catherine de'Medici and targeted French Huguenots.

[75.18] **the stye of contentment**: from Eliot's poem "Marina": "Those who sit in the stye of contentment, meaning / Death" (ll. 10–11).

Kaiserin Theodora [75.21] Empress Theodora [...] died of cancer: (508?–48), wife of Justinian I; source of quotations (probably derived from Procopius's *Secret History*) unknown.

105 **vous m'emmenez?** [...] **discrètement** [75.43]: "Take me home? I'm dirty, the dirtiest in Paris ... You want to touch it? here? Give me some cash ... yes, cash, for the touch ... here ... discreetly ..."

106 **je mon fuh** [76.24] Je mon foo: *Je m'en fous* ("screw you").

Putas, putas, putas [76.24]: Sp. whores.

Göttin der Vernunft [76.36] Goddess of Reason: the cult of Reason was the atheistic French revolutionaries' surrogate for Catholicism, and the Goddess of Reason their surrogate for the Virgin; a famous statute of the Goddess of Reason was indeed modeled after a performer from the Opéra.

Captain de Mun [76.39] Captain de Mun [...] they are hell itself: Albert de Mun (1841–1914), French officer in the Franco-Prussian War and Catholic social reformer. Commenting on the elitist nature of French Catholicism, Marsh gives these extracts from a speech delivered by Captain de Mun in 1873:

> "I affirm that the brutal dogma of equality is a lie; I denounce it as a danger ... It has given birth to the insane theory according to which all offices ought to be open to all, and that all have the right to participate in the government of the commonwealth ... It is not true that the direction of the commonwealth, the exercise of authority, is not the lawful privilege, the hereditary prerogative, of certain classes ... After the civil constitution of the clergy, the greatest crime of the Revolution was the abolition of the corporations [trade-guilds which had the exclusive right of exercising their callings, according to their own regulations] ... The day will come when the vile horde of revolutionists ... will be reduced to utter the imprecation of the apostate, 'Galilæan, thou hast conquered.' Ah, for them no mercy; they are not the people, they are hell itself."

(*MMSM* 113–14; Marsh's ellipses and bracketed note.) The "imprecation" of Julian the Apostate furnishes the epigraph to II.9 (700).

106 **Liberté, égalité, fraternité** [76.41]: Liberty, equality, brotherhood – the motto of the French Revolution (said to have been suggested by Benjamin Franklin).

Friedhof Père Lachaise [77.1] Père Lachaise [...] Byron? Baudelaire?: Paris's largest and most fashionable cemetery, where a great many famous writers, artists, and composers and buried – but neither Byron nor Baudelaire.

107 *Al Misri* [77.17]: Arabic daily newspaper, published in Cairo (?1936–54).

Raymond Lully [77.21]: anglicized form of Ramón Lull (1235?–1315), Spanish ecclesiastic, philosopher, and alchemist (see 131.11, 222.epigraph). The story of his encounter with Ambrosia de Castello is condensed from *EPD* 113–14.

I.3

108 **In den Augen Gottes** [78.epigraph] First of all [...] Clementine *Recognitions*: see 373.1 for *The Recognitions*. In a short chapter entitled "Self-Love the Foundation of Goodness" (book 3, chap. 53), Peter explains why Simon Magus, "whose thoughts are against God, is able to do so great marvels":

> "First of all, then, he is evil, in the judgment of God, who will not inquire what is advantageous to himself. For how can any one love another, if he does not love himself? Or to whom will that man not be an enemy, who cannot be a friend to himself? In order, therefore, that there might be a distinction between those who choose good and those who choose evil, God has concealed that which is profitable to men, i.e., the possession of the kingdom of heaven, and has laid it up and hidden it as a secret treasure, so that no one can easily attain it by his own power or knowledge. Yet He has brought the report of it, under various names and opinions, through successive generations, to the hearing of all: so that whosoever should be lovers of good, hearing it, might inquire and discover what

is profitable and salutary to them; but that they should ask it, not from themselves, but from Him who has hidden it, and should pray that access and the way of knowledge might be given to them: which way is opened to those only who love it above all the good things of this world; and on no other condition can any one even understand it, however wise he may seem; but that those who neglect to inquire what is profitable and salutary to themselves, as self-haters and self-enemies, should be deprived of its good things, as lovers of evil things."

108 Esther [78.3]: contributing to her name may be the biblical Esther, the young Jewish woman who becomes queen of Persia and saves her people from destruction (subject of Handel's oratorio *Esther*); Ishtar, the Babylonian goddess of sexual love with whom Frazer associates the biblical Esther (an identification Lang questions); and, less likely, the protagonist of Henry Adams's novel *Esther* (1884), a free-thinking young painter who falls in love with a clergyman named Stephen Hazard but later breaks their engagement (a curious mirror image of the Wyatt/Esther relationship).

[78.5] women in love: title of a well-known novel (1920) by D. H. Lawrence, an author Esther "trusts" (82.28).

110 die zivilisierte Version jenes urzeitlich-kannibalischen Freßrituals [79.38] comrades who eat their victims: a practice noted by both Frazer and Haggard (*DDD* 318).

vagina dentata [79.44]: the "toothed vagina," prevalent in myth and folklore both as a symbol of ravenous sexual appetite of the female and of male fears of castration.

Animus [80.5] animus: in Jungian psychology, the masculine component in the female psyche (*IP* 19).

[80.12] but not for love: cf. the words of Rosalind quoted at 503.11–13.

111 *Call him louder!* [80.29] *Call him louder!* [...] *Like a hammer that breaketh the stone*: from German composer Felix Mendelssohn's (1809–47) oratorio *Elijah*, first produced in England in 1846. The first quotation is from section 12, where Elijah taunts the priests of Baal to call upon their unresponsive god (from 1 Kings 18:26); the two that follow are from section 17, in which Elijah glorifies his own god's wrath (based on Jer. 23:29).

Händel [80.31] Handel: George Frederick Handel (1685–1759), German composer; many of his works will be mentioned later in *R*.

Mozart [80.36]: Wolfgang Amadeus Mozart (1756–91), Austrian composer.

111 *Tosca* [81.1]: opera by Giacomo Puccini (1858–1924), libretto by Giuseppe Giacosa and Luigi Illica (based on a play by Victorien Sardou), first performed in Rome in 1900. Like *R*, it features an irreligious painter involved in criminal activities; lines from the opera are sprinkled

throughout the novel. (Gaddis once told me he disliked opera, with the exception of *Tosca*.)

111 **Diogenes Laërtius** [81.7]: fl. early third century; his *Lives and Opinions of the Eminent Philosophers* is valuable in that it is the sole source of information on many of the philosophers it treats; a number of his epigrams are in *The Greek Anthology*.

Keine Blumen für Miss Blandish [81.8] *No Orchids for Miss Blandish*: trashy, cliché-ridden detective novel (1939) by British writer James Hadley Chase (pseud. for René Raymond, 1906–85); "while trashy & cliché I recall it being regarded as seminal in the wave of sex/sadism (Justine notwithstanding)" (WG/SM; see 183.40 for Sade's *Justine*). In his essay "Raffles and Miss Blandish," George Orwell points out the great similarity (approaching plagiarism) between the novel and Faulkner's *Sanctuary* (1931).

Berkeleys *New Theory of Vision* [81.9] Berkeley's *New Theory of Vision*: George Berkeley (1685–1753), Anglo-Irish philosopher; his *Essay towards a New Theory of Vision* (1709) maintains that material objects are only ideas in the mind with no independent existence, and that all "reality" consists, finally, of ideas in the mind of God.

112 **Fort** [81.10] Charles Fort: American "phenomenologist" (1874–1932), author of four unusual books that tabulate oddities ignored by scientists. The first and best known of his works, *The Book of the Damned* (1919), from which Wyatt quotes below, is an eccentric attack on dogmatism in science. It records unusual objects that have fallen from the sky but have not been adequately explained, and is written in a unique style that combines epigrammatic quasi-philosophy and a droll sense of humor with exhaustive listings of data. The principal feature of his "supercelestial geography" is a hypothetical cosmic Sargasso Sea floating above the earth.

Die Verdammten [81.11] *Les Damnés de la Terre*: The Wretched of the Earth (1935) by French popular writer Henri Poulaille (1896–??).

»Die Verdammten, das sind für mich die Ausgeschlossenen« [81.14] Fort says, "By the damned, I mean the excluded": *The Book of the Damned* begins:

A procession of the damned.
By the damned, I mean the excluded.
We shall have a procession of data that Science has excluded.
Battalions of the accursed, captained by pallid data that I have exhumed, will march. You'll read them – or they'll march. […]
The Power that has said to all these things that they are damned, is Dogmatic Science.
(Reprinted in *The Complete Books of Charles Fort* [New York: Dover, 1974], 3.)

112 Und die Prostitution ist allem Anschein nach eine nützliche Tätigkeit [81.16] "By prostitution, I seem to mean usefulness": from chap. 3 of *The Book of the Damned*; Fort chides scientists for not pursuing "pure science" and instead tempering their findings to the needs of society, as if "nothing has justification for being, unless it serve, or function for, or express the relation of, some higher aggregate. So Science functions for and serves society at large, and would, from society at large, receive no support, unless it did so divert itself or dissipate and prostitute itself. It seems by prostitution I mean usefulness" (38).

Mozarts Sinfonie Nummer 37 [81.23] Mozart's Symphony Number 37, Köchel Listing 444: long attributed to Mozart, the symphony was actually written by Michael Hayden (1737–1806), Joseph's brother. Mozart furnished only the slow introduction.

113 ein Buch über Mumien vgl. S. 116 [82.6] a book on mummies: see 84.28.

114 Boyles *Skeptical Chemist* [83.21]: Robert Boyle (1627–91), English physician and chemist. *The Skeptical Chemist* (1661) challenged the two prevalent chemical approaches at that time (Aristotelian and alchemical) and helped alchemy mature into modern chemistry.

Jallands *Papst und Papsttum* [83.22] Jalland's *The Church and the Papacy*: a historical study (1944) by Catholic theologian Trevor Gervase Jalland (1898–??).

Cenninis *Libro dell' Arte* [83.22] Cennino Cennini's *Libro dell' Arte*: Cennini's (c. 1370 – c. 1440) technical treatise on painting emphasizes tempera technique. Otto reads from it on the bottom of p. 146.

La Chimie au Moyen Age [83.24]: Chemistry in the Middle Ages (1893) is an important three-volume collection of alchemical texts with commentary by French chemist and historian Marcelin Berthelot (1827–1907); cited often in Jung's *IP*.

Grimorium Verum [83.24]: the True Grimoire is a spell book, of uncertain date, based for the most part on the *Clavicula Salomonis* (The Key of Solomon, also known as The Book of Pentacles) and uncritically attributed (like many similar works) to King Solomon. It is cited throughout Waite's *Book of Ceremonial Magic* (see 139.15).

Turba Philosophorum [83.25]: the Uproar (or Crowd) of the Sages is a medieval alchemical work in the form of an allegorical discussion between Greek alchemists and their Platonist forerunners, all filtered through Sufism. It is cited in *IP*.

115 *Fabrica* des Vesalius [83.29] an arm in dissection from a woodcut in the *Fabrica* of Vesalius: reproduced on p. 148 of *DDD*. Andreas Vesalius (1514–64) was

a Belgian anatomist condemned by the Inquisition. His *De Humani Corporis Fabrica* is a treatise on the structure of the body.

115 eine zeitgenössische Erste-Hilfe-Tafel, betitelt »Der Wund-Mensch« [83.31] *Surgery* of Paré [...] "the wound man": Ambroise Paré (1517–90), French surgeon, often called the father of modern surgery. His career is treated at length in Haggard's *DDD* (31–43), where several illustrations from Paré's *Surgery* are reproduced, including his first-aid chart "the wound man" on p. 134.

Melozzo da Forlì [83.34]: (1438–95?), Italian painter of the Umbrian school, known for his skill in perspective.

Leptis Magna [83.35]: city in Tripolitania (Libya); *EB* notes its lavish public swimming pool (3:205).

116 *Die königlichen Mumien* [84.28] *Royal Mummies*: by Sir Grafton Elliot Smith (1871–1937), published in Cairo in 1912. It is cited in a discussion of Egyptian mummies of the New Kingdom in *EB* (15:954); one of Gaddis's sources for the mummification details later in the novel.

119 wir sind möglicherweise nur Fang für außerirdische Wesen [87.8] Charles Fort says maybe we're fished for: Fort's tongue-in-cheek response to a report of a triangular-shaped UFO with chains attached to the bottom, which was dismissed by the authorities as a partly collapsed balloon. Fort wonders if "something was trawling overhead?" then wryly speculates: "I think we're fished for. It may be that we're highly esteemed by super-epicures somewhere. It makes me more cheerful when I think that we may be of some use after all" (*Book of the Damned*, 264–65). The phrase "maybe we're fished for" will recur throughout the novel.

Orientation sidérale [87.12]: navigation based on the position of astronomical bodies relative to the horizon.

Experimente mit Ameisen [87.13] man who experimented with ants in the desert in Morocco: unidentified; see 110.17–19.

[89.32] auswendig wissen Sie: Ger.: "you know them by heart."

124 Rilke [91.8]: Rainer Maria Rilke (1875–1926), Austrian poet. The first of his famous *Duino Elegies* (1922) will be quoted later (277.34 ff., 622.16 ff.).

125 Echo zwischen den Gesichtern, Laternen und den Bugsprieten der Boote [91.13] faces and lanterns and the prows of boats: from Picasso's *Night Fishing in Antibes* (below).

125 Sopranstimme, die nel massimo dolore sang [91.17] soprano singing [...] mia preghiera: from Puccini's *Tosca* (81.1). In act 2 the tyrannical police chief Scarpia tells the singer Floria Tosca that he will lift the death sentence on her lover only if she agrees to have sex with him. Bewailing her position, Tosca delivers her famous "Vissi d'arte, vissi d'amore" aria, from which the present quotation (and many others to follow) comes:

Vissi d'arte, vissi d'amore,	I lived for art, I lived for love:
Non feci mai male ad anima viva!	Never did I harm a living creature!
Con man furtiva	Whatever misfortunes I encountered
Quante miserie conobbi, aiutai.	I sought with secret hand to succor.
Sempre con fè sincera	Ever in pure faith
La mia preghiera	My prayers rose
Ai santi tabernacoli salì,	In the holy chapels,
Sempre con fè sincera	Ever in pure faith
Diede fiori agli altar.	I brought flowers to the altar.
Nell'ora del dolore perchè,	In this hour of pain, why,
Perchè Signore, perchè	Why, oh Lord, why
Me ne rimuneri così	Dost thou repay me thus?

(Trans. Winston Burdett)

125 *Nächtlicher Fischfang in Antibes* [91.26] Picasso's [...] *Night Fishing in Antibes*: a 1939 work, now in New York's Museum of Modern Art, where it was first seen in the exhibit "Masterworks Acquired through the Mrs. Simon Guggenheim Fund" (29 January-23 March 1952). In a letter Gaddis admitted "I'd probably have seen it just then (1952) & in similar sleepless circumstances" (WG/SM) and allowed the anachronism to stand even though *R*'s chronology suggests Wyatt sees it some five years earlier.

126 aufgehoben in einer einzigen großen Erkenntnis [92.5] all of a sudden everything was freed into one recognition: cf. Berenson's *A&H* (84–85):

In visual art the aesthetic moment is that flitting instant, so brief as to be almost timeless, when the spectator is at one with the work of art he is looking at, or with actuality of any kind that the spectator himself sees in terms of art, as form and colour. He ceases to be his ordinary self, and the picture or building, statue, landscape, or aesthetic actuality is no longer outside himself. The two become one entity; time and space are abolished and the spectator is possessed by one awareness. When he recovers workaday consciousness it is as if he had been initiated into illuminating, exalting, formative mysteries. In short, the aesthetic moment is a moment of mystic vision.

questo è il bacio di Tosca! [92.23]: as she stabs Scarpia at the end of act 2, Tosca hisses: "This is the kiss of Tosca!"

Don Giovanni [92.25]: famous opera by Mozart, libretto by Lorenzo Da Ponte, concerning the last days of the Spanish libertine Don Juan; cf. 941.11.

126 **nicht mehr als siebenmal. Magische Zahl!** [92.26] seven [...] Magic number!: see *R* 265 and notes there; Lethaby records a number of instances of the universal sacredness of the number (*AMM* 122 ff.).

127 **Spinoza** [93.1]: Baruch Spinoza (1632–77), Dutch philosopher (of Portuguese-Jewish parents); excommunicated for transgressing the Law (see 536.31 ff.). Saltus's *AN* contains a digest of his life and teachings (110–19).

Schlittenfahrt [93.4] *Sleigh Ride*: a piece by Leopold Mozart (1719–87), Wolfgang's father.

die Zahl Null existiert nicht [93.14] Zero doesn't exist: Vaihinger (see 120.16, 530.19 ff.) cites the nonexistence of zero as an example of a fictional construct in mathematics (*Philosophy of "As If,"* chap. 12).

schlechtes Geld treibt gutes aus [93.16] bad money drives out good: Gresham's law: see 364.6.

128 *Egmont* [93.22]: overture composed by Beethoven (1810), intended for Goethe's drama of the same name dealing with the Netherlands' struggle for independence.

Der Fliegende Holländer [93.22]: Richard Wagner's (1813–83) first major opera *The Flying Dutchman* (1843) concerns an old Dutch sea captain who, having sworn an impious oath to round the Cape of Good Hope even if it takes an eternity to do so, is allowed to make port only once every seven years until he can find a woman willing to sacrifice everything for his sake. He finds his salvation in the young Norwegian woman Senta. See 551.3 ff. and 895.7–8.

Die Ägyptische Helena [93.23]: a rarely performed opera by German composer Richard Strauss (1864–1949), libretto by Hugo von Hofmannsthal. *The Egyptian Helen,* first performed in Dresden in 1928, is a fanciful drama on the Helen and Menelaus theme.

Han [93.30]: in a section that was cut from the final version, Han was Wyatt's companion in his student days in Munich studying under Herr Koppel. "What we cannot get from the published version," Koenig says (but see 877–78), "is that Han was a totally brutalized and brutal companion of Wyatt in Germany. Han, a homosexual, was to be the first of many characters who would try to use Wyatt. [...] In the deleted section, Wyatt and Han travel from Munich on an excursion to the Jungfrau [a mountain resort] in Switzerland, where Han attempts to make love to Wyatt. Wyatt leaves Han and goes to Paris, where we actually find him in the published version of the novel" ("The Writing of *The Recognitions,*" 29–30).

128 Sibelius s.S.764 [94.1]: Jean Sibelius (1865–1957), Finnish composer, most of whose music attempts to capture the spirit of Finland and its legendary past. He composed seven symphonies; see 574.25–26.

Substanz und Akzidenz vgl.»Akzidentien« S.82 [94.7] substance and accident: see 58.16.

130 Fichte s.S.163 [95.32]: Johann Gottlieb Fichte (1762–1814), German Romantic philosopher; see 120.20ff.

131 Der engste Vertraute einer Heiligen s.S.737 [96.11] Who's the intimate of a saint, it's her Jesuit confessor: see 550.36–38.

für Descartes war Rückzug die einzige Möglichkeit [96.21] Descartes "retiring to prove his own existence," his "cogito ergo sum": René Descartes (1596–1650), eminent French mathematician and philosopher. Source of first quotation unknown; his axiom "I think, therefore I am" (from part 4 of *The Discourse on Method* [1637]) exemplified the importance of intuition in his philosophical method. Cf. this passage with 800.9–11.

132 Der Bogen einer Brücke schläft nie [96.44] Arab saying, "The arch never sleeps": in J. R. Ackerley's *Hindoo Holiday* (see 733.epigraph), Gaddis read:

The Hindoo never builds an arch; he prefers the rectangular form, the straight stone beam resting on uprights; for then there is pressure in only one direction, downwards.
The Mohammedan builds arches, but the Hindoo despises them. There is pressure in two directions, downwards and outwards, and the Hindoo considers this self-destructive.
"The arch never sleeps," he says. (205)

Wyatt interprets the proverb as a favorable remark by the Arab, though it seems obvious it is a disparaging remark by the Hindu.

Maillart s.S.809 [97.6]: see 601.3–5.

133 Händel und Palestrina, William Boyce, Henry Purcell, Vivaldi, Couperin [97.18] Handel and Palestrina, William Boyce, Henry Purcell, Vivaldi, Couperin: all composers: Handel was German, Giovanni Palestrina (ca. 1525–94) and Antonio Vivaldi (ca. 1675–1741) Italian, Boyce (1710–79) and Purcell (1659–95) English, and François Couperin (1668–1733) French.

When I am laid [97.25]: from Dido's famous final aria in Purcell's opera *Dido and Aeneas* (1689), libretto by Nahum Tate:

When I am laid in earth, may my wrongs create
No trouble in thy breast!
Remember me! – But ah! forget my fate!

134 Persephone [98.6]: daughter of Zeus and Demeter, Persephone was abducted by Hades and taken to his "infernal kingdom," where she became queen of the dead. After a long search Demeter finally found her daughter, and a bargain was reached that allowed Persephone to spend half the year (spring-summer) on earth and the other half in the underworld.

[98.29] *the child is father to the man*: the well-known line is from Wordsworth's "My Heart Leaps Up" (1802) and was used in the epigraph to his "Ode: Intimations of Immortality" (1804).

The Secret of the Golden Flower [98.32]: *T'ai I Chin Hua Tsung Chih* is an ancient Taoist meditation text cited in *IP* for Chinese parallels to Western alchemy. In the standard German and English translations it is accompanied by a psychological commentary by Jung.

Problems of Mysticism and Its Symbolism [98.33]: the first major psychological investigation of alchemy, written by German psychologist Herbert Silberer and first published in America in 1917; cited, but given scant credit, in *IP*.

Prometheus and Epimetheus [98.34]: a prose epic (1881) by Swiss poet and novelist Carl Spitteler (pen name of Felix Tandem, 1845–1924), thrice mentioned in *IP* in a comparison of academic rejection of alchemy with the rejection of the jewel in *Prometheus* "for which reason, also, it is unrecognized by all the worldly-wise" (119).

135 *Cantilena Riplæi* [98.34]: Ripley's Song is an alchemical parable of spiritual rebirth by Sir George Ripley (1415–90), canon of Bridlington. Jung paraphrases the poem in *IP* (262–66).

[98.39] *There was a man of double deed*: an anonymous children's "rhyme of strange fascination; many people have recalled the awe-inspiring effect it had on them when children, and yet how they continued to want it repeated to them" (Iona and Peter Opie, eds., *The Oxford Dictionary of Nursery Rhymes* [Oxford: Clarendon Press, 1951], 286). Number 75 in *The Annotated Mother Goose*, where the rhyme begins: "A man of words and not of deeds / Is like a garden full of weeds."

137 chinesisches Neujahrsfest auf Hawaii [100.21] Narcissus Festival: a colorful fête held annually in celebration of the Chinese New Year in January, sometimes extending into February. This nameless tall woman will continue to miss the festival throughout the novel (553.32, 568.20, 887.10).

[100.30] *teeshans red*: that is, Titian red.

Pollyotch [101.2]: Pagliacci (see 105.3).

137 **Ladonnamobile** [101.4] ladonnamobilay: nonsense words corrupted from the popular aria in Verdi's *Rigoletto* ("La donna è mobile, qual piuma al vento").

138 **Otto** [101.10]: to the extent that Otto is a partial self-portrait of the younger Gaddis, "Otto" is a pun on the Latin prefix *auto-* (self), just as Gaddis would use *Eigen* (Ger. oneself) for his persona in *JR*.

The World Is Waiting for the Sunrise [101.23]: 1919 song by Ernest Seitz (music) and Eugene Lockhart (words). "The classic rendering [...] was by Ted Lewis" (WG/SM). The song is also heard in Tennessee Williams's *The Glass Menagerie* (1944), sc. 5.

139 **Was war zuerst da?** [101.43] Who made the first one? [...] First Cause: "We merely pay ourselves with words when we talk about the necessity of a First Cause" (*MMM* 342).

[102.24] *The Origin of Design*: unidentified; the phrase is used earlier at 98.31.

[102.31] Hark the herald angels sing: *PH* #91, words by Charles Wesley, music adapted from Mendelssohn.

[102.37] As it had been, and apparently shall ever be: a laconic version of "As it was in the beginning, is now, and ever shall be; world without end," the concluding words of the Gloria Patri, or lesser doxology.

140 **daß die gestürzten Götter im neuen System als Teufel überleben** [102.37] gods, superseded, become the devils: "It is a well-known fact that when a new religion is established in any country, the god or gods of the old religion becomes the devil of the new" – from the article on witchcraft in *EB* (23:686) by the eminent authority Margaret A. Murray. Cf. 536.2–12.

sich ganz und gar der Magie verschrieben vgl. S. 19 [102.40] magic has not despaired: see 12.2.

[103.1] wearing winter hearts on their sleeves: "But I will wear my heart upon my sleeve / For daws to peck at" (*Othello* 1.1.64–65), that is, to make one's feelings obvious.

Origenes [103.3] Origen: (185?–254?), Christian writer and teacher at Alexandria, one of the Greek fathers of the church, and author of many works (see 420.12). His self-castration is said to have been the result of a too literal reading of Matt. 19:12.

hoc est corpus meum, Dominus vgl. »Hokuspokus« S. 141 [103.5]: "this is my body, Lord" (from the Eucharist). It has been suggested that "hocus pocus" (103.25) is derived from *hoc est corpus*.

Miserere nobis s. S. 855 [103.13]: "Have mercy on us" (from the Agnus Dei of the Mass; see 643.39).

140 *Vae victis* [103.14]: "Woe to the vanquished," a famous quotation from Livy's *History* (*ODQ*).

[103.17] fear of belonging to another, or to others, or to God: from Eliot's "East Coker": "Do not let me hear / Of the wisdom of old men, but rather of their folly, / Their fear of fear and frenzy, their fear of possession, / Of belonging to another, or to others, or to God."

141 Anselm s.S. 481, 856 [103.34]: this major character, whose real name is Arthur (356.19, 642.35), takes his name from Saint Anselm of Canterbury (ca. 1033–1109), Piedmont-born English clergyman and theologian, best known for his ontological argument for the existence of God. See 382.30 ff. and 458.28 ff.

143 Pagliacci [105.3]: Pagliaccio is the jealous husband in Leoncavallo's opera (*I*) *Pagliacci* (The Clowns, 1892).

Eine gesamtgesellschaftlich verankerte, praktische Religionskultur [105.13] extensive leisure [...] religious ritual: this argument can be found in part 5 of Josef Pieper's *Leisure: The Basis of Culture*, introduction by T. S. Eliot (New York: Pantheon, 1952).

Platons Idee vom Staat [105.16] Plato's state [...] the artist: in book 10 of *The Republic* Plato advises the banishment of the artist for the health of the state.

Schopenhauers *Transcendentale Spekulationen* [105.19] Schopenhauer's *Transcendental Speculations on Apparent Design in the Fate of the Individual*: Arthur Schopenhauer (1788–1860) is considered the chief exponent of philosophic pessimism. This title – which Wyatt will later force a traveler to take down at gunpoint (881.15–34, 887.16–20) – is a book version translated by David Irvine (London: Watts, 1913) of an essay in Schopenhauer's *Parerga und Paralipomena* (1851). Briefly, Schopenhauer argues that what appears in retrospect to be an apparent design in the fate of an individual is the result of "the inner guidance, the secret pull, which directs everyone accurately to the only path suitable for him" and "that the systematic connectedness which we believe to have apprehended in the events of our lives is no more than an unconscious effect of our regulative and schematising fantasy" (22, 23).

bis zu den griechischen Skeptikern [105.21] Greek skeptics: not a school of philosophy but rather a tradition of opposition to dogmatic teachings (usually on the grounds of agnosticism or empiricism). One of the chief representatives of this tradition is Pyrrho of Elis (130.7).

Juan Gris [105.27]: (1887–1927), Spanish painter and lithographer, identified with the Cubists.

144 Symposion [...] über Religion s. S. 476 [105.29] symposium on religion: cf. the symposium "Religion and the Intellectuals" in *Partisan Review*, February 1950. Cf. 352–53 below.

das mit den Mumien [105.32] mummies [...] shaped like a man: these details are from Haggard's *DDD* (128–29).

147 Prozeß der Individuation [108.8] process of individuation: a Jungian concept: by "the so-called *process of individuation* [...] I mean the psychological process that makes of a human being an 'individual' – a unique, indivisible unit or 'whole man'" (*IP* 3). Jung considers alchemy to be an allegory of this process.

149 La Guita [109.40]: Spanish slang for money: "dough, bread."

150 Sangre negro en mi corazón [110.11]: Sp.: "Black blood in my heart" (though *negro* should be *negra*).

Esteban [110.35]: the Spanish form of "Stephen," Wyatt's originally intended name and the one he will assume at the end of the novel.

154 alter, unrasierter Mann in einem Boot [113.37] one unshaven man alone in a boat: cf. Hemingway's *Old Man and the Sea* (1952).

156 Wir auf dem Grund eines gewaltigen Himmelsmeers vgl. S. 346 [115.9] great celestial sea: Lethaby records many instances of the belief of the sky as a celestial sea (*AMM* 15–16), a belief shared by Charles Fort (87.8). Cf. 257.1–10.

160 Wyatt [118.12]: this is the last appearance of his name; he will be nameless until he receives the name Stephan from Mr. Yák (Sinisterra) at the bottom of p. 785, which he later Anglicizes to Stephen. Both the difficulties and advantages of allowing Wyatt to go nameless through most of the novel were delineated by Gaddis in a note to himself (quoted in Koenig's "'Splinters from the Yew Tree,'" 99–100):

There are troubles with pronouns, especially "he," in those scenes which, when at all extended, the no-hero – that is Wyatt, becomes lost or confused. To a strong degree this should be so, as, with Valentine (and all the others, but pointedly Basil Valentine) he, the no-hero or not-yet-hero, is what the other person might be: in Valentine's case, the self-who-can-do-more, the creative self if it had not been killed by the other, in Valentine's case, Reason, in Brown's case, material gain; in Otto's case, vanity and ambition; in Stanley's case, the Church; in Anselm's case, religion, &c. &c.

163 heiliger Hieronymus auf dem Bild von El Greco [120.11] Saint Jerome in El Greco's painting: an almost naked Saint Jerome, as a penitent before the opening of a cave, painted between 1597 and 1603, and now in the National Gallery in Washington.

163 **Vainiger** [120.16]: vain Otto consistently mispronounces the surname of Hans Vaihinger (1852–1933), German philosopher. Wyatt has been telling Otto of Vaihinger's *The Philosophy of "As If"* (see 530.19ff.).

Fichte [120.20]: a loose paraphrase of one of the conclusions reached by Fichte (95.32) in his *Die Bestimmung des Menschen* (*The Vocation of Man*, 1800), book 3 ("Faith").

166 **D Form ein Steins kann ma nicht erfind s.S. 619** [123.10] You cannt invnt t shpe of a stone: see 463.28.

167 **Dierick Bouts vgl. S. 387** [123.35]: see 75.6; Wyatt will later forge two Bouts imitations (288.27).

168 **van Eyck [...] Arnolfinis Frau** [124.1] van Eyck [...] Arnolfini's wife: the famous Arnolfini marriage portrait by Jan van Eyck (1494).

Cicero [124.6] Cicero's *Paradoxa* [...] Praxiteles: see 57.20 for Praxiteles, where Rev. Gwyon alludes to the same anecdote (from *GAF* 41):

In *Paradoxa*, a collection of philosophical thoughts called Socratic in style by Cicero [106–43 B.C.], [...] Cicero has the courage to write the following paragraph in defense of Carneades, who maintained that a head of a Faun had been found in the raw marble of a quarry at Chios:

"One calls the thing imaginary, a freak of chance, just as if marble could not contain the forms of all kinds of heads, even those of Praxiteles. It is a fact that these heads are made by taking away the superfluous marble, and in modelling them even a Praxiteles does not add anything of his own, because when much marble has been taken away one reaches the real form, and we see the accomplished work which was there before. This is what may have happened in the quarry of Chios."

Nobili ridicules such an attitude, but Wyatt approves and adds Cicero's questionable aesthetics to his own concept of "recognition."

der Jünger ist nicht über seinem Meister [124.11] The disciple [...] his master [...] Saint Luke: Luke 6:40. Berenson quotes this verse in his discussion of the "originality of incompetence" (*A&H* 170); his views are consonant with (if not the source of) Herr Koppel's opinion of originality quoted by Wyatt earlier (89.23–22).

ihre Disziplin, die Liebe zum Detail [124.24] the force and the flaw [...] recreate the atmosphere: an editorial intern at Harcourt named David Chandler wrote a reader's report on *R* in which he stated: "[In this section,] what I expect to be the ultimate problem of the book exposes itself thoroughly. The problem, which is at once the force and the flaw of the novel, arises from the thoroughness with which Gaddis feels obligated to recreate his atmosphere" (quoted in Koenig's "'Splinters from the Yew Tree,'" 43). Apparently Gaddis liked the phrase and incorporated it into his manuscript. Cf. 460.15–21.

168 Memling vgl. S. 98 [124.26]: see 70.35.

169 Kritik, die Katherine Mansfield mal geschrieben hat vgl. S. 407 [125.2] a lovely passage [...] of Katherine Mansfield's: (1888–1923), New Zealand-born short-story writer; the "lovely passage" (a favorite of Gaddis's, quoted thrice in *R* and once in *JR*) is given at 304.38–40.

Kant [125.16]: Immanuel Kant (1724–1804), German philosopher, a great influence on Fichte, and best known for his *Critique of Pure Reason*. "Quiddity" means essence.

170 Homunkulus s. S. 353 [125.29] homunculus: see 262.17.

Suite Nummer eins in C-Dur [126.3] Suite Number One in C Major of Bach: an orchestra suite for woodwinds, strings, and continuo (of unknown date); a bright, ebullient piece.

173 wie ich daran glauben soll, daß Christus auch für mich gestorben ist vgl. S. 470, 589 [127.35] I am the man for whom Christ died: the source of this sobering thought (repeated at 348.24–25 and 440.25), if not a theological commonplace, is uncertain.

174 Lorenzo di Credi [128.26] a portrait of a lady [...] Lorenzo di Credi: (ca. 1456–1537), Florentine painter, a pupil of Verrocchio. In 1497 he burned many of his paintings on secular subjects, but two paintings entitled *Portrait of a Lady* are extant (one in Florence, one in Forlì).

176 Pyrrho von Elis [130.7] Pyrrho of Elis: (365–275? B.C.), Greek skeptic philosopher; Otto repeats the anecdote (from *LEP* 9) on 466.

177 Leiden [...] ist ein billiger Luxus s. S. 707 [130.38] Suffering [...] more refined state: see 530.14.

Sosimus [131.10] Zosimus: (fl. third century A.D.), Gnostic alchemist, apparently the first to use Hermes (see below). His writings combine laboratory directions with much mystical symbolism. (Zosimus and all the alchemists that follow are named in *IP* and/or Gaddis's two other major sources for alchemy: *EB*'s article "Alchemy" [1:534–37] and Mackay's *EPD* ["The Alchymists," 98–256].)

Albertus Magnus [131.10]: (1193? or 1206?–80), German scholastic philosopher, theologian, and scientist, one of the major figures in medieval alchemy (*IP* 247); canonized in 1931. See also 132.8–12 below.

Geber [131.10]: Jabir ibn-Hayyan (fl. 721–76), Arab alchemist, one of the first to believe base materials could be transmuted into nobler ones, though his books are more noted for their metaphysics than their chemistry (*IP* 206, 217; *EPD* 102–3). As with Albertus Magnus, several works ascribed to Geber are forgeries; the practice of ascribing a work to a past master was as common with the alchemists as it was with early Christian writers.

177 **Bernhardus Trevisanus** [131.10]: Bernard of Trèves (as he is called below) (1406–90) devoted his entire life and fortune to alchemy but only experienced repeated failure.

Basilius Valentinus [131.11]: although alleged to have been a Benedictine monk who lived in Saint Peter's cloister in Erfut in the early fifteenth century, "Basil Valentine" is now known to be a pseudonym, probably of Johann Thölden, who published the works ascribed to Valentine. The most important of the many writings ascribed to him – all of which show a great debt (approaching plagiary at times) to Paracelsus – is *The Triumphal Car* (or *Chariot*) *of Antimony* (see 384.3).

Raymond Lully [131.11]: see 77.21. As with the other alchemists, many of the works ascribed to Lully were the works of disciples. A quotation from his *Codicillus* (via *IP*) stands as the epigraph to I.7 (222).

Khalid ben Yezid [131.11]: (635–704), an Omayyad prince, one of the earliest Arab writers on alchemy, said to have been a pupil of the Syrian monk Morienus; cited by Jung (*IP* 218–19).

Hermes Trismegistos [131.11]: "Thrice-great Hermes," the name given to the alleged author of a large body of alchemical, mystical, and occult writings that were actually written by Greeks in ancient Alexandria. Jung calls Hermes "the Thoth of Hermetic literature," aligning him with the Egyptian god of writing (*IP* 88), identified with the Greek god Hermes.

Bernhardus Trevisanus [131.17] Bernard of Trèves and an unnamed Franciscan are pictured seeking the universal solvent: not a reference to an actual illustration (as I first assumed) but to Mackay's prose sketch of Bernard: "Among all the crowd of pretended men of science who surrounded him, there was but one as enthusiastic and as disinterested as himself. With this man, who was a monk of the order of St. Francis, he contracted an intimate friendship and spent nearly all his time. [...] They afterwards imagined that there was a marvellous virtue in all excrement, especially the human, and actually employed more than two years in experimentalising upon it with mercury, salt, and molten lead!" (*EPD* 132).

178 *Chemā* [131.27]: this myth is related in *EB*'s discussion of the various legends accounting for the origin of alchemy.

Michael Majer [131.43] Michael Majer [...] the image of God: Majer (or Mayer, Maier; 1568–1622) was a German physician, composer, and voluminous writer on alchemy. Paraphrased here is Jung's paraphrase of a passage in Majer's *De Circulo physico quadrato* (1616):

The sun has spun the gold in the earth by many millions of rotations around it. The sun has gradually imprinted in the earth its image, which is the gold. The sun is the image of God, and the heart is the image of the sun in man. Gold is the sun's image in the earth, and is also called *deus terrenus;* God can be recognized in the gold. This image of God appearing in gold is no doubt the *anima aurea,* which, instilled into ordinary quicksilver, changes it into gold. (*IP* 246)

178 **Albertus Magnus** [132.8] Albertus Magnus [...] seven exposures to fire: the skeptical "Albertus Magnus in his *De Mineralibus* – the *De Alchemia* attributed to him is spurious – stated that alchemy cannot change species but merely imitates them – for instance, colours a metal white to make it resemble silver or yellow to give it the appearance of gold. He has, he adds, tested gold made by alchemists, and found that it will not withstand six or seven exposures to fire" (*EB* 1:536).

Werk über Geburtshilfe [132.12] a book on the care of child-bearing mothers [...] alive long enough for baptism: "In the medieval times religion took over the supervision of the prostitutes and the oversight of the practices of the midwives," Dr. Haggard notes. "Thus the Dominican monk, Albertus Magnus (Albert von Bollstädt, 1193–1280), wrote a book for the guidance of midwives, and the Church councils passed edicts on their practices. These instructions were not, however, for the better care of the childbearing woman, for the relief of her suffering or the prevention of her death. They were designed to save the child's life for a sufficient time to allow it to be baptized" (*DDD* 27).

179 **Theophrastus Bombastus von Hohenheim** [132.20] Theophrastus Bombastus von Hohenheim ("better known as Paracelsus"): (1493–1541), German physician and alchemist, whose interest in alchemy was more medical than metaphysical. *DDD* (345–49, 367) is Gaddis's source for the colorful details of Paracelsus' life.

Doktor Ehrlich [132.28] Doctor Ehrlich: Paul Ehrlich (1854–1915), German bacteriologist; discovered "606," a remedy for syphilis. Cf. *DDD* 368.

ignis nostra [133.1]: "'our' fire (*ignis noster*), the philosophical or mercurial fire, and which is thus distinguished from the common one" (*IP* 209).

180 **die heilige Luzia** [133.22] Saint Lucy holds in that Ferrara painting: a portrait by Francesco del Cossa (1435–77), Italian painter of the Ferrarese school. A striking reproduction can be seen in Fern Rusk Shapley's *Paintings from the Samuel H. Kress Collection: Italian Schools XIII-XV Century* (London: Phaidon, 1966), vol. 1, fig. 223.

Wie die aufgedunsene Eule [...] **den heiligen Hieronymus beobachtet** [133.24] the swollen owl [...] watching Saint Jerome: probably Bosch's *Saint Jerome in Prayer* (ca. 1505, Museum of Fine Arts, Ghent).

181 *Adolphe* [133.44]: a novel (1815) by French writer Benjamin Constant (1767–1830). It foreshadows the modern psychological novel in its examination of the relationship between Adolphe, a young man, and Ellénore, a count's mistress (which has its parallel in the relationship between Otto and Esther). "The point here of course is that Otto has not read it & is vainly & sublimely unaware of the parallel" (WG/SM).

183 als ob uns der Hund da nachläuft [135.17] that dog's following us: as earlier critics have noted, a deliberate echo of *Faust* 1147–77, where Mephistopheles appears in the guise of a black poodle. The following scene ("Study") opens with the poodle entering with Faust, as Brown's poodle does with Wyatt.

184 ein Oratorium, *Judas Makkabäus* [136.5] Handel's [...] *Judas Maccabaeus*: first produced in London in 1747, libretto (in English) by Thomas Morrell, concerning the exploits of the second-century B.C. Jewish rebel.

Lo the conqueror comes [136.8]: the high point of the oratorio, this majestic chorus was originally written for a different oratorio.

Die Gleichung x^n plus y^n ist ungleich Null s.S.488 [136.26] The equation [...] greater than 2: see 361.20–23.

[137.25] "The first discovery" [...] foretelling things to come": source unknown.

186 das nächste Glas Brandy [137.39] brandy: included in the necessary accessories to the "Grand Conjuration" (below), according to Waite, is "half a bottle of brandy" (243).

I A O, I A E [137.43]: variants of the Hebrew tetragrammaton (YHWH), used in a variety of magic formulas. See next note.

187 I A O, I A E, im Namen des Vaters [139.1] I A O, I A E, in the name of the father [...] opsakion aklana thalila i a o, i a e: "Matthew vii.22 indicates that it was not long before many outside the pale of the Church used Jesus's name in their exorcisms: [...] In some of the magical papyri lately discovered in Egypt we find the name of Jesus so invoked. I adduce one such incantation from an ancient source, wherein also the demon is addressed in his own tongue: –

Here is a goodly gift of Apsyrtus, a saving remedy, wonderfully effective for cattle. IAO, IAE, in the name of the father and of our Lord Jesus Christ and holy spirit, iriterli estather, nochthai brasax salolam nakarzeo masa areons daron charael aklanathal aketh thruth tou malath poumedoin chthon litiotan mazabates maner opsakion aklana thalila iao, iae.... And write the same with a brass pencil on a clean, smooth plate of tin." (*MMM* 239)

Demonolatria des Remigius [139.10] Remigius' *Demonolatria*: a 1595 study by Nicholas Remy (Lat. Remigius, 1530–1612), a French magistrate. Similar in many respects to *MM* (and likewise translated into English by Montague Summers), it is even more lurid and credulous.

187 *Libro dell' Arte* s. S. 114 [139.11]: see 83.22.

Herrscher [...] durch die Kraft des großen ADONAI [139.15] Emperor [...] by the power of the grand ADONAY [...] P. M. S.: a conjuration of Emperor Lucifer (or "thy Messenger Astarôt") from the *Grand Grimoire,* as recorded in Arthur Edward Waite's *The Book of Ceremonial Magic* (London: Rider, 1911), 248–49. (The initials, it will be noticed, are those of the individual names.) Part 2 of Waite's study, in which this invocation appears, is entitled "The Complete Grimoire," based on the *Grimorium Verum* (see 83.24), the *Key of Solomon* (Goethe's source for Faust's conjuration [ll. 1271 ff.]), and similar works. This particular spell is entitled "Grand Conjuration: Extracted from the Veritable Clavicle," supposedly one of the most potent invocations.

188 du Ausgeburt der Hölle [140.2] Damned ... animal out of hell: Wyatt's asides to the dog during the preceding pages parallel those of Faust to the poodle Mephistopheles (ll. 1178 ff.).

189 Recktall Brown [140.28]: the name puns raunchily on the Freudian connection between money and anality; collectors are usually classified as anal-retentives.

195 der heilige Paulus [...] Zeit auskaufen [144.28] Saint Paul tells us to redeem time: see Eph. 5:15–16 ("See then that ye walk circumspectly, not as fools, but as wise, redeeming the time, because the days are evil") and/or Col. 4:5 ("Walk in wisdom toward them that are without, redeeming the time"). Both letters were traditionally ascribed to Paul, but their authenticity is now in doubt. Eliot too tells us to redeem the time in part 4 of "Ash Wednesday."

196 Der Meister der Maria Magdalena [145.14] Master of the Magdalene Legend: a "second-rate" painter of the late fifteenth century, so named for "a couple of panels with scenes from the legend of Mary Magdalen, which were exhibited at Bruges" (*VEF* 268–69).

198 Gehen sie gar an die Verschönerung einer Wand [146.29] "Most people make a practice [...] *Libro dell' Arte*: see 83.22; the quotation is adapted from chap. 96 of Daniel Thompson's translation *The Craftsman's Handbook: The Italian "Il Libro dell' Arte"* (1933), 60–61.

199 *Dog Days* [147.31]: fictitious.

200 Eitelkeit der Zeit s. S. 59 [148.26] vanity of time: from Rev. Gwyon's sermon: see 41.16.

200 *prima materia* [149.2]: the unresolved, unredeemed, chaotic state – of man or mineral – at which the alchemical process begins; Jung associates the term with elements from the unconscious striving to be integrated into consciousness.

Im Steine schläft mir ein Bild [149.4] "For me an image slumbers in the stone," said Zarathustra: from Nietzsche's *Thus Spoke Zarathustra*, quoted by Jung as an alchemical metaphor (*IP* 228).

205 animalische Ekstasen [152.10] animal ecstasies: cf. "the ecstasy of the animals" in Eliot's "Marina."

Bild Johannes' des Täufers [152.13] Saint John Baptist [...] leaping for joy in his mother's womb: Luke 1:41.

in einem Kleid von Kamelhaaren [152.16] he stands steady in a camel's hair loincloth [...] upbraiding the flesh: see the third chapter of Matthew.

Mein Gott, mein Gott, warum hast du mich verlassen? [152.23] My God, why dost thou shame me: cf. Matt. 27:46, Mark 15:34 (quoting Ps. 22:1); "forsaken" in most translations.

von einem epileptischen Zeltmacher [152.24] an epileptic tent-maker: Saint Paul (see Acts 18:1–3).

Konzert Nummer sieben [152.36] Mozart's, the Concerto Number Seven in F Major: a 1776 composition (K.242; now called #3), generally considered the least interesting of his early piano concerti.

206 wie ein Dolchstoß ins Herz dringt s. S. 135 [153.7] penknife in the heart: the penknife recalls "The Man of Double Deed" (99.13) and foreshadows Wyatt's use of Brown's penknife on Valentine at the end of II.8.

I.4

207 Les femmes soignent [...] Rimbaud [154.epigraph]: Arthur Rimbaud (1854–91), precocious French symbolist poet. The quotation is from his major work, *A Season in Hell* (1873), a prose-poetic vigil through the dark night of the soul: "I'll return with limbs of iron, dark skin and furious eye; people will think to look at me that I am of a strong race. I will have gold: I will be idle and brutal. *Women nurse those fierce invalids, home from the hot countries.* I'll be mixed up in politics. Saved" (from part 2: "Bad Blood" [epigraph italicized], trans. Louise Varèse).

208 italienische Renaissance s. S. 225 [155.7] an Italian Renaissance: later identified as *Lady of the Junipers* (168.10).

209 Die größte Herausforderung des Ideals [156.7] The most difficult challenge [...] ceases to be an ideal: a condensation of *LWW*, book 6: "The Myth v. Marriage."

209 **siehe Petrarca und seine Laura** [156.16] a bit of verse [...] concerning Petrarch and his Laura: probably this couplet from Byron's *Don Juan* (quoted in ODQ):
Think you, if Laura had been Petrarch's wife,
He would have written sonnets all his life?
Lord Byron's name, George Gordon, probably provided that of Otto's Byronic protagonist.

Virginie [...] Paul [156.17] Virginia [...] Paul: from *Paul et Virginie* (1787), the famous idyllic romance by the French writer Jacques Henri Bernardin de Saint-Pierre (1737–1814).

214 *sursum corda* s. S. 448 [160.8]: Lat.: "lift up your hearts" (from the Mass); used similarly at 332.6.

215 **Enescos Rumänische Rhapsodie** [160.27] Enesco's Third Rumanian Rhapsody played on a harmonica: Georges Enesco (1881–1955), Rumanian composer; he wrote only two Rumanian rhapsodies, so either his Third Symphony is meant or (more likely if played on a harmonica) the reference is facetious.

Paulus wollte, daß wir die Zeit auskaufen [160.30] Saint Paul would have us redeem time: see 144.38.

wenn Gegenwart und Vergangenheit gleichermaßen gegenwärtig sind in der Zukunft [160.30] present and past are both present in time future [...] no redemption but one: from the opening of Eliot's "Burnt Norton," the first of *Four Quartets*: "Time present and time past / Are both perhaps present in time future / And time future contained in time past. / If all time is eternally present / All time is unredeemable."

zwei Jahre sind eigentlich gar keine Zeit [160.37] Two years isn't long, not if you say it real fast: a remark Gaddis heard while in Central America in 1947–48 and quoted in his brief memoir "In the Zone" (*New York Times*, 13 March 1978, 21; rpt. in the first edition of this *Reader's Guide*, 301–4). Several details in this chapter and III.1 were reused in the memoir.

217 **Quién limpian mi cuarto mañana** [162.6]: "Who cleaned my room this morning" is what Otto means to ask, though his Spanish here and throughout the chapter is usually incorrect (for example, *limpian* should be *limpió*).

Hay visto una manuscripta aquí? [162.12]: "Did you see a manuscript here?" (should be "¿Han visto un manuscrito aquí?")

Qué dijo? [162.16]: "What did he say?"

playa [162.17]: "beach"; the word Otto wants is *pieza* or *drama*.

El está para la máquina [...] Esta mañana [162.24]: "It was by the typewriter [...]. This morning" (should be "Estaba junto ...").

217 Qué cosa? [162.29]: "What thing?"

Papel [...] al máquina [162.30]: "Paper. [...] Paper on which I wrote my beach on the typewriter."

218 No entiendo [162.41]: "I don't understand."

Tiemplo [162.43]: that is, *tiempo*.

Pero sí [163.7]: "But of course."

Lo pusé aquí [...] o se ensuciara [163.13]: "I set it [should be *puse*] here when I was packing, everything was so unraveled that I was afraid that it would get lost, or get dirty."

222 La limpia [165.39]: "Clean them?"

Una limosnita, por el amor de Dios [166.11]: "A small almsgiving, for the love of God." (If Gaddis didn't hear this himself in Central America or Spain, he would have read it in Borrow's *BS* [72].)

Dios se lo pague [166.17]: "May God repay you."

225 *Madonna der Wacholderbeeren* [168.10] *Lady of the Junipers*: unidentified.

Mädchen [...] das in Liebe entbrannt war für seinen Bruder [168.25] girl who loved her brother the sun: source unknown.

I.5

226 Amerika ist das Land junger Männer. – Emerson [169.epigraph] America is the country of young men. – Emerson: from the essay "Old Age" in *Society and Solitude* (1870). The first edition of *R* has "a country," which is how the line is misquoted in *ODQ*.

When Buddha Smiles [169.20]: 1921 song by Arthur Freed (words) and Nacio Herb Brown and King Zany (Jack Dill) (music); a best-selling record for the Paul Whiteman Orchestra.

227 die Akademische Festouvertüre von Tschaikowsky s.S.232 [170.18] Academic Festival Overture by Tschaikovsky: see 174.6.

229 einen brachycephalischen Kopf [171.26] brachycephalic: referring to a short or broad head.

232 die Akademische Festouvertüre von Brahms [174.6] Academic Festival by Brahms: opus 80 (1880) by German composer Johannes Brahms (1833–97), a short, popular piece.

Allah-preß midi Dunn-Fön [174.8] Clair [...] Claude, Debussy [...] dunfon: two of French composer Claude Debussy's (1862–1918) more famous compositions are "Clair de lune" and "Prélude à l'après-midi d'un faune."

234 **L'Ame d'un Chantier** [175.20] *L'Ame d'un Chantier* [...] The soul of a singer: incorrect, as is "the Worker's Soul" (185.33). *Chantier* means workplace; "singer" would be *chanteur*; "worker" would be *travailleur*.

Uccello [175.42]: Paolo Uccello (1397–1475), Florentine painter. His famous *Battle of San Romano* illustrates his use of solids.

[176.29] *The Joy of Cooking*: the ever-popular cookbook by Irma Rombauer and Marion Rombauer Becker, first published in 1931 – probably the only cookbook to begin with an epigraph from Goethe's *Faust*.

236 **Agnes Deigh** [176.43]: *Agnus Dei* ("Lamb of God") is Christ's sacrificial title in the Mass (see 643.39).

»Laß es drucken, und dann fahr zur Hölle.« [177.6] "Publish and be damned," the Duke of Wellington said: his attributed response to Harriette Wilson, a courtesan who threatened to publish her memoirs and a number of Wellington's compromising letters to her (*ODQ*).

»Die Kunst läuft dem Geld nach.« [177.8] "Trade ye no mere moneyed art": a well-known palindrome (a phrase that reads the same backward as forward) and, as Eric Mottram points out in his short sentry on Gaddis in *The Penguin Companion to World Literature* ("American Literature" 103), a major theme of *R* itself.*

Shelley [...] **Laudanum** [177.11] Shelley did drink laudanum: a liquid form of opium, ostensibly for medicinal purposes; its misuse was a fairly common "vice" in nineteenth-century England.

Swinburne [177.12]: Algernon Charles Swinburne (1837–1909), English poet and man of letters, notorious for his dissipated life-style.

die Ähnlichkeit mit der schönen Toten aus der Seine [177.14] *la noyée de la Seine*: Fr.: "the drowned girl of the Seine" – also known as "La Belle inconnue de la Seine" – a deathmask, perhaps fraudulent, popular in the late nineteenth century.

237 **Guy de Maupassant** [...] **Marie Baschkirzew** [177.23] Guy de Maupassant [...] Marie Bashkirtseff: young Marie Bashkirtseff, the animated and talented daughter of Russian aristocracy, was living in Paris in 1884 as an artist when she impulsively decided to write to French author Guy de Maupassant (1850–93), then at the height of his fame. They exchanged a dozen or so letters over a month's time; hers were ebullient and volatile, his intrigued but cautious: "I kept saying to myself all the time: Is it a masked woman who is amusing herself, or a simple joker?" – therefore: "I mask myself

---

* German edition: from G. E. Lessing's *Emilia Galotti*.

among masked people. It is straight fighting" (letter dated 22 April 1884, in *I Kiss Your Hands: The Letters of Guy de Maupassant and Marie Bashkirtseff* [London: Rodale, 1954], 40). In his final letter Maupassant suggests they meet; she apparently never replied, they never met, and by October of that year she was dead.

237 Thomas Becket s. S. 1182 [177.30] Thomas à Becket: see 911.19.

Thomas von Kempen [177.31] à Kempis [...] *Imitation of Christ*: this famous fifteenth-century religious treatise on contemplation is commonly ascribed to Thomas à Kempis (1380–1471), though other candidates for the authorship of the influential mystical work have been suggested.

die besten Sachen von Händel sind auch geklaut [177.33] Handel plagiarized [...] finally stricken blind: the *EB* article on Handel has a subsection devoted to this subject (11:146–47), where it is also noted that Handel did indeed finally go blind.

Wie der Neger von der Narcissus [177.43] the Negro of the Narcissus: from Joseph Conrad's 1897 novella *The Nigger of the "Narcissus."*

jenseits der Vierzehnten Straße [178.1] Fourteenth Street: the northern limit of Greenwich Village.

238 Mister Six-sixty-six s. S. 666 [178.10]: see 499.17.

[178.32] Modernism heresy: Catholic Modernism was an attempt by certain progressives to bring their church out of the dark ages and more in line with modern scientific and humanistic trends of thought. Pope Pius X declared it a heresy in 1907.

240 *Die Bäume der Heimat* [179.30] *The Trees of Home*: fictitious.

241 Proust [...] Odette [180.28]: in French novelist Marcel Proust's monumental *A la recherche du temps perdu* (1912–22), Odette de Crécy is the paramour of Charles Swann, later the wife of de Forcheville, and finally the mistress of the duc de Guermantes. Critics have debated whether Proust did indeed do as Herschel suggests, not so much with Odette as with Albertine later in the novel. Gaddis comments: "I recall hearing Ch[ristopher]. Isherwood did the same in 'Prater Violet'" (WG/SM; Gaddis also told me he had not read *A la recherche* beyond its "overture").

243 Léger [182.5]: Fernand Léger (1881–1955), French painter whose work displays a great faith in modern technology.

Chagall [182.5]: Marc Chagall (1887–1985), Russian-born French painter, noted for his melancholic treatment of Russian and Jewish themes.

Soutine [182.7]: Chaim Soutine (1894–1943), Lithuanian painter, like Chagall a Jewish émigré artist in Paris.

244 »Ils vont prendre le train [...] de huit heures« [182.29]: "They will take the eight o'clock train": line 11 of T. S. Eliot's French poem "Lune de Miel," concerning an American couple honeymooning in Europe.

Stanley [182.30]: "I don't believe his name had any specific source or reason" – WG/SM.

245 Praxiteles jedenfalls hat einmal s.S.168 [182.44] Praxiteles [...] as Cicero says of Prax ...: see 124.6.

246 Psychoanalusche s.S.605 [183.37] psychoanaloser: discounting Joyce's influence, WG wrote Grace Eckley, "No I did not read FINNEGANS WAKE though I think a phrase about 'psychoanaloosing' one's self from it is in THE RECOGNITIONS" (letter dated 3 June 1975). In *Finnegans Wake,* Yawn tells his questioners, "I can psoakoonaloose myself any time I want" (New York: Viking, 1939, 522). Anselm repeats the Joyce pun at 453.31.

Justine [183.40]: extravagant pornophilosophical novel (1791; rev. 1797) by the Marquise de Sade (1740–1814) concerning a young woman who stubbornly clings to virtue as an ideal despite its impracticality in the real world. The incident described by Anselm below is one of many degradations Justine endures as the prisoner of a group of depraved monks: see *The Complete Justine,* trans. Richard Seaver and Austryn Wainhouse (New York: Grove, 1965), 613.

Malthus' Forderungen [184.6] Malthus: in his *Essay on the Principles of Population* (1798), Thomas Robert Malthus (1766–1834) argued that crime, disease, war, and vice were necessary checks on population growth. In the second edition (1803), responding to criticism, he added that moral restraint may be a fifth check, but he remained pessimistic about human progress.

Roland [184.16]: after leaving the monastery and suffering sundry misadventures, Justine rescues a nobleman named Roland, who had been attacked on the road. In feigned gratitude he offers her a servant's position at his castle, but once there he enslaves her and forces on her a variety of "odious eccentricities" (*The Complete Justine,* 667–91; the crucifix Anselm describes is on p. 673). Roland, appropriately enough for *R,* is a counterfeiter as well.

247 Phyrne [185.1]: see 73.19. She is said to have been the model for Praxiteles' Cnidian Venus: illustrated in *EB* (vol. 10, opposite p. 811).

248 Mit schwerem Herzen, leichten Händen, hallt Orgelgebraus [185.23] "Seated one day at the organ," [...] "weary and ill at ease": the opening lines of the once-popular poem "The Lost Chord" (1858) by Adelaide Anne Procter (1825–64); quoted in *ODQ*.

248 Constable [185.32]: John Constable (1776–1837), one of the two (with Turner) greatest English landscape painters of the nineteenth century. See 623.8 ff for Max's use of Constable.

249 Modigliani [186.1]: Amedeo Modigliani (1884–1920), regarded by many as the most important Italian painter of the twentieth century. He worked exclusively with the human figure and was successful in sculpture as well.

Gabrieli s. S. 435 [186.19]: see 322.11.

250 Henry James [186.33] Henry James [...] *a few grave, rigid laws"*: expressing his enthusiasm for dramatic form, James wrote in a review of Tennyson's *Queen Mary*:

The five-act drama ... is like a box of fixed dimensions and inelastic material, into which a mass of precious things are to be packed away.... . The precious things in question seem out of all proportion to the compass of the receptacle; but the artist has an assurance that with patience and skill a place may be made for each, and that nothing need be clipped or crumpled, squeezed or damaged.... To work beneath a few grave, rigid laws is always a strong man's highest ideal of success.

The ellipses are those of Morris Roberts, who quotes the passage in his introduction to *The Art of Fiction and Other Essays* by Henry James (New York: Oxford University Press, 1948), xvi-xvii. (Since James's original review "is not readily accessible," Gaddis probably used this source.) The complete text of "Tennyson's Drama" can be found in James's *Views and Reviews*, ed. Le Roy Phillips (Boston: Ball, 1908).

Schall und Wahn [187.6] *The Sound and the Fury* [...] *Faulkner's novel*: 1929 work noted for its experimental narrative techniques (derived from Joyce's *Ulysses*). Gaddis told me this is the only Faulkner novel he had ever read.

251 Cézanne [187.22]: Paul Cézanne (1839–1906), French painter, considered by some (like Clive Bell) to be the greatest painter of the nineteenth century and the father of modern art.

Limerick über Tizian s. S. 1129 [187.40] a limerick about Titian: Tiziano Vecellio, called Titian (1488?–1576), one of the greatest Venetian painters of his time. "We all study with Titian," Wyatt will say later (872.18). The limerick runs:

While Titian was mixing rose-madder
His model posed nude on a ladder.
Her position, to Titian,
Suggested coition,
So he climbed up the ladder and had 'er.

252 *»I sold my heart to the junkman«* [188.20]: title of a 1935 song by Otis and Leon René; a 1947 hit for the Basin Street Boys. "Junkman" is slang for a heroin dealer.

252 Djuna Barnes s.S.1221 [188.28]: American novelist and short-story writer (1892–1982); see 941.6.

253 Frau nach der man sich sehnt [189.3]: "The title of a novel by Max Brod, *Die Frau nach der man sich sehnt* – the woman of our desire, of our nostalgia – supplies the best definition of Iseult" (*LWW* 268 n.1). Max Brod (1884–1968) is best known for his edition of his friend Kafka's works.

das Ewigweibliche, die neue Helena s.S.637 [189.7] Ewig-Weibliche, the Eternal Helen: the Eternal Feminine, whom Faust associates with Helen of Troy; see 477.30ff.

255 Rund- und Eierköpfe [190.17] round-heads: the English Puritans under Charles I's reign were so named because of their cropped hair (cf. *EPD* 351), but Rodger Cunningham suggests "the main reference here is to the old 'eugenic' view of the inferiority of brachycephalic non-Nordics." Cf. 171.26.

256 *I am going down to Dutch Siam's* [...] *yes I am* [191.10]: song unidentified; Dutch Siam turns out to be the tattoo artist Herschel visits (see 328–40–43).

257 aus Thomas von Brabants *Über die Bienen* [191.33] Thomas of Brabant's *On Bees*: the thirteenth-century *Liber de apibus* records the earliest activities of the Order of Preachers. It is frequently cited in *MM* on incubi, succubi, and the transportation of witches.

Robert Browning [191.34] Robert Browning [...] *at the clavichord?*: from "A Toccata of Galuppi's," stanza six.

der rechte Arm von Ignatius von Loyola s.S.706 [192.8] the right arm of Saint Ignatius of Loyola: see 66.20 for Ignatius, and 529.36 for his left arm.

258 Geburt, Kommutation, Tod, das ist alles [193.9] "birth and copulation and death": from Eliot's "Fragment of an Agon," part of the unfinished *Sweeney Agonistes*. "Birth, and copulation, and death," Sweeney tells Doris. "That's all the facts when you come to brass tacks: / Birth, and copulation, and death."

259 »Das Spiel ist aus!« [193.12] *"Dust and ashes!"* [...] *their bosoms?*: also from Browning's "A Toccata of Galuppi's," fifteenth and final stanza. Gaddis omits the last half of the last line: "I feel chilly and grown old," which finally appears at 797.36.

Nur leider war in all den Jahren [193.18] *He never saw* [...] *meet death with*: from Browning's poem "A Likeness," ll. 63–66.

260 Esme [194.14]: critics have suggested sources for this name (e.g., Salinger's Esmé and Eliot's second wife Esme Valerie Eliot), but Gaddis said "her name had no referent" (WG/SM). Esme was based to a large extent upon a painter, poet, and model named Sheri Martinelli (1918–96); see "Sheri Martinelli: A Modernist Muse," *Gargoyle* 41 (1998): 28–54.

260 *Die kontrazeptive Gesellschaft* [194.33] *Our Contraceptive Society*: fictitious.

261 Orgon-Akkumulatoren [194.37] orgone boxes: Austrian psychologist Wilhelm Reich (1897–1957) coined the term *orgone* to refer not only to unreleased sexual energy in the individual but to energy propelling the cosmos as well. One could supposedly tap this cosmic energy – and unblock individual energy – by sitting in "orgone accumulators" or "orgone boxes," which allegedly could cure cancer and stimulate flagging sexuality as well. The United States Food and Drug Administration declared the orgone box a fraud.

Buster Brown [194.38]: the obnoxious little boy in R. F. Outcault's comic strip (1902–9).

262 »freien«, das deutsche Wort für *to marry* [195.25] German word for marry, *freien*, was to free: a translation noted by de Rougemont in his analysis of Hitler's popularity with the masses, which was based largely on Hitler's implicit promise to rid the German people "of any oppressive sense of moral guilt" (*LWW* 253).

Du hast keine Arme, du hast keine Beine [195.31] *Ye haven't an arm* [...] *a bowl to beg*: the fifth stanza of the anonymous Irish ballad "Johnny, I Hardly Knew Ye" about a soldier who returns mutilated from the war.

263 ein neues Bühnenbild für *den Ring* [196.16] *The Ring* [...] Wagner: Richard Wagner's operatic tetralogy *The Ring of the Nibelung* (*Das Rheingold, Die Walküre, Siegfried, Götterdämmerung*), alluded to both in *R* (552.3, 907–8) and more extensively in *JR*.

ausgewachsene Zwangsneurose [196.33] obsessive neurosis: Freud defines religion as "the obsessional neurosis of humanity" in his *Future of an Illusion* (chap. 8).

264 der heilige Hieronymus [196.42] Saint Jerome [...] need not wash again: Eusebius Hieronymus Sophronius (342?–420), one of the most important figures in early Christianity. "Cleanliness of the body was regarded as a pollution of the soul" by early Christians, Haggard notes. "The attitude was expressed by Jerome in the words 'Does your skin roughen without bath? Who is once washed in the blood of Christ need not wash again'" (*DDD* 271).

Die heilige Teresa [...] auf allen vieren [197.29] Saint Teresa went around on all fours [...] I would create it for thy sake alone": Marsh records several anecdotes concerning Saint Teresa from the *Flos Sanctorum* (a popular collection of saints' legends), concluding: "on another occasion, Christ said to her, 'If I had not already created heaven, I would create it for thy sake alone;'

[...] notwithstanding these exalted favors, this saint was so humble that she habitually performed menial services in the convent, sometimes running about on all fours and carrying a pannier of stones on her back, *ritu quadrupedis* [in the manner of a four-legged animal], and with a halter around her neck" (*MMSM* 75 n.).

265 »unterliegen«, das deutsche Wort für *surrender* [198.1] German word for surrender, *niederlage,* is to lie under: commenting on the close connection between love and war – specifically, how chivalry adapted military terminology – de Rougemont says in a footnote: "The German word for 'defeat' is *Niederlage,* which literally means 'in the position of being on the ground, of lying under'" (*LWW* 225 n.1).

267 Sukkubus [199.44] Succubus: a discussion of succubi and incubi occupies part 1, questions 3 and 4 of *MM* (21–31).

268 nicht dein eigenes Vergnügen [...] zu verderben [200.4] Not for your own delectation [...] a mortal man: "But the reason that devils turn themselves into Incubi or Succubi is not for the cause of pleasure, since a spirit has not flesh and blood; but chiefly it is with this intention, that through the vice of luxury they may work a twofold harm against men, that is, in body and in soul, that so men may be more given to all vices" (*MM* 25).

lies nach beim heiligen Augustinus [200.10] Saint Augustine. *On the Trinity*: on the question "Whether children can be generated by Incubi and Succubi," the authors of *MM* cite Saint Augustine's *On the Trinity* "that devils do indeed collect human semen, by means of which they are able to produce bodily effects" (22).

Die Teufel sind gefallene Engel [200.14] If devils fell from every rank [...] these filthy delights: "Finally, since some are believed to have fallen from every order, it is not unsuitable to maintain that those devils who fell from the lowest choir, and even in that held the lowest rank, are deputed to and perform these and other abominations" (*MM* 29).

Helias [200.16]: as an example "Of those against whom the Power of Witches availeth not at all," *MM* records the following anecdote (93–94):

Again, in the *Lives of the Fathers* collected by that very holy man S. Heraclides, in the book which he calls *Paradise,* he tells of a certain holy Father, a monk named Helias. This man was moved by pity to collect thirty women in a monastery, and began to rule over them. But after two years, when he was thirty years old, he fled from the temptation of the flesh into a hermitage, and fasting there for two days, prayed to God, saying: "O Lord God, either slay me, or deliver me from this temptation." And in the evening a dream came to him, and he saw three Angels approach him; and they asked him why he had fled from that monastery of virgins. But when he did not dare to answer, for shame, the Angels said: If you are set free from temptation, will you return to your cure of those women? And he answered that he would willingly. They then exacted an oath to that effect from him, and made him an eunuch. For one seemed to hold his hands, another his feet, and the third to cut out his testicles with a knife; though this was not really so, but only seemed to be. And when they asked if he felt himself remedied, he answered that he was entirely delivered. So, on the fifth day, he returned to the sorrowing women, and ruled over them for the forty years that he continued to live, and never again felt a spark of that first temptation.

268 der heilige Viktor [200.18] Saint Victor: Saltus notes that through Satan's artifices "St. Victor was seduced by a beautiful girl" (*AN* 89), but does not identify this saint further.

ich exorziere dich, unreiner Geist [200.22] I exorcise thee [...] envy: from the Catholic rite of exorcism (here with the beer as holy water), as recorded in the Roman Ritual: "I exorcise thee, unclean spirit, in the name of Jesus Christ; tremble, O Satan, thou enemy of the faith, thou foe of mankind, who hast brought death into the world, who hast deprived men of life, and hast rebelled against justice, thou seducer of mankind, thou root of evil, thou source of avarice, discord and envy" (*EB* 8:972–73).

269 Eure Tochter und der Mohr [...] das Tier mit zwei Rücken [200.36] I am one [...] beast with two backs: "I am one, sir, that comes to tell you your daughter and the Moor are now making the beast with two backs" (*Othello* 1.1.116–18) – that is, copulating.

allein zur höheren Ehre Gottes [...] den Schöpfungsplan des Allmächtigen zu durchkreuzen [201.1] God for His own glory permits devils to work against His will: so believe the authors of *MM* (23).

Orchideen [201.20] orchids [...] how they got their name: as late as the nineteenth century there were those who "advocated the doctrine that all diseases should be treated with drugs producing like effects. [...] Thus the root of the orchid, because it is shaped like a testicle (in Latin the word *orchid* means testicle), should be used in curing diseases of that organ" (*DDD* 352). Significantly, Anselm crushes an orchid underfoot (635.35) shortly before castrating himself.

Gegenwart Satans im Menschen [201.21] devil's residence in man: *MM* often points out "that the power of the devil lies in the privy parts of men" (26).

[201.23] she drew him down: an allusion to the concluding lines of Dryden's "Alexander's Feast": "He rais'd a mortal to the skies; / She drew an angel down" (*ODQ*; WG/SM).

I.6

270 »Vater«, fragte er [...] *Die Brüder Karamasow* [202.epigraph] "Father," he asked [...] *Brothers Karamazov*. from part 4, chap. 7 (Constance Garnett translation). Captain Snegiryov is relating an anecdote to Alyosha Karamazov concerning his son Ilusha, who is tormented by his fellow students.

»Warum besitzt der Mensch nicht tausend Augen?« [202.1] "Why has not [...] a fly": from Pope's *Essay on Man*, 1:193–94.

[202.11] distracted from distraction by distraction: from Eliot's "Burnt Norton," part 3.

Diptera [202.15]: the order of insects to which the fly belongs.

271 O Gott, was hab ich *getan*? [202.22] O God, what have I *done*? [...] Rhadames: this and the following references are to Verdi's opera *Aïda* (1871). Rhadames, an Egyptian captain, has unwittingly betrayed the Egyptian army while planning to flee with the Ethiopian slave girl Aïda.

Baal-zebub [...] Beelzeboul [203.13]: this etymological sequence is correct, though source unknown.

272 Sankt Wulfstan [203.30] Saint Wulstan [...] to Hell: in his discussion of the medieval clergy's opposition to long hair and beards, Mackay includes this anecdote:

William of Malmesbury relates, that the famous St. Wulstan [ca. 1009–95], Bishop of Worcester, was peculiarly indignant whenever he saw a man with long hair. He declaimed against the practice as one highly immoral, criminal, and beastly. He continually carried a small knife in his pocket, and whenever any body offending in this respect knelt before him to receive his blessing, he would whip it out slily, and cut off a handful, and then, throwing it in his face, tell him to cut off all the rest, or he would go to hell. (*EPD* 347)

274 Ohrfeo-ätt-Eurodieze [205.10] Gluck's Orfeoadoiradeechay: Christoph Gluck's (1714–87) opera *Orfeo ed Euridice* (1762), treating the famous Orpheus myth.

278 Chaby [208.30]: although the name suggests "shabby," Gaddis said "No referent" (WG/SM).

279 Aubusson [209.4]: French carpets of supreme quality.

280 Im Traume küss' ich Ihre Hand, Madame [209.24] *In Dreams I Kiss Your Hand Madam*: also the title of a song popular first in Germany, then in America in the early part of the century.

Bagandafrau [...] Blüte der Plantainbanane [209.36] Baganda woman [...] plantain trees: from *GB* 137 ("rearing" is simply "genital" in Frazer).

281 *Bett Nummer 29* [210.8] Maupassant story [...] *Bed Number 29*: the story of a vain soldier named Captain Epivent, a dandy and ladies' man who, after having an affair with a woman named Irma, returns from the Franco-Prussian War to find her in bed number 29 of the local hospital with syphilis, contracted from the invading Prussians. Once infected, she had deliberately infected many of the invading soldiers, and when Epivent rebukes her for consorting with the enemy, she boasts that she has killed more Prussians in her way than he in his. He leaves confused and humiliated; she dies the next day. Needless to say, this is hardly the kind of story to be included in "An Anthology of Romantic Stories."

284 *Kronos* [212.38] Cronus: after emasculating his father Uranus and setting himself up as lord of the earth, Cronus (Roman Saturn), having been warned his son would kill him, devoured his children until his wife Rhea substituted a stone for Zeus, who grew up to kill his father and become lord of the universe.

[213.12] particles swirling round him [...] eructations of slate-colored lungs: this passage and a later one also using "eructation" (664.6) echo Eliot's "Burnt Norton":

Men and bits of paper, whirled by the cold wind
That blows before and after time,
Wind in and out of unwholesome lungs
Time before and time after.
Eructations of unhealthy souls
Into the faded air, the torpid
Driven on the wind that sweeps the gloomy hills of London

291 *Effluvium* s. S. 470 u. 473 [218.1]: "a faintly noxious emanation" (356.32); for the text of the poem, see 349–51.

292 »Baby and I [...] out of the pot« [219.2]: first collected in Halliwell's *Nursery Rhymes* (1842); #319 in *The Annotated Mother Goose*.

294 dieser bleiche dünne Mann im Park s. S. 47 [220.26] pale thin man: see 32.20.

296 *Palinurus* [221.40] Palinurus [...] murdered by natives ashore: from the end of book 5 of Vergil's *Aeneid*.

I.7

297 Und ganz wie Jesus aus dem Hause David [...] *Codicillus* [222.epigraph] And as Jesus Christ [...] *Codicillus*: for Lully, see 77.21 and 131.11; this passage is quoted by Jung (*IP* 253) as the earliest example in alchemy of the identification of Christ with the philosopher's stone. The quotation itself is from chapter 9 of Lully's book.

299 Littel girl [...] my bachelor room [223.42]: "Was a calypso sort of song I heard

down there & back then, no idea of title &c, went something like Little girl, please leave my bachelor room &c as is" – WG/SM.

302 Basil Valentine s.S.177 [226.1]: named after the alchemist (see 131.11 and 383.41 ff.).

303 *Avaritia* und *Invidia* [227.5] *Avaritia* and *Invidia*: Avarice and Envy, from Bosch's *Seven Deadly Sins*.

304 *Collectors Quarterly* [227.22]: cf. *Print Collectors Quarterly*, an art journal of the time.

305 Patinir [228.6]: Joachim de Patinir (?–1524), early Netherlandish landscape painter; most of his landscapes have a religious setting. See chapter 24 of *VEF*.

[228.20] other voices in other rooms: see 56.23.

306 etwa dreiunddreißig [229.12] He's about thirty-three: traditionally Christ's age at the time of his crucifixion; cf. 876.43.

308 van der Goes [230.1]: Hugo van der Goes (1440–82), with van Eyck, van der Weyden, and Bosch one of the four great masters of fifteenth-century painting in Flanders. He entered the Convent of the Rouge-Cloître at the height of his career and finally lapsed into madness. See chapter 13 of *VEF*, especially pp. 184–85, where his convent life is described. Like Wyatt, van der Goes "suffered under the dread that he was a son of damnation" (185).

309 di Credi s.S.174 [231.17]: see 128.30.

310 Einen echten Memling s.S.310 [231.32] Memling. An original: see 74.30.

Pinakothek s.S.103 [231.38]: see 74.38.

311 Die Ritterrüstung da oben [232.19] That suit of armor up there [...] That's my favorite thing here: cf. *Faust* 2:10554–62, which Cyrus Hamlin annotates: "An anachronistic allusion to the early-nineteenth-century fad, especially among wealthy aristocrats, of collecting medieval armor."

313 der dreibeinige Mann von Velasquez [234.12] three-legged man of Velasquez: unidentified. "I don't recall either; but believe it was a case of the artist overpainting a leg which later faintly showed through" – WG/SM.

314 Dominus providebit [234.37]: "God will provide" (Vulgate, Gen. 22.8).

315 du bist ein Teil der Finsternis [235.23] one comes to grips with reality only through the commission of evil: basically a French literary tradition (Camus, Genet, Gide, et al.) that can be traced back to Sade.

316 Carmina vel caelo s.S.41 [236.19]: see 28.26.

319 *Soberia, Ira, Lujuria, Pereza* [238.10]: Pride, Wrath, Lust, Sloth (in Spanish), again from the *Seven Deadly Sins*.

Es blaut der Tag [238.27] "Here hath been dawning [...] slip useless away?": from English writer Thomas Carlyle's (1795–1881) "Today," his only popular poem, frequently anthologized in the nineteenth century.

320 Solange die Leute glauben [...] Raphael [239.25] "If the public believes [...] then it is a Raphael": source unknown. Raphael Sanzio (1483–1520) was an architect as well as a painter.

324 Tod der Heiligen Jungfrau [241.42] the death of the Virgin [...] in Brussels: van der Goes's *Death of the Virgin* is one of his later works and contains irrational elements indicative of his impending madness. See *VEF* 180–81 for an evaluation of the painting (where its location is identified as Bruges, not Brussels).

325 Fra Angelico [242.31]: (1387–1455), Dominican friar noted for his reverent paintings of angels, childlike saints, and madonnas. Contrasting Jan van Eyck's intellectual approach to painting with that of Fra Angelico's, Conway writes: "Fra Angelico is recorded to have gone down on his knees, his eyes streaming with tears, when he painted Christ on the Cross, and we can well believe it. John's eyes under like circumstances would have remained very dry" (*VEF* 103–4).

»Dies mag des Lasters sauer Löhnung sein« [242.36] "That vice may merit [...] What then? Is ...": from Pope's *An Essay on Man* (4:149–51):
"But sometimes Virtue starves while Vice is fed."
What then? is the reward of Virtue, Bread?
That, Vice may merit; 'tis the price of Toil.

328 vulgus vult decipi [245.2] Vulgus vult decipi [...] let them be deceived: "It is curious to hear the various opinions entertained by collectors and art lovers concerning faking and its alarming and increasing success," Nobili writes. "An old collector who had, no doubt like so many of his colleagues, learned his lesson through being duped, unhesitatingly declared that faking is a grand art with a reason for existence as it seems to meet a real need of society, the need of being, as it were, deluded and cheated by elegance. Queer ethics answering to the Latin saying: *Vulgus vult decipi, ergo decipiatur* (The crowd likes to be deceived, let it be deceived!)" (*GAF* 198).

Süß ist die Frucht der Widerwärtigkeit [245.6] "... ugly and venomous, wears yet a precious jewel in his head": from Shakespeare's *As You Like It*: "Sweet are the uses of adversity, / Which, like the toad, ugly and venomous, / Wears yet a precious jewel in his head" (2.1.12–14).

329 Lucius Mummius [245.10]: "A type of the early ignorant Roman art collector is given by Lucius Mummius, the general who destroyed Corinth [146 B.C.], and of whom Vellius Paterculus tells (I, 13) that in sending to Rome what might be styled the artistic booty of the destroyed city he consigned the statues and paintings to those in charge of the transport with the warning that should the goods be lost they would be held responsible and would have to reproduce them at their own expense" (*GAF* 19). Valentine's comparison of modern art collectors to those of Rome (and that art collecting started in Rome rather than Greece) derives from Nobili's opening chapters.

Wo ein Bild nämlich per Gerichtsbeschluß nicht dem Maler gehörte [245.23] the point Rome reached when a court could award a painting to the man who owned the board: by Roman Emperor Justinian's time (sixth century), says Nobili, "judges had so lost all sense of art appreciation that in a dispute between a painter and the man who had furnished the board on which the work was painted, they decided that the painting belonged to the one who owned the board. Justinian was forced to do justice by stating that if a quarrel arose between the artist and the one who furnished the board the owner of the work was the artist, as the value of the board could not be compared with the artistic one" (*GAF* 64).

332 Ein Roman ohne Held [247.25] A novel without a hero: the subtitle, Craig Werner notes, of *Vanity Fair* by Thackeray, "whose satirical touch resembles Gaddis's" (*Paradoxical Resolutions: American Fiction since James Joyce* [Urbana: University of Illinois Press, 1982], 172).

333 Farben auf Löschpapier gemischt [248.7] I tried mixing my colors on blotting paper, to absorb the oil: this and some of the following details are from *GAF* 227 ff.

335 Hubert van Eyck [249.27]: a quatrain on the frame of the *Ghent Altarpiece* mentions this otherwise unknown painter (though the quatrain itself has been suspected as a seventeenth-century forgery), and a few scholars have attributed paintings to him, but the identity of this possibly nonexistent painter is still a matter of critical debate. Gaddis found the details of the tradition of Hubert's life in *EB* (9:3) and especially *VEF* (51 n, 52–63). "Painters in the Low Countries, and after them those of France," Conway argues, "learnt from him to look with fresh eyes on the world of nature and man about them, and to embody their dreams and recognitions of beauty in the forms of nature herself" (*VEF* 63).

336 Dürer [250.14]: Albrecht Dürer (1471–1528), generally considered the greatest artist of the German Renaissance.

Gilde [250.28] the Guild: this passage is based on Conway's chapter "The Guild System" (*VEF* 85–100), especially p. 93: "He had to take solemn oaths of honesty, and to promise that his work should be done as in the sight of God. [...] He was not allowed to use any except recognized materials and tools. If bad materials were found by the guild inspectors in his possession, they were destroyed and he was fined." Earlier in the chapter Conway points out: "The student in the old days had to know how to make whatever he required. Certain colours, indeed, like ultramarine which came from Venice and brick-red made in Flanders, could be bought; but artists had to know exactly what they wanted, and to be able to discriminate between good and bad materials" (91).

337 Ein Bild merkt, wenn es angesehen wird. [251.17] conscious of being looked at: cf. "the roses / Had the look of flowers that are looked at" – Eliot, "Burnt Norton."

342 Der Duft jedoch verriet dir [254.22] Mansit odor [...] a goddess had appeared": commenting on the distribution of the gift of tongues at the first Pentecost (Acts 2), Conybeare notes: "In the oldest Syriac versions of the passage it is added that a sweet odour pervaded the house, and this feature was, perhaps, eliminated by the Greek editors of Luke's text; it was, however, a familiar idea among the ancient pagans that the epiphany of a god was attended with a sweet smell, and that he left behind an odour of sanctity. Hence the line of Ovid: '*Mansit odor. Posses scire fuisse deam*' ('An odour remained. You could tell that a goddess had appeared')" (*MMM* 100). The quoted line is from part 5 (May) of the *Fasti,* Ovid's poetic commentary on the Roman calendar, and describes Flora (Roman goddess of flowers and spring) at the conclusion of the poet's imaginary interview with her concerning her annual festival (Floralia).

Steenken-Madonna [254.34] Steenken *Madonna*: Conway's 1921 study attributes this painting to Hubert (*VEF* 59), but a 1938 archival study by H. J. J. Scholtens established that the donor as *not* Herman Steenken (d. 1428), as generally believed. The painting is now known as *The Madonna and Child with Saint Elizabeth of Hungary, Saint Barbara and Jan Vos* (also known as the Jan Vos *Madonna* and/or the Rothschild *Madonna*) and is believed to have been begun by Jan van Eyck and completed by Flemish painter Peter Chistus (ca. 1400–1473).

343 Varé tava soskei [...] warum du gekommen bist. [255.24] Varé tava [...] come hither": this quotation heads a list of short Hungarian-Gypsy sentences in a section at the end of George Borrow's *The Zincali: An Account of the Gypsies of Spain* (1841) entitled "Specimens of Gypsy Dialects" (London: Everyman's Library, 1914), 237.

344 *Madonna im Gehäus* [255.34] *Virgin and Child and Donor*: also known as *Chancellor Rolin Adoring the Madonna and Child,* reproduced in *WMA* facing p. 144.

344 Jean de Visch [256.2]: "grand bailli" of Flanders; the will is dated 1413 and bequeathed a painting by Hubert (*VEF* 59).

Jodoc Vyt [256.11]: see *VEF* 53 and note for his connection with the van Eycks. The house torn down in Ghent that Valentine refers to was believed to be Vyt's (*VEF* 57).

[256.41] color of the sixth heaven, jacinth: see 257.32–35.

345 *Otia Imperialia* [257.1] *Otia Imperialia* [...] Gervase of Tilbury: a collection of medieval legends and superstitions recorded for Otto IV of Germany by Gervase (fl. 1211), English ecclesiastic and writer. The anecdote, as noted earlier (28.32), is from Lethaby (*AMM* 15).

346 stellen Sie sich vor, daß Himmel und Erde [257.17] heaven and earth joined by a tree [...] sky is a roof: from *AMM* 12, quoting from Sir Edward Burnett Tylor's *Researches into the Early History of Mankind and the Development of Civilisation* (3d ed., 1878):
"The sky is to most savages, what is called in the South American language, 'the earth on high,' and we can quite understand the thought of some Paraguayans that at death their souls would go up to heaven by the tree which joins earth and sky. There are holes or windows through the sky-roof or firmament where the rain comes through; and if you climb high enough, you can get through and visit the dwellers above, who look and talk and live very much in the same way as the people upon earth."

Fang für außerirdische Wesen s.S. 119 [257.28] Someone, who was it? said maybe we're fished for: Charles Fort; see 87.8.

die sieben Himmel der Araber [257.32] seven heavens of the Arabs: from *AMM* 24, quoting from Stanley Lane-Poole's *The Art of the Saracens in Egypt* (1886):
"According to the common opinion of the Arabs, there are seven heavens, one above another, and seven earths, one beneath another; the earth which we inhabit being the highest of the latter, and next below the lowest heaven. [...] Traditions differ respecting the fabric of the seven heavens. In the most credible account, according to a celebrated historian, the first is described as formed of emerald; the second of white silver; the third of large white pearls; the fourth of ruby; the fifth of red gold; the sixth of yellow jacinth; and the seventh of shining light."

347 Dabei mag ich Lilien grundsätzlich nicht [258.2] Lilies [...] an *Annunciation*: the lily, "the flower of pur-i-ty" as Esme says (271.21–22), is traditionally associated with the Virgin Mary, and particularly associated in painting with the Annunciation, in which lilies either are held by the archangel or (as Wyatt intends) are present in a vase.

Tertullian s.S. 422 [258.17]: (fl. 160–230), Latin ecclesiastical writer; Valentine is reading his *De Virginibus Velandis* (313.6).

348 **Osiris s. S. 79** [258.28] Osiris [...] Isis: see 56.12.

Hab den Trick von einem Spaghettifresser [258.37] glassware, it's been in a manure pile [...] Some wop taught me that trick: Signore Nobili mentions this trick in his *GAF* (254).

Italia irredenta [258.40]: "Unredeemed Italy" was the name given to Italian-speaking areas still under foreign control from 1861 to 1920. The term *irredentism* is thus used for any nationalistic movement seeking to break away from foreign rule and rejoin others of the same nationality.

350 **Bischof namens Borja** [260.19] eighteenth-century Spanish bishop named Borja: unidentified.

351 **den gleichnamigen Papst aus dem neunten Jahrhundert** [261.14] the ninth century Pope: pope in August and September of 827; his election was largely the result of the efforts of the lay nobility.

352 **von einem abtrünnigen Maler** [261.27] the renegade painter: a phrase sometimes used to describe Cavaradossi in *Tosca*.

erst das Geld [...] macht unseren Kontrakt [...] verbindlich [261.37] money [...] binds the contract: Minkoff (247) suggests this is a "parodic debasement" of the blood contract made by Mephistopheles with Faust (ll. 1737–40).

Somerset Maugham s. S. 849 [262.8]: (1874–1965), English writer; his *Razor's Edge* is mentioned at 638.25.

353 **Momos und Vulkan** [262.17] Momus and Vulcan: this anecdote is recorded in one of the satirical dialogues of the Greek author Lucian (ca. 120–ca. 180), but Gaddis's source unknown.

Ein Held meiner Kindheit [...] Jan Hus s. S. 46 [262.28] a hero? John Huss: see 32.20.

355 **Emersons Satz s. S. 425** [264.10] Emerson's advice [...] perhaps they are: "Emerson recommended us to treat people as though they were real, and added, 'Perhaps they are.' But the doubt that lingered in the mind of the stately pantheist never entered into that of the Hindu" (*AN* 6). The quotation is from Emerson's essay "Experience" and is repeated at 315.17.

356 *Was du ein halbes Leben lang vergeblich gesucht hast* [265.2] *What you seek* [...] *you become its prey*: a remark made by Thoreau to Emerson and recorded in the latter's eulogy "Thoreau" (*Atlantic Monthly*, August 1862). Walking one day with his friend, Thoreau

heard a note which he called that of the night-warbler, a bird he had never identified, had been in search of twelve years, which always, when he saw it, was in the act of diving down into a tree or bush, and which it was vain to seek; the only bird which sings indifferently by night and by day. I told him he must beware of finding and booking it, lest life should have nothing more to show him. He said, "What you seek in vain for, half your life, one day you come full upon, all the family at dinner. You seek it like a dream, and as soon as you find it you become its prey."

Valentine appears to be reading *Walden*: Emerson's quotation is cited in Byron Rees's introduction to his frequently reprinted edition of 1910, and in some editions of *Walden* Emerson's essay has been printed in full as an introduction. Gaddis later used this quote as the epigraph to *A Frolic of His Own*.

357 **Sieben himmlische Stoffe** [265.8] Seven celestial fabrics [...] Throne of the Compassionate: "'Traditions differ respecting the fabric of the seven heavens [see note to 257.32]. [...] next above the seventh heaven [are] seven seas of light, then an undefined number of veils or separations of different substances seven of each kind, and then Paradise, which consists of seven stages one above another (these are distinguished by the names of precious gems) canopied by the Throne of the Compassionate'" (*AMM* 24, quoting Lane-Poole).

Klang der Sphären [265.17] music of the spheres: "'The early Pythagoreans further conceived that the heavenly bodies, like other moving bodies, emitted a sound; these they supposed made up a harmonious symphony. Hence they established an analogy between the intervals of the seven planets and the musical scale'" (*AMM* 21, quoting from Sir G. C. Lewis's *An Historical Survey of the Ancients* [1862]).

ein etruskischer Priester [265.32] the Etruscan priest [...] delivering the residence of deity to earth: "'The Etruscan priest who built a sanctuary, traced above in the sky with his wand the foundations which he re-produced on earth – he transported, so to say, upon the earth a part of the sky to make a dwelling for his God'" (*AMM* 42, quoting from the Comte de Vogüé's *La Syrie Centrale* [1865–67]).

Sieben Tage, sieben Siegel [265.36] Seven days, seven seals [...] Abednego: biblical instances of the magicality of the number seven: "Seven days" refers to the days of Creation, the Holy Week, etc.; "seven seals" from Rev. 5:1; "seven bullocks" (Num. 29:32); "seven times Jacob bowed before Esau" (Gen. 33:3); "seven stars [...] in his right hand" (Rev. 1:20; 4:5; 2:1); "seven years in Eden" (apocryphal?); "seven times seven years to the jubilee trumpet" (Lev. 25:8–9); "seven years of plenty [...] famine" (Gen. 41:29–30); "Nebuchadnezzar heated the furnace seven times" (Dan. 3:19); "the golden image" is described in Dan. 3:1, and the quotation " – Blessed be the God of Shadrach, Meshach, and Abednego" (the three in the furnace) is from Dan. 3:28. (It might be noted this passage occurs in the novel's seventh chapter.)

358 *Selbst diejenigen, die andere Götter anbeten* [266.8] *Even those who worship other gods worship me although they know it not*: so boasts Krishna (see 56.12) in the ninth chapter of the *Bhagavad-Gita*.

359 *Let's Do It* [267.13]: "Let's Do It (Let's Fall in Love)" is a 1928 composition by Cole Porter.

360 **von den Lilien könntest du regelrecht was lernen** [267.17] Take a lesson from the lilies: from Matt. 6:28.

361 *Boyma große Mann* [268.27] *Boyma big man* [..] *not so strong as Boyma*: quoted verbatim from *M&R* 37; the passage is Lang's reconstruction of how an Australian aborigine may have described his religion to an early settler named Manning, who later used Christian terminology to describe aborigine beliefs, making explicit parallels between the two religions. But Frazer says of Manning that his "evidence on [many] matters of Australian beliefs is open to grave doubt" (unabridged *GB*, 7:307–8).

363 **Schöpfung unter Schöpfung** [269.31] one creation beneath another [...] seven stages, one beneath another: from *AMM* 24–25, again quoting Lane-Poole on ancient Arab beliefs.

Die Heilige [...] **Der Ruch der Heiligkeit** [270.1] The lady saint [...] odor of sanctity: identified below as Saint Catherine de Ricci (1522–90). "Where St. Catherine of Ricci had walked through the cloister was known to the nuns by the delicious scent that clung even to the flags whereon she had trod." Thus, Summers concludes, "'The odour of sanctity' is more than a mere phrase" (*PMM* 62).

367 **Zu seiner Beruhigung** [...] **Laute gespielt** s.S. 309 [272.40] In the convent where he came, they tried to soothe and comfort him: Hugo van der Goes (see 230.1).

In den alten Zeiten [273.14] In den alten Zeiten [...] "That the sun itself...": from "The Frog King," the first story in the Brothers Grimm's *Kinder- und Hausmarchen* (Nursery and Household Tales, 1812), the tale of a frog who returns a princess's ball from a well in exchange for becoming her friend. Her father the king forces the fickle princess to honor her agreement, but later in a fit of anger she hurls the frog against her bedroom wall, and he falls to the ground a prince. He had been bewitched years before, and upon now being released he marries the princess. The translation that Wyatt interrupts concludes: "that the sun itself, which has seen so much, was astonished whenever it shone on her face."

371 **Francesca de Serrone** [276.1]: (1557–1600), a Franciscan tertiary. Commenting on those stigmatics who receive "the visible Wound in the side only," Summers says of Francesca: "Every Friday the wound gushed forth blood, which was fragrant with the odour of sweetest violets" (*PPM* 169).

373 **Wer, wenn ich schriee** [277.34] Who, if I cried [...] Each single angel...: the opening lines of Rilke's first Duino Elegy (in the Leishman-Spender translation

[1939]). The interrupted seventh line ends: "Each single angel is terrible." Later Max will steal this piece of paper (299.11–13) and, not recognizing it as Rilke's, publish the poem as his own (622.16ff.).

II.1

377 **legen sich tausend Zufälle** [281] A thousand accidents [...] Thomas De Quincey: (1785–1859), English essayist and opium addict. The epigraph is from his famous *Confessions of an English Opium-Eater* (1821; rev. ed. 1856), part 3: "The Pains of Opium." The quotation is from the middle of a sentence that begins: "Of this, at least, I feel assured, that there is no such thing as ultimate *forgetting*; traces once impressed upon the memory are indestructible; a thousand accidents [...]." The passage is a Proustian discussion of involuntary memory, of experiences apparently forgotten but suddenly *"recognized"* in new circumstances (De Quincey's italics).

378 **metaphysische (Bergsonsche) Heiterkeit** [282.17] metaphysical (Bergsonian) hilarity: though best known for his philosophical investigations into the nature of time, the French philosopher Henri Bergson (1859–1941) also wrote an important essay entitled "Laughter," which has been translated into English and published in many anthologies.

in den Kaffeehäusern von Antwerpen [282.20] spawned in the estaminets of Antwerp: from Eliot's "Gerontion" (ll. 7–10):
My house is a decayed house,
And the jew squats on the window sill, the owner
Spawned in some estaminet of Antwerp,
Blistered in Brussels, patched and peeled in London.

384 **Buch [...] mit der Überzeugunskraft von vier Millionen verkauften Exemplaren** s. S. 664 [286.3] a book which had sold four million copies: see 498.3.

O Gott, was hab ich getahaan s. S. 271 [286.11] O God, what have I du-un: see 202.22.

387 **zwei Bilder von Dierick Bouts** [288.27] Dierick Bouts: see 75.6; the "original paintings" are Wyatt's forgeries.

388 **der Schrei der entwurzelten Alraune** [289.12] shriek of the mandrake root [...] drove a man mad: a popular superstition mentioned in *DDD* (95).

Chloroform ein Lockmittel des Satans [289.13] chloroform a decoy of Satan: "The [nineteenth-century] arguments used by the clergy against anesthesia varied," Dr. Haggard notes, "but all centered around the theme that pain, particularly the pain of childbirth, was the ordained lot of mankind; to prevent it was a sacrilege. As one clergyman expressed it, 'chloroform is a decoy of Satan, apparently offering itself to bless women; but in the end it will harden society and rob God of the deep, earnest cries which arise in time of trouble for help'" (*DDD* 108).

388 **Blattern eine Heimsuchung des Herrn** [289.13] smallpox a visitation of God: in his "Answers to the Religious Objection Against the Employment of Anesthetic Agents in Midwifery and Surgery" (1847), Dr. James Y. Simpson "explains that opposition, particularly on theological grounds, had been presented against every humane innovation in the past. He cites as an instance the opposition to the introduction of vaccination against smallpox. Those opposed to its introduction had argued against it on religious grounds. 'Smallpox,' they had said, 'is a visitation from God, and originates in man: but the cowpox [vaccination] is produced by presumptuous, impious man. The former Heaven ordained; the latter is a daring and profane violation of our holy religion'" (*DDD* 109).

390 **der arme Campesino [...] auf jenem Berggipfel in Darién** [290.30] the Indian sat silent [...] on a peak in Darien: a parody of the last line of Keats's "On First Looking into Chapman's Homer," where Cortez's men "Looked at each other with a wild surmise – / Silent, upon a peak in Darien."

die Menschheit würde komplett ausgelöscht [290.32] "If man were wiped out [...] again evolve": source unknown.

[290.36] in the foremost shambles of time Mr. Pivner stood heir: a parody of a famous line in Tennyson's "Locksley Hall" (1842): "I the heir of all the ages, in the foremost files of time" (given more straightforwardly at 559.19).

395 **Da war noch Zeit.** [293.31] there would be time: another quotation from Eliot's "Love Song of J. Alfred Prufrock" (see 15.25).

Adam war immerhin neunhundertdreißig Jahre alt geworden. [293.31] Adam [...] lived for nine hundred thirty years: so alleges Gen. 5:5.

397 **mit freundlicher Unterstützung des Sonnenkönigs** [295.21] Sun King: Louis XIV, king of France (1643–1715); Louis XV's Deer Park (in Versailles) was just such an artificial setting.

Simpotico [295.24] Simpotico [...] simpótico: that is, Sp. *simpática* (or It. *simpàtica*): pleasantly sympathetic, congenial.

398 **Leda und der Schwan s. S. 521** [295.43] Leda and the swan: in Greek mythology, Zeus came to Leda in the guise of a swan while she was bathing; she laid two eggs as a result (see 385.2).

401 *The Compleat Angler* [298.11]: a treatise on the joys of fishing and the pastoral life by English writer Izaak Walton (1593–1683). It does not, however, recommend pumpkin seeds in martinis.

401 Wer bin ich [298.12] "What is mine [...] quiet of the grave": from Robert Louis Stevenson's short story "Olalla" (1885), concerning the deterioration of a Spanish Catholic family. At the end of the family line is a saintly girl named Olalla, who in the quoted passage (as well as in the quotation on p. 302 below) rejects the narrator's marriage proposal in order to allow her ruined family to die out. The story is usually found in collections of Stevenson's supernatural fiction (as is "Thrawn Janet," which Gaddis alludes to elsewhere).

403 Wörter [...] mit ihrer eigenen Bedeutung versehen [299.19] words for themselves, and invest them with her own meaning: just as Humpty Dumpty recommends in *Through the Looking-Glass* (chap. 6).

sprödestes Material, das [...] in tausend Stücke zersprang [299.26] straining and cracking [...] raid on the inarticulate: from two discussions of poetry in Eliot's *Four Quartets*: see "Burnt Norton," sec. 5, and "East Coker," sec. 5.

404 während sie der Stoff aus der Nadel in eine Welt überführte [300.28] that world not world where the needle took her: from Eliot's "Burnt Norton": "Descend lower, descend only / Into the world of perpetual solitude, / World not world, but that which is not world."

wo sie in einem gewaltigen Orgasmus dahintrieb [300.33] the world of ecstasy they all approximated by different paths: see de Rougemont's comparison and contrast between mystics, erotomaniacs, and drug users in *LWW* (141).

Amors Pfeil [...] sterben, weil sie nicht sterben konnte [300.36] "Love's dart" [...] "dying of not being able to die": "If now we turn to the writings of the great Spanish mystics of the sixteenth century," de Rougemont writes (*LWW* 133–34), "Saint Teresa and Saint John of the Cross, we find them employing the whole rhetoric of courtly love, even its most delicate shades of expression. Here are the chief topics common alike to the troubadours and these orthodox mystics:

"To die of not being able to die." [cf. 40.7]
The "sweet cautery."
"Love's dart" that wounds but does not kill. [...]
To complain of an ill that is yet prized more than every joy and worldly good. [...]
The "stolen heart," the "ravished understanding," the "rape of love."
Love treated as an ultimate "understanding" (*conoscenza* in Provençal).

405 Gerbert, Erzbischof von Ravenna [300.41] Gerbert, Archbishop of Ravenna: citing Michelet's *Histoire de France*, Saltus writes (*AN* 90):

According to the gossip of the day, Gerbert, once a Spanish student, afterwards Archbishop of Ravenna, and subsequently Pope [as Sylvester II, 999–1003], entered into an agreement of this kind, and one night the devil came in person to claim him. It was an agreement they had made together long before in Cordova, where Gerbert, finding his studies too arduous, had signed the bond in exchange for the royal road. It was the devil who had taught him all he knew – algebra, clock-making, and how to become a Pope. It was clear as day that he would have known none of these things without infernal assistance. Gerbert resists, but Mephisto proves his claim. "You did not think me a logician, did you?" are said to have been his historic words, and, presto! Gerbert disappeared in a fork of lambent flame.

405 Elisabeth, Mathilda und Brigitta [301.2] SS Elizabeth Matilda Bridget [...] drops of blood 3,000,800]: from the ever-sardonic Marsh (*MMSM* 145–47):

We do not know the original date of the two miraculous documents we next describe. Judging from internal evidence, we should presume them to be of quite modern fabrication, and of Jesuit paternity. [...] The first lays claim to some antiquity, having been found, it is said, in the Holy Sepulchre at Jerusalem, and afterward preserved in a silver casket by the Emperor Charles V. and "His Holiness." The story is that Christ appeared to St. Elizabeth, St. Matilda, and St. Bridget, and delivered to them a written account of the details of his passion, stating the number of soldiers who attended the Crucifixion; of kicks, blows, and wounds inflicted upon the Saviour by them; of punctures from the crown of thorns; and of drops of blood shed and sighs breathed by the sufferer. The fractures of the skull, it is said, were one hundred in number, and the drops of blood thirty-eight thousand four hundred and thirty. [...]
The other miraculous communication is a letter from the Saviour, printed in characters of gold, and sent, through her guardian angel, to a girl of St. Marcel, in France. It was published at Rome "by permission of His Holiness, Pius IX." It resembles the first, of which it appears to be a French amplification, the numbers having been multiplied in some such proportion as the dignity of a pope bears to that of an archbishop; for the drops of blood are reckoned at three millions and eight hundred. [...] These disgusting and profane fables are printed by hundreds of thousands, and exposed for sale, together with vulgar and often immoral ballads, at half the street-corners and bookstalls in Florence, Rome, and other Italian towns.

Ehrentitel der Jungfrau Maria [301.7] Virgin's titles number 305: "the most noticeable feature" of the Reverend Ambrogio Landucci's *Origine del Tempio dedicato in Roma alla Vergine Madre di Dio presso all Porta del Popolo* (1646) says Marsh, who goes on to quote many of the more recherché examples.

Sir Arthur Eddington [301.7]: (1882–1944), English astronomer, author of *The Nature of the Physical World* (1929), source of the Eddington reference on p. 34 of *A Frolic of His Own*.

Sir James Jeans [301.8]: (1887–1946), English astronomer and physicist, author of several books on cosmogony.

Sir William Rowan Hamilton [301.12]: "The Irish mathematician, Sir William Rowan Hamilton [1805–65], once allowed himself to be drawn into the speculation of how far out into space Jesus could proceed in a certain time if he was rising at the moderate rate which the above passage [Acts

1:9] contemplates. When his calculations revealed to him that he would as yet not have reached the nearest of the fixed stars, he began, as a good Christian, to recoil from his speculations, and relegated the matter to faith, as a mystery beyond the reach of human reason" (*MMM* 358–59).

[301.43] "the brethren had only to ring their bells [...] behind the screen": source unknown.

406 **Nicolas von Tolentino** [302.9] *Saint Nicolas of Tolentino*: from Summers (*PPM* 68):
The Augustinian mystic, St. Nicholas of Tolentino, as he lay wasted and weak on his death-bed, exhausted by the broiling August heat, so excited the pity of his sorrowing brethren that they brought him a dish of doves, most delicately dressed, to tempt his appetite. The Saint, however, reproved them, firmly, but in gentle terms. He had never tasted animal food in his life. Painfully raising himself on his poor pallet, he stretched his hands over the dish, and lo! the birds rejoicing were in a flash covered with plumage, and flew out of the window of his little white-washed cell towards the blue sky beyond. But they hovered around until in a few days the Saint breathed his last [10 September 1306], when they were seen mounting into the air, accompanying (as it is piously believed) his soul to Paradise. For as he breathed his last the room was filled with a heavenly fragrance, as of lilies, and gleamed with radiant light.

407 **Du bist ein Mann und gebildet** [302.21] "You are a man [...] and are warned and pity ...": from Stevenson's "Olalla"; see 298.12.

408 **Psycho-Krempel von Ödipus** [303.16] *Oedipus and all the rest*: the search for a physical or spiritual father is a theme running throughout world literature, from Sophocles' Oedipus to Clement in *The Recognitions* to Hamlet to Stephen Dedalus, and now to Otto Pivner.

Vesey Street [303.21]: in lower Manhattan, north of the World Trade Center.

410 **Dies sind die Momente [...] ungebrochen.** [304.38] *These are the moments [...] with its spirit unbroken*: from Mansfield's review in the *Athenæum* (10 September 1920) of E. V. Lucas's *Verena in the Midst,* an epistolary novel about a woman confined to her bed, comforted with letters from a variety of characters. The first paragraph of the review – reprinted in Mansfield's *Novels and Novelists,* ed. J. Middleton Murray (1930), the book Esther shared with Otto on pp. 124–25 – reads:

It is a fearful thing to have to lie in bed. To be sent to bed, to be commanded to stay there – to gaze from a little valley of humiliation, up, up to that ineffable brow that, wreathed with the mists of discretion and vacancy bends over one ... To pipe: "When shall I be allowed to get up again?" and to be answered by: "We had rather postpone our answer for the present." These are moments which set the soul yearning to be taken suddenly, snatched out of the very heart of some fearful joy, and set before its Maker, hatless, dishevelled and gay, with its spirit unbroken. For it is impossible to go condemned to bed in our grown-uppishness without recalling how favourite a remedy it was with our parents and nurses for a spirit that wanted breaking. There, naked between the sheets, prone when all the rest of the world is walking or leaping, conscious, to a hopeless degree, that it certainly isn't for you that the clocks chime, the cups rattle, the lamps are lighted and the door-bell rings, one wages many a fierce battle. But the infants who emerge triumphant are, depend upon it, bound to be attacked by larger nurses and more unyielding parents later on, who will send them back to bed for another tussle, as though it were never too late to break ...

411 **Viareggio** [305.16]: modeled on the San Remo Cafe, formerly on the northwest corner of Bleecker and MacDougal, a favorite gathering place for writers and artists in the late forties and early fifties; "in calling it the Viareggio I simply took the next town up or down the coast [of Italy]" (WG/SM).

[305.37] **Dante had rejuvenated hell six centuries before**: cf. Saltus: "In words that rise and greet and kiss the eye, Dante had rejuvenated hell" (*AN* 101).

Decimus Laberius [305.39] Laberius [...] the public latrine: Decimus Laberius (105?–43 B.C.), Roman knight and writer, author of several farces and verse satires. "In one of the forgotten plays of Laberius, a jester is represented as recommending a smug-faced companion to get a foretaste of philosophy in the latrinæ" (*AN* 109).

eher an Petrarca erinnert [305.43] Petrarch finding the papal court at Avignon a "sewer [...] his sister seduced by a pope: condensed from Saltus (*AN* 100):

Meanwhile, the popes and princes of the Church had lost faith, and decency as well. Petrarch, in his letters *Sine titulo,* speaks of the papal court as follows: "There is here (in Avignon) everything imaginable in the way of confusion, darkness and horror. Avignon is the sewer of every vice, the gully of every wickedness. I know from personal experience that in this place there is neither piety nor charity. Faith is absent; there is nothing holy, nothing just, nothing human. Friendship, modesty and decency are unknown. Houses, squares, temples, courts and pontifical palaces drip with lies. The hope of a future life is considered an illusion; Jesus Christ is looked upon as a useless invention; virtue is regarded as a proof of stupidity, and prostitution leads to fame."
Such is Petrarch's account; but Petrarch was possibly annoyed because his sister had been seduced by the pope.
In his novel *Juliette* (1797), the Marquis de Sade identifies the pope as Benedict XII.

412 **Ernest Hemingway** [306.5]: this apparently is not Hemingway but a character who takes advantage of his physical resemblance to the writer. On the other hand, Hemingway was in New York in November 1949, and his pugnacious, boorish behavior was the subject of a devastating profile by Lillian Ross in the *New Yorker* (13 May 1950), which Gaddis probably read. A copy of *R* was in Hemingway's library at the Finca Vigía in Cuba, no doubt a complimentary copy sent by Gaddis and/or

his publisher; whether Hemingway actually read it or not is unknown; see James D. Brasch and Joseph Sigman's *Hemingway's Library: A Composite Record* (New York: Garland, 1981), 136 (item 2399).

412 **Come Back to Sorrento** [306.16] *Return to Sorrento*: also known as "Come Back to Sorrento," a popular sentimental song written by Ernesto di Curtis (1935).

Twit Twit Twit [306.26]: line 203 of Eliot's *Waste Land* (WG/SM).

419 ***I'm a Little Piece of Leather*** [311.7]: "sung (& recorded) by a cult chanteuse in the 40s named Stella Brooks, she was quite a dish" (WG/SM). Brooks (1915–?) wrote and recorded this song ca. 1946; it appears on an album entitled *Diverse Songs and Moods: Stella Brooks & Greta Keller* (Folkways Records, 1981). A short woman, she is described in the liner notes as having "dark hair in a page-boy bob and blue eyes."

420 **Bronzino** [311.22]: Il Bronzino (real name Agnolo di Cosimo Allori, 1503–72), Florentine portraitist.

[311.24] **Infessura** [...] **Sixtus IV, "puerorum amator et sodomita fuit"**: from Saltus's description of the corruption of the Renaissance papacy: "Of Sextus IV., Infessura says, in words that are best left untranslated, 'Puerum amator et sodomita fuit.' And it would appear, not only that he was guilty of these charming practices, but that he granted indulgences for their general commission" (*AN* 100).* Sixtus IV was pope from 1471–84; Stefano Infessura (ca. 1435–ca. 1500) was an Italian historian; see Summers' note on him in *MM* (xxv, n.). The Latin phrase, which translates "he was a lover of boys and a sodomite," is from his notorious *Diarium urbis Romae*.

die dionysischen Prozessionen [311.31] Dionysian processions [...] Holy Ghost: source unknown.

jus primae noctis [311.40]: the "first night's rights" that a medieval lord could claim over any bride in his domain.

Lupercalien [312.10] Lupercalia [...] naked women whipped: a Roman festival of expiation, later of fertility, celebrated on February 15. Roman women, to ensure fertility (and not necessarily naked), would put forth their hands to be stricken with the leather thongs carried by young men

---

* Gaddis followed Saltus in the first edition of R, but corrected "Sextus" to "Sixtus" and "puerum" to "puerorum" in later editions; these errors appear in the first edition of *The Anatomy of Negation* (New York: Scribner and Welford, 1886) and in Brentano's 1925 reprint, one of which Gaddis obviously used, but were corrected in the revised edition of *AN* published by Belford, Clarke & Company in 1889.

(Luperci) appointed to celebrate the festival. In 494 Pope Gelasius I changed the day to that of the Purification of the Virgin Mary.

421 **wie George Washington ohne Perücke** s. S. 88 [312.25] she looked rather like George Washington [...] for her money: 1759 (cf. 63.2).

Popeye [312.31]: the name of the depraved protagonist of Faulkner's *Sanctuary* (1931), though Gaddis may not have known this (see note to 187.6).

422 **Tertullian [...]** *De Virginibus Velandis* [313.2] Tertullian [...] *De Virginibus Velandis* [...] evil angels: adapted from Conybeare (*MMM* 232–33):

The idea that spirits, especially evil ones, approach women through the ear, which these early legends of the Virgin Mary embody, was an old Rabbinic one, found in the Talmud, in Philo, Josephus, and, above all, in Paul. The latter, in I Corinthians, ch. xi., forbids a woman *"to pray or prophesy with her head unveiled. She must carry on her head a talisman* (lit. power), *because of the angels."* Tertullian, the earliest of the Christian Fathers to comment on this passage, explains that evil angels were ever lurking about ready to assail even married women, much more virgins, through their ears. From this point of view he penned his weighty treatise, *De Virginibus Velandis* – "On the Necessity of Veiling Virgins"; and the Church has been careful, in devising a dress for nuns, who are espoused to Christ, to cover up their ears and protect them from this class of risk.

der Logos ist ihr einfach ins Ohr geschlüpft [313.9] The Virgin conceived that way, the Logos entered her ears: an early Christian belief, based on earlier Egyptian beliefs; see *MMM* 230–34. The Logos is, of course, the Word of God (John 1:1; cf. *Faust* 1224–37).

Vergil [...] daß Stuten vom Wind trächtig werden [313.11] Vergil [...] mares were made pregnant by the wind: Vergil says this of the mares of Boeotia in the third of his *Georgics* (ll. 266–76), quoted in *MMM* 196.

Fuisse deam [313.21] *Fuisse deam* [...] a goddess had just appeared: from Ovid: see 254.22–23.

423 **Pony boy** [314.10]: one who assumes a subservient role in certain sadomasochistic scenarios.

Victoria und Albert Hall [314.11] Victoria and Albert Hall: cf. the Royal Albert Hall, Victoria and Albert Museum, etc.

424 **Seraphina di Brescia** s. S. 83 [314.32]: see 59.36 (and cf. 295.30).

425 **The Boof on the Roof** [315.12]: that is, Le Boeuf sur le Toit – a cabaret in Paris (named after Milhaud's 1919 ballet) known to expatriates as the "Nothing-Doing Bar." The French name appears at 575.21 and in partial translation at the bottom of 608.

425 wenn wir uns Emersons Satz vor Augen halten s.S.355 [315.17] Emerson's advice: see 264.10.

Baby and I [...] wonderful hot s.S.292 [315.21]: see 219.2.

Tarahumara-Indianer [315.28] Tarahumara Indian [...] not having danced enough: verbatim from *FRR* (88). A chosen member of this indigenous Mexican tribe would dance to procure rain for their crops.

426 Clemens von Alexandria [315.35] Greek Clement [...] *generation and death*: from Clement of Alexandria's (see 373.1) *Stromata*, as quoted by Saltus (*AN* 76).

Philippe Auguste [315.43]: Philip II (ruled 1180–1223) married Ingeborg in 1193 but quickly developed a dislike for her; he repudiated the marriage and in 1196 married Agnes, daughter of Bertold IV, duke of Meran. The marriage was opposed by Popes Celestine III and Innocent III, and in 1201 Philip agreed to separate from Agnes (who died later that year). Ingeborg was kept in prison until 1213. The details of Philip's marital history may be from *EB* (17:718); the description of France under the interdict is from Saltus (*AN* 95).

427 Piero di Cosimo [316.25]: (1462?–1521?), unusual Florentine artist who did much to advance landscape painting.

428 versuchte, sich einen Fleck vom Ärmel zu reiben s.S.1010 [317.10] brushing at a spot on his sleeve: see 770.17.

[317.33] dawn's early light: from "The Star-Spangled Banner."

429 Max Schling [317.39]: a well-known florist shop at the time – not, as I assumed in the first edition of this book, the surname of Gaddis's character Max.

431 Leptis Magna s.S.115 [319.44]: see 83.35, where Wyatt owns a ground plan of the Libyan city. Somehow Wyatt comes into possession of this ceramic fragment, or one very similar (see 895.38).

[320.8] the middle sea: the literal meaning of Mediterranean.

434 Heilige Katharina [...] Heiliger Laurenz [321.13] Saint Catherine [...] Saint Lawrence: see 46.15–16.

José de Anchieta [321.42] Jesuit Father Anchieta: José de Anchieta (1534–97), Spanish missionary known as the Apostle of Brazil. "When walking in the sun," Marsh relates, "he would summon flocks of birds to hover over his head and keep pace with him, performing the part of a parasol" (*MMSM* 91).

435 Peter von Alcántara [...] Peter Nolasco [...] Peter Gonzales [322.2] Saint Peter of Alcántara, Saint Peter Nolasco, Saint Peter Gonzalez: "The Franciscan mystic St. Peter of Alcántara, the director of St. Teresa, an ascetic of surprising

holiness, walked upon the waves of the sea as though it were dry land, as also did St. Peter Nolasco [d. 1256], Father of the Mercedarians, and St. María de Cervellione of the same Order, and the Dominican St. Peter Gonzalez [1190–1246]" (*PPM* 68).

435 **die Gabrielis s. S. 249 u. 435** [322.11] the Gabrielis: Andrea Gabrieli (1510?–86) and his nephew Giovanni (1557–1612) were Italian composers and organists at Saint Mark's in Venice. References in the singular (186.19 and 744.18) are probably to the latter (cf. 323.7), considered the more important of the two.

Corelli [322.12]: Arcangelo Corelli (1653–1713), Italian composer.

Dové sei Fenestrula? [322.24]: It., "where is Fenestrula?" Fenestrula is the fictitious Italian town at which Stanley meets his end.

436 **Liber Usualis** [322.29] *Liber Usualis* [...] Quando júdex est ventúrus: the *Liber Usualis* is a modern compilation of the texts and music for the Mass and daily Office; the *Missae pro Defunctis* ("Mass for the Dead") includes the famous medieval hymn "Dies irae" (usually ascribed to Thomas of Celano), which begins:

Dies írae, díes ílla,
Sólvet saéclum in favílla:
Téste Dávid cum Sibÿlla.

Quántus trémor est futúrus,
Quando júdex est ventúrus,
Cúncta stricte discussúrus!

As scanned in the *Liber Usualis*, ed. the Benedictines of Solesmes [Boston: McLaughlin and Reilly, 1950], 1810): "That day of wrath, that dreadful day, / Shall the whole world in ashes lay, / As David and the Sibyls say, // What horror will invade the mind, / When the strict Judge, who would be kind, / Shall have few venial faults to find!" (trans. Wentworth Dillon).

Misereris omnium [322.33]: the only hymn of this title in the *Liber Usualis* is the one for Ash Wednesday (525).

der Teil eines Gedichts von Michelangelo [322.34] verse by Michelangelo: a madrigal; see *The Complete Poems and Selected Letters of Michelangelo*, trans. Creighton Gilbert (New York: Random, 1963), 7. Gaddis's source unknown.

441 **Hestia oder Vesta** [326.18] Hestia, Vestia, virgin-sworn, the hearth and the home: Vesta was the Roman goddess of the hearth (corresponding to the Greek Hestia) and custodian of the sacred fire. Women dedicated to her service ("vestals") were sworn to virginity and buried alive if they violated their vows.

441 Kardinal Spellman [326.25] Cardinal Spellman: Francis Joseph Spellman (1889–1967), American clergyman, made archbishop of New York in 1939 and a cardinal in 1946.

443 ein Kästchen mit der dicken Finsternis [327.34] darkness that Moses called down: see Ex. 10:21–23.

Zwinglis Soldaten [327.36] Zwingli's soldiers: for Zwingli, see 7.2; source of quote unknown.

444 ein ruchloses Frauenzimmer [329.1] Dawn [...] a woman of bad character: source unknown; in most primitive mythologies, the sun is feminine and the moon masculine.

445 Saturnalien [329.23] Saturnalia: the Roman festival of Saturn during the third week in December (the week in which the present chapter is set), when debauchery and role reversals took place.

Der Auftrieb der Knöpfe s.S.508 u.519 [329.26] like buttons from a host of common ladles: probably from Ibsen's *Peer Gynt*: act 5 (scenes 7, 9, 10) features a Button-moulder, an agent of God who melts down the souls of those who are neither good nor bad, to furnish the raw material for new souls, just as defective buttons are melted down in a ladle for new ones. Wyatt repeats this image of the streets filling with people like buttons at 376.1 and 384.15.

446 Pavane eines toten spanischen Komponisten [329.34] a pavan by a dead Spaniard: the phrase recalls Ravel's *Pavan for a Dead Princess*, but this is "just a parody throw away I believe" (WG/SM).

[329.38] Raphael, Tintoretto, Murillo: noted Italian (1483–1520), Venetian (1518–94), and Spanish (1617–82) painters.

Es blaut der Tag s.S.320 [330.15] Another blue day: see 238.27.

447 Loyolas *Geistliche Übungen* s.S.92 [330.34] Loyola's *Spiritual Exercises*: the famous manual of devotions and prayers by Saint Ignatius of Loyola (see 66.20).

448 *La nuit des Rois* [331.22]: Shakespeare's *Twelfth Night* has been translated into French under this title.

449 Boyma s.S.361 [332.14]: see 268.27.

451 Plinius [334.21] Pliny? [...] discourse on colors?: *Natural History*, book 35.

452 Portinari-Triptychon [334.25] Portinari triptych: an enormous work painted 1476–78; a detail from the work is used on the cover of the 1993 Penguin Classics edition of *R*.

wie heißt es bei Valéry [334.29] Valéry's line [...] one only abandons it: an often quoted dictum of Paul Valéry (1871–1945), French poet and critic.

157

453 Wenn selbst die Götter [...] nicht mehr tilgen können [335.15] *if the gods themselves [...] cannot recall their ... gifts*: from Tennyson's poem "Tithonus" (1860), ll. 46–49:

Why wilt thou ever scare me with thy tears,
And make me tremble lest a saying learnt,
In days far-off, on that dark earth, be true?
"The Gods themselves cannot recall their gifts."

[335.38] *a disciplined nostalgia*: this definition of criticism is used later by the British R.A. (670.39).

454 Semper aliquid haeret [336.32] *semper aliquid haeret? something always remains*: a Latin proverb. Bacon, for example, used it thus: "Audacter calumniare, semper aliquid haeret" ("Hurl your calumnies boldly; something is sure to stick" [*De Augmentis Scientiarum*]). The proverb and many variants will recur throughout the novel.

455 der rechte Arm von Hubert van Eyck [336.39] *Hubert van Eyck's right arm [...] Saint Bavon's in Ghent*: the anecdote is recorded in the article on Hubert in *EB* (9:3). The Van Eycks' *Ghent Altarpiece* is in the Church of Saint Bavon's.

Cardinale di San Giorgio [337.9] *Michelangelo's Cardinale di San Giorgio [...] thanked him?*: No. The cardinal demanded his money back from the dealer and refused to countenance Michelangelo when he first came to Rome (*EB* 15:410; cf. *GAF* 82, 89–90).

456 *Heimsuchung Mariens* [338.10] *Visitation*: the Virgin Mary's visit to her kinswoman Elizabeth, mother of John the Baptist (Luke 1:39–56).

Stabat Mater [338.11]: the Virgin weeping for her son on the cross, from the famous poem that begins: "Stabat mater dolorosa" ("The mournful mother stood weeping") attributed to the thirteenth-century monk Jacopone da Todi.

Nikodemus im Johannesevangelium [338.12] *Nicodemus [...] and be born?*": his story is told in John 3:1–14.

das Johannesevangelium ist das unzuverlässigste [338.13] *Saint John, that ... least reliable of the gospels*: cf. Conybeare: "This fourth Gospel enshrines, no doubt, many noble thoughts, but is, on the whole, frigid, insincere, and full of exaggerations. We may safely neglect it in any attempt to get back to the earliest traditions of Jesus" (*MMM* 20).

457 diese Szene im Garten Eden [338.26] *Eden*: unidentified.

Wie sagt doch der Prediger Salomo [338.33] *Ecclesiastes? [...] women have sought out many inventions*: "And I find more bitter than death the woman, whose heart is snares and nets, and her hands as bands: whoso pleaseth God shall escape from her; but the sinner shall be taken by her. [...] Lo, this only have I found, that God hath made man upright; but they have sought out many inventions" (Eccles. 7:26, 29), where "they" refers to "man" (or mankind in general) and not, as Valentine alters it, to women. The first part of this passage is quoted with approval in the misogynistic *Malleus Maleficarum* (47).

462 **Onward Christian Soldiers** [342.14]: famous hymn (1864), words by Sabine Baring-Gould (1834–1924); *PH* 3399.

II.2

463 **Denn dieser ist wie ein Trunkener** [343.epigraph] This is as if [...] *Recognitions,* Book V: from chap. 4, "Ignorance of Evils," which begins: "From all these things, therefore, it is concluded that all evil springs from ignorance; and ignorance herself, the mother of all evils, is sprung from carelessness and sloth, and is nourished, and increased, and rooted in the senses of men by negligence; and if any one teach that she is to be put to flight, she is with difficulty and indignantly torn away, as from an ancient and hereditary abode. And therefore we must labor for a little, that we may search out the presumption of ignorance, and cut them off by means of knowledge, especially in those who are preoccupied with some erroneous opinions, by means of which ignorance is the more firmly rooted in them, as under the appearance of a certain kind of knowledge; for nothing is worse than for one to believe that he knows what he is ignorant of, and to maintain that to be true which is false. This is as if a drunk man [...]" (continues as quoted in epigraph).

464 **Geistermann Saint Louis** [344.23] Saint Louis: Louis IX, king of France 1226–70, a member of the Sixth Crusade (1248–54); source of anecdote unknown; cf. 346.27.

469 **Reverend Gilbert Sullivan** [348.12]: from the British comic opera partnership Gilbert and Sullivan. Wyatt will adopt this name in the next chapter.

472 **Das Lesbennest** [350.17] *Wild Gousse Chase*: in his review for the *Saturday Review* (12 March 1955) Maxwell Geismar said *R*'s plot was reminiscent of Rex Warner's novel *Wild Goose Chase* (1937), but Jack Green insists it does not resemble it in the least (33). *Gousse* is French slang for a lesbian: "dyke"; see 188.28 ff for a synopsis of Max's novel.

Stoff, über den nicht schon [...] geschrieben wurde [350.19] What hasn't been written before?: Minkoff (250 n.10) finds a parallel in Mephistopheles's words after meeting with the newly graduated Baccalaureus: "Who can think anything, obtuse or wise, / That ages was not an ancient story" (6809–10).

472 Mit Worten läßt sich trefflich streiten [350.27] Let me give you some advice: Minkoff again (250) hears an echo of the advice given by Mephistopheles to the student in the first part of *Faust* (1990–96):

> In sum – have words to lean upon,
> And through that trusty gateway, lexicon,
> You pass into the shrine of certainty.
> STUDENT: Yet with each word there must a concept be.
> MEPHISTOPHELES: Oh, quite – no need, though, to be racking
> One's brain, for just where concept's lacking
> A word in time supplies the remedy.

474 Menander s.S. 13 [351.36]: see 7.40.

475 Ennius [352.30]: Quintus Ennius (239–169? B.C.), Roman poet; only fragments of his work are extant. (Vergil has often been charged with plagiarism.)

Chrysippus [352.30]: Greek Stoic philosopher of the third century B.C. The anecdote is recorded in *LEP 7*, where the play is identified as *Medea*.

[353.10] **diary of dead souls**: compound literary allusion to Russian author Nikolay Gogol's (1809–52) story "Diary of a Madman" and his novel *Dead Souls*.

[354.8] **All the world loves …**: a sentiment derived from Emerson's "All mankind love a lover" (*ODQ*).

478 Lex Cornelia [354.33]: a series of laws established by the Roman dictator Sulla in the first century B.C., which restored to the Senate its former power and laid the foundations of Roman criminal law.

[359.5] **supralapsarian**: one who holds the Calvinist doctrine that God's plan of salvation for some preceded the fall of man from grace, which had been predestined. (Infralapsarians believe salvation followed – and was a result of – the fall.)

487 Brown, dein Töchter waren alle schön s.S. 376 [360.43] your daughters all were fair: see 273.32.

488 Wenn gelten soll: x hoch n plus y hoch n [361.20] The equation of x […] Fermat's last theorem: Pierre de Fermat (1601–65), French mathematician, called the founder of the modern theory of numbers. There is a short article in *EB* entitled "Fermat's Last Theorem" (9:173–74), but Gaddis seems to be quoting a different source.

Den Heiligen Petrus aber bitte umgedreht [362.3] Saint Peter, upside-down: "Jerome saith that he was crucified, his head being down and his feet upward, himself so requiring, because he was (he said) unworthy to be crucified after the same form and manner as the Lord was" (*BM* 4).

489 **Old Crucifer** [362.12] crucifer: the cross-bearer in a religious procession.

[363.19] Caligula: see 383.9.

492 **Greshams Gesetz** [364.6] Gresham's law: the tendency of money of lower intrinsic value to circulate more freely than money of higher intrinsic and equal face value (e. g., a paper dollar circulates more freely than a silver dollar), after English financier Sir Thomas Gresham (d. 1579), though first formulated by Copernicus.

494 **die Heilige Agatha vom Kreuz** [365.41] the saint [...] Agatha of the Cross: "Agatha of the Cross (1547–1621), a Spanish Dominicaness, for the last eight years of her life did not sleep at all" (*PPM* 63). Agatha, however, was never canonized.

495 **Cuff** [366.16]: from an old "witticism": When a woman was suspected of having dyed hair, it was wondered if "collars and cuffs" matched.

über den Seligen Dodo von Hascha [366.25] Blessed Dodo of Hascha: "Little is known of this Beato, but it is chronicled that at his death in 1231, it was discovered that his hands, feet, and side, were marked with the Five Sacred Wounds" (*PPM* 185).

496 **Vulgär?** [...] **Lateinisch vulgus: die Leute** [367.10] vulgar means, people: from Latin *vulgus*.

497 **Selige Didée** [367.36] Blessed Didée: Summers only says of this beato the "pus [...] of the Blessed Didée gave forth a strong scent of Madonna lilies" (*PPM* 175).

Seliger Bartolo von San Gimignano [367.36] Blessed Bartolo of San Gimignano: from Summers (*PPM* 175):

Blessed Bartolo of San Gimignano, who lived about 1300, when fifty-two years old, was attacked with leprosy in its most virulent form. The holy man, "the Job of Tuscany" as he was called, literally rotted to pieces with the inroads of the horrible disease. And yet there was no contagion. Moreover a most heavenly perfume exhaled from his poor body, the *odor del paradiso* as the Italian phrase goes. When he died his little hermitage became radiant with light, and the air laden with the fragrance of beds of violets.

Doktor Biggs von Lima Peru [367.39] Doctor Biggs of Lima Peru: dismissing various scientific investigations into stigmatization (and especially its relation to self-induced hypnosis), Summers says: "Of no account and not worth detailing are the experiments of Dr. Biggs of Lima as reported in the S[ociety for]. P[sychical]. R[esearch]. *Journal*, May, 1887" (*PPM* 121).

Die Heilige Rose von Lima [368.2] Saint Rose of Lima: Peruvian recluse (1586–1617) who subjected herself to severe penances but had many mystical experiences as a reward; cf. 550.36. Summers reproduces an old portrait of Saint Rose in *PPM* (facing 161).

497 Don Diego Jacinto Paceco [368.2]: Summers (*PPM* 19) contrasts the insubstantial ghosts of antiquity with

the glorious vision of St. Rose of Lima, when she appeared to Diego Jacinto Paceco [*sic* – should be Pacheco], a copyist who earned his livelihood by engrossing legal documents, but who was seized with agonizing writer's cramp so that his right-hand and whole arm were paralysed. Starvation, or the most abject beggary, seemed his fate. But there entered his room a Dominican nun, who smilingly sat down at his bedside, took the arm in her hands and stroked it gently. There was a spasm of pain, and the arm and hand were perfectly cured, and remained so until the day of his death. He was, in fact, able to write more clearly and with greater speed than ever before. This was not many years after Saint Rose's death, and seeing her portrait he at once recognized his visitant.

Mozart? [...] **Sinfonie Nummer siebenunddreißig. Vulgo vierviervier. s. S. 112** [368.8] Mozart [...] Four four four: see **81.23**.

[369.19] **something new under this sun:** Ecclesiastes insists there's nothing new under the sun (1.9).

501 Damals Persephone, heute Proserpina s. S. 134 [370.30] Persephone [...] Proserpina: Proserpina is the Roman equivalent of the Greek Persephone, for whom see 98.6–16.

502 In Arethusa [371.30] "In Arethusa [...] corn being put into their ...": "In Arethusa [in Greece], several were ripped open, and corn being put into their bellies, swine were brought to feed therein, which, in devouring the grain, likewise devoured the entrails of the martyrs" writes Foxe of Christian persecution under Julian the Apostate in the year 363 (*BM* 35).

nach der Geißelung [371.32] "scourged [...] his body torn with ...": "Romanus, a native of Palestine, was deacon of the church of Caesarea at the time of the commencement of Diocletian's persecution. Being condemned for his faith at Antioch, he was scourged, put to the rack, his body torn with hooks, his flesh cut with knives, his face scarified, his teeth beaten from their sockets, and his hair plucked up by the roots. Soon after he was ordered to be strangled, November 17, A.D. 303" (*BM* 27).

Martha Constantine [371.32]: from *BM* 109, under the heading "An Account of the Persecutions in the Valleys of Piedmont, in the Seventeenth Century":

Martha Constantine, a handsome young woman, was treated with great indecency and cruelty by several of the troops, who first ravished, and then killed her by cutting off her breasts. These they fried, and set before some of their comrades, who ate them without knowing what they were. When they had done eating, the others told them what they had made a meal of, in consequence of which a quarrel ensued, swords were drawn, and a battle took place. Several were killed in the fray, the greater part of whom were those concerned in the horrid massacre of the woman, and who had practiced such an inhuman deception on their companions.

502 **mit Beuteln voller Schießpulver behängt** [371.38] the guy they tie little bags of gunpowder: "Peter Gabriola, a Protestant gentleman of considerable eminence, being seized by a troop of soldiers, and refusing to renounce his religion, they hung a great number of little bags of gunpowder about his body, and then setting fire to them, blew him up" (*BM* 114 – "Further Persecutions in the Valleys of Piedmont, in the Seventeenth Century").

503 **Martin Luther einmal beinahe von einem Blitz erschlagen** [372.15] Martin Luther was struck by lightning: "Walking out into the fields one day, he was struck by lightning so as to fall to the ground, while a companion was killed by his side; and this affected him so sensibly, that, without communicating his purpose to any of his friends, he withdrew himself from the world, and retired into the order of the hermits of St. Augustine" (*BM* 159).

Heilige Katharina von Racconigi [372.21] Blessed Catherine de Racconigi: documenting those who "endured the Wound of the left shoulder caused by the weight of the Cross and the friction of the wood when Our Lord carried His Rood on the way to Calvary," Summers instances "the Dominicaness, Blessed Catherine de Racconigi, one of whose shoulders was so notably lower than the other thereafter that she seemed hunchbacked" (*PPM* 172). See also 634.16.

Jedes Wort wird einfach nur rückwärts ausgesprochen [372.31] Spelled backwards [...] profaning the Eucharist: traditional elements of the Black Mass. Valentine paraphrases Michelet's *S&W* (102, 106):

The *Black Mass*, in its primary aspect, would seem to be this redemption of Eve from the curse Christianity had laid upon her. At the Witches' Sabbath woman fulfills every office. She is priest, and altar, and consecrated host, whereof all the people communicate. [...] By her prostrate body and humiliated person, by the vast silken net of her hair, draggled in the dust, she (that proud Proserpine) offered up herself as a sacrifice. On her loins a demon performed Mass, pronounced the *Credo*, deposited the offertory of the faithful.

Michelet speculates the Eucharist used in a Black Mass consisted of the same *confarreatio* used as a love potion. The witch would oblige a female customer thus: "On her loins she lays a board, and on it a miniature oven, in which she bakes the magic cake.... 'Sweet friend, I can bear no more. Quick, quick, I cannot stay like this!' 'Nay, madam, [...] 'twill be heated of your very body, the hot flame of your passion!'" (97).

504 **Willie** [372.41]: William Gaddis, who makes a few cameo appearances in the novel.

504 Die *Recognitiones* [373.1] The *Recognitions*: though traditionally ascribed to Clement of Rome, the original author of this "theological romance" is unknown; it probably came to be attributed to Clement as a result of confounding the first-century pope and martyr (see 23.25) with Flavius Clement, a kinsman of the Roman emperor Domitian. Others have attributed it to Bardesanes. Internal evidence suggests the first quarter of the third century as a date of composition.

Gaddis may have first learned of the Clementine *Recognitions* from Graves, who writes: "According to the Clementines, whose religious theory is popularized in a novel called *The Recognitions,* the identity of true religion in all ages depends on a series of incarnations of the Wisdom of God, of which Adam was the first and Jesus the last." He adds in a note: "Voltaire modelled his *Candide* on it; and it has the distinction of appearing in the select list of books in Milton's *Areopagitica,* along with John Skelton's *Poems,* as deserving of permanent suppression" (*WG* 132 and note; but Milton's reference is to the books of Clement of *Alexandria* – see next annotation).

Frazer and Lethaby also refer to the novel, as does James, who gives this convenient summary (*ANT* xxiv-xxv):

The setting is derived from secular romance; it is the ancient theme of the members of a family parted from one another by a series of accidents for many years, and in the end reunited: in this case it is Clement's family. His parents, his brothers, and himself are brought together by the agency of St. Peter. This setting is filled in, and indeed completely overlaid, by the matter which conveys the real purpose of the book, namely, the discourses of Peter; partly his debates with Simon Magus, and partly his unopposed expositions of doctrine. ["Mostly talk, talk, talk," as Valentine correctly observes.]

The body of the doctrine thus set forth is not orthodox. It is, in fact, eccentric. At one time it was contended that these books were precious monuments of a condition of the Church in primitive times, when the Twelve were in opposition to Paul; it being doubtless the case that Simon Magus in these books is to some extent Paul under a mask. But it is now recognized that the books are not only rather late in date (not earlier than the end of the third or beginning of the fourth century), but also that they do not represent the views of a large school of thought, but of a small and obscure sect.

The Greek form of the romance consists of twenty so-called Homilies – the Clementine *Homilies.* The Latin is a version of another form, expurgated and translated by Rufinus in the fourth century. It is in ten books, and is called the Clementine *Recognitions.*

An English translation by the Reverend Thomas Smith appeared in 1906 in vol. 8 of *The Ante-Nicene Fathers,* ed. Alexander Roberts and James Donaldson (New York: Scribner's).

Clemens *Romanus* [373.1] Clement of *Rome*: as opposed to Clement of *Alexandria* (fl. 150–217), head of the catechetical school of Alexandria and author of numerous works (see 315.35).

504 **daß er schließlich nach Ägypten aufbricht** [373.3] he goes to Egypt: in 1.5 Clement announces his intention to go to Egypt to "cultivate the friendship of the hierophants or prophets, who preside at the shrines. Then I shall win over a magician by money, and entreat him, by what they call the necromantic art, to bring me a soul from the infernal regions, as if I were desirous of consulting it about some business. But this shall be my consultation, whether the soul be immortal." But shortly thereafter he hears of Christ and abandons his plans for Egypt.

der Ursprung der Faustlegende [373.5] beginning of the whole Faust legend: Clement's father is named Faustinianus, and Clement has a set of young twin brothers named Faustinus and Faustus (9.5). But it is Clement's initial assumption that the magicians of Egypt (rather than God) can lead him to salvation and his plan to summon "a soul from the infernal regions" that anticipate Faust's pact with Mephistopheles and thus originates the Faust legend.

[373.25] "suck": sycophant (used thus in Joyce's *Portrait* in a similar Jesuit setting).

505 *Oft grüble ich über deine* s. S. 343 [373.42] *Much I ponder*: see 255.28.

[374.5] Sie kocht schlecht: Ger: "She cooks badly."

El pudridero [374.13] pudridero [...] Charles the Second: king of Spain 1665–1700; died childless. "The deformed and retarded 'Charles the Bewitched' was a notorious example of Hapsburg inbreeding" (Rodger Cunningham).

506 **der sechste Himmel** s. S. 346 [374.19] the sixth heaven all enclosed [...] the seventh, of shining light: see note on "the seven heavens of the Arabs" (257.32).

[374.28] We are all in the dumps [...] built without walls: an anonymous children's rhyme; #322 in *The Annotated Mother Goose*.

Allegro ma non troppo [374.33]: "Lively, but not too fast": a musical indication of tempo.

Martha Constantine s. S. 502 [374.37]: see 371.32.

507 **Transdanubien** [375.5] Transdanubia: a region of Hungary.

am Grund des Sees [375.14] bottom of a tank: the residence of the Frog King (see 273.14); "tank" is an Anglo-Indian term for "lake," which Gaddis would have come across in Ackerley's *Hindoo Holiday* (see 733.epigraph).

König der Trolle [375.15] troll king [...] fine and brave": in act 2, scene 6 of Ibsen's drama *Peer Gynt* (1867), Peer visits the mountain domain of the troll king to ask for his daughter's hand. The king insists Peer must first become like a troll and gives him a tail and a special drink. But Peer's human nature persists:

> THE OLD MAN [troll king]: My son-in-law, now, is as pliant as any;
>   he's willingly thrown off his Christian-man's garb,
>   he's willingly drunk from our chalice of mead,
>   he's willingly tied on the tail to his back, –
>   so willing, in short, did we find him in all things,
>   I thought to myself the old Adam, for certain,
>   had for good and all been kicked out of doors;
>   but lo! in two shakes he's atop again!
>   Ay ay, my son, we must treat you, I see,
>   to cure this pestilent human nature.
> PEER: What will you do?
> THE OLD MAN: In your left eye, first,
>   I'll scratch you a bit, till you see awry;
>   but all that you see will seem fine and brave.

(Trans. William and Charles Archer; see Gaddis's own gloss at 545.27.)

507 **I min Tro** [375.31] "I min Tro [...] Solveig: Solveig is a young woman who leaves her family to join the fugitive Peer, then patiently waits for him (and, more importantly, believes in him) while he is off on his adventures. When he finally returns at the end of the play, Peer asks: "Where was I, as myself, as the whole man, the true man? / Where was I, with God's sigil upon my brow?" and Solveig answers: "In my faith, in my hope, and in my love" (the translators give the Norwegian original, quoted by Wyatt, in a footnote). Valentine later mocks this line (551.8).

Zeno [375.36]: founder of the Stoic school of philosophy (fl. late fourth-early third centuries B.C.). *LEP* 7 records the anecdote but says he broke a toe, not a finger.

508 **Cleanthes** [376.21]: Greek Stoic philosopher of the third century B.C.; he succeeded Zeno as the head of the Stoic school. His last words are recorded in *LEP*.

509 **Kardinal Richelieu wurde noch auf dem Sterbebett s. S. 66** [376.44] Cardinal Richelieu [...] on his death bed: see 46.36.

mit dem Urin treuer Ehegattinen kuriert [377.2] in Egypt [...] We treated sore eyes with the urine of a faithful wife: "The early Egyptian physicians made considerable use of drugs. [...] It is said that the urine of a faithful wife was with them effective in the treatment of sore eyes. The tale concerning the difficulty in obtaining this remedy (or the ineffectiveness of its cures) has come down with variations through folk tales" (*DDD* 336).

510 **Mara** [377.25]: in Hindu mythology, the god of temptation who tries to turn Buddha away from his path. In a famous myth, the daughters of

Mara – Lust, Delight, and Pining – tried in vain to entice Buddha out from under the Bodhi-tree.

510 **bevor der Buddhismus zum Götzendienst verkam** [377.26] That was before Buddhism was corrupted by idolatry: commenting on the eventual concretization of the Hindu trinity, Saltus writes: "Female counterparts were found for them, and the most poetic of the creeds of man was lowered in a sensuous idolatry" (*AN* 8). Cf. 497.30 and note.

Varé tava soskei s. S. 343 [377.30]: see 255.24.

diese Stierfigur, die das Ei auf die Hörner nimmt? [377.32] gold bull busting an egg [...] to give birth to the earth: from *AMM* (264–65), quoting/translating from Eugène Marie Dognée's *Les Symboles Antiques, l'Œuf* (1865):
"In Japan, in the Pagoda of Miaco," he says, "upon a large square altar is placed a bull of massive gold on a block of rock; the animal is ornamented by a rich collar, and pushes with its horns an egg floating in the water contained in a cavity of the rock. To explain this image, the following is told by the Priests. At the time of chaos, before the creation, the world was concealed and inert in an egg which floated on the surface of the waters.... The divine bull image of creative force broke the egg by a stroke of its horns, and from the egg issued the terrestrial globe."

511 **Religion ist die Verzweiflung an der Magie s. S. 19** [377.44] Before death came into the world [...] religion is the despair of magic: see 11.44–12.1.

[378.1] **Night and Chaos**: "The story of Leda and the parallel one of Latona are but distorted cosmic myths and Night and Chaos, from which is formed the egg mundane" (*AMM* 266).

Religion ist die Mutter der Sünde [378.3] Religion is the mother of sin. [...] That's Lucretius: in the first book of *De Rerum Natura* (On the Nature of Things), the Roman poet and philosopher Lucretius (d. 54 B.C.) speaks of the evils committed in the name of religion. Gaddis found the line in Saltus: "To those who objected that in devastating the skies [of gods] a high-road was opened to crime, Lucretius, pointing to the holocausts, the hecatombs and the sacrifices, answered, 'It is religion that is the mother of sin.'
"'Religio peperit scelerosa atque impia facta.'"
(*AN* 62). The Latin is quoted at 392.37.

Greifeneier [378.5] griffin's egg [...] a clear liquid: Wyatt runs together several quotations from Lethaby: "The 'Griffin's egg' was a common ornament in our own mediæval churches" (*AMM* 257); "[The Christians of Egypt] 'consider them [ostrich eggs] the emblems of watchfulness: sometimes they use them with a different view; the rope of their lamps is passed through an ostrich egg shell in order to prevent rats coming down and drinking the oil, as we were assured by the monks of Dayr Antonios'" (265, quoting from Sir J. F. Wilkinson's *Many Bones of Egypt viz: A Popular Account of the Ancient Egyptians* [1854]); "The 'Griffin's eggs' were not necessarily ostrich eggs; in one instance they are described as having a brown and hairy exterior, the inside white, with a clear liquid yelk [*sic*]. We can buy them now for four-pence, as cocoa-nuts" (258).

511 *Die Geschichte der fränkischen Könige Childerich und Clodovech* [378.14]: History of the Frankish Kings Childeric and Clovis, an 1857 study by W. Junghans, cited in the bibliography to *EB*'s article on Clovis, the source for the anecdote that follows.

Am Weihnachtstag des Jahres vierhundertsechsundneunzig [378.15] Christmas day [...] His wife converted him: "The legend runs that, in the thickest of the fight, Clovis swore that he would be converted to the God of Clotilda if her God would grant him the victory. After subduing a part of the Alamanni, Clovis went to Reims, where he was baptized by St. Remigius on Christmas day 496, together with 3,000 Franks. The story of the phial of holy oil (the *Sainte Ampoule*) brought from heaven by a white dove for the baptism of Clovis was invented by archbishop Hincmar of Reims three centuries after the event" (*EB* 5:856).

die Stoiker hatten die Sonne als [...] intelligenten Himmelskörper betrachtet [378.21] even the Stoics believed the sun was animated and intelligent: the Stoic Zeno (375.36) held this belief (*LEP* 7).

Pilgrim Hymnal [378.26] *Pilgrim Hymnal.* [...] wilt not despise": from the conclusion of "A Prayer for Forgiveness and Renewal," "Responsive Readings" no. 618 (adapted from Psalm 51), *PH* 71:
Deliver me from bloodguiltiness, O God, thou God of my salvation:
   And my tongue shall sing aloud of thy righteousness.
O Lord, open thou my lips;
   And my mouth shall show forth thy praise.
For thou desirest not sacrifice; else would I give it:
   Thou delightest not in burnt offering.
The sacrifices of God are a broken spirit:
   A broken and a contrite heart, O God, thou wilt not despise.
The boldface lines (printed thus in *PH*) are the congregation's responses; note that Wyatt confuses the fifth line for a response.

512 **Mother Shipton** [379.5]: fictitious English prophetess said to have lived during the reign of Henry VIII and to have made a number of extraordinary predictions. Her life and prophecies are recounted in *EPD* 267–69.

513 **Yetzer Hara, das böse Herz** [379.21] Yetzer hara, the evil heart: a kind of evil angel that, according to Jewish legend, attends every person.

513 **Novalis** [379.41] Novalis [...] appealed to all the most dangerous parts of me: Novalis was the pen name of Friedrich von Hardenburg (1772–1801), German poet and novelist, the leading poet of early German Romanticism. *LWW* singles out Novalis as the chief advocate of blending death with love; romanticism is dangerous, then, insofar as it caters to the death instinct.

514 **in der ganzen griechischen Literatur keine einzige Szene** [380.27] no scene in all Greek literature [...] our Christian culture: apparently the reference is to the death of Socrates (379.23) as reported in Plato's *Phaedo*.

515 **The Stars and Stripes Forever** [380.35] *The Stars and Stripes Forever* [...] *Thunder and Lightning Polka*: the first is a famous Sousa march, the second a popular instrumental by Johann Strauss, Jr.

Juan de Valdés Leal s. S. 1133 [381.5]: (1630–91), Spanish painter and engraver; mentioned again at 873.21.

516 **Zeno** [382.6] Zeno wouldn't have [...] add anything to infinity: Zeno and the Stoics believed "time is incorporeal, being the measure of the world's motion. And time past and time future are infinite, but time present is finite" (*LEP* 7; trans. R. D. Hicks, Loeb Classical Library [1925], 2:245).

homo- oder homoi s. S. 16 [382.11] homo- or homoi-: see 9.30 ff.

517 **Wer gewinnt? Jesus oder die Schildkröte?** [382.11] who wins? Christ or the tortoise?: from Zeno's famous parable about the infinite subdivisibility of time, featuring Achilles and a tortoise (see *EB* 23:945). The paradox is that Achilles can never overtake the tortoise in a race.

O mein süßes Gold! [382.12] O my sweet gold!: from Marlowe's *Doctor Faustus*: see 425.13.

Gettato a mare s. S. 62 [382.17] "gettato a mare" [...] and martyred: the legendary martyrdom of Saint Clement (see 44.3–6).

Vielleicht sind wir ja nur Fang für außerirdische Wesen s. S. 119 [382.19] maybe we're fished for: see 87.8.

Averroes [382.29]: the Latin name of ibn-Rushd (1126–98), Spanish Arab philosopher and physician. His Neoplatonic view of Aristotle gave rise to several doctrines that were formally anathematized in 1270.

Glauben wir, um zu begreifen? [382.30] believe in order to understand? [...] Saint Anselm, Credo ut intelligam: for Saint Anselm (see 103.34); "the starting-point of all theological speculation must be faith, *Credo ut intelligam*. 'He who does not believe will not experience, and he who has not experienced will not understand.' And once confirmed in faith it is our duty to demonstrate by reason the truth of that which we believe" (*EB* 2:11). Wyatt's attribution of this line to Averroes is repeated by Anselm later (458.28–30); apparently Averroes and Saint Anselm borrowed (plagiarized?) from the same source, for in Saint Augustine's *On the Gospel of Saint John* we read: "Understanding is the reward of faith. Therefore seek not to understand that thou mayest believe, but believe that thou mayest understand." Saint Anselm's formulation appears in his famous *Proslogion,* which is again quoted at 535.6ff.

517 **O Fleisch, Fleisch, wie bist du verfischt worden** [382.35] flesh, how thou art fishified: from Shakespeare's *Romeo and Juliet*; see 392.22.

Auf diesen Felsen will ich bauen meine Gemeinde [382.37] On this rock, remember? and I shall make thee a fisher of men: Jesus is reported to have punned: "Thou art Peter, and upon this rock I will build my church" (Matt. 16:18); earlier he had told Peter and his brother Andrew: "Follow me, and I will make you fishers of men" (4:9). Conybeare questions the authenticity of this invitation (*MMM* 29).

Nach Philippi. Meine erste Mission [382.40] with Paul, to Philippi: Acts 16:9–40 relates how Paul, inspired by a vision, travels to Philippi (in Macedonia), where he and his comrades are imprisoned. Their prayers and singing at night cause an earthquake to destroy the prison, after which the Roman authorities ask them to leave. The episode has been called "patently unhistorical."

518 **Ish Kerioth** [382.43] Ish Kerioth bought a cemetery with his ... thirty pieces: in Matthew 27, Judas Iscariot (Hebrew Ish Kerioth: "the man of Kerioth") hangs himself; the chief priests thereupon take his silver and buy a field "to bury strangers in." But in Acts 1:18, Judas himself buys "a field with the reward of iniquity; and falling headlong, he burst asunder in the midst, and all his bowels gushed out." In their *Nazarene Gospel Restored,* Robert Graves and Joshua Podro (they who found Paul's adventure "patently unhistorical") find Matthew's account the more "historically acceptable," the Acts version being indebted to the apocryphal *Book of Ahikar.*

[383.8] **Nothing can be given, which cannot also be withheld:** cf. "Nothing is a gift unless it might also be withheld from us" – the dedication in Corneille's play *La Place royale,* which de Rougemont quotes (*LWW* 174).

wenn sie nur einen einzigen Hals hätten [383.9] if they had but one neck: according to Roman historian Suetonius, the emperor Caligula once prayed: "Would that the Roman people had but one neck!" (*ODQ*).

Shabbetai Zebi s.S. 736 [383.10]: see 545.40ff.

518 **Dominis ac Redemptor** [383.12] Dominis ac Redemptor [...] Clement the fourteenth: from *EB*'s article on the Jesuits (13:13):

On July 21, 1773, appeared the Brief of Suppression, *Dominus ac Redemptor Noster*. This Brief (not a Bull) is narrative rather than judicial in tone. Clement XIV. cited certain past difficulties of the Society and enumerated present complaints against it, notably charges of political and mercantile activities and the hostility of the Bourbon Courts and of Portugal. The Pope thus concluded the Brief: "For the sake of peace, and because the Society can no longer attain the aims for which it was founded, and on secret grounds which we enclose in our heart, we suppress the said Society."

The order was revived in 1814.

die Kirche muß strafen [383.16] the Church must punish, to prove it has the power to punish: a Spanish priest in Borrow's *Bible of Spain* justifies his church's persecution of sorcery: "The Church has power, Don Jorge, or at least, it had power, to punish for anything, real or unreal; and as it was necessary to punish in order to prove it had the power of punishing, of what consequence, whether it punished for sorcery or any other crime?" (165).

519 **Die Schwalbe singt bis zum Martinstag** [383.29] Lent! Martin's? Martins?: the martin is a kind of swallow that appears (in England) about Lent and disappears about Martinmas (11 November). Cf. 392.29.

doch vorher hegst und pflegst du sie gewiß zu Tod [383.29] you killed him with much cherishing?: Juliet wishes Romeo were her pet bird but fears: "Yet I should kill thee with much cherishing" (2.2.184). Cf. 392.29.

Ici Castel Gandolfo [383.41]: Fr.: "Gandolfo Castle here" (the pope's summer residence).

Ein Mister Inononu s. S. 859 ff. [383.41] Mister Inononu: see 647 ff.

die vierzig Tage sind fast abgelaufen [383.42] forty days: Christ's temptation by the devil took place during his forty-day sojourn in the desert (cf. 431.28–30).

Der antimonische Triumphwagen [384.3] *The Triumphal Car of Antimony* [...] anathema to monks: Jung refers to the book under this title (*IP* 211), but Gaddis's source for the anecdote appears to be Haggard (*DDD* 349):

Paracelsus had used antimony under the name of stibium, but later the name was changed and the drug popularized by a medical book published in 1604 and entitled *The Triumphant Chariot of Antimony*. The author's name was given as Basile Valentine, a monk, but it is doubtful if such a person existed, and it is believed that an alchemist wrote the book. The origin of the name antimony as given in this book is as follows: The author alleges that he had observed that some pigs which had eaten food containing antimony became very fat. He was led by this observation to try what effect it would have on some monks who had become emaciated as a result of prolonged fasting. He tried the experiment; the monks all died. Hence the name stibium was replaced by antimony, meaning antagonist to monks.

519 **Am-ha-aretz** [384.16]: a Hebrew phrase meaning "one from the land" and used pejoratively by the Pharisees of Jesus' time for an ignorant or sinful man, a man living outside the Law.

[384.17] as the composer predicted, there's nothing left but knowledge and evidence: source unknown.

520 **daß Petrus eines natürlichen Todes gestorben ist s. S. 488** [384.20] Peter died an old man, and right side up: cf. 362.3.

Maria erst mit einem römischen Soldaten namens Panthera fremdgegangen [384.20] Mary [...] Panthera [...] his son: commenting on the lack of historical evidence for the existence of Jesus, Saltus notes (*AN* 67):

An early legend has, however, been handed down from Celsus, a Jew who lived about the time of Hadrian. The work containing this legend has been lost, and is known only through fragments which Origen has preserved [in his *Contra Celsum*: see 420.12]. In substance it amounts to this. A beautiful young woman lived with her mother in a neglected caphar. This young woman, whose name was Mirjam – Mary – supported herself by needlework. She became betrothed to a carpenter, broke her vows in favor of a soldier named Panthera, and wandering away gave birth to a male child called Jeschu, – Jeschu being a contraction of the Hebrew Jehoshua, of which Jesus is the Greek form.

der ganze Gottesglaube ruht auf einem äußerst wackligen Fundament [384.25] the whole thing hangs on a resurrection that only one lunatic saw [...] visions are contagious: "On the experience of Cephas [Peter], then, the entire history of the resurrection hinges," writes Conybeare (*MMM* 289), who cites Paul's version as the earliest account: "And that he was buried, and that he rose again the third day according to the scriptures: And that he was seen of Cephas, then of the twelve: After that, he was seen above five hundred brethren at once" (1 Cor. 15:4–6, quoted in *MMM* 288). Conybeare explains:

In the earliest form of gospel tradition Peter is the leader and spokesman of Jesus's followers; if he was once convinced that Jesus had been raised from the dead and had appeared to him, he was sure to suggestionise the rest of the twelve companions into seeing visions like his own; they in turn would be capable of suggestionising the much larger number specified by Paul, of whom many were yet alive when the letter to the Corinthians was written. In the history of religious enthusiasm we find nothing so contagious as visions. (*MMM* 288)

Conybeare describes the psychological state Peter had reached by the time of Christ's crucifixion – a state in which hallucinations might occur – but Wyatt's description of Peter as a "lunatic" is perhaps going too far. See *MMM* 289–93 for the development of the resurrection legend by way of the Gospels' conflicting accounts.

520 **Auf jedem Marktplatz standen irgendwelche Messiahs** [384.28] the streets were full of messiahs spreading discontent: cf. Conybeare: "It need hardly be observed that, if Pilate was really convinced of Jesus's innocence, he could have released him at once. But Jesus's admission before him that he was King of the Jews or Messiah, in a period when the Roman Government was perpetually menaced by such pretenders, left no alternative but to condemn him" (*MMM* 280).

daß Jesus in einem Massengrab für gewöhnliche Kriminelle gelandet ist [384.31] Christ was thrown into a pit for common malefactors: finding the Gospels' account of Christ's burial unacceptable, the French priest and scholar "Abbé Loisy suggests that Jesus was more probably thrown into the common pit reserved for crucified malefactors, and that the episode of his burial by Joseph [of Arimathea in Luke 23:50–53] was invented by his followers at a later day to save him from the reproach of a dishonourable interment" (*MMM* 297).

daß nicht die Macht den Menschen korrumpiert [384.32] not that power corrupts men, but men corrupt power: George Bernard Shaw somewhere writes: "Power does not corrupt men; but fools, if they get into a position of power, corrupt power."

grabe mit einem Stichel von Messing in eine glänzende Kupferplatte: I A O, I A E s. S. 186 [384.38] write with a brass pencil on a clean tin plate, I A O, I A E: see 139.1.

Earl of Atholl [384.40] Atholl's coronation: the earl of Atholl claimed the Scottish throne at the death of James I in 1437 but was instead tortured to death with a red-hot iron crown (*M&R* 203).

von den Ägyptern, die alle Rothaarigen verbrannten [384.41] Egyptians burned red-haired men: "With regard to the ancient Egyptians we have it on the authority of Manetho that they used to burn red-haired men and scatter their ashes with winnowing fans, and it is highly significant that this barbarous sacrifice was offered by the kings at the grave of Osiris. We may conjecture that the victims represented Osiris himself, who was annually slain, dismembered, and buried in their persons that he might quicken the seed in the earth" (*GB* 378). Lang disagrees with Frazer's interpretation (*M&R* 128).

Fliesen in der Kirche der Heiligen Sophia [384.42] Justinian's pavement [...] Saint Sophia fell in: "In the church [of Saint Sophia], as finished by Justinian, 'the varied hues of the pavement were like the ocean,' This was destroyed when the roof fell in" (*AMM* 202, quoting Codinus).

520 **Sohn des Herrschers von Kairo** [384.44] son of the ruler of Cairo [...] lake of quicksilver: also from Lethaby: "One of the rulers of Cairo, the son of Ibn-Tulun, who succeeded him in 883, seems to have set himself to rival the garden of delights in a 'paradise.' [...] 'But the chief wonder [...] was a lake of quicksilver; on the surface of this lake lay a feather bed inflated with air, fastened by silk bands to four silver supports at the corners; here alone the insomnolent sovereign could take his rest" (*AMM* 104, quoting Lane-Poole's *Art of the Saracens*).

521 **Erzähl ihnen von Antiope und dem Satyr, von Parsiphae und dem Stier** [385.1] Antiope and the goat, of Pasiphaë and the bull, and the egg that Leda laid: cf. Ortega y Gasset: "The romantics of every period have been excited by those scenes of violation, in which the natural and infrahuman assaults the white form of woman, and they have depicted Leda and the swan, Pasiphae and the bull, Antiope and the goat" (*RM* 88).

der mehr vermöchte, als ich vermag s. S. 436 [385.26] I became the one who could do more than I could: cf. Michelangelo's poem at the bottom of 322.

522 **Meg van [...] holnap reggel** [385.43]: Hungarian: "I have the necessary information, the papers are here. Eh ... ? not now, call tomorrow morning ..."

seit Fabius den Herkules von Lysippus [386.21] Hercules of Lysippus that Fabius brought back: the anecdote is related in *GAF* (19) in illustration of the early Romans' ignorance of art. Lysippus was a Greek sculptor of Sicyon (fourth century B.C.) credited with developing a new system of bodily proportions.

S P Q R & Co. [386.23] S P Q R: *Senatus Populusque Romanus* (Lat: "the Roman Senate and People"), initials inscribed on Roman standards.

523 **eine Weisheit, die Wotan einst an seinen Sohn weitergab** s. S. 736 f. [387.3] the secret that Wotan taught to his son: see 552.3–5.

524 **vergleichbar dem festen Firmament bei den frühen Juden** [387.21] solid firmament of early Jews where stars were nailed lest they fall: from Lethaby, quoting *Smith's Bible Dictionary*: "'The word translated [in the Old Testament] firmament is the Hebrew word *rakia*. [...] A secondary purpose of the *rakia* was to support the heavenly bodies – sun, moon, and stars – in which they were fixed as nails, and from which, consequently, they might be said to drop off'" (*AMM* 28).

sieben Tauben auf der ständigen Flucht vor Orion [387.22] the flight of the seven doves Orion hunts: "One myth concerning the Pleiades relates that they were so beautiful in appearance that Orion unceasingly pursued them, much to their discomfiture. They appealed to Jupiter for assistance and he pitying them changed them into doves. Thereupon they flew into the sky and found a refuge among the stars" (*SL* 419).

524 der Felsen, den Alexander in Indien erklomm [387.31] the cliff that Alexander climbed in India: Lethaby (*AMM* 112–13) thus summarizes a portion of the medieval *Romance of Alexander* by Pseudo-Callisthenes:

In India, Alexander and his army came to two paths, eastward and north; they try eastward, but it is impassable, and they go back and attempt the other to the north, by which at last they reach a cliff covered with diamonds, with hanging chains of red gold. Two thousand five hundred steps there were, which they ascend, and reach the clouds and "wait for wonders." They see "a palais, one of the precioussest and proudest in earth, and built, as the book says, with two broad gates and seventy windows, of gold, carven, and clustered with gems."

There was a temple surrounded by a garden of golden vines full of great fruit of carbuncle stones; it was the "house of the sun" and paradise. Alexander enters, and on a gorgeous bed he finds a god, who asks him if he would have his future known by inquiry of the trees of the sun and moon; on his consenting, they approach two enormous trees, that of the moon was silver; the tree of the sun was gold, and on its crest sat "a proud bird." "All gilded was her gorge with golden feathers." "Yon is a fearless fowl, a Fenix we call." It is predicted that Alexander will never return.

Sir John Mandeville [387.34] Sir John Mandeville [...] *Travels*: purporting to be a travel guide to the Holy Lands and the Orient, this popular medieval book is actually a collection of imaginative legends and superstitions. Although the author claims to be an Englishman from Saint Albans, "Sir John Mandeville" was a physician of Liège named Jehan de Bourgogne who wrote the book in 1356–57. The English version is a translation from the French made sometime before 1500. Combining a vivid imagination with genuine travel accounts, the author collected many of the legends of Prester John (see 408.14ff.). The quoted remark about Paradise is from chap. 33, as quoted by Lethaby (*AMM* 113, immediately following the Alexander episode quoted above).

525 Verirrte Seelen in der Welt der Nacht [388.3] Through the world of night [...] corridors dark and dangerous: a condensation of an extract from Gaston Maspero's *Egyptian Archaeology* (1887), as quoted by Lethaby (*AMM* 169–70):

"During the day the pure soul was in no serious danger, but in the evening, when the eternal waters which flow along the vaulted heavens fall in vast cascades adown the west and are engulphed in the bowels of the earth, the soul follows the escort of the sun and the other luminary gods into the lower world bristling with ambuscades and perils. For twelve hours the divine squadron defiles through long and gloomy corridors, where numerous genii, some hostile, some friendly, now struggle to bar the way, and now to aid it in surmounting the difficulties of the journey. Great doors, each guarded by a gigantic serpent, were stationed at intervals, and led to an immense hall full of flame and fire, peopled by hideous monsters and executioners, whose office it was to torture the damned. Then came more dark and narrow passages, more blind gropings in the gloom, more strife with malevolent genii, and again the welcoming of the propitious gods. At midnight began the upward journey towards the eastern region of the world; and in the morning, having reached the confines of the Land of Darkness, the sun emerged from the east to light another day." "The tombs of the kings were constructed upon the model of the world of night. They had their passages, their doors, their vaulted halls, which plunged down into the depths of the mountain."

525 **das Totenbuch umklammert s.S.70** [388.3] lost souls clutching their guidebooks: "the guide-book for the dead was laid in the coffin, telling them of all the turnings, and of all the *ruses* of the wicked spirits who would entice them away from the one true path" (*AMM* 172). Earlier (157) Lethaby identified the guidebook as the *Book of the Dead* (see 49.13).

Gruft tief unter der Erde [388.5] so the king built his tomb deep in earth [...] So Egypt: "The Tomb of Seti I. penetrates 470 feet and is 180 feet deep in the earth; another has some 24,000 square feet taken up by the passages, halls, staircases, pits, and chambers of the tomb" (*AMM* 171).

Abendrot [...] Morgenrot [388.9] Red in the west [...] roses of Eden: *AMM* 110; see 53.14.

Sonne, Mond und Sterne durch eine Schleuse im Osten [388.15] sun and the moon [...] through a subterranean passage: "The general early view, however, was that there were two openings – the Gates of the East, and the Gates of the West. Through the one the sun enters in the morning the mundane temple, to pass out at the other in the evening, and thence pursue its way back by the dark path of the under world" (*AMM* 174).

Gefangen am Firmament, wüten die Himmelskörper [388.19] Raging up and down the sky [...] exit only at opposite ends: "In the Talmud an exactly similar account [to that of the Persian *Bundahish*] is given. The sun rages up and down the eastern and western horizon like a mighty beast prisoned in a cage; it cannot go farther because of the enclosing sides of the firmament. The gates for it to pass to the lower world and rise again are only found in the ends of the box" (*AMM* 66–67).

hinab in die Unterwelt stieg Tammuz [388.25] Down: down went Tammuz (slain by the boar's tusk) [...] to the lower world: "In Babylon also it was at the world's centre that Tammuz made his descent, for here is the lid stone of the lower world" (*AMM* 78). The parenthetical remark is from *AMM* 160–61: "'One of the most popular of old Babylonian myths,' says Professor Sayce, 'told how Istar had wedded the young and beautiful sun-god Tammuz, and had descended into Hades in search of him when he had been slain by the boar's tusk of winter.'"

525 Piute-Indianer [388.33] the Piute Indians followed the sun [...] distended with stars: also from Lethaby (*AMM* 165):

> Mr A[ndrew] Lang quotes, in his "Myth and Ritual," an account given by the Piute Indians: "Down, deep under the ground, deep, deep, under all the ground, is a great hole. At night, when he has passed over the world, looking down on everything, and finished his work, he, the sun, goes into his hole, and he crawls and creeps along it till he comes to his bed in the middle part of the earth. So then he, the sun, stops there in his bed all night. This hole is so little, and he, the sun, is so big, that he cannot turn round in it; and so he must, when he has had all his sleep, pass on through, and in the morning we see him come out in the east. When he, the sun, has so come out, he begins to hunt up through the sky to catch and eat any he can of the stars, his children, for if he does not so catch and eat he cannot live. He, the sun, is not all seen. The shape of him is like a snake or lizard. It is not his head that we can see, but his belly, filled up with the stars that times and times he has swallowed."

526 Mag der Stier des Glücks, der Genius des günstigen Geschicks [388.41] May the bull of good fortune [...] Never more may its care cease: verbatim from *AMM* 192, quoting Lenormant.

Esar-Haddon [388.44] Esar-Haddon [...] refurbish its gods: Esar-Haddon ruled 681–669 B.C.; the details of his reign seem to be from *EB*'s article on him (8:700).

Baal hat Seinen Tempel betreten [389.4] Thrown open [...] His Temple: from Lethaby's dramatic reconstruction of what the morning ritual of sunrise might have been like in ancient Assyria (*AMM* 200):

> It is the moment of sunrise, chill and expectant; all the gates are thrown open to the east. The worshippers are waiting, and the golden tips of the obelisks are already burning. The sun shows its red rim through the open ceremonial gate of the outer court. They prostrate themselves.
> There is a sudden awaking sense of heat and life and light, a passing vibration in the air. The little bells festooned from pillar to pillar shiver out silver notes; a deep strain vibrates from the sanctuary. They stand on their feet. The great gates of the temple close with a clangour that reverberates like thunder.
> Baal has entered into his temple.

II.3

527 An diesem Baum hat man den Jüngling aufgehängt [...] *Die spanische Tragödie* [390.epigraph] It was a man [...] *The Spanish Tragedy*: Thomas Kyd's (1558–94) popular Elizabethan play was first produced sometime between 1584 and 1589. In the second act, Hieronimo's son Horatio is slain by his beloved's brother and the prince of Portugal. His body is left hanging in the arbor where his father sees it (he is mad at this point and has trouble at first recognizing the corpse as his son's), utters the quoted lines, and vows revenge. The quotation (2.5.85–88) is from a passage that, among others, was added to the play at a later date by an unknown hand.

527 der Wetterhahn [390.1] weathercock [...] cock of fire rising from its own ashes: the mythical bird the phoenix was said to live five hundred years, at which time it would beat its wings until a fire started. From the ashes a new phoenix would emerge – there was only one in the world at a time – and repeat the cycle. (See 700.3 for more details.) "We may remark here," says Lethaby, "that the weathercocks on every church are gilded birds that greet the sun" (*AMM* 186).

Die Gnade aber des Herrn [390.10] The Lord's mercy [...] unto those that fear him: Ps. 103:17.

[390.14] O God be-neath Thy guid-ing hand [...] crossed the sea: the opening verses of *PH* #347, words by Leonard Bacon (1833), music by John Hatton (1793).

[391.20] Mirabile dictu: Lat.: "wonderful to tell," a common exclamation.

[391.23] God of our Fa-thers [...] hymn no 383: words by Rudyard Kipling (his famous "Recessional"), music by John H. Gower (1903).

529 Adeste – ad esse fidelis [391.31]: "Adeste Fideles" ("O Come All Ye Faithful," *PH* #105) and *ad bene esse,* an ecclesiastical phrase meaning "for the well-being of."

[391.31] hymn no 223 [...] Oh for a Faith that Will Not Shrink: words by William H. Bathurst (1831), music by John B. Dykes (1875).

A,M,D,G s. S. 532 [391.32]: see 393.38, 40.

infra dig dominocus [391.32]: "infra dig" is a common abbreviation for *infra dignitatem* (Lat.: "beneath [one's] dignity); "dominocus" is apparently a variant (or pun?) of *dominicus* (Lat: "lord's, master's"), yielding "beneath the Lord's dignity."

Die Staubteilchen in einem Sonnenstrahl [391.33] Demons the motes in a sunbea[m], said Blessed Reichelm: "Abbot Richalm explains how evil spirits are everywhere: 'they swarm like motes in the sunbeam; they are scattered all over like particles of dust; they shower down on the world like drops of pelting rain; their numbers fill and crowd out the whole world; the very air we breathe is infected thick with devils'" (Montague Summers, *Witchcraft and Black Magic* [1946]; but Gaddis's spelling Reichelm indicates a different source). Blessed Richalm (d. 1219) was abbot of Schönthal in the Neckar Valley; the quoted remarks are from his *Liber de insidiis dæmonum.* (The current edition of *R* has "sunbean," a typo lingering from the first edition.)

[391.35] Saxons driven through a river: see 56.1.

529 **Blessed Leo X., could nicht anders** [391.36] Blessed Leo X, could nicht anders, the 95 Thæces stuck to the door: Pope Leo X issued the bull excommunicating Luther in 1520; the ninety-five theses Luther nailed to the church door in Wittenburg on 31 October 1517 questioned the value of indulgences and the methods by which they were sold. "Ich kann nicht anders" (I cannot do otherwise) is from Luther's speech at the Diet of Worms (18 April 1521) and is inscribed on his monument there (*ODQ*).

in the beginning this end [391.37]: cf. "In my beginning is my end," the first line of Eliot's "East Coker."

annus mirabilis [391.38]: Lat.: "wondrous year."

infra supra [391.39] infra supra sub: Lat. prepositions "below, above, under."

seit er das Dintenfaß nach dem Leibhaftigen geschleudert [391.40] threw the inkpot: Luther reputedly threw his inkpot at a devil that was tormenting him: see *AN* 102.

führt uns garantiert nicht in Versuchung [391.43] leadeth us not into temptation: from the Lord's Prayer: Matt. 6:13.

Abscondam faciem meam s. S. 71 [392.1] Abscondam faciem meam [...] et considerabo novissima eorum: "I will hide my face from them, I will see what their end shall be"; see 50.16.

frag die schöne Helena [392.3] ask Helen for a piece, she found it: that is, a piece of the True Cross, allegedly found by Saint Helen (ca. 250–ca. 330), mother of Constantine the Great (next line). See *EPD* 696 for an account.

Dann gut rubbeln vor Gebrauch [392.4] rub it, Aladdin: the magic lamp of popular Arabian legend; cf. *AMM* 269ff.

Konstantin [392.4] **Constantine**: probably the emperor Constantine, upon whose conversion Catholicism became the official religion of the Roman Empire. Dante chastises Constantine for allowing wealth to taint the church (*Inferno* 19:109–11).

[392.4] Nicodemus: see 338.12–16.

Geburt einer Nation [392.6] birth of a nation: title of a D. W. Griffith film on the Civil War and the rise of the Ku Klux Klan.

530 **Hyperduliacs** [392.19] hyperduliacs: those who pay special homage to the Virgin Mary.

das stinkende falsche Vlies [392.20] wear a stinking merkin for a beard: Brownson explains: "from a scurrilous poem formerly attributed to John Wilmot,

Earl of Rochester, but actually written by John Oldham, entitled 'To the Author of a Play called Sodom.' Nine lines suffice to give the context of the line in question:

Sure Nature made, or meant to 'ave don't,
Thy tongue a Clitoris, thy mouth a Cunt;
How well a Dildoe wou'd that Place become,
To gag it up, and make't for ever dumb?
At least it should be syring'd Womb
Or wear some stinking Merkin for a Beard,
That all from its base converse might be scar'd,
As they a door shut up, and mark't, Beware,
That tells infection and the Plague is there.

Because a 'merkin' is counterfeit pubic hair for a woman, used to hide the effects of syphilis, the line fits into Gaddis' theme of falsification; also, the poem itself has been the subject of disputes for years, as both it and the play it attacks were attributed to Rochester" (67).

530 Frau bleibt Frau [392.20] she is only a woman (but a good cigar is a smoke): forced to choose between cigar-smoking and his fiancée, the narrator of Rudyard Kipling's poem "The Betrothed" ponders:

Open the old cigar-box – let me consider anew –
Old friends, and who is Maggie that I should abandon *you*?
A million surplus Maggies are willing to bear the yoke;
And a woman is only a woman, but a good cigar is a Smoke.

(The final line is quoted in *ODQ*.)

ist schon Eva dran hängengeblieben [392.21] Eve caught by the furbelow, Hae cunni (the oldest catch we know): "The line referred to I think was a catch (or glee) of Purcell's: 'Adam caught Eve by the fur below / And that's the oldest catch we know" – WG quoted in *The Oxter English Dictionary* by George Stone Saussy III (New York: Facts on File Publications, 1984), 103–4. "Hae cunni" is "apparently bad Latin for 'these cunts'" (Brownson 68).

Dido ein Trutschel, Cleopatra eine Zigeunerin [392.22] Dido a dowdy [...] Thisbe's gray eye: Mercutio greets Romeo thus: "Without his roe, like a dried herring. Oh, flesh, flesh how art thou fishified! Now he for the numbers that Petrarch flowed in. Laura to his lady was but a kitchen-wench – marry, she had a better love to berhyme her – Dido, a dowdy; Cleopatra, a gypsy; Helen and Hero, hildings and harlots; Thisbe, a gray eye or so, but not to the purpose" (*Romeo and Juliet* 2.4.39–45).

praebeat ille nates [392.23]: Lat: "let that one offer his rump" (Brownson 68); source unknown.

180

530 (allem Anschein nach ein nützliche Tätigkeit) s.S. 112 [392.23] (I seem to mean usefulness): Fort's definition of prostitution (see 81.16).

Alfonso Liguori s.S. 35 [392.24] Alfonso Liguori – There is no mysticism without Mary: see 23.35.

[392.25] **shrouded in the decent obscurity of a learned language**: in his *Autobiography*, Edward Gibbon (author of *The Decline and Fall of the Roman Empire*) writes: "My English text is chaste, and all licentious passages are left in the decent obscurity of a learned language" (*ODQ*).

[392.25] **Stabat Mater [...] dolorosa**: see 338.11.

fœmina si [...] puerque [392.26]: Lat.: "if a woman – and a man and a boy – will do the wicked deed for me" (Brownson 69); perhaps from the same source as "praebeat ille nates" above.

[392.27] **Origenal sin**: a pun on original sin and Origen's method for dealing with it (see 103.3 ff.).

[392.27] **Carnelevarium**: a day of abstentation from meat, etymologically related to "carnival" (see 428.2).

das Herz kommt erst später dran s.S. 113 u. 517 [392.28] (the heart came out very late): from the process of mummification; see 84.28 and cf. 382.22–25.

Polymastie [392.28] polymastia: Lat. "many-breasted."

Zwei Brüste wohnen, ach! in meiner Seele [392.29]: "Two breasts reside, alas! in my soul," a reversal of Faust's complaint that

Two souls, alas, are dwelling in my breast
And either would be severed from its brother;
The one holds fast with joyous earthly lust
Onto the world of man with organs clinging;
The other soars impassioned from the dust,
To realms of lofty forebears winging. (ll. 1112–17)

[392.29] **Martinmas, Saint Martin's [...] Lent**: cf. 383.29. Martinmas (Saint Martin's Day) is 11 November; Lent is the forty days from Ash Wednesday to Easter. Saint Martin of Tours lived in the fourth century.

Pelagia [392.30]: "There is no man in the world who studies so hard to please the good God as even an ordinary woman studies by her vanities to please men," lament the authors of *MM*. "An example of this is to be found in the life of Pelagia, a worldly woman who was wont to go about Antioch tired [*sic*] and adorned most extravagantly. A holy father, named Nonnus, saw her and began to weep, saying to his companions, that never in all his life had he used such diligence to please God; and much more he added to this effect, which is preserved in his orations" (*MM* 46–47). Translator Summers provides the following gloss:

> "Pelagia meretrix" or "Pelagia mima," a beautiful actress who led the life of a prostitute at Antioch. She was converted by the holy bishop Nonnus, and disguised as a man went on pilgrimage to Jerusalem, where for many years she led a life of extreme mortification and penance in a grotto on the Mount of Olives. This "bienheureuse pécheresse" attained to such heights of sanctity that she was canonized, and in the East, where her cult was long very popular, her festival is kept on 8 October, which is also the day of her commemoration in the Roman Martyrology.

530 **Mary of Egypt** [392.30]: see 826.41–44 and note.

Thaïs [392.31]: Saint Thaïs of Alexandria (d. ca. 348), like Saints Pelagia and Mary of Egypt, was an actress and courtesan (the two professions were often synonymous) before converting and becoming a penitent; her story is the subject of a novel by Anatole France and an opera by Jules Massenet.

Kundry [392.31]: in Arthurian legend, a female counterpart to the Wandering Jew. She seduced Grail knights for Klingsor until finally redeemed by Parsifal (see von Eschenbach, Wagner).

Salome [392.31]: the daughter of Herod who shed her veils for the head of Saint John the Baptist (see Wilde, Strauss).

Heilige Irene [392.31] Saint Irene: Foxe relates the martyrdom of Irene and her two sisters under Diocletian in A.D. 304. She was first "exposed naked in the streets" (or, in other accounts, forced into a brothel) before being burned to death (*BM* 28).

Costanza [392.31]: "may refer to Flavia Julia Constantina, daughter of Constantine the Great by his second wife, Fausta. Cruel and ambitious, she played a powerful part in the complicated politics of her day" (Brownson 70–71).

Ds ac Redemptor, S.J. [392.32]: see 383.12.

Valeria Messalina [392.32] Valeria Messalina [...] in the gardens of Lucullus hic jaceted age 26 years: "Valeria Messalina, third wife of the emperor Claudius, possessed a character similar to Costanza's. She was executed for her crimes in the gardens of Lucullus – her own property, gained through evil trickery – at the age of 26. Hence, hic jacet – 'here lies'" (Brownson 71).

Marozia [392.32]: "yet another powerful woman. She lived in the tenth century, and replaced Pope John X with her son, Pope John XI" (Brownson 71).

530 der schwarze Mann der Fallsüchtigen Janet [392.34] Thrawn Janet's [...] garden wall: "Thrawn Janet" (1881) is a short story by Robert Louis Stevenson concerning Satanic possession in eighteenth-century Scotland, written in the Scots vernacular. A loose woman of the town named Janet M'Clour is saved by the town's new minister from a harrowing experience, apparently only to die that night. Her body is then inhabited by "the black man" (the devil) and in that condition she becomes the minister's house servant, the only noticeable difference being her "thrawn" (twisted) neck. The minister eventually discovers the ruse and calls upon the help of heaven, which obligingly kills the possessed woman with a thunderbolt. The next morning the black man is seen leaving town, never to return again.

et ardet [392.35]: Saltus notes that during the Middle Ages "bishops received orders to visit personally or by delegate any portion of their diocese in which they suspected that heretics might lurk. When this decretal was made, the Inquisition was established. 'Et ardet' [Burn them], said the pseudo St. John; and those two words were sufficient to send over half-a-million of human beings to the stake" (*AN* 98–99).

Anaxagoras [392.35]: (500–428 B.C.), Greek philosopher, teacher of Pericles, Thucydides, Euripides, and possibly Socrates. Though he made Athens the center of philosophic inquiry, he was banished from the city for questioning the state religion.

in contemptu Christianae fidei [392.35]: the Codex Theodosianus (A.D. 438) made any act *in contemptu Christianæ fidei* ("in contempt of the Christian religion") a punishable offense (*M&R* 154).

Lukrez [392.36] Lucretius [...] impia facta: see 378.3–4 for the Latin phrase. Saint Jerome records the legend (followed in Tennyson's *Lucretius*) that he committed suicide in a fit of madness induced by a love potion administered by his wife.

Exhomologesis (c. 218) nach Papst Calixtus I. [392.37] exhomologesis (c. 218) by Calixtus I: in his discussion of baptism Conybeare notes that the first Christians held "the belief that mortal sin, committed after baptism, could no longer be expatiated," then continues:

Such puritanism was too much for human frailty. The baptised, in spite of it, must often have relapsed into idolatry, homicide, fornication, and other sins; and nearly as often have repented. Something had to be done in order to reclaim them and restore them to the Church. Rome, as always, made the change – in this case most necessary, if the Church was to continue to exist. Pope Calixtus, therefore, invented about A.D. 218, a rite of *Exhomologesis* – *i.e.*, of outright confession – which is yet to be found in some old service-books; *e.g.*, in those of the Armenian Church. It was a repetition of the rite of baptism, of which all the formalities were repeated except the use of water. But this "medicine of repentance," as the rubrics which still exist prescribe, could be used only once. If the Christian relapsed a second time, then he was really lost. Old-fashioned believers, like Tertullian and Hippolytus, railed against this innovation, which yet later generations found insufficient. Re-admission but once was not enough for sinners, and it was found necessary to permit it a second and third and fourth time; and finally it became the existing sacrament of penitence, which is inspired by the very convenient and roomy doctrine that, no matter how often and how wilfully a man sins, he can always, by confession and penance, expiate his guilt and be reconciled to the Church.

(*MMM* 320, 321–22.) "Exhomolojesuis" below brings in the Jesuits, who made confession easier still (attacked in Pascal's *Provincial Letters*).

[392.38] Pelagic: of/on the sea, but cf. 57.43, 553.17, 806.14, and Saint Pelagia, above.

531 **Berberaffen werfen bereits mit Steinen auf den Y.M.C.A.** s. S. 1103 [392.39] Rock, resident Barbary apes pelt stones at the local Y.M.C.A.: see 848.33–37.

Hinkebein Ignatius von Loyola [392.40] Ignatius' militant limp: the result of being wounded at the siege of Pampeluna in 1521.

Inquisitor De Arbues [392.41]: Saint Peter de Arbues (1442–85), inquisitor of Aragon. "De Arbues is reported to have been eminently successful in inventing methods of torture which inflicted the keenest agony on the victim without a wound or even breaking the skin" (*MMSM* 62 n).

ex hac Petri cathedrâ [392.42]: Lat.: "from this chair of Peter," formula used for papal proclamations (the phrase occurs in Marsh: *MMSM* 282).

[392.42] Welt: capitalized, Ger.: "world."

Amor perfectissimus [392.42]: Lat.: "most perfect love," a phrase used by the alchemist Morienus to describe the proper attitude of the alchemist to his work (*IP* 219).

definiert das Dunkle anhand des Dunkleren [392.43] explaining what is dark by what is darker still: "Slowly, in the course of the eighteenth century," Jung writes, "alchemy wasted away through its own obscurity. It tried to explain everything on the principle of: *obscurum per obscurius, ignotum per ignotius* (what is dark by what is darker still, what is unknown by what is still more unknown); and this principle agreed very badly with the spirit of enlightenment and especially with the dawning of chemistry as a science towards the end of the century" (*IP* 205).

Wo war denn da der Edelmann? [392.43] Who then was the gentleman?: in his discussion of the movement toward social equality in the Middle Ages,

Huizinga writes: "In quoting the text of John Ball, who preached the revolt of 1381, 'When Adam delved and Eve span, who was then the gentleman?' one is inclined to fancy that the nobles must have trembled on hearing it. But, in fact, it was the nobility themselves who for a long time had been repeating this ancient theme" (*WMA* 53).

531 (Ich meine den Ausgeschlossenen.) s. S. 112 [392.44] (I mean the excluded): see 81.14

Philo, De Exsecrationibus [392.44]: Philo Judaeus was a contemporary of Jesus and is often quoted by Conybeare; he explains (*MMM* 40–43) that *De Exsecrationibus* (About the Curses)

is a testimony [...] written, it would seem, not before A.D. 35 and not after A.D. 42 by a Jew of Alexandria deeply versed in old Greek philosophy and literature, and so Hellenised that he could not understand his own tongue. [...] In Palestine he sees realised in all their dreadful intensity the curses proclaimed in Deut. xxviii. against those who break the statutes and law of Jehovah. [...] His only hope was in a supernatural liberator, descending from heaven and rescuing from their oppressors the chosen race of Israel. But Israel must first repent and fulfil all righteousness – that is, discharge faithfully all the works of the law; in particular, keep the sabbaths holy and observe the rule of circumcision. Then, and not before, will the heavenly Messiah appear and establish on earth the kingdom of David.

Aristobulus [393.1] Aristobulus [...] plagiarized from Moses: describing the efforts made by some Hellenized Jews of Alexandria to gloss over "not a few of the worst anthropomorphic traits of Jahveh," Conybeare gives this instance (*MMM* 331):

As early as 150 B.C. an Alexandrine Jew, named Aristobulus, issued for Gentile reading a commentary on the Pentateuch, in which he at once sought to prove that the Greek philosophers, Pythagoras, Socrates, and Plato, even Homer and Hesiod, had plagiarised the best of their wisdom from Moses, and also explained away such passages as attributed to the Jewish God hands and arms, face and feet, and represented him as coming down and walking about in the Garden of Eden.

Pues díme Sigismundo, dí: [...] haber nacido [393.3]: from Calderón's play *La Vida es sueño* (see 820.37): "So tell me, Sigismundo, speak: Man's greatest sin is to have been born."

No, no don't listen to them 1870 [393.5] No, no [...] 1870! Nono the winner: infallible [...] Arkansas, crying Non Placet: at the Vatican Council of 1869–70 the dogma of papal infallibility was proclaimed by Pope Pius IX (Pio Nono in Italian). At the final ballot, two votes had remained *non placet* ("it displeases" – a nay vote): those of an Italian bishop from Naples and Bishop Edward Fitzgerald of Little Rock, Arkansas. Both bishops submitted immediately after the definition passed.

The pun "No, no" recalls that in Samuel Butler's *The Way of All Flesh* (a novel Gaddis has said he admires):

The Pope's action in the matter of the Sicilian revolution naturally led the Doctor to the reforms which his Holiness had introduced into his dominions, and he laughed consumedly over the joke which had not long since appeared in *Punch*, to the effect that Pio "No, No," should rather have been named Pio "Yes, Yes," because, as the Doctor explained, he granted everything his subjects asked for. Anything like a pun went straight to Dr. Skinner's heart.

(Chap. 28; see 393.38 below for another reference to the same page of Butler's novel.)

[393.11] **disdain simple ruses**: from Esme's letter (see bottom of p. 471): "Since paintings are in the service of my desires, I can disdain no ruse to accomplish them."

531 **Gebt mir Energie und Materie** [393.12] Give me force and matter, and I will refurbish the world! Blame Descartes, then!: Saltus praises Descartes as one of "a handful of thinkers" free of the "mental stagnation" of the seventeenth century: "'Give me force and matter,' he cried, 'and I will refurbish the world.' Force and matter were not forthcoming, but in that magnificent boast was the accouchement of modern thought" (*AN* 108).

532 **Der Doktor Aeskulap war so blitzgescheit** [393.25] Æsculapius [...] lightningstruck: see 46.24–26.

Senta zieht sich mit sabinisch erfülltem Lächeln zurück [393.28] Senta retires with Sabine smile of satiety, Thankyou ma'am: the heroine of Wagner's *Flying Dutchman* (see 551.3 ff.); the women of the Sabine tribe were abducted by Romans needing wives; "Thankyou ma'am" is from the coarse description of casual sex: "Wham, bam, thank you ma'am."

E ucciso [...] Son la Diva! [393.29]: from *Tosca*, act 2; after stabbing Scarpia (see 92.23), Tosca gloats:

Ti soffoca il sangue?	Is your blood choking you?
E ucciso da una donna!	And killed by a woman?
M'hai assai torturata?	Did you torment me enough?
Odi tu ancora? Parla!	Can you still hear me? Speak!
Guardami! Son Tosca! O Scarpia!	Look at me! I am Tosca! Oh Scarpia!
SCARPIA (*fa un ultimo sforzo, poi cade riverso*) Soccorso! Aiuto!	(*after a last effort, he falls back*) Help! Help!
TOSCA (*chinandosi verso Scarpia*) Ti soffoca il sangue?	(*bending over Scarpia*) Is your blood choking you?
Muori dannato! Muori! Muori! Muori!	Die accursed! Die! Die! Die!

La Diva ("The Goddess") is a name Scarpia applies to her in act 2.

Frarsch den Heiligen Bernhard [393.31] Saint Bernard about women [...] the hissing of serpents: quoted from *MM* 47.

(**fa un ultimo sforzo:**) **Soccorso!** [393.34]: from *Tosca* (see above).

532 Chrysippus. Cleanthes. Zeno. Pyrrho [393.35]: see 352.30, 376.21, 375.36, and 130.7, respectively.

[393.36] Hipparchia's courtship [...] Telephus and Crates: Hipparchia was a female Greek philosopher of the late fourth century B.C.; her "courtship" is described in *LEP* 6:

> She fell in love with the discourses and the life of Crates, and would not pay attention to any of her suitors, their wealth, their high birth or their beauty. But to her Crates was everything. She used even to threaten her parents she would make away with herself, unless she were given in marriage to him. Crates therefore was implored by her parents to dissuade the girl, and did all he could, and at last, failing to persuade her, got up, took off his clothes before her face and said, "This is the bridegroom, here are his possessions; make your choice accordingly; for you will be no helpmeet of mine, unless you share my pursuits."

Earlier, Crates is said to have been converted to the Cynic philosophy after "having once, in a certain tragedy, seen Telephus holding a date basket, and in a miserable plight in other respects" – the only reference to Telephus in *LEP*.

A,M,D,G, [393.38] A,M,D,G, [...] Ad Mariam Dei Genetricem: A.M.D.G. usually stands for *Ad Majorem Dei Gloriam* ("For the Greater Glory of God" – motto of the Jesuit order), but the Latin phrase here translates "To Mary Mother of God," and is apparently from Butler's *The Way of All Flesh* (chap. 28):

> Dr. Skinner had lately published a pamphlet upon this subject ["a reconciliation between the Churches of England and Rome"], which had shown great learning, and had attacked the Church of Rome in a way which did not promise much hope of reconciliation. He had grounded his attack upon the letters A.M.D.G., which he had seen outside a Roman Catholic chapel, and which of course stood for *Ad Mariam Dei Genetricem*. Could anything be more idolatrous?
> I am told, by the way, that I must have let my memory play me one of the tricks it often does play me, when I said the Doctor proposed *Ad Mariam Dei Genetricem* as the full harmonies, so to speak, which should be constructed upon the bass A.M.D.G., for that this is bad Latin, and that the doctor really harmonised the letters thus: *Ave Maria Dei Genetrix*. No doubt the doctor did what was right in the matter of Latinity – I have forgotten the little Latin I ever knew, and am not going to look the matter up, but I believe the doctor said *Ad Mariam Dei Genetricem*, and if so we may be sure that *Ad Mariam Dei Genetricem* is good enough Latin at any rate for ecclesiastical purposes.

Lao-tses 84jährige Gedanken-Schwangerschaft [393.39] (Lao-tse's 84–year gestation): or Lao Tzu (ca. 600–530 B.C.), Chinese philosopher, traditional author of the *Tao Te Ching*. Saltus writes (*AN* 29–30):

> The life of this early thinker has been as liberally interwoven with legends as that of the Buddha. The Orient seems to have had a mania for attributing the birth of reformers to immaculate conceptions; and one learns with the weariness that comes of a thrice-told tale, that the mother of Laou-tze, finding herself one day

alone, conceived suddenly through the vivifying influence of Nature. But though the conception was abrupt, the gestation was prolonged, lasting, it is said, eighty-four years; and when at last the miraculous child was born, his hair was white – whence his name, Laou-tze, the Aged Baby.

532 Unter dem brennenden Dornbusch [393.40] burning bush: the form Yahweh took to speak to Moses (Exod. 3:2).

dixIt, pinxIt [393.41]: traditional elements of Latin signatures, "written by" and "painted by," respectively.

Varé tava soskei [393.42]: see 255.24.

[393.42] Mermaid mahn stole my heart away: see 347.3.

(verso:) Ti soffoca il sangue? [393.44]: see 393.29 above.

Arsch Alexander VI. [394.4] Alexander VI [...] the rape of (Christian) girls: from Saltus's description of the corruption of the Renaissance papacy: "Of Alexander VI. [pope 1492–1503], the father and lover of Lucretia Borgia, little that is favorable can be said, except perhaps that he was the most magnificent ruffian that Rome had seen since the days when Nero, with a concave emerald for monocle, watched the rape of Christian girls" (*AN* 101).

Ah! è morto! [...] tutta Roma! [394.5]: after stabbing Scarpia, Tosca says: "Ah! he is dead! ... Now I forgive him! ... And it was before him that all Rome trembled!"

533 Jupiter [...] Baal [394.42]: "the names of the sun" (395.6); the many Old Testament references to sun worship in this chapter were no doubt developed from a concordance, and the present listing of solar deities may be based in part on the headnote to "sun" in *Cruden's Complete Concordance* (New York: Holt, Rinehart, 1930), 647:

The *sun* has been the object of worship and adoration to the greatest part of the people of the East. It is thought to be the sun that the Phenicians [*sic*] worshipped under the name *Baal*, the Moabites under the name of Chemosh, the Ammonites by that of Moloch, and the Israelites under the name of Baal and by *the king of the hosts of heaven*. They did not separate his worship from that of the moon, whom they called *Astarte*, and the *queen of heaven*.

jemand gefunden wird [...] der da tut, was dem Herrn, deinem Gott, mißfällt [395.9] man or woman [...] host of heaven: see Deut. 17:2–3, 5.

534 hebe auch nicht deine Augen auf gen Himmel [395.13] And lest thou [...] Lord thy God ...: "... hath divided unto all nations under the whole heaven" (Deut. 4:19).

536 Der christliche Tempel in Tyros [397.7] Christian temple at Tyre: from Lethaby (*AMM* 197):

The earliest Christian buildings naturally looked to the temple as a type, and it would appear from Eusebius, that even the toran found a place in the new structures. Describing the Church of Tyre, he says that a magnificent propylon was built, far off toward the sun-rising, to attract the passer-by; passing through the court and other gates, the entrance to the temple itself was reached, which also fronted the rising sun, and was covered with brass.

[398.9] the departing back: perhaps a reference to Moses being favored with a glimpse of Yahweh's backside (Exod. 33:23).

537 **Geh bring in Ooorooma!** [398.16] Ooorooma way? [...] Ballima way?: see 268.27 ff.

Krakatau und der gelbe Tag in Boston [398.16] Krakatao and the yellow day in Boston: see 60.43.

[398.17] Grand Climacteric: age sixty-three. Lethaby writes: "At three times seven – twenty-one – we become 'of age.' Three times twenty-one is the 'grand climacteric;' and seventy years is put as the time to die" (*AMM* 123, in a discussion of the sacred number seven [cf. 92.26]).

[398.17] Valerian: see 74.40 and cf. 405.6–10 and 421.18 ff.

Cave, cave [398.21] Cave, cave [...] dominus vulgus vult: a combination of two Latin phrases previously quoted: see 25.40 and 254.2.

Tyndale [398.26]: see 46.17.

[398.31] the vigilant conspiracy of inanimate things: cf. "The total depravity of inanimate things," attributed to E. M. Forster in *JR* (486).

538 **Im Obergeschoß blaute der Tag** s. S. 319 [399.1] another blue day: see 238.27.

O Phantom der Stabat mater [399.4] spectral stabat mater: see 338.11; Wyatt's "spectral" mother visited him on p. 20 (and cf. 52.4 ff.).

[399.16] skipping dancing and foretelling things to come all ye faithful: see 137.32–33 and 391.31.

[399.17] of thine own give we back to thee: from the hymn heard at 21.26–27.

539 **Welt der Formen und Gerüche** s. S. 353 [399.36] world of shapes and smells provided force and matter to touch a line without changing it: see 262.42, 393.12, and 138.38–39.

Reichtum und Fülle wird in ihrem Haus sein [399.40] The prosperity of the godly shall be an eyesore to the wicked: apparently a paraphrase of Ps. 112:10 using the diction of Psalm 73. The quotation that follows is Ps. 112:3.

GLORIA! schmettert der Händelsopran [400.1] *GLORIA!* sings Handel's soprano: unidentified: could be any number of works.

540 **Wie lieb ist mir der Mutter Bibel!** [400.27] "Ah, that dear old mother's Bible [...] *in the grave*: an unidentified temperance song.

[401.12] careful and troubled about many things [...] cumbered with much serving: from the description in Luke 10:38–42 of the active Martha, who is compared (to her disadvantage) to the contemplative Mary. Cf. *PPM* 28.

541 **Nymphe, schließ in dein Gebet all meine Sünden ein** [401.18] "Nymph in thy orisons, be all my sins remembered": *Hamlet* 3.1.97–98.

Tom Swift [401.19]: inventive hero of a series of boys' novels by Edward Stratemeyer (1862–1930).

klagen um die Tochter Jephthahs [401.36] daughter of Jephthah [...] bewailing her virginity: see Judg. 11.1–12:7. Graves says that in Wales in the 1850s "the hills of Fan Fach and South Barrule in Carmarthenshire were crowded with mourners for Llew Llaw on the first Sunday in August, their excuse being that they were 'going up to bewail Jephthah's daughter on the mountain!'" (*WG* 251).

542 **Manichäer** [402.28] Manichee: a follower of the dualistic Oriental religion of Manichaeism, which centers on the conflict between light/good and dark/evil. "The fundamental dogma of all Manichaean sects is that the soul is divine or angelic, and is *imprisoned* in created forms – in terrestrial matter, which is Night" (*LWW* 60; de Rougemont goes on to demonstrate the influence of Manichaeism on Christianity in general and on courtly love in particular).

543 **Prester John** [403.9]: see note to 408.14; Janet's rhyming riddle is Gaddis's own, he believes (WG/SM).

Maran-atha! [403.12]: the earliest Christians, Saltus notes, lived "in a state of constant expectation. Their watchword was *Maran atha*, The Lord cometh" (*AN* 73). See 1 Cor. 16:22.

Bin zwar nur ein Klumpen Erde [403.20] "I am but a lump of clay [...] caught its fragrance": source unknown.

544 **Stier** [403.31] bull: this bull, along with Wyatt's golden bull, reflects the symbolic importance of the bull to Mithraism. The Tauroctonous ("Bull-Slaying") Mithra is the most common subject of Mithraic art, for from the wound in the bull's side came all the plants and grains of the earth. "What," Graves notes, "for the early Church Councils, seemed the most diabolical and unpardonable heresy of all was the identification of the Hercules-Dionysus-Mithra bull, whose living flesh the Orphic ascetics tore and ate in their initiation ceremony, with Jesus Christ whose living flesh was symbolically torn and eaten in the Holy Communion" (*WG* 116).

[404.13] O pirate ships [...] of wicked gain!: unidentified.

545 Al-shira-al-jamânija s. S. 38 [404.35] Al-Shira-al-jamânija [...] Dog Star: see 27.19.

Tod oder Islam [404.36] death? or Islam: the choice offered Shabbetai Zebi (see 546.3).

Zarathustra [405.8] Zoroaster [...] Ahriman, and the hosts of evil: more properly Zarathustra, semi-legendary founder of the religion of the ancient Persians. Conybeare parallels his career with that of Jesus (*MMM* 177–78). See *EB* 23:988–89 for the conflict between Ormazd and Ahriman.

[405.31] hero came forth from the desert to call "the hesitating retinue of finer shades": in his introduction to Doughty's *Travels* (43.13), T. E. Lawrence (see 581.20) described the Arabs as follows: "They are a certain people, despising doubt, our modern crown of thorns. They do not understand our metaphysical difficulties, our self-questionings. They know only truth and untruth, belief and unbelief, without our hesitating retinue of finer shades" ([New York: Random House, 1947] 21–22). Lawrence repeated this passage in chap. 3 of his *Seven Pillars of Wisdom* (1926).

547 Lieder der Unschuld, Lieder der Erfahrung [406.7] Songs of innocence and experience: *Songs of Innocence* (1789) and *Songs of Experience* (1794) are two series of poems (subtitled *Showing the Two Contrary States of the Human Soul*) by English poet and artist William Blake (1757–1827).

Händels *Almira* [406.10] Pleasant and Unpleasant Thoughts in Handel's *Almira*: his first opera, libretto by F. C. Feustking, produced in 1705.

Er schaffte also die Rosse ab [406.13] he took away the horses [...] host of heaven: 2 Kings 23:11ff. describes King Josiah's sweeping religious reforms after discovering the forgotten "book of the covenant" (i.e., Deuteronomy). Cf. 418.35.

548 Rabbuni [406.42] Rabboni: a variant of *rabbi* (Heb.: "master"): Mary Magdalene thus addresses Jesus upon his resurrection (John 20:26).

Lappland zum Beispiel s. S. 44 [407.28] Lapland lay, waiting for the Gospel: see 30.18.

549 König Wenzeslaus [407.37] good King Wenceslaus [...] papal interdict [...] pale thin man in mean attire: see 32.20ff.; in March 1411 Pope Alexander V renewed his ban against Huss's preaching at Prague. Huss ignored the ban, and the pope laid the entire city of Prague under interdict (cf. 316.1–2). The interdict was later extended to all places that might give Huss shelter. (The Town Carpenter was first associated with Wenceslaus by Wyatt at 37.12, and will be again at 545.25–26.) Wenceslaus is called "the vacillating" in *EB* (23:512).

[408.14] from Ethiopia and the three Indies: the details both here and on 417 are from the article on Prester John in vol. 18 of *EB*, which the Town Carpenter has borrowed from Rev. Gwyon (420.14; 442.31). The relevant portion reads:

About 1165, a letter was circulated purporting to be addressed by Prester John to the [Byzantine] emperor Manuel. This letter, professing to come from "Presbyter Joannes, by the power and virtue of God and of the Lord Jesus Christ, Lord of Lords," claimed that he was the greatest monarch under heaven, as well as a devout Christian. The letter dealt at length with the wonders of his empire. It was his desire to visit the Holy Sepulchre with a great host, and to subdue the enemies of the Cross. Seventy-two kings, reigning over as many kingdoms, were his tributaries. His empire extended over the three Indies, including that Farther India where lay the body of St. Thomas, to the sun-rising, and back again down the slope to the ruins of Babylon and the tower of Babel. In war thirteen great crosses made of gold and jewels were carried in wagons before him as his standards, and each was followed by 10,000 knights and 100,000 footmen. There were no poor in his dominions, no thief or robber, no flatterer or miser, no dissensions, no lies, and no vices. His palace was built after the plan of that which St. Thomas erected for the Indian king Gondopharus. Before it was a marvellous mirror erected on a many-storeyed pedestal; in this speculum he could discern everything that went on throughout his dominions, and detect conspiracies. He was waited on by 7 kings at a time, by 60 dukes and 365 counts; 12 archbishops sat on his right hand, and 20 bishops on his left, besides the patriarch of St. Thomas's the protopote of the Sarmagantians (Samarcand?), and the archprotopope of Susa, where the royal residence was. Should it be asked why, with all this power and splendour, he calls himself merely "presbyter," this is because of his humility, and because it was not fitting for one whose chamberlain was a bishop and king, and whose chief cook was an abbot and king, to be called by such titles as these.

550 Startrampe für den Fesselballon [409.3] his balloon ascension stand: the juxtaposition of references to balloons and Prester John recalls the first stanza of Eliot's "Conversation Galante":

I observe: "Our sentimental friend the moon!
Or possibly (fantastic, I confess)
It may be Prester John's balloon
Or an old battered lantern hung aloft
To light poor travellers to their distress."
She then: "How you digress!"

552 Camelus bactrianus [409.44] camel [...] Bactrian: cf. 48.41–42. Hamlet, with whom Wyatt has much in common (indecision, ambivalence toward parents, feigned [?] madness; cf. Esme as Ophelia), also notices a cloud in the shape of a camel (3.2.393–94).

553 Aldebaran [410.23] Aldebaran [...] keeping watch on the Pleiades: the Arab name for the principal star of the constellation Taurus, meaning "'leader,' or the attendant or follower, *i.e.*, of the Pleiades" (*SL* 340).

Wir müssen alles radikal vereinfachen [411.9] We must simplify: the major theme of Thoreau's *Walden*, chap. 2 ("Where I Lived, and What I Lived For"); cf. 441.41.

554 **Johan Hus** [412.1] John Huss [...] seeking tangible evidence of Christ's presence instead of in His enduring word: quoted from *EB*'s summary of Huss's *De Omni Sanguine Christi Glorificato* (see 651.7).

555 **Denn dieser Tag ist ein Tag des Grimms** [412.15] That day is a day of wrath [...] saith the Lord: Zeph. 1:15; 1:17; 2:1; 2:11; 3:20 (final verse).

[412.39] a Figure Who brooked no nonsense, lurking, "ravin in tooth and claw": quoting from Harnack's *History of Dogma,* Conybeare finds that "in the history of Jahveh, as it is pictured in the Old Testament, and in nature, 'red in tooth and claw with ravine,' we have all shades of conduct, ranging from bare justice and resentment to arbitrary malice, from tenacious obstinacy to crass stupidity, but all alike falling short of real goodness" (*MMM* 330). Harnack/Conybeare/Gaddis quote Tennyson's *In Memoriam* (56:15).

556 **mochte sein Name auch noch so oft in zweiundsiebzig Buchstaben zerfieselt worden sein** [412.41] His seventy-two-letter masquerade in the Old: "The Name [of God secretly] taught in the Academies is likely to have been a complicated one of either 42 or 72 letters" (*WG* 240); cf. 499.16.

Haggai [412.41] Haggai anticipates Him shaking the earth [...] the nations: Hag. 2:6–7.

558 *Osservatore Romano* [414.22] *Osservatore Romano* [...] Cardinal Tedeschini [...] eloquent messages to the Vicar of Christ": at the thirty-fourth anniversary of the miracle of Fátima (see 917.1), "the big news about the Pope [Pius XII] was delivered by Cardinal Tedeschini who reported that the Pope himself had had the same kind of vision as the Portuguese children. He had looked directly into the sun and it was 'quivering with life, all movement, transmitting mute but eloquent messages to the Vicar of Christ'" ("A Million Faithful at Fátima," *Life,* 5 November 1951, 53; Gaddis is quoting from a similar article, as 917.1 ff. indicates, but I have not traced it or the *Osservatore Romano* original).

Scientific American [414.32] *Scientific American* for 11 April 1891 [...] worms of the grave": in an article entitled "Electroplating the Dead," M. Edant describes the efforts of French physician Dr. Variot to promote "the use of electro-metallurgic processes for obtaining indestructible mummies." The gruesome details of the process are accompanied by an equally gruesome engraving of a child's body undergoing electroplating. The article concludes: "The inventor of the process just described, however, accords to the total metallization of the body but slight importance. The object of his researches has been more especially to give the museums and laboratories of our faculties of medicine very faithful, very exact specimens, rather than to rescue our cadavers from the worms of the grave" (227).

[415.6] *Drink, drink!* [...] *Devil's Chain*: unidentified; "don't know the source but I believe the same temperance ditty as 404.13" (WG/SM).

559 Otium cum dignitate [415.29]: Lat.: "Leisure with dignity," Cicero's famous description of retirement (*ODQ* gives its more correct form: "cum dignitate otium").

560 Die Resurrektionisten [416.1] Resurrectionists [...] grave-robbers: Resurrectionists are members of the Congregation of the Resurrection, which began in 1842 as a Catholic lay apostolate movement and continues today with missionary activities. In the eighteenth and nineteenth centuries, grave-robbers who sold corpses to surgeons for dissection were called "resurrection men" (e.g., in Stevenson's "The Body-Snatchers"). See *DDD* 149, 154–55.

wie man aus Mumien Medikamente macht [416.4] medicine made from mummies: the medicinal use of mummy is discussed in both *EB* (15:955) and *DDD* (324); Haggard points out "most of the mummy used was adulterated or counterfeited."

wo sie in der Schweiz einen Hahn verbrannt haben [416.11] Swiss rooster is condemned [...] Fourteen seventy-four: "One of the most comical witch-persecutions took place in 1474 against a diabolical rooster who had been so presumptuous as to lay an egg. The poor creature was solemnly tried, whereupon he was condemned to die at the stake and publicly burned by order of the authorities of the good city of Basel" – Paul Carus, *The History of the Devil and the Idea of Evil* (Chicago: Open Court, 1900), 337.

weder hic noch ubique [416.17] hic, et ubique: Lat: "here, and everywhere."

561 daß es nach der Sintflut keinen Gott gab [417.3] after the Great Deluge [...] above their empty heads: as every student of *Finnegans Wake* knows, a paraphrase of the origin of religion and civilization according to Italian historian Giambattista Vico (1668–1744) as set forth in his *La Scienza nuova* (*The New Science*, 1725–30).

564 Und ließ verbrennen den Thron der Sonne [418.35] he burnt the throne of the sun with fire: "when Josiah cleared the Temple of Jerusalem of the idolatrous objects and symbols that had been set up there by his apostate predecessor, it was from the eastern gate that the symbolic chariot of the sun was removed. 'And he took away the horses that the kings of Judah had given to the sun at the *entering in* of the house of the Lord [...] and burned the chariots of the sun with fire.' It was, doubtless, a throne for the sun like that at Mabog" (*AMM* 198, quoting 2 Kings 23:11).

Briefe des Kaisers Flavius Claudius Julianus [419.1] *Letters* of the Emperor Flavius Claudius Julianus: Julian the Apostate, emperor of Rome from 361 to 363 and a devotee of Mithraism. He was the author of a number of letters as well as a "Hymn to Helios." Himerius's tribute to him is quoted at 719.24 ff.

564 **Neunzehn ... vier ... Er hat der Sonne ein Zelt gemacht** [419.3] Nineteen ... four [...] the heat thereof: Ps. 19:4b-6.

Sieben ... elf ... Weisheit ist gut mit einem Erbgut [419.8] Seven ... eleven ... and by it there is profit to them that see the sun: Eccles. 7:11b.

elf ... sieben [...] **Es ist das Licht süß** [419.10] eleven ... seven ... Truly the light is sweet [...] behold the sun: Eccles. 11:7.

565 [419.27] make full proof of his ministry: 2 Tim. 4:5 (cf. 49.18).

Sor Patrocinio s. S. 71 [419.39]: see 50.12.

Contra Celsum [420.12] Origen's *Contra Celsum*: a defense of Christianity by Origen (see 103.3) against the attacks made by the Platonist philosopher Celsus in his *True Word* (or *True Account*), the first notable attack on the new religion (see 384.20). It is cited by Graves (*WG* 382) in a discussion of the guarding of religious mysteries.

PLANTS bis RAYM [420.14] Volume eighteen [...] PLANTS to RAYM: of *EB*, which the Town Carpenter has borrowed to read up on Prester John.

Tertullian's *De Coronâ* [420.15]: The Chaplet (204?) is a tract discussing the participation of Christians in military service; it is cited twice in *M*.

Cathemerinon [420.17] *Cathemerinon* [...] Kindly Guide [...] faithful followers: a devotional guide by Aurelius Clemens Prudentius (348–410?), a Latin Christian poet. The book features twelve long hymns for devotional use; Rev. Gwyon translates the first four lines of the fifth hymn, "Hymnus ad Incensum Lucernae" (Brownson 230).

567 **Predigt über die Druiden** [421.41] Druids [...] often struck by lightning: see 55.31. Actually, the oak tree is struck more often than others simply because it has vertical roots that provide a more direct route to groundwater.

[423.31] *The Toast* [...] *who beg for bread*: unidentified.

571 **Superbia ... Ira ... Invidia** [425.10] Superbia [...] "I would desire [...] O my sweet gold!" [...] Covetousness: in Christopher Marlowe's (1564–93) play *Doctor Faustus* (1592?), Lucifer arranges for Faustus a parade of the Seven Deadly Sins, the second of which introduces itself thus: "I am Covetousness, begotten of an old churl, in an old leathern bag: and might I have my wish, I would desire that this house and all the people in it were turned to gold, that I might lock you up in my good chest: O, my sweet gold!" (*Marlowe's Plays and Poems*, ed. M. R. Ridley, Everyman's Library [New York: Dutton, 1955], 138–39).

572 Μείθρας [...] Αβραξάς s. S. 581 [425.34]: see 433.1.

Das ist das Brot, und das ist der Fisch [426.1] bread [...] fish [...] waiting for something to happen: cf. the miraculous multiplication of bread and fish in Mark 6:37ff.

573 **vor einem Teller weißer Bohnen** [426.37] white navy beans: see *WG* 51–52 for possible significance: in ancient Greece and Rome, it was believed ghosts entered beans, to be eaten by women for rebirth; thus "for a man to eat a bean might be an impious frustration of his dead parents' designs" to be reborn.

575 **Was, wenn ich unter die Räuber fiele** [427.40] If I fell among thieves: quoted from the story of the Good Samaritan in Luke 10:30–37.

Ein regelrechter Karneval. [...] Lebwohl, o Fleisch! [428.2] carnival [...] O flesh, farewell: "carnival" originally referred to the days preceding Lent, after which time meat was to be put away (It. *carne levare*). "The explanations 'farewell flesh, farewell to flesh' (from L. *vale*) [...] belong to the domain of popular etymology" (*OED*). Cf. 800.8ff.

das Glitzern im Auge [428.9] glittering eye: the most noticeable feature of Coleridge's Ancient Mariner (ll. 3, 13, etc.). Sinisterra likewise possesses a "glittering eye" (794.25).

in der Hölle kann man es sich sehr kurzweilig machen [428.12] "in hell is all manner of delight": from Marlowe's *Doctor Faustus*; see note to 441.34.

als die Saat war aufgegangen s. S. 135 [428.23] And when the seed began to grow: see 98.41.

576 **Schönheit lockt Diebe schneller noch als Gold** [428.44] And if beauty did provoke thieves, sooner than gold?: deciding to take to the road with Celia, Rosalind asks: "Alas, what danger will it be to us, / Maids as we are, to travel forth so far! / Beauty provoketh thieves sooner than gold" (*As You Like It*, 1.3.110–12.)

sie brächte selbst die Natur um ihre Kunden [429.1] ape to nature: perhaps another Shakespearean allusion: "Julio Romano [...] would beguile Nature of her custom, so perfectly he is her ape" (*Winter's Tale*, 5.2.105–8; Romano was a famous Italian artist of the sixteenth century).

577 **die Hexen von Thessaloniki** s. S. 41 [429.36] Thessalonian witches: see 28.15ff.

Ihr habt aus dem Mond eine Frau gemacht [429.41] "The moon [...] Arnobius [...] a thousand forms": Arnobius (fl. A.D. 300), early Christian apologist, whose only known work is *Adversus Gentes* (Against the Heathens; also called *Adversus Nationes*, as at 436.40]), a devastating attack on the Roman religion. The present quotation is from book 6, chap. 10, a discussion of the futility of trying to create images of the gods; which of the moon's thousand forms, for example, is to be rendered in a statute devoted to her?

578 **den Heiligen Bernhard in Grund und Boden predigen** [430.18] Saint Bernard: (1090–1153), French abbot and theologian, a founder of the Cistercian order; quoted earlier on feminine charm (393.31–33).

ein Bruder den anderen zum Tod überantworten [430.22] "And the brother [...] put to death": Matt. 10:21.

Laodicea [430.25]: one of the seven churches in Asia singled out in the Book of Revelation; it is criticized for being "neither cold nor hot" in religious matters (3:14 ff.).

Narr um Christi willen [430.25] God's fool: cf. 1 Cor. 4:10.

Zaunkönig [430.28] the wren: see 47.33.

579 **Bereit für die Prüfungen [...] Nur die Starken können Priester sein.** [431.6] The trials before you, for the priesthood: an extended series of extracts from Phythian-Adams's *Mithraism* (83–92) is necessary to annotate the Mithraic elements of *R* 431–32. (The location of Gaddis's borrowings will be indicated in brackets; footnotes have been eliminated.) The most striking feature of Mithraism, says Phythian-Adams, is what "may be called the Tests or Trials of Fortitude":

Of these there were twelve in all [432.1] (or, as some writers aver, eighty!); and in the old days, in the mountains of the Near East, they must have been more than moderately severe. The Neophyte was exposed to scorching heat and biting cold [431.41, 43], to hunger, thirst, the terrors of drowning [432.2–3], to every torment (they were also called *"cruciatus"* [432.18]) which the wit of man could devise to render the human body "Passionless" [431.8, 22], [...] to inure it to hardship, and strengthen it against temptation [431.21]. Such was the candidate's entry into the mysteries. [...]

Thus far, then, the neophyte had learned two lessons – Fortitude, and Subdual of Passions [432.9–10]. His next lesson was Renunciation [431.37]. At some point, presumably as the last test had been triumphantly surmounted, a Crown of Victory was presented to the elated youth [431.26]; yet ere he could accept it, he was warned to thrust it from him with the words "Mithras is my crown." So even in the moment of success, he learned entire submission and self dedication to his god. It is not surprising that Tertullian [420.15] held up this custom as an example and reproach to his "Fellow soldiers in Christ."

When the act of Renunciation had been made, the candidate was Sealed upon the forehead [432.4] and became a "tried soldier" of Mithras. It was perhaps then also that he was Baptized to the Remission of Sins [431.12]. Justin Martyr tells us that "Bread and a cup of water" [431.15] were placed with certain incantations in the rite of initiation. If this statement is correct, it describes an imperfect or preliminary act of Communion [431.15], which foreshadowed that fuller Participation which only those who had reached the grade of Lion [432.20] were allowed to experience.

Yet before the neophyte had climbed to this spiritual eminence, a last and greatest trial of his fortitude and fidelity still awaited him. [...] Now he had to Die [436.16, 22].

That the Mithraic mysteries (in common with all others before and since) contained a Mystical Death appears perhaps a somewhat hazardous suggestion. In reality, *the fact* is practically undeniable. Tertullian speaks of an "image of Resurrection" [432.33] which the Devil had introduced into the Mithraic rites with the object of overthrowing and contaminating the Truth. The other side of the same ritual act is fortunately preserved for us by the chronologist of Commodus. That Emperor, we are told, "polluted the mysteries of Mithras by a real homicide, when something of the kind is done or spoken there to produce terror." Interpreting this sentence in the light of our previous knowledge we obtain two facts: (1) that there was a symbolic *murder*, (2) that it was performed by the *Pater Patrum* [432.27], who was the *direct representative* of Mithras (since it must be presumed that Commodus would be content with none but the chief rôle in this as in all else). The mythical explanation of this act would then run as follows: [...] "By suffering 'death' at the hands of the Pater Patrum, the initiate passes into true 'life.'" [...]

We have now surveyed, in however cursory a manner, the vital principles of the Mithraic creed. We have seen that it contains in "outward and visible form" the sacred "Rock" [431.11], Baptism, the Sign on the Brow, Communion of Bread and Cup [431.14–15]; and on its inward and spiritual side the doctrine of Sin, Redemption, Sacramentary Grace and Salvation to Everlasting Life [431.15–16]. Is it surprising that in the face of this astonishing similarity the Christian apologists denounced the Mysteries as a most crafty and insidious attack upon the Truth, made not, be it observed, by men (human plagiarism is never suggested), but by that great Counterfeiter, the Devil himself?

579 **Felsgeborener** [431.11] Born of the Rock: Mithra was said to have been born from a rock, as illustrated in various Mithraic bas-reliefs (e.g., *M* 54); see the reaction of Firmicus Maternus to this belief below (436.40).

Die dritte Versuchung Jesu [431.28] the third temptation, "All these things will I give thee": "[...] if thou wilt fall down and worship me" (Matt. 4:9). Similarly, Mephistopheles tempts Faust (ll. 10130–33):

You have surveyed immeasurable stretches,
The kingdoms of this world and all their riches;
And yet, insatiable as you are,
You've felt no appetite so far?

Earlier (i.e., the night before), Wyatt had said, "hurry ... the forty days is almost done ..." (383.41).

580 **und liegt doch hinter mir** [431.30] he's behind me: after the third temptation, Jesus says: "Get thee behind me, Satan" (Luke 4:8).

[432.3] sacramentum: "We learn from Tertullian [*De Coronâ*, 15] that Mithraism exacted an Oath of Allegiance (*sacramentum*) from the recruits for its 'sacred warfare,' and signed or sealed them on the forehead as a memorial of their vow" (*M* 76). Phythian-Adams later cites

Tertullian's *De Præscriptione Hæreticorum* (chap. 40) on the same point (*M* 84 n.2); Rev. Gwyon's library contains both works.

580 **Nonnus […]** *In Sancta Lumina* [432.9]: Phythian-Adams makes a passing reference to Nonnus (*M* 83 n.1) but makes no mention of this work. Nonnus was a Greek poet and mythographer who lived in Egypt in the late fourth or early fifth century. (The bishop Nonnus who converted Pelagia [392.30] is unrelated.)

Pater Patrum [432.15]: "Father of Fathers," the head of those Mithraic initiates who reached the father (*pater*) degree (see next note). "Pater Patratus" (432.27) Phythian-Adams gives as a variant of Pater Patrum.

Cryphius […] Heliodromus [432.20]: from *EB*'s article on Mithra (15:620):

As regards the organization of Mithraism, S. Jerome (*Epist.* 107, 2) and inscriptions preserve the knowledge that the mystic, *sacratus*, passed through seven degrees, which probably corresponded to the seven planetary spheres traversed by the soul in its ascent; *Corax*, Raven; *Cryphius*, Hidden ([…] the initiate was perhaps veiled); *Miles*, Soldier, signifying the holy warfare against evil in the service of the god; *Leo*, Lion, symbolic of the element of fire; *Perses*, Persian (*cf.* the Christian use of "Israel," "Zion," etc.); *Heliodromus*, Courier of the Sun; *Pater*, Father, a degree bringing the mystic among those who had the general direction of the cult for the rest of their lives.

581 **Natalis invicti** [432.37]: the birthday of the sun at the winter solstice, celebrated on 25 December (*M* 58); Graves notes: "That the Sun-gods Dionysus, Apollo and Mithra were all also reputedly born at the Winter solstice is well known, and the Christian Church first fixed the Nativity feast of Jesus Christ at the same season, in the year 273 A.D. " (*WG* 262).

Abraxas [433.1] Abraxas […] the resident of the highest Gnostic heaven: *abraxas* was a symbolic word used by Basilides of Alexandria (fl. third century) as a title for the divinity; later it became a proper name. There seems to have been seven heavens or spheres in the Gnostic system, though Basilides for one counted no less than 365 heavens – obviously reflecting the solar year (see *EB* 1:62).

Gnosticism (Greek *gnosis*, knowledge) augmented Christianity with the speculations of Pythagoras, Plato, and other Greek and Oriental philosophers, which resulted in an esoteric "religion" available only to initiates. (Its elitism alienated many of the more democratic early Christians.) Emphasizing knowledge rather than faith, Gnosticism involved magic, occult symbolism, and what later would develop into alchemy. Several early church fathers attacked Gnosticism, the most thorough being Saint Irenaeus, whose *Against Heresies* furnishes *R*'s motto. In spite of Irenaeus's definitive exposé of the cult's contradictions and absurdities, Gnosticism continued to attract certain temperaments, as it does to this very day.

581 **Der menschlichen Rasse sind die Götter freundlich gesinnt** [433.8] "The gods are benevolent [...] Elisæus [...] by the hands of the king: source unknown; Elisæus was a fifth-century Armenian religious writer.

Mithras bedeutet Freund [433.15] *Mithras means friend* [...] mediator between the gods and the lower world: in one footnote Phythian-Adams notes "Mitra in Sanskrit ='Friendship' or 'Friend'" (*M* 6, n.1), and in another: "As the god of Light, M[ithras]. occupied a *'middle'* place in the air (Vayu) between the splendour of Heaven and the gloom of Hell. He was thus called the Mediator (Mesiths)(Plutarch de Isid, c. 46), a title later transferred by Mazdaeans to his relations between Ormuzd and mankind. There is no trace of this doctrine in Mithraism, and Christian writers do not refer to it in spite of the obvious parallel in their own religion" (*M* 8, n.1). Cf. Weston: "Mithra is the mediator, who stands between 'the inaccessible and unknowable God, who reigns in the ethereal spheres, and the human race which suffers here below'" (*FRR* 165–66, quoting Cumont).

585 **gab es da nicht diese Frauengilde** [...] *Hyæna* [436.24] *woman's grade* [...] Porphyry [...] Hyena: Phythian-Adams cites a confusing reference in Porphyry's *De Abstinentia* as the only argument against the apparent fact that Mithraism "was a system solely and entirely devoted to the needs of the Male" (*M* 82 and n.1). Porphry (232?–304?), Greek scholar and Neoplatonic philosopher, vigorously defended paganism and opposed Christianity in his many books.

Und der Mond wird sich verwundern [436.28] Then the moon shall be confounded and the sun ashamed: Isa. 24:23.

Die Sonne soll nicht mehr dein Licht sein [436.30] The sun shall be no more [...] for the Lord shall be: Isa. 60:19–20.

586 **Tertullian's *De Præscriptione Hæreticorum*** [436.39]: The Prescription against Heretics argues that those who base their religious beliefs on unorthodox interpretations of the scriptures (as the Gnostics did) thereby forfeit their right to use the scriptures at all. Cited in *M*.

das *Adversus Nationes* des Arnobius s.S. 577 [436.40] Arnobius' *Adversus Nationes*: see 429.41.

***De Errore Profanarum Religionum* von Firmicus Maternus** [436.40] *De Errore Profanarum Religionum* of Firmicus Maternus: Julius Firmicus Maternus was a Latin writer of the fourth century A.D.; the cited work, written around 346, is an attack on paganism. Phythian-Adams refers to *De Errore* in an a discussion of the Mithraic "Rock Mother," whence comes Mithra, "Born of the Rock" (431.11), a concept that "was denounced by the Christian writers [Firmicus Maternus and Justin Martyr] as a blasphemous caricature of their 'sacred and venerable' secret, that there was but one 'Rock hewn without hands,' one 'Living Stone,' which was Christ himself" (*M* 90).

586 Dunklen Nacht der Seele s. S. 35 [437.1] Saint John of the Cross [...] *Dark Night of the Soul*: see 23.40.

Sonnengott, Mithra, Serapis [...] *abraalbabachaebechi* [437.9] Herakles star-adorned [...] abraalbabachaebechi: the source of Rev. Gwyon's prayer and the meaning of the final word are unknown.

Kapitel vierundzwanzig, Vers acht [437.32] verse eight [...] according to Saint Matthew: this chapter concerns the sign of the Second Coming.

587 Vers vierundzwanzig [437.36] verse twenty-four: "For there shall arise false wonders, and false prophets, and shall shew great signs and wonders; insomuch that, if it were possible, they shall deceive the very elect."

nun, da wir uns allmählich dem ewigen Wanderer zuwenden [438.21] "While we go now [...] *The Prince of India*: a 300,000–word novel (1893) suggested by President Garfield to popular novelist Lew Wallace (1827–1905), best known as the author of *Ben Hur*. Very successful in its day, *The Prince of India* reworks the Wandering Jew theme; the quotation is the final paragraph of book 2, chap. 1.

591 Fort, fort, zur Hölle, zur Hölle! [441.34] "Away, to hell, to hell! [...] How happy were I then": in Marlowe's *Doctor Faustus,* Faustus dismisses the Seven Deadly Sins (see 425.10ff.) thus (140 in Everyman's ed.):

FAUST: Away, to hell, to hell!   [*Exeunt the Sins.*
LUCIFER: Now, Faustus, how dost thou like this?
FAUST: O, this feeds my soul!
LUCIFER: Tut, Faustus, in hell is all manner of delight.
FAUST: O, might I see hell, and return again,
    How happy were I then!

[442.5] harrowing of hell: the apocryphal legend of the Harrowing of Hell (based on an enigmatic statement in 1 Peter 3:19) has it that Jesus, on the day after his crucifixion (Holy Saturday), descended to hell and took with him to heaven the first souls to be saved. Vergil speaks nostalgically of the event in Dante's *Inferno* and names several of the lucky souls (4:52ff.). The subject has been treated often in apocryphal writings (see *Acts of Pilate*, 23.38) and religious literature (see epigraph to II.8 [647]). For the pagan origin of Christ's infernal descent, see *MMM* 286.

II.4

596 Ich hatte einen schönen Traum [...] *Die Brüder Karamasow* [446.epigraph] "I've had a good dream [...] *Brothers Karamazov*: the last sentence of part 9, chap. 8. Mitya falls asleep at the end of the examination of witnesses at his trial and dreams of poor peasants. "And he felt that a passion of pity, such as he had never known before, was rising in his heart, that he wanted to cry, that he wanted to do something for them all, so that the babe should weep no more, so that the dark-faced, dried-up mother should not weep, that no one should shed tears again from that moment, and he wanted to do it at once, at once, regardless of all obstacles, with all the recklessness of the Karamazovs" (Constance Garnett translation). Upon waking, he discovers that someone has placed a pillow beneath his head. Under the dual influence of the unexpected kindness and the inspiring dream, he agrees to sign whatever the authorities wish.

Sempre con fè sincera [446.1] Sempre con fè sincera [...] perchè me ne rimuneri così?: from *Tosca*; see 91.17.

[447.23] **that isn't what I meant [...] That isn't what I meant at all**: a refrain in Eliot's "Love Song of J. Alfred Prufrock."

602 den falschen Tizian [450.38] a forged Titian: from a "newspaper story which Gaddis saw when *The Recognitions* was already at the printer, and which he felt so central to what his novel was about that he inserted it at some added expense," except that the "worthless old painting" (450.40) was actually "a fairly good 19th century painting" (Koenig, "'Splinters from the Yew Tree,'" 12).

603 der Heilige Johannes vom Kreuz [451.35] Saint John of the Cross [...] take out love": in a discussion of Saint Gregory's distinction between the active and the contemplative life (see 488.10), Summers writes (*PPM* 29):

In a letter dated 6th July, 1591, only five months before his death, when already he had been "thrown into a corner like an old rag" – to use his own phrase – St. John says to a nun [María de la Encarnación], who bewailed the seeming triumph of his persecutors and enemies, "As to my affairs, daughter, let them not trouble you, for none of them trouble me. [...] These things are not done by men, but by God, Who knows what is meet for us and ordains things for our good. Think only that God ordains all. And where there is no love, stablish love there, and you will find love."

604 Tolstojs *Und das Licht leuchtet in der Finsternis* [452.23] Tolstoy's *Kingdom of God*: *The Kingdom of God Is within You; or, Christianity Not as a Mystical Teaching but as a New Concept of Life* (1893) is Tolstoy's interpretation of the Sermon on the Mount and an exposition of the principles of civic nonresistance (which greatly influenced Gandhi). It also attacks institutional Christianity and advocates a return to Christ's basic teachings.

605 Psychoanalusche s.S.246 [453.31] a three time psychoanaloser: repeated from 183.37.

regelmäßig als kleines Mädchen verkleidet [453.35] little girl's clothes and rape her. – Too much Dostoevski: in a chapter of *The Possessed* long suppressed, Stavrogin describes a sexual encounter with a twelve-year-old girl who, feeling afterward that she has "killed God" as a result, hangs herself. Similarly, the profligate Svidrigaylov in *Crime and Punishment* admits to having sexually abused young girls, one of whom committed suicide afterward. Toward the end of the novel he dreams of rescuing a shivering, crying, five-year-old girl, undressing her, and allowing her to take his bed to recover. He soon sees in her countenance, however, "the face of a courtesan, the brazen face of a mercenary French harlot." Shortly after waking from this nightmare, Svidrigaylov shoots himself.

[454.21] Zheed: André Gide (1869–1951), French novelist and critic. Gaddis admits reading *The Counterfeiters* when young, but doubts it had any influence on his work.

[455.11] common asphodel: *The Common Asphodel* (1949) is a collection of essays on poetry by Robert Graves.

608 Schönheit, die gelassen verschmäht [455.18] Beauty, serenely disdains to destroy us: from Rilke's first Duino Elegy; see 277.34ff., 622.16ff.

609 *Venus und Cupido* von Velázquez [456.27] Velasquez, *Venus and Cupid*: Diego Velásquez (1599–1660), the greatest Spanish painter of the seventeenth century. This painting, also known as the *Rokeby Venus*, dates from 1648–51.

612 Averroes s.S.517 [458.28] Averroes [...] believe in order to understand: see 382.29–30.

Skulptur von Lippchitz mit dem Titel *Mother and Child II*. [458.32] sculpture by Lipchitz, titled *Mother and Child II*: Jacques Lipchitz (1891–1973), Lithuanian-born French sculptor. A reproduction of the sculpture is featured in the February 1952 issue of *Art News* – an issue Gaddis read (see 888.8) – but the critical remarks quoted by Max are not from *Art News* (which states: "the lunge of its savagely truncated arms and the double image it forms of a bull's head are deeply moving, but might repel superficially delicate tastes").

615 Das ist wie bei van Gogh [461.4] van Gogh says about painting [...] "vague consonance of colors": in a letter to his brother Theo, van Gogh wrote: "I pose the black and white of Delacroix or Millet before me as a subject and impro-

vise colour on it, not, you understand, altogether as myself, but searching for memories of *their* pictures – the memory, 'the vague consonance of colours which are at least right in feeling'; that is my own interpretation" (*Dear Theo: The Autobiography of Vincent Van Gogh*, ed. Irving Stone [1937; rpt. New York: New American Library, 1969], 451). Eugène Delacroix (1798–1863), the major painter of the French Romantic movement, was greatly admired by van Gogh; for Millet, see 73.26.

616 **ein grottenhohler Tenor mit »I'm dreaming of a white Christmas ...«** [461.10] a vacuous tenor [...] I'm dreaming of a white Christmas: Bing Crosby introduced the song "White Christmas" in the 1942 film *Holiday Inn*.

Cherubini [461.13]: Maria Luigi Cherubini (1760–1842), Italian composer.

Yes We Have No Bananas [461.26] *Yes We Have No Bananas* [...] from *The Messiah*: after the 1923 Silver-Cohen song became a hit, the Westman Company, which published Handel's music, took the song's publishers to court and successfully proved that the melody was indeed a direct steal from a portion of *The Messiah*. The Westman Company was awarded a share of the song's profits.

619 **Die Form eines Steins kann man nicht erfinden** [463.28] Ben Shahn's, "You cannot invent the shape of a stone": Lithuanian-born American painter (1898–1969), a very social-minded artist. Source of quotation (first used at 123.10) unknown.

Wie Stevenson schon sagte: Wir alle müssen verkaufen. [463.32] Stevenson says, we all live by selling something: in an essay entitled "Beggars"(in *Across the Plains*, 1892), Stevenson writes: "Every one lives by selling something, whatever be his right to it" (first half quoted in *ODQ*).

Sherlock Holmes [463.44] Sherlock Holmes [...] Doylean literary tricks: Adrian Conan Doyle and John Dickson Carr's "The Adventure of the Seven Clocks" appeared in the 29 December 1952 issue of *Life* (54–61). "How Holmes Was Reborn," by Herbert Brean, follows the story (62–66) and is the source for Max's quotation on the reproduction of Doyle's style.

621 **Der Teufel ist der Vater der falschen Künste** [464.34] The devil is the father of false art: "The Devil is the father of false art, of all those works which are 'neither good nor bad,' because the act of which they were born suppresses the very measures of beauty" (*DS* 40–41).

ein jeder tötet, was er liebt [464.41] you kill the thing you love: cf. Oscar Wilde's once-famous line, "Yet each man kills the thing he loves" ("Ballad of Reading Gaol," *ODQ*). Cf. Juliet's concern (383.29).

[466.6] it's difficult to shed our human nature: see 130.7–10.

623 **wie gesagt, irgend etwas bleibt immer kleben** [466.9] A little always sticks: a vulgarization of the *semper aliquid haeret* motif (see 336.32).

624 **kalte Hölle** [467.5] "chilly hell" of the poet's *Elegy on the Thousand Children*: Graves (*WG* 77) quotes four lines from Gwion's (see 3.9) "Marwnad y Milveib" (Elegy on the Thousand Children):
Incomprehensible numbers there were
Maintained in a chilly hell
Until the Fifth Age of the world,
Until Christ should release the captives.

Boreas [467.6]: the personification of the north wind in Greek mythology.

625 *Frank, Bishop of Zanzibar* [468.26]: a biography of Frank Weston (1871–1924), an Anglican missionary in Africa and a leader of the Anglo-Catholic party. The biography is by H. Maynard Smith and was published in 1926. (Though appropriate reading for one considering a life of missionary work – as Wyatt is rather wildly doing at this point – Gaddis seems to have taken nothing from this book but its title.)

628 *Kinder- und Hausmärchen* s.S. 367 [470.34]: see 275.12ff.

semper aliquid haeret s.S. 628 [470.44]: see 336.32.

[471.24] You: The demands of painting [...] *absolute* death: an actual letter written by Sheri Martinelli (see note on Esme at 194.14) to WG in the late 1940s.

629 **De Chirico** [471.11]: Giorgio di Chirico (1888–1978), Italian painter, considered the creator of "metaphysical" painting.

631 **wie ein Vogel, der zerbrochene Eier in sich trägt** [472.45] a bird with broken eggs inside: asked about this striking phrase, Martinelli told me it was an image from one of Anaïs Nin's books.

634 **Rudy Vallee mit *Love Made a Gypsy Out of Me*** [475.11] Rudy Vallee singing, *Love Made a Gypsy Out of Me*: Rudy Vallee (1901–86) was a popular singer and bandleader; the song is unidentified.

Phylogynie [475.27] Philogyny? [...] misogyny recapitulates philogyny [...] misologist?: philogyny=fondness for women; phylogeny=racial history of a related group of organisms; misogyny=hatred of women; misogamy=hatred of marriage; misologist=one who hates reasoning or enlightenment. A variant on Haeckel's biogenetic law "ontogeny recapitulates phylogeny" is intended, and apparently "Willie" Gaddis himself is making the clever but unappreciated pun; cf. 478.28–29.

Baedeckers *Babel* [475.32] Baedeker's *Babel*: Karl Baedeker (1801–59) was the author of a famous series of travel guide books, noted for their reliability and thoroughness. Babel (Genesis 11; i.e., Babylon) never merited a Baedeker's guide; the name is, of course, used figuratively for any confused, noisy place. For the relevance of the Tower of Babel myth to modern civilization (as well as a justification for the title "Baedeker's *Babel*" – Willie's fictional counterpart to *R*), see the chapter entitled "The Tower of Babel" in de Rougemont's *DS*.

634 Tiffany's [475.39]: the fashionable New York jewelers.

635 wie Archimedes in seiner verdammten Wanne [476.24] Archimedes in his [...] bathtub: the principle of the displacement of water is said to have occurred to Greek mathematician and inventor Archimedes (ca. 287–212 B.C.) as he stepped into his bath.

636 Warum solltest du Sünder zur Welt bringen? [477.1] wouldst thou be a breeder of sinners [...] into a nunnery: *Hamlet* 3.1.122–23.

der Heilige Hieronymus über die Frauen [477.5] Saint Jerome say about women? [...] She's the gate of Hell: de Rougemont attributes these words to Tertullian (*DS* 177).

Ein Feind der Freundschaft [477.6] "A foe to friendship [...] says Chrysostom: Saint John, surnamed Chrysostom ("Golden Mouthed")(347–407), one of the fathers of the Greek church, provided the following gloss on Matt. 19:10: "What else is woman but a foe to friendship, an unescapable punishment, a necessary evil, a natural temptation, a desirable calamity, a domestic danger, a delectable detriment, an evil of nature, painted with fair colours!" (*MM* 43).

Bruckner [477.10]: Anton Bruckner (1824–96), Austrian organist and composer of church and symphonic music.

Nach Pascal besteht das ganze Malheur des Menschen [477.15] Pascal [...] alone in a small room: from his *Pensées* (#139).

637 Ich bin einer, Herr, der Euch zu melden kommt [477.24] I am one to tell you [...] beast with two backs: repeated from 200.36. Hannah is a palindromic name.

[477.30] Das Unbeschreibliche [...] Das ewig-Weibliche: Goethe's *Faust* ends with the "Chorus mysticus" intoning:

Alles Vergängliche	All in transition
Ist nur ein Gleichnis;	Is but reflection;
Das Unzulängliche,	What is deficient
Hier wird's Ereignis;	Here becomes action;
Das Unbeschreibliche,	Human discernment
Hier ist's getan;	Here is passed by;
Das Ewig-Weibliche	Woman Eternal
Zieht uns hinan.	Draw us on high.

638 Mary Baker Eddy [478.23]: (1821–1910), American religious leader, founder of Christian Science, the basic tenets of which were set forth in her book *Science and Health* (1875)(see 532.7) and continued in its organ, the *Christian Science Monitor* (1908–). See Mark Twain's critical book *Christian Science* (1907), which Gaddis says he read (WG/SM).

in Platons Staat s. S. 143 [478.32] Plato's Republic: see 105.16.

639 *Onkel Toms Hütte* [479.12] *Uncle Tom's Cabin*: the popular novel (1852) by Harriet Beecher Stowe (1811–96), subject of a lame joke a few pages later (482.11–13). See also 826.35–37, 913.30.

642 Zieht aus den alten Menschen mit seinen Werken [481.19] Put off the old man, says the Bible: "Lie not to one another, seeing that ye have put off the old man with his deeds; and have put on the new man, which is renewed in knowledge after the image of him that created him" (Col. 3:9–10; reworded in Eph. 4:22–24).

wie der Eiter des Heiligen Johannes vom Kreuz s. S. 1075 [482.1] the pus of Saint John of the Cross: see 827.6.

644 Denn wir sind ja nur die Zigeuner [482.40] gypsies: the "lore" Esme relates is from popular superstition rather than actual history; her "They" refers to the Holy Family during their Egyptian sojourn. See Borrow's *The Zincali*, especially pp. 90–91 for the Gypsies' alleged origin.

645 Ich meine, wenn man jemanden verliert s. S. 203 [484.9] when you lose someone ... lose contact with someone you love: see 151.10.

[485.24] *Eine kleine Taverne im Golf von Napoli*: "A Little Tavern on the Bay of Naples" – unidentified.

647 toot sweet [485.34]: *tout de suite* (Fr.: "immediately, right away").

[486.2] C.I.D.: Criminal Investigation Department (Scotland Yard).

648 Sir Walter Raleighs listenreiche Avance [486.27] Sir Walter Raleigh's cunning advance [...] yet fear I to fall": under this Queen Elizabeth wrote in reply: "If thy heart fails thee, climb not at all" (*ODQ*).

[486.30] *Fliege mit mir in die Heimat*: "Fly with Me to the Homeland" (or "Fly Home with Me") – unidentified.

II.5

649 Das Gottvertrauen unseres Volkes [...] Direktor der amerikanischen Münze [487.epigraph] "The trust of our people [...] director of the Mint: from Laurence Dwight Smith's *Counterfeiting: Crime against the People* (196–97), the source for many details in the first ten pages of this chapter:

Fearful that the Republic might be utterly destroyed by the [Civil War], the Reverend M. R. Watkinson wrote to Salmon P. Chase, who was then Secretary of the Treasury under Lincoln, pointing out that no mention of the Almighty God appeared on our coins. "Antiquarians of succeeding generation" might believe, he declared, when they examined the coinage of the country, that we were a "heathen nation." Chase promptly wrote to Pollock, Director of the Mint: "The trust of our people [... as above ...] national recognition." On April 22, 1864 an act was passed authorizing the coinage of two-cent bronze pieces with the inscription, "In God we trust."

649 am Fuße des Janiculum [487.3] ancestors had gathered at the foot of the Janiculum [...] on the Tiber bank: from the opening paragraph of Saltus's third chapter, "The Convulsions of the Church" (*AN* 66):

The earliest barbarian that invaded Rome was a Jew. He did not thunder at the gates; he went unheralded to the Taberna [sic] Meritoria – a squalid inn on the Tiber that reeked with garlic – broke his fast, and then sauntered forth, as any modern traveler might do, to view the city. His first visit was to his compatriots at the foot of the Janiculum. To them he whispered something, went away, returned and whispered again. After a while he spoke out loud. Some of his hearers contradicted him; he spoke louder. The peddlars, the rag-pickers, the valets-de-place and hook-nosed porters grew tumultuous at his words. The ghetto was raided, and a complaint for inciting disorder was lodged against a certain Christus, of whom nothing was known and who had managed to elude arrest.

Wie kann dieser uns sein Fleisch zu essen geben? [487.9] "How can this man give us his flesh to eat?": the Jews' response to Jesus's declaration: "and the bread I will give is my flesh" (John 6:51–52). The line is quoted by Conybeare in his discussion of the Eucharist (*MMM* 271).

[487.17] a scream so ghastly [...] as the book said: source unknown.

A.M.D.G. s.S.529 [487.22]: see 393.38–40.

650 der Heilige Augustinus [488.8] Saint Augustine [...] Tagaste: "When he was dwelling in community near Tagaste, he utterly withdrew from the world, 'living for God alone, wholly occupied in fasting, prayer, and similar good works, meditating day and night upon the things of God, and closely following the manner of life of the solitaries of the Egyptian desert'" (*PPM* 30–31, quoting from Père Hélyot's *Histoire des ordres monastiques* [1715]).

die Worte des Heiligen Gregor [488.10] Saint Gregory ("the Contemplative Life [...] the active"): Saint Gregory the Great, pope 590–604. The famous dictum is quoted by Summers (*PPM* 30), who cites Gregory's *Homily on Ezechiel* as the source.

Atlanta [488.17]: location of one of three Federal penitentiaries maintained by the U.S. government at the time.

650 **das Eremitendasein des Heiligen Giles** [488.18] Saint Giles's retirement to the desert: apparently the Saint Giles who died about 712, about whom many legends were told. Summers notes "the hermit was companioned by a hind which he loved" (*PPM* 68) but gives no further details concerning his "retirement."

mit der Bescheidenheit des Propheten Jeremia [488.21] Jeremiah [...] "go and cry in the ears of Jerusalem": Jer. 2:2; cited by Summers on the same page (*PPM* 30) as the Saint Gregory quotation above.

651 **Cavalieri** [488.36] Cavalieri as Tosca: Lina Cavalieri (1874–1944), Italian operatic soprano who sang often in America in the early part of the century. A photograph of Cavalieri as Tosca appears in Gustave Kobbé's *The Complete Opera Book*, rev. ed. (New York: Putnam's, 1935), a book Gaddis later used for some Wagner references in *JR*.

Pius IX., jenem beliebten Pio Nono [488.37] Pius IX, the Pio Nono: the Italian form of the popular pope (in office 1846–78, the longest pontificate in church history). Cf. 5.37, 393.5. His *Bolla di Composizione* is noted and discussed in *MMSM* (141 n).

Drachenblut [488.44] "dragon's blood": in printing, a powdered resin applied to a block for processing that prevents the etching of the covered portion (*CCP* 216).

***Theologia Moralis* von Alfonso Liguori** [489.4] *Theologia Moralis* of Alfonso Liguori: a multivolume study in moral theology (nine revisions from 1748 to 1785), considered a classic in its field. See 5.37 for Liguori, and *MMSM* 131–33 for a discussion of this work.

***Counterfeit Detector* von 1839 s.S. 660** [489.5] Bicknall's *Counterfeit Detector* for 1839: see 495.23 ff.

Jim the Penman [489.17]: real name Emanuel Ninger; some of the details that follow are from Smith (*CCP* 87–88), but another (unknown) source was used as well. (The Jim the Penman mentioned by Benstock ["On William Gaddis," 180] is a different person.)

652 *National Counterfeit Detector* s.S. 652 [489.41]: see 5.44.

[490.5] less than kin [...] more than kind: Hamlet's first line, describing his stepfather King Claudius, is: "A little more than kin and less than kind" (1.2.65).

654 **Scheol mit seinen üblen Miasmen** [491.13] Sheol: in Judaism, the gloomy place of the dead, though without the punishments and tortures of the Christian hell – more akin to the Greek Hades. Geographically it was associated with the Valley of Ben-himmom outside the south wall of Jerusalem, where sacrifices to Moloch were sometimes made (2 Kings 23:10).

It might be noted that this passage is a Christian-Judaic version of the earlier Classical infernal kingdom in which Wyatt dwelt (98.6–16, 370.30–32); the smell of lavender is common to both. Also, cf. Sinisterra's "a little always sticks" (492.9) with Wyatt's motto *semper aliquid haeret* (336.32, 470.44, etc.).

656 die One-Penny Antigua [492.32] one-penny Antigua stamp [...] puce: from Robert Graves's *Antigua, Penny, Puce* (1936; U.S. title: *The Antigua Stamp*), a novel about stamp-collecting and sibling rivalry centering on a unique stamp such as Sinisterra describes.

658 Pete McCartney und Fred Biebusch oder Big Bill the Queersman [493.32] Pete McCartney and Fred Biebusch, and Big Bill the Queersman [...] Brockway: American forgers of the 1870s whose exploits are described by Smith (*CCP* 85–86).

Johnnie the Gent s.S. 692 [493.35]: see 519.20–31; otherwise unidentified.

Längsschraffur auf dem Hamilton-Zehner [493.41] spaces behind Hamilton on the ten [...] one one-hundred-twentieth of an inch: a detail noted by Smith (*CCP* 153).

wie es schärfer nagt als Schlangenzahn [494.1] How sharper than a snake's tooth it is to have a kid like that: adapted from Shakespeare's *King Lear*: "How sharper than a serpent's tooth it is / To have a thankless child!" (1.4.310–11).

Jenes Schwein [...] es zierte auch die Krawatte [494.6] The pig [...] of purification: "The pig was so important [to the Eleusinian Mysteries] that when Eleusis minted her autonomous money, 350–327 B.C., the pig of purification is stamped upon one face of her coins" (*PPM* 21). As Otto later notes, Sinisterra is wearing the club tie of Harvard's Porcellian society (517.13).

Salerno [494.12]: city and port in southern Italy.

Viele Generationen lang gingen unsere Berufsgeheimnisse vom Vater auf den Sohn über [494.12] every secret [...] from father to son: for Italian counterfeiters, Smith writes, "the making of spurious notes and coins was not merely a profitable enterprise; counterfeiting was a family or clan tradition. For generations the craft passed from father to son" (*CCP* 94–95).

659 die Protokolle der Ältesten von Zion [494.17] Protocols of the Elders of Zion: a document purporting to outline secret Jewish plans for world domination by taking over international finance and undermining Gentile morality. It

first appeared in a trashy German novel entitled *Biarritz* (1868) by Hermann Goedsche (under the pseudonym Sir John Retcliffe), reemerged around 1905 in Russia (probably concocted by the Imperial secret police), then circulated rapidly throughout Europe and the United States.

659 Konstantinische Schenkung [494.18] grant of Constantine [...] bequeath all of western Europe to the Papacy: the "Donation of Constantine," supposedly bequeathing to Pope Sylvester and his successors temporal jurisdiction over western Europe, was later discovered to be an eighth-century forgery. See *MMSM* 208–9 for details.

Polykrates [494.25] Polycrates [...] talented ecclesiastics: a condensation of material in *CCP* 44–47.

indem sie ihren Wampum mit gefälschten Muscheln [...] aufbesserten [495.1] forging wampum of porcelain and bone: *CCP* 56.

660 dekretierte der Staat Pennsylvania die Wiedereinführung des Prangers [495.4] Pennsylvania decreed the pillory [...] and a fine: a decree of 21 February 1767, excerpted in *CCP* 62–63.

Egal, ob Krämer, Barbier oder Gastwirt, jeder [...] brachte auf einmal sein eigenes Geld heraus [495.8] tradesmen, barbers, and barkeeps issued money: *CCP* 75, quoting A. B. Hepburn.

den staatlichen Kontrolleuren oft nur um wenige Stunden voraus [495.14] inspectors went from one bank to another [...] broken glass: *CCP* 76.

counterfeit detectors [495.18]: books that grouped banks by states and described the counterfeits made on them, but of little practical value according to Smith (*CCP* 77, 81).

Bicknalls *Counterfeit Detector* [495.23] Bicknall's *Counterfeit Detector* for 1839 [...] 1395 varieties of counterfeit notes: the book and the statistics that follow are cited in *CCP* 78.

Anatomie des Galenus [495.25] Galen's *Anatomy*: Greek physician of the second century A.D. The anatomical details that follow are from the article on Galen in *EB* (9:973–74).

661 die Zahl der italienischen Einwanderer etwa fünfmal höher [495.38] Italians: Smith often notes the disproportionate number of Italian immigrants involved in counterfeiting (*CCP* 90–91, 94–95).

die mit Abstand modernste Fälscherwerkstatt der Welt [495.39] New York [...] greatest modern center of counterfeiting: "New York is the Mecca of counterfeiters, to which pilgrimages are made from the remotest corners of the earth.

It is the greatest distribution center for spurious currency in the world" (*CCP* 54).

661 **Heiliges Jahr** [496.2] Holy Year: a year in which the pope grants the Jubilee indulgence to all Catholics who fulfill the prescribed conditions. Holy Year has been proclaimed every twenty-five years since 1450; the Holy Year of 1950 was extended to 1951.

Schlacht am Hanging Rock [496.14] Battle of Hanging Rock: 6 August 1780.

Kampf gegen das Geldmonopol der Bank of the United States [496.18] his rousing battle with wealth, and the Bank of the United States: recounted in *CCP* 75; Jackson attacked the Second Bank of the United States as an organ of privilege and monopoly.

663 **Demokrit gelesen [...] daß meistens das Unerwartete eintraf** [497.14] Democritus [...] it is the unexpected which occurs: these remarks on the Greek philosopher of the fifth century B.C. are from *EB*'s article on him (7:187–88) – which furnished the Hippocrates anecdote and the composition of the soul as "round, smooth, specially mobile atoms" – and from Saltus (*AN* 36–40), who calls Democritus "the grandsire of materialism" rather than "sire," sees in his philosophy portents of atheism, and notes the philosopher's discovery "that it is the unexpected that occurs" (*AN* 40).

Nirwana [497.28] Nirvana? [...] a goal where nothing was: "In the ears of not a few modern thinkers," writes Saltus of the Buddha's conception of Nirvana, "this promise of annihilation has sounded like a gigantic paradox. It has seemed inconceivable that men could be found who would strive unremittingly their whole lives through to reach a goal where nothing was" (*AN* 25).

Buddhismus [497.30] Buddhism [...] its tangible (idolatrous) form [...] – *Life is suffering*: with concessions in Buddhism to popular superstition, Saltus feels, "Idolatry had begun [...] and today before a gilded statue a wheel of prayers is turned while through the dim temples, domed like a vase, the initiates murmur, 'Life is evil'" (*AN* 23). For Gaddis's variant *"Life is suffering,"* see 764.3.

das große *Vielleicht* [497.33] What sense in the Buddhists? They who affirm. What sense in the Gainas? They who say *Perhaps*: "Another religion without a God, and one which is a twin-sister to Buddhism, is that of the Gainas," writes Saltus, who discusses their philosophy (Jainism) over the next few pages (*AN* 27–29). Similar to the Buddhists, they are more rigorous and austere in their observances, and like the Gnostics have an abhorrence of matter. "In Gainism it is not existence that is an affliction," Saltus concludes, "it is life; and the Nirvāna is less an annihilation than an entrance into eternal beatitude. To distinguish between the two faiths, the Brahmans called the Buddhists, 'They who affirm,' and the Gainas, 'They who say, Perhaps'" (*AN* 29).

663 **Prinz von Kapilavastu** [497.35] Prince of Kapilavastu: that is, Gautama (the Buddha), born in the city of Kapilavastu.

die schier endlose Kette der Wiedergeburten [497.36] the chain of twenty-four lakhs [...] might be severed: in an effort to explain the existence of pain, writes Saltus, "the Hindu accepted an unfathered idea that he is expiating the sins of anterior and unremembered existences, and that he will continue to expiate them until all past transgressions are absolved and the soul is released from the chain of its migrations. According to the popular theory, the chain of migrations consists in twenty-four lakhs of birth, a lakh being one hundred thousand" (*AN* 11); and later: "while the Buddha agreed with the Brahmans that life formed a chain of existences, it was the former who brought the hope that the chain might be severed" (*AN* 21).

Nazarener [497.37] the Nazarene (who, agreeing with the Buddha that life was a sore thing: cf. Saltus: "To him [Jesus], as to the Buddha, life was a tribulation" (*AN* 75).

664 **Cesare Borgia** [497.43] Cesare Borgia Machiavelli: Borgia is spoken highly of in the seventh chapter of Machiavelli's *The Prince*.

Pater Dinet [498.1] Father Dinet: a teacher at the Jesuit school at La Flèche "to whose special care" the young Descartes was entrusted. "Later, during his controversies with Bourdin and Voetius, he tuned to his former school teacher, Father Dinet, for advice" (*EB* 7:244–45).

Schiller [498.2]: Johann Cristoph Friedrich von Schiller (1759–1805), German poet and playwright, second in importance only to Goethe in German literature.

Dale Carnegie [498.3]: (1880–1958) author of the well-known *How to Win Friends and Influence People* (1936), discussed over the next few pages. De Rougemont, in *DS* ("The Demon of Popularity," 110–13), also discusses Carnegie's book in order "to measure to its full extent the dwindling of proper spiritual energy which our 'moral progress' represents."

Mutter der Salome [...] **nicht mal so unrecht hatte** [498.5] Salome's mother was right: Herodias advised her daughter Salome to ask for the head of John the Baptist to stop his slanders against her (Matt. 14:3 ff.).

Damon [498.6] Damon [...] Phintias: "Phintias" is the correct form of the more common Phythias, who, condemned to death by Dionysius, arranged to have his friend Damon take his place to be executed should he not return from a journey. Return he did, and the tyrant was so struck by their trust and friendship that he released them both.

664 **eine halbe Million Meter Polsterstoff** [498.9] a half-million yards of upholstery (aggregate value $1,600,000): from an anecdote illustrating "how richly it sometimes pays to let the other fellow do the talking" (*HWF* 3.6).

Packard [498.11] a Packard car [...] the Connecticut attorney: his reward for showing interest in an aunt's house and antiques (*HWF* 2.6).

Ich wiederhole [...] eine neue Lebenseinstellung. [498.15] "Let me repeat: [...] a new way of life": concluding paragraph of *HWF* 5.

Betrachten Sie es als Gebrauchsanweisung [498.18] "Regard this as [...] specific problem": from *HWF* 1, "Nine Suggestions on How to Get the Most out of This Book."

Sie versuchen wirklich, ein neues Leben anzufangen [498.22] "Ah yes, you are attempting a new way of life": ibid.

Descartes s. S. 131 [498.24] Descartes [...] (cogitans, ergo sum-ing): see 96.21.

665 **Roger Bacon** s. S. 13 [498.29] Roger Bacon [...] geometrical proofs of God: see 7.42.

als potentieller Käufer [...] *Hotel Greeters of America* [498.30] a potential buyer [...] head of the Hotel Greeters of America: a baker had failed for years to sell his goods to the manager of a New York hotel until he learned the manager was president of the Hotel Greeters. He then feigned an interest in the Greeters, after which he was invited to bring samples over to the hitherto recalcitrant manager (*HWF* 2.5).

[498.38] an *action* book: citing Herbert Spencer ("the great aim of education is not knowledge but action"), Carnegie declares: "And this is an *action* book" ("How This Book Was Written – and Why").

Wir verstehen darunter das sogenannte *echte* **Lächeln** [498.40] "I am talking about a real smile [...] in the market place": *HWF* 2.2.

Erwerb von Eigenschaften in den Erwerb von Gütern verwandeln ließ [499.8] exchanged the things worth being for the things worth having: cf. E. E. Cummings's description of a woman "cruel as only she who has exchanged being for having can be cruel" in *Eimi* (New York: Sloane, 1933), 239.

666 **Kapila** [499.14]: (perhaps fl. 600 B.C.) founder of the so-called Sankhya philosophy (which the Buddha used as a point of departure). Saltus writes: "Kapila was the fist serious thinker who looked up into the archaic skies and declared them to be void" (*AN* 10) – that is, void of god(s).

Anaxagoras [499.15] of what the Athenians accused Anaxagoras: impiety: see 392.35.

den geheimen Namen von Jahwe [499.16] the secret name of Jahveh: the name of the god of the Hebrews was represented only by the letters YHWH (now usually rendered Yahweh, Jahveh, etc.; Jehovah is a poor but popular transliteration). The name was never to be pronounced for fear of its falling into enemy hands and being used against him in sorcery, and as a result the original pronunciation is now unknown. In addition, 12–letter, 42–letter, and 72–letter names of Yahweh were known to initiates. (Some of these appear in Waite's *Book of Ceremonial Magic*.) See the chapter entitled "The Holy Unspeakable Name of God" in Graves's *WG*.

666 **wer den Gordischen Knoten zersäbelt** [499.16] who cleft the Gordian knot: Alexander the Great, in "an act of far greater moral significance than is generally realized" (*WG* x; see Graves's long footnote on 380 for significance). There is also an echo here of the line "who cleft the Devil's foot" from John Donne's famous "Song" ("Go and catch a falling star"), which likewise enumerates "strange wonders" similar to Gaddis's.

die Zahl 666 [499.17] the meaning of 666: in the Book of Revelation, the Beast of the Apocalypse is associated with this number – probably, Graves argues (*WG* 281–84), a numerical code for Domitian, emperor of Rome at the time Revelation was written (ca. 95).

Reizworte wie »Vergil« [499.20] calculus. Vergil: "Most men go through college and learn to read Virgil and master the mysteries of calculus without ever discovering how their own minds function" (*HWF* 1.3).

Sie brauchen nicht vier Jahre in Harvard studiert zu haben [499.22] "You don't have to study for four years in Harvard to discover that": Carnegie's response to Harvard president Charles W. Eliot's secret to a successful business interview ("Exclusive attention to the person who is speaking to you is very important. Nothing else is so flattering as that")(*HWF* 2.4).

Andrew Carnegie [499.29] Andrew Carnegie […] Cyrus H. K. Curtis […] George Eastman: see *HWF* 1.3, 3.10, and 2.6 respectively.

667 **etwa bei Bettnässen** [499.42] fraud practiced on a bed-wetting child: his parents allowed him to think he purchased his own new bed, which of course he would not want to wet (*HWF* 1.3).

Umgang mit besonders schwierigen Leuten wie Opernsängern [499.44] deceit practiced on a great opera singer: feigned sympathy was sometimes necessary to get bass Feodor Chaliapin out on stage (*HWF* 3.9).

[500.1] author had read "everything […] to win friends and influence people": from the introductory "How This Book Was Written – and Why."

Charles Schwab [500.10]: (1862–1939), American industrialist, mentioned throughout *HWF*.

667 **Dutch Schultz [...] Al Capone [...] Two-Gun Crowley** [500.10]: noting that even criminals have high opinions of themselves, Carnegie asks: "If Al Capone, 'Two Gun' Crowley, Dutch Schultz, the desperate men behind prison bars don't blame themselves for anything – what about the people with whom you and I come in contact?" (*HWF* 1.1).

Pola Negri [500.11]: (1899–1987), Polish-born American actress, quoted on the importance of flattery (*HWF* 1.2).

Daniel Webster [500.14] ("Daniel Webster [...] most successful ..."): *HWF* 3.4.

[500.17] "You owe it to yourself [...] TO YOUR INCOME!": untraced, perhaps from the cover of the edition of *HWF* Gaddis used.

über den ägyptischen König Akhtoi [500.18] "old King Akhtoi": "And 2,200 years before Christ was born, old King Akhtoi of Egypt gave his son some shrewd advice – advice that is sorely needed today. Old King Akhtoi said one afternoon, between drinks, four thousand years ago: 'Be diplomatic. It will help you gain your point'" (*HWF* 3.2).

die sokratische Methode [500.22] The Socratic method [...] a 'yes, yes' response": *HWF* 3.5.

In ähnlicher Manier sagten Jesus und Konfuzius ihren jeweiligen Spruch [500.26] Christ and Confucius appeared, to recite the Golden Rule: *HWF* 2.6.

[500.35] Nietzsche's idea of the Christian: best illustrated in his *Antichrist*.

668 **Spuren von Jod** [500.42] "A little iodine [...] for five cents": *HWF* 3.6.

für das Kamel, das dort durchs Nadelöhr bugsiert werden sollte [501.1] camel passing through the eye of the needle: see Matt. 19:24.

Reformationssinfonie [501.8] Reformation Symphony: Mendelssohn's Symphony No. 5, composed in 1830 for the tercentenary of the Augsburg Conference (at which Luther announced the establishment of the German Reformed church).

in einem Land, wo Geisteskrankheiten mehr Menschen dahinrafften [501.11] a land where mental diseases tolled more people than all other human ills combined: *HWF* 1.2.

670 **der Pförtner in jenem Bürohaus** [502.32] the janitor [...] call him by his first name: one of Carnegie's success stories boasts: "'When I used to walk through my establishment, no one greeted me. My employees actually looked the other way when they saw me approaching. But now they are all my friends and even the janitor calls me by my first name'" (*HWF*, "How This Book Was Written – and Why").

671 **Was aber hatte David gesagt** [503.3] King David, what did he say: "O my son Absalom, my son, my son Absalom! would God I had died for thee, O Absalom, my son! my son!" (2 Sam. 18:33). See 513.13.

671 Rosalinds Entgegnung beispielsweise [503.11] the words of Rosalind [...] but not for love": *As You Like It*, 4.1.106–8.

672 Welche Form hatte wohl Mr. Pivners Seele [503.32] what was the shape of Mr. Pivner's soul? round, or oblong?: ridiculing early church councils, Saltus writes: "Meanwhile, in a corner of the Orient whither some of the flotsam and jetsam of civilization had drifted, a college of charlatans wearied the centuries with abstractions and discussions on words. Their earlier disputes are legendary. One of them concerned the soul. Was the soul round or oblong? This question was never satisfactorily determined" (*AN* 84–85).

[503.34] round, smooth, and especially mobile?: repeated from 497.22.

[504.36] chapter nine: *HWF* 3.9.

676 König Albert von Belgien [507.12] Albert, King of the Belgians, was killed mountain-climbing: died 1934.

682 Prokrustes [508.15] Procrustes: in Greek legend, a robber who would place his victims on an iron bed and stretch them to fit if too short, and cut off the excess if too long; finally slain by Theseus. He is also called Damastes, as at 511.23.

Theseus [511.24] Theseus [...] the sword his father had left behind: see Ovid's *Metamorphoses*, book 7.

jenes proteische Bild seines Vaters [511.31] Proteus [...] the curious caught him: in book 4 of Homer's *Odyssey*, Menelaus succeeds in holding Proteus long enough to wrest a prophecy from him.

683 Malleus Maleficarum [512.6] *Malleus Maleficarum* [...] sight and touch": *MM* 173, though the "phenomenon" is more fully discussed earlier in the book.

684 Demokrit [513.5] Democritus [...] less liable to dissolution": "Democritus rejected the notion of a deity taking part in the creation or government of the universe, but yielded to popular prejudice so far as to admit the existence of a class of beings, of the same form as men, grander, composed of very subtle atoms, less liable to dissolution, but still mortal, dwelling in the upper regions of the air" (*EB* 7:188).

Anatole [513.9]: undoubtedly named after journalist Anatole Broyard (d. 1990), Gaddis's rival for Sheri Martinelli's affections in the late 1940s. Broyard's affair with her is described in his posthumous memoir *Kafka Was the Rage* (1993).

[513.12] the green muffler: cf. Dostoevski's *The Idiot* (see 937.30 ff.), where Kolya borrows Ganya's new green scarf to deliver Myshkin's letter to Aglaia (2.1).

684 **Absalom** [513.13] Absalom [...] Joab: see 2 Sam. 18:14.

685 *March of the Sardar* [514.2]: final and best-known section of Mikhail Ippolitov-Ivanov's (1859–1935) orchestral suite *Caucasian Sketches* (1895).

686 **Wer geduldig ist, der ist weise** [514.35] "He that is slow to wrath [...] exalteth folly": Prov. 14:29.

687 **die Musik spielte Mozarts** *Türkischen Marsch* [515.12] Mozart's *Turkish March*: the "Allegro all turca" from the Piano Sonata in A Major, K. 300.

691 **die** *Schöne blaue Donau* [518.4] *Blue Danube* waltz: the popular piece by Johann Strauss, Jr. (1825–99).

693 **Vissi d'arte** [520.1] Vissi d'arte [...] ad anima viva: from *Tosca*; see 91.17.

696 **Jones Street** [522.16]: Sheri Martinelli lived on this short street in the West Village.

697 **Muskelmann Rex / Der hatte da diesen Komplex** [523.1] the one about the muscular fellow named Rex: "There was a young fellow named Rex / With diminutive organs of sex; / When charged with exposure / He said with composure, / '*De minimus non curat lex*!'" ("The law does not concern itself with trifles" – a legal maxim).

Il y avait une jeune fille de Dijon [523.3]: a variant of: "Il y avait un jeune homme de Dijon, / Qui n'avait que peu de religion. / It dit, 'Quant à moi, / Je m'encule tous les trois – / Le Père, et le Fils, et le Pigeon.'"

Es gibt ein Arbeiter von Linz [523.4]: a variant of: "Es giebt ein Arbeiter von Tinz, / Er schläft mit ein Mädel von Linz. / Sie sagt, 'Halt sein' plummen, / Ich höre Mann kommen.' / 'Jacht, jacht,' sagt der Plummer, 'Ich binz.'"

698 *Und ewig seufzt der Tiber* [523.5] "The whole gripping story [...] *The Moan of the Tiber*: unidentified.

Too Much Mustard [523.32] *Too Much Mustard* [...] Bach: a 1911 song by Cecil Macklin, featured in the 1939 movie *The Story of Vernon and Irene Castle*. See 537.17 ff. for Bach.

I Can Give You Anything But Love s. S. 793 [523.33]: see 594.11.

700 **Zwei Gefangene Musik hörend** [524.41] Kollwitz print, *"Zwei Gefangene Musik hörend"*: "Two Prisoners Listening to Music" (1925) by Käthe Kollwitz (1867–1945), German painter and lithographer.

Vertreter sind Leute, die zu gefallen stinken [525.11] Cummings' poem, *a salesman is an it that stinks to please*: from *1 X 1* (1944).

703 alles ist entweder konkav oder konvex [526.44] Everything is either concave or convex: a rhyming quip that concludes "... So whatever you dream will be something with sex." That is, in Freudian psychology everything is either a masculine or a feminine symbol; for example, "men raised cigarettes in erect threat; women proffered the olive-tongued cavities of empty glasses" (572.13–14).

der Heilige Franz Xaver wäre nicht einmal eins vierzig groß gewesen s. S. 531 [527.21] Saint Francis Xavier was only four and a half feet tall: see 392.40.

704 das wilde Tier im Dschungel, Tier mit den zwei Rücken [528.13] the beast in the jungle. The beast with two backs [...] the number of the beast: references to a Henry James story (1903), Iago's description of fornication (see 200.36), and Revelations 13:18 (see 499.17), respectively.

706 *Old Masses* [529.17]: cf. *New Masses*, a weekly periodical that appeared in 1926 (the successor to the communist-oriented *Liberator*, which succeeded the original *The Masses*), revamped as a monthly in 1948 under the name *Masses & Mainstream*.

707 Montherlant [530.14] Montherlant [...] Le bonheur [...] de médiocre qualité: Henry de Montherlant (1896–1972), French novelist. Although I could not locate this exact quotation (the French original of Gordon's epigram) in Montherlant's major writings, it is possible Max is misquoting or paraphrasing, for there are many similar sentiments in Montherlant's tetralogy *Les Jeunes filles* (1936–39; translated into English in 1938–40 and again in 1968 – I shall quote from the latter: *The Girls*, trans. Terence Kilmartin [New York: Harper & Row]). For example, compare the present quotation with: "For melancholy is the luxury of the poor in spirit" (437). (Gaddis later commented: "the only other book of Montherlant I remember reading is Les Célibataires though your derivation from Les jeunes filles in another translation sounds likely" [WG/SM].) Other possible borrowings from *The Girls* are Esther's complaint "A woman is always waiting" (128.21; Montherlant: "Women are always waiting, hopefully up to a certain age, hopelessly thereafter" [108]) and the orgasmic possibilities in decapitating a duck (76.13–14; Montherlant: "How he loved to take them [consumptive girls] as they coughed, like those perverts who take ducks as they decapitate them!" [536]).

Vainiger [530.19] Vainiger [...] *Die Philosophie des Als Ob*: *The Philosophy of "As If": A System of the Theoretical, Practical and Religious Fictions of Mankind* (1911) by German philosopher Hans Vaihinger, whom Wyatt and Otto discussed earlier (120.16). The book is recommended in Huxley's *Eyeless in Gaza*, alluded to later (644.37).

708 *The buttons say U.S.* [530.30] The buttons say U.S. [...] and Mo-therrr: song unidentified.

ich bin ihm nicht gewachsen [530.40] als ob [...] nicht gewachsen: Ger. "as if, I give you my word, [...] I am not a match for him." The last phrase is the German original of section 185 of *Why Not Try God*Nietzsche's *Beyond Good and Evil,* which translates: "'I dislike him.' – Why? – 'I am not a match for him.' – Did any one ever answer so?"

709 *Why Not Try God* [531.16] *Why Not Try God?* [...] by Mary Pickford: (1893–1979), popular actress in the early days of movies. Her slight book is highly recommended by Carnegie (*HWF* 2.2).

710 die Katharer, die Albigenser [532.5] Catharism [...] Albigensians: heretical medieval sects that held dualistic beliefs similar to those of the Gnostics and Manichaens (see 433.1 and 402.28, respectively), namely, a good spirit created the spiritual world and an evil one the material world, which includes the human body. For this reason, they held marriage and generation in contempt and commended suicide as a refusal to participate in a world ruled by evil. See *LWW* 74–78.

Bishop Berkeley [532.6]: see 81.9. Haggard notes that both Mary Baker Eddy (author of *Science and Health*) and Bishop Berkeley believed "Matter is merely an illusion" (*DDD* 314).

Science and Health [532.7]: see 478.23. Haggard offers a scathing review of Eddy's personal life and the various editions of her *Science and Health* (*DDD* 310–15).

714 die *Wildente* [534.41] Ibsen [...] *The Wild Duck*: a play (1884) examining the nature of reality, especially when distorted by idealism and romanticism. It has a number of thematic points in common with *R*.

der Heilige Anselm [535.6] Saint Anselm [...] part of his understanding itself": from Saint Anselm's *Proslogion,* chap. 2, an argument for the existence of God.

715 Der Heilige Augustinus [535.14] Saint Augustine [...] before they are produced": source unknown.

Nola [535.22]: popular piano instrumental, written by Felix Arndt.

Save the bones for Henry Jones [535.33] Save the bones for Henry Jones [...] Cause Henry don't eat no meat: lyrics from a song; recorded by Ray Charles on his album *Just Between Us.*

Na ja, wie Frazer schon sagte [535.40] Frazer says [...] absurd practices: *GB* 477 (slightly misquoted).

715 **der Heilige Augustinus [...] für seine Zwecke imitieren** [535.43] Saint Augustine [...] imitating the sacraments: see 719.13.

716 **Die getötete Gottheit** [536.6] The god killed [...] the god's death: paraphrased from Frazer (*GB* 469).

Justin der Märtyrer [536.16] Justin Martyr [...] "the evil spirits practice mimicry": from the *Apology* of Saint Justin the Martyr (114?–165?), who opened the first Christian school in Rome. Gaddis's source unknown.

dieser Gott-trunkene Mensch [536.31] Gott-trunkener Mensch: "A man drunk with God" is what Novalis called Spinoza (*ODQ*)(see 93.1), and what Jack Gibbs calls "Herr Bahnhofmeister Teets" in *JR* (189).

für ein bißchen öffentliche Selbstkritik [536.33] what they offered Spinoza to reform? [...] the Schammatha: from Saltus (*AN* 112–13) who, unlike Anselm, greatly admired the Dutch-Jewish philosopher:

Spinoza was educated to be a rabbi, but with increasing years he grew too big for Jewish theology and declined to visit the synagogue. It was then that some zealot tried to stab him. This argument being insufficient, the elders offered him an annual pension of a thousand florins, on condition that now and then he would appear in the synagogue and keep his opinions to himself. Spinoza was very poor, but his opinions were to him more precious than money. He refused therefore, and was excommunicated at once. The great ban, the Schammatha, was publicly pronounced upon him. For half-an-hour, to the blare of trumpets, he was cursed in the name which contains forty-two letters; in the name of Him who said, *I am that I am and who shall be*; in the name of the Lord of Hosts, the Tetragrammaton; in the name of the Globes, the Wheels, Mysterious Beasts and Ministering Angels; in the name of the great Prince Michael; in the name of Metateron, whose name is like that of his master; in the name of Achthariel Jah. The Seraphim and Ofanim were called upon to give mouth to the malediction. Jehovah was supplicated never to forgive his sin, to let all the curses in the Book of the Law fall upon him and blot him from under the heavens. Then, as the music swooned in a shudder of brass, the candles were reversed, and through the darkness the whole congregation chanted in unison, Amen!
After that, Spinoza, being no longer a Jew, changed his name from Baruch to Benedictus, and turned his thoughts from the Kabbala to Descartes.

718 **Wir eilen mit schwachen, doch emsigen Schritten** [537.17] Bach [...] feeble but diligent footsteps": from the cantata "Jesu, der du meine Seele" (1724), text based on a hymn by Johann Rist. The animated duet (for soprano and alto) translates (by Charles Enderby):

We hasten with feeble yet eager footsteps
O Jesu, O Master, to crave Thine aid
Diligently seekest Thou the sick and those that stray
O hear us as we, our voices raised, for succour pray.
May Thy merciful countenance be gracious unto us.

über der Campagna, wo sich Attilas Hunnenheer [538.7] the sky over the Campagna where Attila's Huns [...] unburied dead: from Conybeare: "The legend, however, that it was on the third day or after three days that Jesus was raised from the dead, was not generated by prophecy alone; for it was a popular belief that the spirit or soul of a man remains by his corpse for a period of three days – a belief glanced at in the legend of the raising of Lazarus" (*MMM* 296). He continues in a note (373–74):

> This belief is quaintly illustrated in a story told by Damascius (about A.D. 450) in his life of Isidore. The Huns, under Attila, fought in the Campagna against the armies of Rome. The battle was so fierce and prolonged that no combatants were left alive on either side. But the fray did not then cease, for the spirits of the slain proceeded to fall on one another; and for three days and nights a ghostly battle raged over the waste plain on which their bodies were stretched unburied. And there were those, says Damascius, who were witnesses of the phantom warfare, and heard the war-cries of the dead as they continued, with unabated fury, to rain blows upon one another.

722 *Zauberlehrling* [540.23] *Sorcerer's Apprentice*: symphonic work by French composer Paul Dukas (1897), based on Goethe's ballad "Der Zauberlehrling."

II.6

724 Des gens passent. On a des yeux. On les voit [542.epigraph]: Fr.: "People pass by. One has eyes. One sees them"; source unknown.

725 Carnot [543.33]: Sadi Carnot (1837–94), fourth president of the French Republic.

727 es stammt von den Gebrüdern Grimm [544.32] Grimm Brothers? the *Froschkönig*: "The Frog King," the story Esme reads on page 273.

728 Dasselbe wie mit Johan Hus [545.18] What happened to Huss? [...] the Antichrist is to be found in Rome: from *EB*'s account (11:942–43) of Huss's trial and death; cf. *BM* 140–44 and *MMSM* 26ff.

O sancta simplicitas! s.S. 66 [545.25]: see 46.18.

der Boyg [545.27] Boyg: Gaddis provided the following gloss for his Italian translator (quoted in Koenig's "'Splinters from the Yew Treee,'" 92):

> p. 545 l.27 the "Boyg" was the troll king in Ibsen's "Peer Gynt" who wanted Peer to marry his ugly troll daughter and, in order to cure Peer of his 'pestilent nature' and make him see as trolls do, says he will scratch his eyes so that Peer will "see awry; but all that you see will seem fair and brave."
> The reference is to Brown, as elaborated on page 375 lines 15–19, Brown as the Boyg-troll king having perverted Wyatt's vision so that the false looks beautiful.

However, the Boyg and the troll king are not the same; the former is a mysterious voice in the darkness, an insubstantial substance, that advises Peer to go around rather than through it. (In act 4 Peer sees a resemblance between the Boyg and the Egyptian sphinx.) The translators of the edition Gaddis used interpret the Boyg chiefly "as the Spirit of Compromise among other things."

728 **Sein Schicksal sei, daß er keinen Namen habe** [545.32] "I lay this destiny [...] receives from me": from "The Romance of Llew Llaw Gyffes," a story from the Welsh collection of legends *The Mabinogion*, in Lady Charlotte Guest's translation as quoted by Graves (*WG* 251–58). In a kind of virgin birth, a young boy is born to Arianrhod, who later denies any kinship and refuses to name him. But when the boy (like Wyatt) skillfully kills a wren, she says: "Verily, with a steady hand did the lion aim at it." Thereafter, the boy is called "Llew Llaw Gyffes" – the Lion with the Steady Hand.

talitha cumi [545.35]: the Aramaic words ("Damsel, arise") Jesus used to raise Jairus's twelve-year-old daughter from death (Mark 5:41).

diese kluge Jungfrau [545.35] wise virgin: from the parable of the wise and foolish virgins (Matt. 25); like Janet, wise virgins look for Christ's coming.

Shabbetai Zebi [545.40]: these details are from Conybeare's sketch of the career of the seventeenth-century Jewish messiah Sabatai Levi (as he spells it), illustrating "how constant and unvarying in character continued to be the expectations and aspirations of this downtrodden race" (*MMM* 363–66). Forced to choose between death or Islam, he "chose the latter; and Felure [Conybeare's source] testifies to the despair with which the apostasy of their Messiah filled the Jews of Turkey."

729 **Ein Tag mit dem Papst** [546.22] *A Day with the Pope*: a slim picture-book by Canadian author Charles Hugo Doyle, published in 1950, which describes the daily duties of the pope.

mi piace [546.27: It., "I like it."

Der Gedanke an den Selbstmord ist ein starkes Trostmittel [546.31] the thought of suicide [...] Nietzsche: from *Beyond Good and Evil*, section 157.

732 **Die Sieben Todsünden** [548.30] The Seven Sins [...] "field full of folk": in William Langland (fl. 1330–86) famous narrative poem *Piers Plowman*, the narrator falls asleep and dreams of "a fair felde ful of folke" between a lofty tower and a deep dungeon (Prologue); the phrase is repeated in passus 5 (Piers's second dream), in which Reason preaches, then Repentance hears the confessions of the Seven Deadly Sins.

734 **Der goldenen Esel** [549.42] Lucius in the *Golden Ass* [...] "odoriferous feet": Lucius Apuleius's second-century satirical romance *Metamorphoses* (more commonly known as *The Golden Ass*) concerns a young man named Lucius who is accidentally turned into an ass, in which form he has

many adventures. He is eventually restored to human form by Isis: Graves (*WG* 53–54) excerpts this famous section from William Adlington's 1566 translation.

735 wie die Rose von Lima s.S. 497 [550.36] Rose of Lima: see 368.2. For the details of her "innocency," see *PPM* 107–9.

Die düstre Glut [...] *Der Fliegende Holländer* [551.3] "somber glow" [...] Flying Dutchman [...] go to heaven in a wave: upon being introduced to Senta (see 93.22), the Dutchman sings (in Paul England's 1895 translation; the one Gaddis used is unknown):

How like the voice of long-forgotten ages
Her gentle presence speaks to me!
All that my dreams have writ in memory's pages,
All that I longed for, here I see!
Oft through the gloom there broke upon my vision
One radiant form, a woman sweet and fair;
But evermore 'twould prove some fiend's derision,
Soon fled the dream, and left me to despair!
In this dull glow that in my heart is burning
Dare I believe the fires of love returning?
Ah no! redemption now is all I crave;
Has this dear angel come my soul to save?

This opens the duet that closes the second act. The opera ends as Senta (in the words of the libretto) "throws herself into the sea. Immediately the Dutchman's ship disappears in the waves. In the red light of the rising sun, the glorified forms of Senta and the Dutchman are seen, in a close embrace, rising from the wreck of the vessel, and soaring upwards."

I min Tro s.S. 507 [551.8] "I min Tro [...] Solveig: see 375.31.

736 das Geheimnis, das auch Wotan nur seinem Sohn anvertraute [552.3] What Wotan taught his son [...] The power of doing without happiness: from George Bernard Shaw's *The Perfect Wagnerite* (4th ed., 1923), a commentary on Wagner's *Ring* (see 196.16). In his synopsis of *The Valkyrie*, Shaw writes: "With the son [Siegmund] he himself [Wotan] leads the life of a wolf, and teaches him the only power a god can teach, the power of doing without happiness" (New York: Dover, 1967, 35).

Frääre dschaake [552.30] Frerra jacka [...] soney malatina: a phonetic rendering of the popular nursery song: "Frère Jacques, Frère Jacques, / Dormez-vous, dormez-vous? / Sonnez les mâtines, sonnez les mâtines, / Ding dang dong."

738 *Gratziääh* [552.40] grot-zy, grot-sy: *grazie* (It.: "thanks").

Der Mithraskult [...] hatte im Grunde nie eine reelle Chance [553.8] Mithraism [...]

failed because it lacked central authority: "There was," Phythian-Adams points out, "as far as we know, no central supreme authority, which could combine the scattered units into a compact and formidable whole. Thus, when the crisis came, Mithraism, though it numbered countless adherents, though it boasted generals, governors, and emperors among the faithful, was helpless before the ordered onset of the Church Militant: isolated and impotent, its small communities could be attacked and crushed in detail" (*M* 67).

738 Chrysipp s. S. 475 [553.14] Chrysippus: see 352.30.

Aber wie sagt Pascal doch so richtig [553.21] Pascal said, There's as much difference [...] but that was Montaigne: from the conclusion of Michel de Montaigne's (1533–92) essay "On the Inconstancy of Our Actions." Pascal borrowed much from Montaigne; Gaddis said he found this quote ascribed to Pascal in a book on Pirandello, which I've not identified.

739 *Morro Castle* [553.29]: a luxury liner that caught fire 7 September 1934 off the coast of New Jersey. Only 85 of the 219 passengers survived.

Narzissenfest in Hawaii s. S. 137 [553.32] Narcissus Festival in Hawaii: see 100.21.

Zu Philippi? [554.2] At Philippi? [...] Why, I will see thee at Philippi, then: cf. 382.40; here the allusion is to Shakespeare's *Julius Caesar*. The ghost of Caesar appears to Brutus as his "evil spirit" and warns him that he will reappear at Philippi, to which Brutus responds: "Why, I will see thee at Philippi then" (4.3.286).

745 Chavenet s. S. 836 [558.29]: see 628.29.

746 alljährliches Fest von Adam und Eva [558.37] SS Adam and Eve: their feast day is given different days in the martyrologies, but 24 December is the most common.

vierzig Jungfrauen von Antiochien [558.37] 40 Maidens martyred at Antioch: the forty Christian virgins put to death under Decius in Antioch about 251 (*BM* 17).

sah aus wie eine gigantische Heidi [559.11] Heidi: the Swiss girl in the novel of the same name by Johanna Spyri (1881), portrayed by Shirley Temple in a popular movie (1937).

Puritanerdenkmal von Augustus Saint-Gaudens [559.18] Saint-Gaudens' statue of the Puritan: Augustus Saint-Gaudens (1848–1907), Irish-born American sculptor. The famous statue is now in Merrick Park, Springfield, Massachusetts.

[559.19] heirs to all the ages and the foremost files of time: from Tennyson's "Locksley Hall" (see 290.36), a poem often quoted in *JR*.

747 *Seid aber Täter des Worts und nicht Hörer allein* [559.27] *Be Ye Doers of the word, and not hearers only*: "… deceiving your own selves" (James 1:22); the line is quoted in an anecdote in *MM* (128).

748 *In der U-Bahn-Station Vierzehnte Straße* [560.12] the Fourteenth Street I.R.T.-B.M.T. subway station: at Union Square (Fourteenth Street and Broadway), a large station for both the Lexington Avenue line (formerly known as the East Side I.R.T. [Interborough Rapid Transit]) and the Broadway Metro Transit, which runs NW-SE through Manhattan.

750 *der ewige Moment des cartesischen Gottes: die Quadratur des Kreises* [561.34] the Cartesian God, Who can will a circle to be square: in his discussion of the Cartesian doctrine of eternal truths, Jacques Maritain notes: "If in the last analysis these truths depend, as Descartes insists, not on divine essence itself as the eternal object of divine intellection, but on creative liberty – in such a way that God might have been able to make possible a square circle or a mountain without a valley – our knowledge of these truths no longer derives its certainty from essences, but rather that it results from a natural revelation instructing us in what, effectively, divine liberty has chosen" (*The Dream of Descartes*, trans. Mabelle L. Andison [New York: Philosophical Library, 1944], 193 n.28; cf. 46).

751 *Tragik satt für Jahrzehnte* [563.9] the evil thereof is sufficient unto the day: see Matt. 6:34.

752 *Weihnachtskonzert von Francesco Manfredini* [563.26] Francesco Manfredini's Christmas Concerto: Italian violinist and composer (ca. 1680–1748); the 1718 work is also known as *Concerto Grosso per il santissimo natale*.

753 *U. Nu (Thakin Nu)* [564.2]: prime minister of Burma at the time.

II.7

759 *Betrachten wir nun den Kampf ums Überleben* [...] *Die Entstehung der Arten* [568.epigraph] We will now discuss [...] *Origin of Species*: from *ODQ*; cf. 626.27–30.

Es erinnert mich eher an dieses Kloster [568.1] that convent [...] that was turned into a madhouse: the location of Claas Sluter's (fl. 1385–404) sculpture *Puits de Moïse*, discussed by Conway (*VEF* 30), who heard the cries of madmen when visiting the sculpture.

Händel [...] *The Triumph of Truth and Justice* [568.17] Handel [...] *The Triumph of Truth and Justice*: that is, *The Triumph of Time and Truth*, an oratorio. (The man is perhaps confusing Handel's oratorio with Superman's "never-ending battle for truth, justice, and the American way.")

760 einen von diesen entzückenden Renaults gekauft [...] Ein Original? [569.14] Renaults [...] An original?: the automobile is confused with the painter Georges Rouault (1871–1958). A similar gag appears at 940.25.

Murti-Bing [569.21]: "The Pill of Murti-Bing" is the title of the first chapter of Czeslaw Milosz's *The Captive Mind* (trans. Jane Zielonko [New York: Knopf, 1953]). Gaddis informed me it first "appeared as 'The Happiness Pill' in Partisan Review Sept-Oct 1951 which must be where I saw it. Milosz is describing a 1932 novel of Witkiewicz titled INSATIABILITY with which I'm not familiar" (WG/SM). Milosz describes his fellow Pole's dystopian novel (actually published in 1930; an English translation appeared in 1977) as follows:

Witkiewicz's heroes are unhappy in that they have no faith and no sense of meaning in their work. This atmosphere of decay and senselessness extends throughout the entire country. And at that moment, a great number of hawkers appear in the cities peddling Murti-Bing pills. Murti-Bing was a Mongolian philosopher who had succeeded in producing an organic means of transporting a "philosophy of life." This Murti-Bing "philosophy of life," which constituted the strength of the Sino-Mongolian army, was contained in pills in an extremely condensed form. A man who used these pills changed completely. He became serene and happy. [...] A man who swallowed Murti-Bing pills became impervious to any metaphysical concerns. The excesses into which art falls when people vainly seek in form the wherewithal to appease their spiritual hunger were but outmoded stupidities for him.

Milosz compares those who embrace communism – especially intellectuals – to Witkiewicz's Murti-Bing addicts.

762 Er unterhielt sich mit einem flattrigen blonden Boy [570.12] a fluttering blond boy who [...] resembled an oeuf-dur-mayonnaise: sounds like Truman Capote.

Edna St. Vincent Millay [570.39]: (1892–1950), American poet. Arnold Genthe's well-known photograph of her "posing with magnolias" is now at the Museum of Modern Art.

Pyramus und Thisbe [571.10] Pyramus and Thisbe: famous thwarted lovers, recounted in Ovid's *Metamorphoses,* travestied in Shakespeare's *Midsummer Night's Dream.*

764 Ruskin [571.35] Ruskin [...] a book about stones: John Ruskin (1819–1900), prominent English art critic, author of *The Stones of Venice* (1851–53). He dated his "entry into life" from his first sight of the Alps (*VEF* 60–61).

lauschte den festlichen Klängen jenes Bartscherersohns [572.17] barber's son who had learned to play on a dumb spinet: according to *EB* (11:143), Handel was the son of a barber-surgeon and learned to play on a clavichord smuggled into his attic.

768 **Jupiter-Sinfonie** [575.1] *Jupiter Symphony*: Mozart's forty-first (and last) symphony (1788). (Coincidentally, it is playing on the radio at Brown's party, which is taking place at the same time as Esther's: see 655.13.)

769 **Da hat Göring auch gerne getafelt!** [575.22] *Goering's*: Hermann Göring (1893–1946), a high-ranking member of Hitler's Third Reich.

770 **Yaddo** [576.26]: a mansion in Saratoga Springs, New York, since 1926 a working place for invited writers and other artists.

771 **Victor Hugo wollte, daß man ganz Paris nach ihm benennt** [577.10] *Victor Hugo wanting the whole city of Paris renamed for him*: Carnegie cites this as an example of how various people "got their feeling of importance" (*HWF* 2.2).

774 **Geschichte des mechanischen Klaviers** [579.21] *player pianos*: the subject of an amusing article Gaddis published while in Europe working on *R*, entitled "'Stop Player. Joke No. 4'" (*Atlantic Monthly*, July 1951). They were at the heart of book on technology and the arts that Gaddis planned to write, fragments of which appear as Jack Gibbs's *Agapē Agape* in *JR*.

775 **Bathysiderodromophobie** [580.13] *Bathysiderodromophobia*: this seems to mean "deep-iron-road-fear," that is, a fear of subways: see 618.8–9.

[580.34] *What's he to Hecuba*: marveling at an actor's identification with his role, Hamlet asks: "What's Hecuba to him or he to Hecuba, / That he should weep for her?" (2.2.585–86).

777 *Sieben Säulen der Weisheit* [581.20] *Seven Pillars of Wisdom*: T. E. Lawrence's (1888–1935) lengthy account of the Arab revolt against the Turks and his own adventures as "Lawrence of Arabia." It was edited by his friend Bernard Shaw and is somewhat indebted to Doughty's *Travels in Arabia Deserta* (43.13), for which Lawrence wrote an introduction (see 405.31 ff.).

[581.28] *lost horizon*: title of a popular novel by English writer James Hilton (1900–54).

780 *Nearer My God to Thee* [583.37]: well-known hymn (*PH* #200), words by Sarah Flower Adams.

781 *Mit Kanone und Kamera durch Flatbush and Greenpoint* [584.11] James Leak [...] *With Gun and Camera in Flatbush and Greenpoint*: fictitious.

Charles Reade [584.19]: (1814–82), English novelist, best known for his medieval romance *The Cloister and the Hearth* (1861).

George Borrow s. S. 1157 [584.20]: see 892.11.

Ischia [584.28]: island resort off Naples, favored at that time by homosexuals.

782 *The Great Elopement* [585.18]: like *The Gods Go A-Begging* (600.26), a suite of Handel's music arranged by English conductor Sir Thomas Beecham.

789 *Und er verbarg sich* von Ignazio Silone [590.44] a play by Silone called *And He Hid Himself*: Ignazio Silone (1900–78), anti-fascist Italian writer, best known for his novel *Bread and Wine*. Inspired by that novel, *And He Hid Himself* (*Ed Egli Si Nascose*, 1945) concerns a leftist agitator in Mussolini's Italy named Murica who betrays his comrades to the police. He develops a "horror of impunity" and, after years of disbelief, begins yearning for the existence of God. "If I finally decided to confess everything," he tells the leftist leader who threatens to kill him, "taking no thought of the consequences, it was with the deliberate and clear-cut intent of setting up order once again between the world and myself, of restoring the ancient boundary between good and evil, without which I couldn't go on living any more" (trans. Darina Tranquilli [New York: Harper Bros., 1945], 100). Murica rejoins his comrades, is arrested by the police, and dies from their brutality (with heavy crucifixion imagery), but his death mobilizes the peasants for further resistance.

791 *Was macht der Magnet bei den Eisenteilen* [593.4] "A magnet hung in a hardware shop": "a silly song from gilbert & sullivan," says Jack Green (51). See *Patience*, act 2.

[593.44] *faggot* [...] Greek *phagein*: the Greek etymology is more ingenious than plausible. "Faggot," which began as a contemptuous term for a woman, is thought to have become associated with gay men either because "fags" (British slang for cigarettes) favored by gays were considered effeminate by cigar and pipe smokers when first introduced at the end of World War I, or from "fag," meaning a boy servant or lackey in the British school system.

793 *I Can't Give You Anything But Love* [594.11]: 1926 song by Dorothy Fields (words) and Jimmy McHugh (music), featured in several films of the 1930s and 1940s. Cf. 523.33.

[594.15] *Enthousiazein* [...] spirit of God: cf. de Rougemont's discussion of Platonic love (*LWW* 55):

Plato, alike in the *Phaedrus* and in the *Symposium*, speaks of a frenzy that, spreading from the body, infects the spirit with malignant humors. This is not love as he commends it. But there is, he says, another kind of frenzy or delirium which is neither conceived nor born in a man's soul except by the inspiration of heaven. It is alien to us, its spell is wrought from without; it is a transport, an infinite rapture away from reason and natural sense. It is therefore to be called *enthusiasm*, a word which actually means "possessed by a god," for the frenzy not only is of heavenly origin, but culminates at its highest in a new attainment of the divine.
Such is Platonic love.

[594.28] I never wanted to see him [...] I have to see him: "dialogue that echoes Edward in [Eliot's play] *The Cocktail Party*," commented James J. Stathis in his review of the Meridian *R* in *Critique* (5 [1962]: 92).

796 **Händels Cembalo-Suite Nr. 5** [596.28] *Harmonious Blacksmith*: popular name for the air and variations from Handel's harpsichord suite no. 5 (1720).

Frothinghams Aratos [597.10]: American theologian and writer Nathaniel Langdon Frothingham's (1793–1870) verse translation of the *Phenomena* of Aratos, quoted earlier at 6.29–30. Frothingham's translation is included in his *Metrical Pieces, Translated and Original* (1855).

799 **Melancholie alles Fertigen** [599.4] Nietzsche [...] "the melancholia of things completed": section 277 of Nietzsche's *Beyond Good and Evil* translates: "It is too bad! Always the old story! When a man has finished building his house, he finds that he has learnt unawares something which he *ought* absolutely to have known before he – began to build. The eternal, fatal 'Too late!' The melancholia of everything *completed*!"

[599.20] killing the one thing you ... love: see 464.41.

Die Negation als Prinzip [599.32] negation [...] the Eternal No: Stanley has it backward: Nietzsche (especially in *Antichrist*) says *Christianity* is the Eternal No and the embodiment of negation.

800 **Einstein** [...] **Epstein** [...] **Gertrude** [600.12]: cf. this anonymous limerick: "There's a wonderful family called Stein, / There's Gert and there's Epp and there's Ein; / Gert's poems are bunk, / Epp's statues are junk, / And no one can understand Ein." "Epp" is American-born British sculptor Sir Jacob Epstein (1880–1959); Gertrude Stein (1874–1946) will be alluded to later (757.41).

Heisenbergs Unschärferelation [600.15] Heisenberg's Principle of Uncertainty: states that any observation of a system inevitably disturbs the system under observation. It was formulated in relation to the measurement of atomic systems by German physicist Werner Heisenberg (1901–76).

ein wenig niedriger als Engel [600.20] "a little lower than the angels" [...] That was Pope: Alexander Pope's couplet "What would this Man? now upward will he soar, / And little less than Angel would be more" (*Essay on Man*, 1:173–74) is based on Ps. 8:4–5: "What is man, that thou art mindful of him? and the son of man, that thou visitest him? For thou has made him a little lower than the angels, and has crowned him with glory and honour."

[600.29] Handel. *The Gods Go A-Begging*: see 585.18.

801 **dieser also auch keine feste Burg, sondern ein** [...] **hastig errichtetes Verteidigungswerk** [600.40] the interior castle: title (*El castillo interior*, 1583) of a

famous mystical treatise by Saint Teresa of Avila, considered by many to be her finest work (and cited occasionally in *LWW*). She envisions the soul as "a castle made of a single diamond [...] in which there are many rooms, just as in Heaven there are many mansions."

801 **Robert Maillart** [601.3]: (1872–1940), Swiss engineer and bridge designer. His Schwandbach Bridge is featured on pp. 90–91 of Max Bill's *Robert Maillart* (1949; trans. W. P. M. Keatinge Clay [New York: Praeger, 1969]).

806 **Und grauenvoll, was sie getan [...] Stopfte sie mit Käfern voll** s.S. 831 [604.33] A dreadful crime she did commit [...] Black beetles in walnut shells: apparently from "Hannah the Horror of Hampstead" (624.29).

807 **Fedja aus Tolstoijs *Auferstehung*** [605.22] Fedya [...] Tolstoy's *Redemption* [...] hate them for the harm: Fedya, separated from his wife Lisa, fakes a suicide to leave her free to marry a childhood sweetheart. He relates the story in a bar (2.1: the scene from which Feddle quotes), where he is overheard and arrested. Learning at his trial that either exile or an annulment of Lisa's second marriage will occur, Fedya shoots himself.
The play's Russian title, *Zhivoi trup* (1900), is properly translated *The Living Corpse*; *Redemption* is the title Arthur Hopkins used when first producing the play in New York (1918); Gaddis's use of the latter title stresses the importance of redemption to his novel.

809 **Es gab da diese schreckliche Kluft zwischen dem, was ich fühlte, und dem, was ich leisten konnte** [606.31] "There was something terribly lacking between what I felt and what I could do": from an exchange between Fedya and Prince Sergius (1.4), which reveals many similarities between Fedya and Wyatt:

PRINCE SERGIUS (*after a pause*): I must confess that you bewilder me. You with your gifts and charm and really au fond – a wonderful sense of what's right. How could you have permitted yourself to plunge into such tawdry distractions? How could you have forgotten so far what you owed to yourself? Tell me, why did you let your life fall into this ruin?

FEDYA (*suppressing emotion*): ... Ah, yes, my ruin. Well, first, drink, not because it tasted well, because everything I did disappointed me so, made me so ashamed of myself. I feel ashamed now, while I talk to you. Whenever I drank, shame was drowned in the first glass, and sadness. Then music, not opera or Beethoven, buy gypsy music; the passion of it poured energy into my body, while those dark bewitching eyes looked into the bottom of my soul. (*He sighs*) And the more alluring it all was, the more shame I felt afterwards.

PRINCE SERGIUS (*after a pause*): But what about your career?

FEDYA: My career? This seems to be it. Once I was a director of a bank. There was something terribly lacking between what I felt and what I could do. (*Abruptly*) But enough, enough of myself. It makes me rather nervous to think about myself.

809 Maillart [...] Brücke von Salginatobel [606.36] Maillart's bridge at Salginatobel: featured on pp. 60–64 of Bill's *Robert Maillart*.

Der Bogen einer Brücke schläft nie s. S. 132 [606.39] *The arch never sleeps*: see 96.44.

813 Sappho [610.11]: famous woman poet (sixth century B.C.) from the Greek island of Lesbos (whence lesbian).

814 Feenspuk im Garten [611.10] fairies in the bottom of your garden: from Rose Fyleman's (1877–1957) once-popular poem for children, "The Fairies" (*ODQ*).

817 Händelsche Feuerwerksmusik [613.23] Handel's *Royal Fireworks Music*: one of the more popular of Handel's orchestral suites.

Bye Bye Blackbird [613.23]: 1926 song by Mort Dixon (words) and Ray Henderson (music), popularized by Eddie Cantor and later identified with Georgie Price.

On the Sunny Side of the Street [613.26]: 1930 song by Dorothy Fields (words) and Jimmy McHugh, featured in a number of films in the 1940s and 1950s, including the movie of the same name (1951).

821 die Einheit der Handlung, wie Aristoteles sagt [616.4] on whole, and express an entire perfect action, as Aristotle says: in chap. 7 of his *Poetics*, Aristotle states: "The truth is that, just as in the other imitative arts one imitation is of one thing, so in poetry the story, as an imitation of action, must represent one action, a complete whole, with its several incidents so closely connected that the transposal or withdrawal of any one of them will disjoin and dislocate the whole" (trans. Ingram Bywater).

Maubeuge [616.15] Mauberge: that is, Maubeuge, city in northern France.

822 Wir eilen mit schwachen, doch emsigen Schritten s. S. 718 [617.20] "We hasten with feeble but diligent footsteps": see 537.22.

823 Wenn es keinen Gott gäbe, müßte man ihn erfinden [617.22] Voltaire [...] it would be necessary to invent him": the well-known saying is from *Epîtres: a l'auteur du nouveau livre des trois imposteurs* (1769) and is quoted (but translated differently) in *ODQ* and *AN* 194–95. Stanley doesn't "read Voltaire of course" because his works were on the Catholic *Index*.

Simon [617.34] Simon Magus: Peter's chief adversary in the Clementine *Recognitions* (see 373.1). In book 2, chap. 9, a disciple of Peter's named Aquila reveals that Simon once promised, in return for helping him to win the love of a woman named Luna, that he would allow Aquila and his friends "'to be invested with the highest honours, and we should be believed by men to be gods.'"

824 *Musica Donum Dei* [618.35]: "Music is the Gift of God."

826 "Wer, wenn ich schriee ..." s. S. 826 ff. [620.28]: see 622.16 ff.

Evolutionäre Adaptionsleistungen [620.33] *The Vertebrate Eye and its Adaptive Radiation*: a thick volume on comparative ocular biology by Gordon L. Walls, published in 1942.

828 *Duineser Elegien* [622.16] Duino Elegies [...] Die erste: the opening lines of the first ("Die erste") of Rilke's *Duino Elegies*; see 277.34 ff. for a translation of the first seven lines.

829 *Sonette an Orpheus* [622.34]: Rilke's *Sonnets to Orpheus* (also 1922), after the *Elegies* his greatest poetic achievement.

"Weisst du's noch nicht? [622.44]: "Don't you know *yet*?" ("First Elegy," l. 22).

830 so eine Art Scheinschwangerschaft [623.42] hysterical pregnancy: "Hysterical persons involuntarily counterfeit the symptoms of physical disease as a means of attracting attention to themselves," Dr. Haggard notes, "of attaining sympathy, and of avoiding disagreeable situations. [...] Hysterical women may believe themselves pregnant and show all the signs of that condition [...]" (*DDD* 288).

831 Irgendwo auf der Welt ist immer Morgen [624.22] It's always morning somewhere [...] That's Longfellow: the line "'Tis always morning somewhere in the world" is from Richard Hengist Horne's *Orion* (1843; *ODQ*). The man in uniform is probably thinking of Longfellow's last poem, "The Bells of San Blas" (1882): "Out of the shadows of night / The world rolls into light; / It is daybreak everywhere."

Hannah the Horror of Hampstead [624.29]: apparently a British ballad.

[625.14] as though he'd never seen [...] what was able to take his breath away: from Browning's "A Likeness" (see 193.18).

832 Limerick [...] mit *Phoebe* und *einer* Amöbe [625.22] the campiest limerick about an a-*mee*ba and the queen of *She*-ba: cf. "There was a young lady named Sheba, / Fell in love with an eager amoeba. / This queer bit of jelly / Crept into her belly, / And ecstatically murmured, *"Ich liebe!"*

833 Einstein sagt [...] Spielchen treibt [626.10] Einstein says [...] the universe: in a letter to his colleague Max Born, Albert Einstein wrote: "I cannot believe that God would choose to play dice with the universe."

[626.38] time past and future, both contained in this limicolous present: cf. the opening lines of Eliot's "Burnt Norton" (see 160.30); "limicolous" means "mud-dwelling."

834 **Daddys Grab wird umgebettet, umgebettet** [626.40] They're moving Father's grave: source unknown.

835 **ein Wort wie *venerisch*** [627.17] Derive veneral: Middle English *venerealle*, Latin *venereus*, *Venus* (goddess of love).

was deinen Emerson angeht [627.35] Emerson [...] that eclectic digger: perhaps an allusion to Emerson's observation: "There is no way to success in our art but to take off your coat, grind paint, and work like a digger on the railroad, all day and every day" (*ODQ*).

836 *Judas Maccabaeus* s. S. 184 [628.27]: see 136.6.

Hapteron [628.33]: the attaching organ that allows aquatic plants to fasten onto rocks.

[628.38] Mickey Mouse semaphored annul: five or ten minutes after six.

837 **Suckling** [629.24] Suckling [...] 'tis let loose": the conclusion of "Love's Offense"; the full text of the poem can be found in *The Works of Sir John Suckling*, ed. Thomas Clayton (Oxford: Clarendon Press, 1971), 1:52–53.

839 **Carruthers seine Stute** s. S. 91 [631.6] Carruthers had a mare: see 66.2.

Cómo? qué dice ... ? [631.10]: "What? what did you say?"

840 **ein bißchen Gras und zwei Bennys obendrauf** [631.28] take two strips of benny [...] a connection uptown we can probably catch: taken from William S. Burroughs's first novel, *Junkie* (1953; Gaddis owns the first Ace edition published under the pseudonym William Lee; I'm citing the later Ace edition published under his real name): "'Benzedrine is a good kick,' [a woman named Mary] said. 'Three strips of the paper or about ten tablets. Or take two strips of benny and two goof balls. They get down there and have a fight. It's a good drive.' [...] 'Why don't we go uptown? I know several good connections we can probably catch about now'" (28–29).

eine Führernatur s. S. 229 [631.36] leader of men: see 171.38.

841 **Er starb ganz still in meinem Apartment** s. S. 89 [632.4] He died in my apartment in Paris when I was having my first one-man show: see 63.28.

[632.11] B. M. T.: the Broadway subway line; see 560.12.

Füllet die Wasserkrüge mit Wasser [632.26] There's no more to drink [...] Woman! what have I to do: a parody of Jesus' first miracle at the wedding at Cana (John 2).

Denn ich bin gekommen, den Menschen zu erregen [632.37] For I am come [...] his own household: Matt. 10:35–36. Wyatt earlier quoted from the same chapter (430.22).

[633.20] caul: a membrane that sometimes envelops the head at birth, considered a good omen by the superstitious.

[633.41] Arse gratias artis: a ribald version of *ars gratia artis* (Lat.: "art for art's sake").

843 Ferita [634.14]: in mysticism, "the heart-wound, or transverberation of the heart" (*PPM* 118).

Blutschwitzen im Garten Gethsemane [634.14] sweat of blood in Gethsemane: "Certain stigmaticas," Summers notes, "for example St. Lutgarde of Tongres, the Cistercian nun who died in 1246; the Capuchiness St. Veronica Giuliani, 1660–1727; Blessed Catherine of Racconigi, a Domicaness of the Third Order, 1486–1547; and many others suffered the sweat of blood in Gethsemane" (*PPM* 127).

[634.41] Lupercalia: see 312.10.

845 Anselm [...] zertrat die Orchidee s. S. 269 [635.35] the orchid under foot: see 201.20.

846 Daß er gelassen verschmäht, uns zu zerstören [636.1] Und wir bewundern [...] uns zu zerstören: "And why we adore it so is because it serenely / disdains to destroy us" ("First Elegy," ll. 6–7).

849 *Auf Messers Schneide* [638.24] *The Razor's Edge*: 1944 novel by Somerset Maugham (see 262.8) concerning two Americans abroad: the elder a determined social climber, the younger a man in search of spiritual values, which he eventually finds in India.

[638.28] philander: unlike the earlier derivation of "faggot" (593.44), this one is correct.

Iphigenie [638.36] Iphigenia: daughter of Agamemnon, sacrificed by him to gain favorable winds for the Greek fleet on its way to Troy; however, she was spirited away from her funeral pyre by Artemis and lived to be united with her brother Orestes; she is the subject of plays by Euripides, Racine, Goethe, and others.

851 und dann ziehen wir uns ein paar Bennys rein [640.15] We'll just go [...] and get high on benny: another quotation from Burroughs's *Junkie* (see 631.28), also spoken by Mary: "'Let's buy some benny tubes and go over to Denny's. They have some gone numbers on the box. We can order coffee and get high on benny'" (29).

Fedja [640.31] Fedya [...] the deed was mine": see 605.22; although Fedya does commit suicide, the quoted lines are Nikíta's in *The Power of Darkness*, as Feddle realizes.

Was nutzen dem Vogel die Schwingen [640.37] "When the claw is caught, the bird is lost": the subtitle of Tolstoy's play *The Power of Darkness* (1886), concerning a man named Nikíta who commits a series of crimes but finally makes a public confession. He repeats the proverb at the end of the play as the light of redemption vanquishes the power of darkness.

852 Pokheepsie [641.3]: that is, Poughkeepsie, 65 miles north of New York City.

[641.12] Today is the day they give babies away: "The Day They Gave Babies Away" is a story by Dale Eunson that appeared in the Christmas 1946 number of *Cosmopolitan*, their most successful Christmas story ever. It was published as a book the following year.

853 *Stars and Stripes Forever* [641.37]: a Sousa march (1897).

Violets [641.37]: turn-of-the-century song by Julian Fane (words, adapted from a poem by Heine) and Ellen Wright (music). The middle part of the song was appropriated by Bernice Petkere for her popular song "Starlight," which resulted in a plagiarism suit.

855 qui tollis peccata mundi [...] dona nobis pacem [643.39]: from the Agnes Dei of the Mass: "Lamb of God, You who take away the sins of the world, have mercy on us. / (Repeat) / Lamb of God, You who take away the sins of the world, grant us peace."

856 Solcherart geblendet (in Gaza, was?) [644.37] eyeless enough in this reduction of Gaza: *Eyeless in Gaza* (1936) is a novel by Aldous Huxley (1894–1963) concerning a young man whose meaningless life takes on new meaning when he converts to mystical doctrines not unlike Huxley's own. The title is from Milton's *Samson Agonistes*, in which Samson is "Eyeless in Gaza, at the mill with slaves" (*ODQ*).

857 in nomine ... [645.18]: "In the name of ..." Anselm's self-castration recalls that of Origen: see 103.3 ff., the same page on which Anselm first appears.

[645.30] Cozy fan tooty: *Così fan tutti* (It.: "Everybody does it") – the title of an opera by Mozart (1790).

Yom Kipper ist um Halloween [645.37] Yom Kippur was around Hallowe'en: it falls in late September or early October; the patron is mistaking Yom Kippur with Hanukkah, which coincides with the Christmas season.

II.8

[647.epigraph] *Then Adam* [...] *The Harrowing of Hell*: from the Chester (England) Cooks' and Innkeepers' passion play; "hert" means promised. Gaddis's text is from *Chief Pre-Shakespearean Dramas*, ed. Joseph Quincey Adams (Cambridge: Houghton Mifflin, 1924), 187–90.

859 Mr. Inononu [647.9]: cf. Ismet Inönü (1884–1973), Turkish statesman.

Fas et Nefas [647.12] Fas et Nefas [...] quadam singulari: the first stanza of "Vagans loquitur" (The Gift of Giving), one of the *Carmina Burana*, a medieval anthology of anonymous poems and student drinking songs:

Fas et Nefas ambulant	Right and Wrong they go about
pene passu pari;	Cheek by jowl together.
prodigus non redimit	Lavishness can't keep in step
vitium avari;	Avarice his brother.
virtus temperantia	Virtue, even in the most unusual moderation,
quadam singulari	Seeking for the middle course,
debet medium	Vice on either side it, must
ad utrumque vitium	Look about her with the most
caute contemplari.	Cautious contemplation.

Trans. Helen Waddell, in *Mediæval Latin Lyrics* (New York: Holt, 1948), 188–89, which Gaddis has identified as his source (WG/SM).

860 *Az igazi pozitiv filozófia* [648.28]: The True Positive Philosophy (1896) by Hungarian scholar Samuel Brassai. (The title should be spelled *Az igazi pozitiv filozófia*: Gaddis's spelling is from the article on Hungarian literature in *EB*, which is the source for the other Hungarian material that follows.)

Was, bitte, hat Móricz neben Gárdonyi zu suchen [648.29] Móricz, side by side with Gárdonyi?: "The realistic [Hungarian] novelists found a successor in Sigismond Móricz [1879–1942], whose preoccupation with brutish peasants and corrupt petty tradesmen reflect[s] his political tendencies. His work is the antithesis of that of idealistic novelists such as Géza Gárdonyi (d. 1923) and Cécile Tormay" (*EB* 11:897).

A Véres költö [648.32] *A Véres költö* [...] Kosztolányi: Dezso Kosztolányi (1885–1936), Hungarian poet and writer. His *A Véres költö* (1924; English trans. *The Bloody Poet*, 1927) is a novel about Nero; aspiring to be the preeminent poet, he kills all his artistic rivals.

Bródy [...] *Faust orvos* [648.34] Bródy [...] *Faust orvos*, his *Don Quixote kisasszony*: Sándor Bródy (1863–1924), Hungarian writer. His Doctor Faust dates from 1910, his Miss Don Quixote from 1905.

861 demotische Schriftzeichen [649.26] Demotic: a simplified form of ancient Egyptian hieratic writing.
[649.26] Saite period: the Thirty-fourth and Thirty-sixth Egyptian dynasties (718–712, 663–525 B.C.).

Einerseits kooperieren Sie mit dem gegenwärtigen Regime [650.14] the present regime [...] restore the monarchy of the Hapsburgs: the Hapsburg-Lorraine house ruled Austria-Hungary from 1848 to 1918, when Charles I abdicated. He made two unsuccessful attempts to regain the throne in 1921, and after World War II there were those (like Valentine) who hoped to see the monarchy restored. Hungary was declared a republic in 1946.

863 **Pázmány** [650.22]: Péter Pázmány (1570–1637), Hungarian Roman Catholic prelate and writer, leader of the counterreformation in Hungary.

864 *De Omni Sanguine Christi Glorificato* [651.7]: "In 1405, while still unconscious of any opposition to Catholicism, Huss published his *De Omni Sanguine Christi Glorificato*, in which he declaimed against forged miracles and ecclesiastical greed, and urged Christians to desist from looking for sensible signs of Christ's presence, but rather to seek Him in His enduring word" (*EB* 11:942). Cf. 412.1–4.

865 die Prophezeiungen in der **Cheopspyramide** [652.11] prophecies contained in the Great Pyramid of Cheops: see, if concerned, David Davidson's *Judgement of the Nations in the Great Pyramid's Prophecy* (1940).

Molnárs *Liliom* [652.26] Molnár [...] *Liliom*: Ferenc Molnár (1878–1952), Hungarian playwright. His *Liliom* (1909), a dramatic mystery play, was the basis of the Rogers and Hammerstein musical *Carousel* (1945).

866 *Szent Peter esernyoje* [652.39] Mikszáth, *Szent Peter esernyoje*: Kálmán Mikszáth (1847–1910), Hungarian novelist. *Saint Peter's Umbrella* (1895; Eng. trans. 1962) centers on a tattered red umbrella that is mysteriously placed over a priest's infant sister to protect her from a rainstorm. The townsfolk assume it was placed there by Saint Peter himself (actually by an old wandering Jew), and the umbrella is soon invested with miraculous properties and later becomes part of a disputed will.

Székesfehérvár [653.14]: a large city in Hungary, the coronation and burial place of Hungarian kings from the tenth to the sixteenth century.

867 der Sprecher sagte Kerkel oder Körchel oder so [653.32] Kerkel: "Köchel," that is, a work of Mozart's as catalogued by Ludwig von Köchel.

869 **Mais cette** [...] **Pas si bête** [656.2]: "But that painting there, I want to buy it, you know, but the price! ... of course it is a Memlinc, granted, but the price he's asking is foolish!" "You're telling me ..." (This Memlinc is not an original but Wyatt's art-school imitation: see 74.30 ff.)

871 umgeben von lautlosen Schatten [656.38] surrounded by shades: the first of many allusions in this chapter to Dante's *Inferno*.

Ganymed [657.6] Ganymede: Zeus's boy cupbearer.

872 Thutmosis [...] Ink-naton [657.43] Tuthmosis [...] Ikhnaton [...] let his politics go out the window: these details are from the article on Egyptian history in *EB* (8:72–73).

873 den alten Tutenchamun ausgebuddelt [658.29] Lord [...] dug up old King Tut: Howard Carter and his patron Lord Carnarvon were the first to uncover the tomb of Egyptian king Tutankhamen (1922).

Sohn von diesem Echnaton [658.30] Tutankhamen [...] son of [...] Ikhnaton: actually, son-in-law.

874 Con permiso, señor [659.19] Con permiso, señor [...] nada, gracias: "Excuse me, sir. Do you know Mr. Brown?" [...] "Nothing ... nothing, thanks."

Iført den uovervinnelige rustning [659.20]: Norwegian: "Arrayed in the invincible suit of armor" – evidently a scrap of poetry.

Oui, à vendre [659.25] Oui, à vendre [...] tendresse: "Yes, to sell privately, you know, at the price of a restoration of ... Hubert van Eyck." "Memlinc, of course. [...] Strength, you see, but also ... tenderness."

Royal Academy, wie das nachgestellte R.A. zeigte [659.43] R.A.: Royal Academician, that is, a member of England's Royal Academy of Arts.

875 et surtout, vous savez [660.23]: "and especially, you know."

Bleu de Prusse, alors [660.26] Prussian blue [...] eighteenth-century color: "The presence of Prussian blue, for example, in a painting supposedly of the 15th or even the 17th century is absolute evidence of forgery or repainting" (*EB* 17:65).

876 was Michel-Ange über die flämischen Maler gesagt hat [660.44] what Michel-Ange has to say about these painters [...] vraie harmonie: Michelangelo's harsh criticism of Flemish art, as reported by Portuguese artist Francesco de Holanda, is recorded in *WMA* (244; Crémer's quotation is italicized):

"Flemish painting pleases all the devout better than Italian. The latter evokes no tears, the former makes them weep copiously. This is not a result of the merits of this art; the only cause is the extreme sensibility of the devout spectators. *The Flemish pictures please women, especially the old and very young ones, and also monks and nuns, and lastly men of the world who are not capable of understanding true harmony.* In Flanders they paint, before all things, to render exactly and deceptively the outward appearance of things. The painters choose, by preference, subjects provoking transports of piety, like the figures of saints or of prophets. But most of the time they paint what are called landscapes with plenty of figures. Though the eye is agreeably impressed, these pictures have neither art nor reason; neither symmetry nor proportion; neither choice or values nor grandeur. In short, this art is without power and without distinction; it aims at rendering minutely many things at the same time, of which a single one would have sufficed to call forth a man's whole application."

876 On va faire des zigzags [661.19]: "One is making zigzags."

877 Remake von *Faust* [661.36] *Faust* [...] a sort of bop version: cf. Orson Welles's *Time Runs* (1950), a stage production based in part on Marlowe's *Doctor Faustus* with music by Duke Ellington. It played in Paris while Gaddis was living there.

Kuvetli [662.6]: cf. Turkish *küvvetli* (strong, powerful).

878 Racinien [...] qu'en France [663.24]: "Racinian [in the classical manner of French dramatist Jean Racine (1639–99)], you know ... leaning toward that taste. The instinct of ... of Atticism, if you will. Like Corot, like Seurat, you know, it is Racinian. As I have written, the supreme flower of French genius and which could grow only in France." Georges Seurat (1859–91): French neo-impressionist painter.

880 quelle drôlerie [664.27]: "What nonsense!"

Ah mais oui, mais [...] **c'est charmant** [664.35]: "Oh but yes, but ... it's charming."

Martin Schongauer [665.15] Martin Schongauer's etchings: also known as Martin Schön (1445?–91), German engraver and painter, reputed to be the greatest engraver of the fifteenth century. He is mentioned in passing in *VEF*.

881 bien entendu, les visage de la Vierge [665.32]: "of course, the Virgin's face."

Un sacrilège [...] **Résurrection** [665.38]: repeated (with slight variation) from 74.25.

882 Il va sans dire [...] faux [666.12]: "It goes without saying, [...] everybody knows the great paintings of Goya that one finds in the Jockey Club of Buenos Aires are ... fake." See 631.13.

Leonardo-Madonna [666.16] *Madonna of the Rocks*: the central panel of Leonardo da Vinci's altar painting for the Church of Saint Francesco in Milan; it exists today in two versions, one in the Louvre and one in London's National Gallery.

Porträt von Doktor Arnolfini und Frau s. S. 168 [666.24] portraits of Doctor Arnolfini and his wife: see 124.1.

886 Bilder sind eine Goldmine s.S.101 [670.20] Coulanges [...] pictures are bullion: repeated from 73.8.

887 unter dem Gesichtspunkt [...] einer disziplinierten Wertschätzung s.S. 453 [670.39] disciplined nostalgia: see 335.38.

888 Après tout, chargé de défendre [671.33]: "After all, self-defense."

889 *Papilio cynorta* [672.42] The female of *Papilo cynorta*, in the Uganda: from *EB*'s article on mimicry (15:517).

890 Et ce vieux moricaud ... où se cathe-t-il? [673.30]: "And the old darkie ... where is he hiding himself?"

Men den himmelske rustning [673.39]: Norwegian: "But the heavenly armor ..."; apparently from the same source as the line quoted at 659.20.

891 Ravels *L'Enfant et les Sortilèges* [674.29] Ravel, *L'Enfant et les Sortilèges*: The Child and the Sorceries (1925; also known as The Bewitched Child), a short opera by French composer Maurice Ravel (1875–1937) with libretto by Colette.

Don Quiche [674.32] Don [...] the Spanish fellow: Cervantes's Don Quixote.

[675.11] *son métier*: "his business."

[675.27] all of a piece, as Dryden puts it: from English poet and dramatist John Dryden's (1631–1700) "Secular Masque" (1700), l. 86.

893 Sie wissen doch, der Pferdefuß, deshalb die falschen Waden [676.21] devil, wearing false calves [...] Mephistopheles: the devil appears in the Witch's Kitchen disguised (ll. 2498–2502):
Those talons, horns, and tail – all vanished!
As for the foot I cannot be without,
It would impair my social chances;
For some years now I have eked it out,
Like many young men, with false appurtenances.
"An allusion," explains Cyrus Hamlin (editor of the Norton Critical Edition), "to the eighteenth-century practice among men of padding their stockings to make their calves appear more muscular" (61, n.8).

[678.13] that grimpen [...] where is no secure foothold: a quotation from Eliot's "East Coker" (which in turn quotes to the opening of Dante's *Inferno*):
We are only undeceived
Of that which, deceiving, could no longer harm.
In the middle, not only in the middle of the way
But all the way, in a dark wood, in a bramble,
On the edge of a grimpen, where is no secure foothold,
And menaced by monsters, fancy lights,
Risking enchantment.

896 Les pieds [...] allemande [679.3]: "The feet, you see, the feet of that armor, he stumbled, you know. [...] And without his (eye)glasses ... The feet? the

feet? you see? Kraut-style ["Boches" is French slang for Germans], right? See what German clumsiness... ."

896 **das Taschenmesser** [679.34] penknife: the penknife recalls "The Man of Double Deed" (99.13); the stabbing recalls *Tosca* (cf. 683.39).

897 **Il faut [...] vous savez** [680.18]: "It is imperative that I leave, I just remembered an ... heh heh assignation, you understand, but the Memlinc, you see, the Memlinc, I want to buy it you know [...] At any price, you understand."

[680.33] **ghood night [...] goo night**: perhaps an echo of the adieux at the end of "The Fire Sermon" in Eliot's *Waste Land* (which are in turn an echo of Ophelia's farewells in *Hamlet*).

[680.37] **"as week as Moses"**: a cliché based on Num. 12:3.

898 **Attention?** [681.3] Attention? [...] tu es fou: "Listen? eh? what do you want then! go on ... let me by ..." "Money, you know, [...] you should always have some on you" [cf. 69.43]. "In that case, you're crazy, eh?"

899 **die Zeit von Sir Walter Scott** [682.1] Sir Walter Scott's past: if this is an allusion to an incident in one of the English author's (1771–1832) novels, it eludes me.

901 **Ja, deine Töchter waren alle schön s. S. 367** [683.17] your daughters all were fair: see 273.14.

Stille Nacht, heilige Nacht [683.28] *Silent Night*: 1818 composition by Joseph Mohr (words) and Franz Gruber (music), apparently as sung by Bing Crosby (cf. 461.10).

Beethovens *Missa Solemnis* [683.29]: an 1823 mass, the culmination of the composer's "second style."

When the Saints Go Marching In [683.31]: classic Dixieland tune, of unknown authorship.

il sangue [...] un artista [683.39]: see 393.29 for the first part. During what she thinks is merely a mock execution, Tosca admires her lover's playing dead, saying: "Là! Muori! Ecco un artista!" ("There! Die! Behold an artist!). Upon discovering that the execution was real, she throws herself off a parapet.

die Stelle, an der sie auch den Zaunkönig an den Baum nageln [683.42] there's where they nailed the wren: "The child Llew Llaw's exact aim was praised by his mother Arianrhod [see 545.32] because as the New Year Robin, *alias* Belin, he transfixed his father the Wren, *alias* Bran to whom the wren was sacred, 'between the sinew and the bone' of his leg" (*WG* 261 – a discussion of the Roman method of crucifixion).

902 **gegen die Verschwörung der Hierophanten hattest du keine Chance** [684.6] what chance had you, when hierophants conspired?: repeated from 376.11 (but not a quotation: WG/SM).

ich hab mir williglich einen Schwanz an den Steiß geheftet s. S. 507 [684.9] I willingly fastened a tail [...] fine and brave: see 375.15 ff.

903 **Ich hab Kopfschmerzen, wahnsinnige Kopfschmerzen** [685.20] I've got a rotten headache: it may be only coincidental that Jake Barnes says exactly the same thing to Lady Brett Ashley in chap. 4 of Hemingway's *The Sun Also Rises* (1924).

905 **In dieser kleinen privaten Genizah** [686.41] genizah: a room attached to a synagogue where damaged and heretical books and sacred relics are stored.

Ah oui [...] monde des truqueurs [687.7]: "Ah yes, he wanted a souvenir, you know, a tiny little souvenir for memory's sake from the world of counterfeiters."

Bleu de Prusse [...] vous savez [687.13]: "Prussian blue, then, it means nothing you know, the sky of Prussian blue, simply retouched you know." See 660.26.

907 **Gold macht man am besten aus Gold** [689.4] Thank God there was the gold to forge: in his *Paris Review* interview, Gaddis identified this as "very much the key line to the whole book" (66).

908 **Wie eine fette, widerliche Kröte** s. S. 329 [689.13] ugly venomous toad with the precious jewel in its head: see 245.6.

Kanzler Rolin [689.30] Chancellor Rolin [...] for vanity and avarice and lust: see 255.34. Rolin, writes Huizinga, "combined rigid piety with excesses of pride, of avarice and of lust" (*WMA* 240). In fact, Valentine's harangue on fifteenth-century Flanders owes much to *WMA*, especially the chapter "Art and Life."

[689.37] Adoration of the Mystic Lamb: by the brothers Van Eyck.

909 *horror vacui* [690.19] this terror of emptiness: Huizinga writes that form in Burgundo-French art "develops at the expense of the idea, the ornament grows rank, hiding all the lines and all the surfaces. A *horror vacui* [terror of emptiness] reigns, always a symptom of artistic decline" (*WMA* 228).

912 **die einzige Lektion, welche die Götter für uns bereithalten** s. S. 736 f, [692.31] the only lesson the gods can teach: see 552.3.

914 **cave, caveat emptor, Dominus videt** [693.31]: "Beware, let the buyer beware, God is watching."

915 weil er nicht wußte, in welchen dunklen Wald es sie verschlagen hatte [694.40] uncertain where he was in the dark wood: from this point to the end of the chapter Otto's course parodies that of Dante in the *Inferno*. Here, the "dark wood" of Central Park corresponds to that in the first stanza of the *Inferno*:

> Midway in our life's journey, I went astray
> from the straight road and woke to find myself
> alone in a dark wood.

Ich fahr Sie hin, aber dann müssen Sie aussteigen [694.41] the driver [...] we'll go down: parallels Vergil's role as Dante's guide through the underworld.

916 in diesem eisstarren Malstrom [695.21] this concentric ice-ridden chaos: Dante's hell descends concentrically like a funnel; at the bottom is Satan, trapped in ice.

Wind stieß aus großer Höhe hinab [...] das rote Licht einer Bar über den nassen Asphalt [695.22] The wind bellowed [...] red lights: *Inferno* 3:130–31: "the tear-soaked ground gave out a sigh of wind / that spewed itself in a flame on a red sky."

Vor dem Eingang dehnte sich eine größere Pfütze [695.25] stumble around the dark edge of a pool: upon reaching the Acheron, Dante "stumbled into darkness and went down" (3:134).

Besitzer und Barkeeper des Lokals gerieten sich in die Haare [695.28] owner and the bartender swore at each other: *Inferno* 7:25–30:

> Here, too, I saw a nation of lost souls,
> far more than were above: they strained their chests
> against enormous weights, and with mad howls
>
> rolled them at one another. Then in haste
> they rolled them back, one party shouting out:
> "Why do you hoard" and the other: "Why do you waste?"

Der Fußboden schwamm von verschütteten Drinks [...] und genauso roch es auch [695.31] The place was foul-smelling [...] a clogged drain: recalls the infernal habitat of the Gluttons (canto 6).

Eine kümmerliche Gestalt [...] fixierte ihn mit ihrem Silberblick [695.33] A small figure [...] fixed him with a strabismic stare: from Dante's description of the Sodomites (15:16–21):

> ... a company of shades came into sight
> walking beside the bank. They stared at us
> as men at evening by the new moon's light
>
> stare at one another when they pass by
> on a dark road, pointing their eyebrows toward us
> as an old tailor squints at his needle's eye.

916 **die Schlägerei begann** [695.37] *a fight started* [...] *mud-spattered anger*: in canto 7, the Wrathful fight each other in muddy slime.

das zerlassene Rot auf dem Asphalt wie flüssige Flammen [695.41] *wet flame*: from 8:1–6, where the flames signal Phlegyas, boatman of the Styx:

... I say we came
to the foot of a Great Tower; but long before
we reached it through the marsh, two horns of flame

flared from the summit, one from either side,
and then, far off, so far we scarce could see it
across the mist, another flame replied.

als er den düsteren Tümpel überqueren wollte [695.42] *the dark lake*: canto 8 opens with Dante standing at the edge of a swamp (the river Styx).

[696.4] *Dis*: crossing the marsh in canto 8, Dante sees the towers of Dis, the capital of hell. The walls of Dis separate upper from lower hell.

917 **Ich bin Wahrsager** [696.21] *fortune teller*: though this interlude is not part of Otto's infernal descent, the fortune teller recalls those of his profession in circle 8 of Dante's hell (canto 20).

919 **am Bordstein entlang wie am Rand eines Abgrunds** [698.4] *edge of a chasm* [...] *dazzled by fire and pitch*: cf. 21:16–24:

so, but by Art Divine and not by fire,
a viscid pitch boiled in the fosse below
and coated all the bank with gluey mire.

I saw the pitch; but I saw nothing in it
except the enormous bubbles of its boiling,
which swelled and sank, like breathing, through all the pit.

And as I stood and stared into that sink,
my Master cried, "Take care!" and drew me back
from my exposed position on the brink.

Sein Jackett [...] **hing ihm bleischwer an den Schultern** [698.7] *his coat* [...] *hung heavy as lead*: from the description of the Hypocrites (23:58–62):

All wore great cloaks cut to as ample a size
as those worn by the Benedictines of Cluny.
The enormous hoods were drawn over their eyes.

The outside is all dazzle, golden and fair;
the inside, lead.

als sei er aus einem Spalt in der Erde gekommen [698.9] *as though risen from an exposure of pavement*: the metaphor recalls the tombs of the Heretics in cantos 9–11.

[698.26] counterfeit: in canto 30, Adam of Brescia (see 5.30) is featured as an example of a counterfeiter; like Tantalus, he is condemned to eternal thirst.

920 Wind [699.7] wind: perhaps this wind corresponds with that Dante feels (33:103) as he approaches Satan, the source of the wind. After his meeting with Wyatt Otto notices "the wind had gone down" (699.35), which suggests Wyatt is being equated with the ice-bound Satan; similarly, Otto's reaction to Wyatt's face recalls that of Dante toward Satan's (34:37ff.).

in den verstümmelten Schatten an der Ecke [699.10] mutilated shadows: in canto 28, the Sowers of Discord are characterized by their mutilated bodies. In the following canto, Vergil asks Dante: "'What are you waiting for? Why do you stare / as if you could not tear your eyes away / from the mutilated shadows passing there?'"

921 Dunkelheit, die sie auf einmal wie ein finsterer Hauch umhüllte [699.27] thick gloom: the central pit of Malebolge is thick with gloom (31:11, 14).

Eis [699.29] ice: as noted above, the bottom of hell is a lake of ice (32:22–24).

umzingelt von gefrorenen Häusergiganten [699.37] frozen giants of buildings: in canto 31, Dante sees "what seemed a cluster of great towers," but is told by Vergil that "they are not towers but giants."

[699.38] head over heels: this describes the manner in which Dante and Vergil climb over Satan to the opening that leads to Purgatory (34:76–84).

das himmlische Blendwerk der Sterne [699.39] in the stars: the *Inferno* ends (as do the other two sections) with a reference to the stars – "God's shining symbols of hope and virtue" (translator Ciardi's note, p. 181).

II.9

922 Vicisti, Galilæe – Letzte Worte des Kaisers Julian [700.epigraph] Vicisti, Galilæa. – Julian, dying words: "'Thou hast prevailed, O man of Galilee.'" Thus Phythian-Adams ends his *Mithraism*, quoting the "dying words of [Sol Invictus's] noblest and most devoted follower, that bitter cry of one who saw in his own untimely end the doom of all the hopes that he had cherished for the ultimate salvation of his Empire – " (*M* 95). See 419.1 for Julian the Apostate, and cf. Captain de Mun's use of the Latin phrase at 76.39.

[700.3] cock of fire: a repetition of the phoenix allusion that opens II.3 (see 390.1).

923 Kartäuserkloster [...] Abd-er-Rahman s. S. 15 [701.36] Carthusian monastery [...] Abd-er-Rahman: all these rumors are repeated from p. 9.

in einem Baum vor der Scheune [...] eine große, weiße Gestalt [702.28] figure in the branches of a tree [...] up the lawn toward the parsonage: from the Mithraic "Episode of the Bull" as described in *M* (56–57):

The god is first seen in the branches of a tree, apparently on the look out for his prey. The Bull is in the safe shelter of its stable, but Mithras contrives to elude its shepherd guardian [...], and compels the animal to break cover. A wild pursuit ensues. The Hero-god, clasping his quarry round the neck, is at first carried away by its headlong rush: his feet leave the ground, and he literally flies through the air. At last his valour and perseverance are rewarded: the beast is overcome and submits to being mounted or led by its captor. But, *for some reason,* Mithras is little satisfied with this method of progress. First he flings the animal round his shoulders and carries it in the well-known attitude of the "Hermes Criophoros" or the "Good Shepherd": then, as he nears his Cave, he grasps its hind legs and drags it backwards into the place of Sacrifice where with glances of mingled fear and triumph he consummates the Demiurgic Act.

[703.3] **charity** [...] a voice sounding like a tinkling cymbal, and another sounding brass: from 1 Cor. 13:1.

925 Der Schock traf sie erst, als sie das Gotteshaus betraten [703.17] interior of the church: the description of the church's conversion into a Mithræum follows *M* 44–46.

Natalis Invicti Solis s. S. 581 [703.29]: "Birthday of the Invincible Sun"; see 432.37.

926 Transitus dei [704.1]: "The long pursuit and wearisome return of the hunter [Mithra] was called by the Initiated the Transit of the God (*Transitus dei*)" (*M* 58).

Cultores Solis Invicti Mithrae [704.6]: the designation of members of Mithraism's religious communities (*M* 65).

Mithras wollen wir unser Opfer weihen [704.13] We sacrifice unto Mithra [...] a God invoked by his own name: this and the liturgy that follows are adapted from the Avesta (see 718.6) as translated by James Darmesteter and L. H. Mills for the *Sacred Books of the East,* ed. F. Max Müller, vols. 23 and 31 (Oxford: Clarendon Press, 1883 and 1887). Most of the following formulas are from the "Mihir Yast" (Hymn to Mithra, Yast no. 10), a sacrificial liturgy dating from the fifth century B.C., addressed to Mithra (*SBE* 23:119–58). Rev. Gwyon quotes first not from the Mihir Yast, however, but verbatim from Sîrôzah 2, 16 (*SBE* 23:17), a prayer addressed to Mithra as the presiding deity of the sixteenth day of the month. The Mihir Yast opens in much the same manner: "Unto Mithra, the lord of the wide pastures, who has a thousand ears, ten thousand eyes, a Yazata invoked by his own name, and unto Râma *Hv*âstra, / Be propitiation, with sacrifice, prayer, propitiation, and glorification" (23:119); see 705.17.

926 **Mithras wollen wir unser Opfer darbringen** [704.16] We sacrifice unto Mithra [...] ever awake: Mihir Ya*s*t 2.7 (23:121), a refrain repeated thereafter at the beginning of each chapter.

Mithras wollen wir unser Opfer weihen [704.20] We sacrifice unto Mithra [...] swift-horsed sun: Mithra is not addressed as "the lord of all countries" until the last chapter (35.145 [23:158]); the Khôrsh*ê*d Ya*s*t (Hymn to the Sun, Ya*s*t no. 6) begins: "We sacrifice unto the undying, shining, swift-horsed Sun" (23:85); this hymn was recited particularly on days consecrated to Mithra and/or the sun.

Seht, ich weihe Mithras ein Opfer [704.22] For his brightness and glory [...] of wide pastures: 1.4 (23:120), a refrain repeated thereafter at the end of each chapter (though the verb in the original is "will offer" rather than "have offered").

927 **Möge Er uns zu Hilfe kommen** [704.26] May he come to us for help [...] of wide pastures: 1.5 (23:120–21); in the original, each statement is followed by an exclamation point rather than a period.

Den Menschen, die Ihn zuerst verehren [704.36] On whichever side [...] the wise: 2.9 (23:122).

Ich rufe dich bei deinem Namen, mildtätiger Mithras [704.43] With a sacrifice [...] beneficent Mithra: 8.31 (23:127); "will" rather than "do" in the original.

Und wären die bösen Gedanken [...] auch hundertmal schlimmer [705.1] Should the evil thoughts [...] evil words [...] evil deeds [...] of the heavenly Mithra: 27.106 (23:146–47); good thoughts, good words, and good deeds were the three basic commandments of Zoroaster.

928 **Mithras, dem Herrn der weiten Weiden [...] Yazad, dein Name ist** [705.17] To Mithra [...] the Yazad of the spoken name [...] and praise: from the Gâh Hâvan, the first of the five Gâhs (prayers to be said during the five divisions of the day; the Hâvani was from six to ten A.M.). Verse two reads: "And to Mithra of the wide pastures, of the thousand ears, of the myriad eyes, the Yazad of the spoken name, be sacrifice, homage, propitiation, and praise, and to Râman *Hv*âstra" (31:379). "Yazad" (like Yazata) means a god; Râma(n) *Hv*âstra, whose name is often linked with Mithra's, is described elsewhere as "the Genius that gives good abodes and good pastures" (23:249).

931 **Geschichte vom armen Lazarus** [708.13] Saint John, and that vernal episode involving Lazarus [...] and the Life: John 11.

931 **den ersten Vers von Psalm 110** [708.24] Psalm Number 89, – Till I thy foes thy footstool make: from Psalm 110, not 89; no hymn in *PH* is based on either psalm.

932 **Rondo aus der *Kleinen Nachtmusik*** [708.41] Mozart's *Eine Kleine Nachtmusik*: "A Little Night Music" is one of Mozart's most popular orchestral pieces.

934 ***Malay Magic* oder *Libellus de Terrificationibus Nocturnisque Tumultibus* s. S. 34** [710.22] *Malay Magic* and *Libellus* [...] *Tumultibus*: see 23.30–31.

Baxters *Everlasting Rest* [710.27]: Richard Baxter (1615–91), English Puritan scholar and writer, author of *The Saint's Everlasting Rest* (1650), a spirited case for the Christian life.

Katechismus von Fisher [710.27] Fisher's *Catechism*: unidentified.

Die *Penetralia* des Andrew Jackson Davis s. S. 51 [710.29] Andrew Jackson Davis's *Penetralia*: see 35.40.

Dick [710.30] "Dick" [...] Richard: a satire, says Gaddis, on Richard "Dick" Nixon (1913–94), then senator from California (WG/SM).

Buffons Naturgeschichte s. S. 52 [710.33] Buffon's *Natural History*: see 29.32.

***Histoire des ballons* von Tissandiers s. S. 75** [710.37] Tissandier's *Histoire des ballons*: see 53.8.

Zwei Bände Lewis Wallace s. S. 587 [710.40] two volumes of Lew Wallace: see 438.25.

Jules Verne [710.41] Jules Verne's *Tour of the Moon, Round the World in Eighty Days*, and *Five Weeks in a Balloon*: English translations of three novels by the famous French adventure-story writer (1828–1905).

937 **Mister Farisy** [712.35]: cf. Pharisee, a member of the orthodox Jewish sect accused of complacency and hypocrisy in the Gospels (especially Matt. 23). Mr. Farisy's experiment, described below, was actually performed in the late 1970s (and featured on an episode of the television series *In Search Of*), from which it was concluded that the nails were driven through the wrists.

hinsichtlich eines Forschungsauftrags für die römische Kurie [712.42] Congregation of the Sacred Rites: the *Sacrorum Rituum Congregatio*, established in 1588, supervises the beatification and canonization of saints and everything relating to holy relics, as well as liturgical matters.

wenn Pilatus den Barabbas tatsächlich losgegeben hat [713.14] did Barabbas go free?: apparently: see Matt. 27:26.

939 **zum erstenmal seit der Ermordung von Präsident James A. Garfield** [715.3] the assassination of James A. Garfield: in 1881.

940 Hatte nicht bereits Jakob der Erste [...] gegen das Übel des Rauchens gewettert [715.35] felt every bit as strongly about tobacco as did [...] King James: three quotations from the monarch's *A Counterblast to Tobacco* (1604) are given in *ODQ*.

941 Lied [...] Nr. 347 s. S. 527 [715.43] Hymn Number 347 [...] Our ex-iled fa-thers crossed the sea: heard earlier at 390.14.

[716.23] *SENSATION*: fictitious; "I'd thought that one day I might write a novel with this title & so a little advance billing" (WG/SM).

eine Passage von Katherine Mansfield s. S. 410 [716.28] a passage [...] from Katherine Mansfield: see 304.38.

942 Kontakt mit dem (nach Petrus) »schwächeren Geschlecht« [716.33] Saint Peter [...] "weaker vessel": 1 Pet. 3:7.

[717.20] "these quaint and curious volumes of forgotten lore": the second line of Poe's famous poem "The Raven."

943 den Tertullian, den Origines s. S. 565 u. 586 [718.4] Tertullian and Origen: see 420.12, 15–16; 436.39.

Sosomen [718.5] Sozomen: Salaminius Hermias Sozomen (fl. early fifth century), Greek Christian historian; he continued the work of Eusebius with a nine-volume *Ecclesiastical History*, most of which was plagiarized from other historians. (See note on the hermit Paul at 843.26.)

Sosismus s. S. 177 [718.5] Zosimus: see 131.10.

Avesta [718.6]: the sacred texts of Zoroastrianism; Phythian-Adams guesses that Mithraic liturgies resembled (or were derived from) the hymns in the Avesta (*M* 6).

im ersten Korintherbrief [718.13] I Corinthians: see 1:18–25 to unscramble Dick's quotations.

944 Justinus [...] Arnobius, Firmicus Maternus s. S. 716, 577, 586 [719.8] Justin Martyr [...] Arnobius, Firmicus Maternus: see 536.16, 429.41, and 436.40 respectively.

Augustinus [719.9] Augustine Bishop of Hippo [...] the ex-Manichee Hippian bishop: shortly after reading Cicero's *Hortensius* in 373, Augustine joined the Manichee sect; but after he met a Manichee leader named Faustus of Milevis, doubts began to assail him, and he finally converted to Christianity in 385. He later wrote several anti-Manichaean books, including *On Free Will* and *Against Faustus the Manichee*.

Paulinus Nolanus [719.10] Paul of Nola: Meropius Pontius Paulinus of Nola (353–431), Christian Latin writer, a correspondent with Saint Augustine. Cited at 903.16.

944 **denn böse Geister erscheinen im Gewand des Erhabenen** [719.13] "For evil spirits [...] followers of Christ": source unknown, but similar to a passage in Saint Augustine's *On the Trinity* (4.11).

945 **Ode des Himerius auf Kaiser Julian** [719.19] panegyric upon Julian written by Himerius [...] a better life": Himerius (fl. fourth century), Greek Sophist and rhetorician, was a secretary to Julian; source of quotation unknown.

III.1

949 **Es gibt viele Manii in Aricia** [723. epigraph] "There are many Manii at Aricia": a proverb that Frazer explains as follows (*GB* 491–92):
> Certain loaves made in the shape of men were called by the Romans *maniae*, and it appears this kind of loaf was especially made at Aricia [in Italy]. Now, Mania, the name of one of these loaves, was also the name of the Mother or Grandmother of Ghosts, to whom woollen effigies of men and women were dedicated at the festival of the Compitalia. [...] The tradition that the founder of the sacred grove at Aricia was a man named Manius, from whom many Manii were descended, would thus be an etymological myth invented to explain the name *maniae* as applied to these sacramental loaves.

Gaddis compounds the pun below with *mani*, a Spanish-American word meaning peanut.

Tibieza de Dios [723.4]: I doubt any city is actually called the Tepidity (or Lukewarmness) of God.

[725.18] **the quiet limit of the world**: from Tennyson's "Tithonus," l. 7.

953 **Crassus** [726.22]: Marcus Licinius Crassus (115?–53 B.C.), surnamed Dives ("the Rich"), Roman financier and politician. After Crassus was beheaded in battle, the Parthian king Orodes made an example of his avarice by pouring molten gold down his throat.

[730.30] **ravin in tooth and claw**: see 412.39.

960 **Hören Sie Geräusche [...] Klingeln im Ohr [...] Ménièresche Krankheit** [731.36] Do you hear noises in your ear? [...] Ménière's disease: "a form of auditory vertigo, first described in 1861. [...] The attack usually sets in with dizziness, noises in the ear, nausea, vomiting and staggering gait, and the patient may suddenly fall down unconscious" (*EB* 15:249).

961 **Angenehm, ich bin Doktor Fell** s. S. 60 ER [732.15] Doctor Fell: see 42.19.

III.2

962 **»Miss Potter, wo ist Gott?« [...] *Indisches Tagebuch*** [733.epigraph] "Miss Porter [...] *Hindoo Holiday*: J. R. Ackerley's (1896–1967) *Hindoo Holiday: An Indian Journal* (1932) is a charming and often amusing account of Ackerley's stay in India in 1930 as private secretary to "His Highness the Mahara-

jah Sahib of Chhokrapur." The epigraph records a short interview with Miss Porter, a missionary; her rejoinder to His Highness's query, if any, is unrecorded (New York: Viking, 1932, 212 ["me" is italicized in the original]). A revised version of the book appeared in 1952.

962 diese Heilige Klara [733.7] Saint Clare: Saint Clare of Assisi (ca. 1193–1253), a nobleman's daughter who became a religious (with the help of Saint Francis) and later founded the Poor Clares.

Portiuncula [733.17]: a small church (also called Saint Mary of the Angels, as at 830.11) near Assisi, where on 24 February 1209 the Holy Spirit revealed to Saint Francis the Gospel of the Mass. It was at that chapel that Saint Francis gave the religious habit to Clare; cf. 830.10ff.

963 *Die Zerstörung der Philosophen [...] Die Zerstörung der Zerstörung* [734.12] *The Destruction of the Philosophers* [...] *The Destruction of the Destruction*: the first title is by Arab philosopher al-Ghazzali (Lat., Algazel, 1058–1111) and is a refutation of philosophies that oppose the teachings of the Koran. The second is by Averroes (see 382.29) and is a refutation of al-Ghazzali's anti-intellectual attack (Green 50).

[734.29] Skull and Bones man: that is, from Yale; Skull and Bones is the oldest of Yale's secret societies.

969 *The End of a Perfect Day* [738.6]: "The Perfect Day" (1910) by Carrie Jacobs-Bond.

970 Twenty-one [738.41]: the 21 Club restaurant at 21 West 52nd Street.

[741.6] *It was roses, roses, all the way*: the first line of Robert Browning's poem "The Patriot" (*ODQ*).

[741.11] Cleopatra's gnathic index, or Nefertiti's cephalic index: measurements of the jaw and head, respectively.

974 *The Bells of Saint Mary's* [741.37]: 1945 song by Douglas Ferber and A. Emmett Adams from the movie of the same name.

975 en este momento [742.33]: Sp.: "at this moment."

[743.5] hope: the only thing left in Pandora's box (742.42) after she let everything else escape.

976 Paganinis Konzertallegro *Moto perpetuo* [743.13] Paganini's *Perpetual Motion*: Niccolò Paganini (1782–1840), Italian violin virtuoso; his "Moto perpetuo: Allegro de concert" for violin and orchestra was published posthumously.

Er ward verachtet ... und verschmähet [743.18] He was despiséd [...] and acquainted with grief: from the text of Handel's *Messiah*, based on Isa. 53:3.

976 **in welcher klassischen Fabel eine Ameise die Hauptfigur sei** [743.20] a fable with an ant for its hero: Aesop's and/or La Fontaine's story "The Ant and the Grasshopper." (Crotcher appeared earlier at Esther's party in II.7.)

977 *Beautiful Dreamer* [744.16]: well-known song by American composer Stephen Foster (1826–64), who died destitute in Bellevue's charity ward.

982 **Er spielt den Heiligen Sebastian** [748.12] Saint Sebastian: one of the more renowned of early Roman martyrs and a popular subject with Renaissance artists (who would often depict their patron's "favorite" as the martyr). According to unreliable legends, he was tied to a tree, shot at by Roman archers, and finally clubbed to death (in the year 288 according to some martyrologies). Cf. *BM* 25–26.

984 **Teile [...] sind Gott weiß wo verstreut** [749.28] little parts of me all over the place: cf. the dismembered Osiris, scattered all over Egypt and reconstructed by Isis.

[750.6] Chrahst I mean, how long?: cf. the opening of Ps. 13 and/or Rev. 6:10.

986 **Verklärte Nacht** [751.15]: *Transfigured Night* (1899), Arnold Schoenberg's famous tone poem.

987 **Eine regelrechte Walpurgisnacht** [751.23] Walpurgis: Walpurgisnacht (30 April), the night on witches gathered in German folklore; two Walpurgisnachts figure in *Faust*.

990 *Elmira* [753.31]: city in southern New York.

Sweet Betsy from Pike [753.41]: old American folk song.

Ischia s.S. 781 [754.14]: see 584.28.

hieße Eulen nach Athen tragen [754.14] taking an ow-wel to A-thens: a proverb, like carrying coals to Newcastle, indicating an unnecessary effort.

995 **Ehe die Blumen der Freundschaft welken** [757.41] Before the flowers of friendship faded friendship faded: a phrase first used by Gertrude Stein in her *A Novel of Thank You* (1926) and then as a book title in 1931. *Flowers of Friendship* is also the title of a collection of Stein's correspondence, published in 1952.

Wir alle sind eine einzige Verweigerung [757.42] the great refusal: "Il gran rifiuto" from canto 3 of Dante's *Inferno* (*ODQ*), which Ciardi suggests is a reference to "Celestine V, who became Pope in 1294. He was a man of saintly life, but allowed himself to be convinced by a priest named Benedetto that his soul was in danger since no man could live in the world without being damned. In fear for his soul he withdrew from all worldly affairs and renounced the papacy. [...] Celestine's great guilt is that his cowardice (in selfish terror for his own welfare) served as the door through which so much evil entered the church" (17).

997 **Es ist verboten, mit Blumen den Garten zu betreten** [759.19] It is forbidden to enter the garden with flowers in the hand: this notice posted at the entrance to the public garden in Tarbes in southern France – to prevent people from stealing the garden's flowers and then claiming to have brought them – is the subject of an allegory that frames Jean Paulhan's *Les fleurs de Tarbes* (1941); Maurice Blanchot's review of this critical work led to an important debate in France on the status of literature. JR makes an unwitting reference to this practice (*JR* 661).

[759.30] frabjously: a "portmanteau" word from Lewis Carroll's poem "Jabberwocky" (*Through the Looking-Glass*, chap. 1).

998 *The Deserter* [...] *Sadlers Wells* [760.8] The Deserter [...] at Sadlers Wells in 1785: an opera by Charles Dibdin (1745–1814), based on *Le deserteur* by Monsigny and Sedaine.

Rue Gît le Coeur [760.29]: "Street Where the Heart Lies," near Notre Dame. Henri IV, passing the street in his carriage on the Quai des Grands Augustins, remarked to his companion: "Ici gist mon coeur," for his mistress lived there.

1000 **Der stille Teilhaber** [762.17] the secret sharer: title of a famous short story by Joseph Conrad (1912) concerning a sea captain and his "double," a murderer.

1002 **die vier edlen Wahrheiten, der achtfach edle Weg** [764.3] The Four Noble Truths! and the Eightfold Path! Why, life *is* suffering: at the sermon at Benares the Buddha expounded the basic tenets of his philosophy. The "Four Noble Truths" can be summarized: (1) Life is suffering; (2) Suffering is caused by desire (i.e., selfish craving); (3) Desire can be eliminated; (4), it is eliminated by adhering to an eightfold path: (i), right understanding, (ii) right purpose, (iii) right speech, (iv) right conduct, (v) right vocation, (vi) right effort, (vii) right alertness, and (viii) right concentration. Cf. *AN* 22–23.

Bischof von Whutley oder so [764.8] Bishop ... Whutley?: Richard Whately (1787–1863), English theologian and logician, archbishop of Dublin (1831–63).

1005 *Die Geschichte der Barbara Ubrick* [766.2] *The Story of Barbara Ubrick*: there are several books in German and Polish on this Cracow nun, but I don't know of anything in English.

[766.18] Or I shall wear a cockleshell [...] and he will know me well: from an unidentified ballad.

Santiago de Compostela [766.20]: the church in Spain at which the relics of Saint James the Greater were enshrined after his corpse was miraculously transported from Jerusalem to Spain. During the Middle Ages it was the most famous place of pilgrimage after Jerusalem and Rome. In art Saint James is represented as a pilgrim in a cloak covered with shells.

1005 **das Herz der Heiligen Gertrud** [766.23] Saint Gertrude's heart: Saint Gertrude of Nirelles (626–59); her emblem is a pastoral staff with a mouse running up it. Summers notes her receiving the stigmata on her heart (*PPM* 187) but makes no mention of mice.

1006 *ritu quadrupedis* s. S. 264 [766.41]: used by Anselm earlier at 197.31.

1007 *blessed Mary went a-walking* [768.11]: listing the seven conditions under which prayer and benediction may be employed to heal the sick, the authors of *MM* caution (181):

Thirdly, there must be nothing in the words that is untrue; for if there is, the effect of them cannot be from God, Who is not a witness to a lie. But some old women in their incantations use some such jingling doggerel as the following:
Blessed MARY went a-walking
Over Jordan river.
Stephen met her, and fell a-talking, etc.

1008 **Pater noster qui es in coelis** [768.25]: the opening of the Lord's Prayer (Matt. 6:9–13).

III.3

1009 **Die letzte Drehung der Schraube** s. S. 7 [769.title] THE LAST TURN OF THE SCREW: see 5.19.

¡Así por la calle [...] *Amar sin saber a quién* [769.epigraph]: Lope de Vega (1562–1635), Spanish dramatist and poet, considered the greatest figure in Spanish literature after Cervantes. *Amar sin saber a quién* (roughly, To Love without Knowing Whom [to Love]) concerns Don Juan's quest for a veiled lady, who turns out to be the sister of his friend Fernando. At the beginning of act 3, Don Juan is stopped by Fernando, who rebukes him with the quoted line ("So that's the way you pass in the street someone to whom you owe affection!"), then invites him inside his house, where Don Juan finally meets the veiled lady.

Spanien ist kein Land für Reisende s. S. 576 [769.1] Spain is a land to flee across: so said Rev. Gwyon earlier (429.21–22).

1010 **einen Flecken Mondlicht vom Ärmel zu wischen** s. S. 428 u. 1038 [770.17] brush a spot of moonlight off the sleeve: perhaps an allusion to a poem from *Pierrot Lunaire*, a cycle of poems by Belgian dramatist and critic Albert Giraud (1860–1929), best known in their musical setting by German composer

Arnold Schoenberg (1912). The poem is entitled "The Moonfleck" (trans. Robert E. Wolf):

With a fleck of white – bright patch of moonlight –
On the back of his black jacket,
Pierrot strolls about in the mid evening air
On his night-time hunt for fun and good pickings.
Suddenly something strikes him as wrong;
He checks his clothes over and sure enough finds
A fleck of white – bright patch of moonlight –
On the back of his black jacket.
Damn! he thinks, There's a spot of white plaster!
Rubs and rubs, but he can't get rid of it,
So goes on his way, his pleasure poisoned,
Rubbing and rubbing till dawn comes up –
At a fleck of white, a bright patch of moonlight!

Cf. 317.10 and 794.1.

1010 **sangre negro en mi corazón** s. S. 150 [770.18]: see 110.11.

[770.30] **specter-ships of the sea to sail forever unable to make port:** here and on p. 816 Gaddis quotes from *EB*'s short article (9:431):
"FLYING DUTCHMAN," a spectre-ship popularly believed to haunt the waters around the Cape of Good Hope. Its appearance is considered by sailors as ominous of disaster. The commonest legend declares that the captain of the vessel, Vanderdecken, was condemned for his blasphemy to sail round the cape for ever, unable to "make" a port. The legend was used by Wagner in his opera *Der fliegende Holländer*.
The German legend makes one Herr von Falkenberg the hero and alleges that he is condemned to sail for ever round the North Sea, in a ship without helm or steersman, playing at dice for his soul with the devil.

Dinah [770.37]: 1924 song by Sam Lewis and Joe Young (words) and Harry Akst (music); there are classic jazz recordings both by Ethel Waters (who introduced the song in her nightclub act) and by Louis Armstrong.

1011 **paso doble** [771.26] pasa doble: a dance step in 6/8 time popular in the 1920s (*pasa* should be *paso*).

La Tani [771.27]: a song heard throughout the chapter; see Sinisterra's explanation on p. 813.

1012 **quiere comer?** [771.39]: "Do you want to eat?"

una y una dos [...] **No sale la cuenta** [772.7]: "One and a two ... two and a three [...]. The count doesn't come out."

España, Arriba, ABC [772.30]: Spanish newspapers.

dos iguales para hoy! [772.31]: "Two of the same today!"

1013 Intuneric şi Lumină [773.9] I. Al. Bratescu-Voinesti's [...] *In Tuneric si Lumină*: Darkness and Light (1912) by Ioan Alexandru Bratescu-Voinesti (1868–1946). (*In Tuneric* should be *Intuneric* – Gaddis's spelling indicates his source: the article on Rumanian literature in *EB* [19:656]; the preposition *si* was properly spelled with a cedilla beneath the *s* in the first edition of *R* but somehow got dropped in the latest edition.)

1014 Pensión Las Cenizas [774.3]: "The Ashes Pension": cf. Stephan Asche (795.39) and the phoenix rising from the ashes.

1015 Goya [774.20]: Francisco de Goya (1746–1828), Spanish artists, one of the greatest (and most prolific) of European artists.

Digame [774.34]: Tell Me – apparently another Spanish newspaper.

1016 Marga [775.10]: cf. Gretchen (a German diminutive of Margaret) in Goethe's *Faust*.

1017 Segovia [776.1]: city and province northwest of Madrid.

1018 das junge Mädchen, die Frau, die Greisin, als letztes der Totenschädel [776.38] the girl, the woman, the hag, and the skull: cf. Graves's description of the Triple Goddess: "As the New Moon or Spring she was girl; as the Full Moon or Summer she was woman; as the Old Moon or Winter she was hag" (*WG* 320).

Ausculta [776.39]: Lat.: "Listen; pay attention."

Mira Señor [776.40]: Sp. "Look sir."

die Worte *la guerra* und *los rojos* [777.29] *la guerra* [...] *los rojos*: "the war" (Spanish Civil War) ... "the reds" – Yák/Sinisterra will explain at the bottom of 777.

1019 España ... no hay más que una! [777.40]: "Spain – there's only one" (perhaps a tourist slogan).

Coño, mira [778.3]: "Fuck [literally, cunt], look."

ya no, ya no [...] ya viene! [778.14]: "Not now! (or Not yet!) [...] It's coming! It's coming!"

die erste Station des Kreuzwegs [778.18] first station of the cross: see 3.5; the fourteen stations, some of which are mentioned over the next few pages, are: (1) Jesus is condemned to death. (2) He is made to bear his cross. (3) He falls the first time under the weight of the cross. (4) He meets his mother. (5) Simon of Cyrene helps to carry the cross. (6) Veronica wipes the perspiration from Jesus' face. (7) He falls a second time. (8) He speaks to the daughters of Jerusalem. (9) He falls a third time. (10) He is stripped of his garments. (11) He is nailed to the cross. (12) He dies. (13) He is taken down from the cross. (14) He is laid in the sepulcher.

1022 Hace años [...] cuya presencia [780.19]: "Years ago the prelates of the church came reprimanding the shameful [...] the sanctity of the church is no longer respected, nor the most august and sacred mysteries in whose presence [...]."

1023 Jedesmal, wenn einem ein Leichenwagen begegnet, ist es auch die eigene Beerdigung [780.39] every time a funeral passes, it's your own passing: a paraphrase of John Donne's often-quoted lines: "any man's death diminishes me, because I am involved in mankind; and therefore never send to know for whom the bell tolls; it tolls for thee" (*ODQ*).

vino albus, bianco [781.14] albus. Bianco: "white" in Latin and Italian.

Manzanilla s.S.149 [781.22]: the same white wine Wyatt and Esther once shared (109.40).

1024 *La Sebastiana* s.S.1071 [781.35]: see 822.16–21.

Dama de Elche [782.15]: famous Greco-Phoenician bust of a woman, usually dated between 500 B.C. and A.D. 150, found at the Spanish village of Elche, and now in the Archaeological Museum in Madrid; reproduced in *A&H*, plate 23. However, a recent study argues that the patriotic symbol of Iberia is actually a late-nineteenth-century forgery: see John F. Moffitt's *Art Forgery: The Case of the "Lady of Elche"* (Gainesville: Univ. Press of Florida, 1995).

1026 sie beobachten uns [783.38] these fish [...] watching me: fish are a traditional symbol for Christ, making this a comic aspect of the *Dominus videt* motif.

Sam Hall [784.4]: the murderous chimney-sweep celebrated in an English song popular in the middle of the nineteenth century.

Vaya! Fuera! [784.6]: "Go! Out!"

1028 Denn du hast ja ausgezogen den alten Menschen mit seinen Werken s.S.642 [785.34] putting off the old man: see 481.19.

1029 Stephan s.S.40 u.1051 [785.42] Stephan: see 27.25 and 795.39.

1030 Zunächst wird die Leiche aufgebahrt [...] Einsatz von Farbe [787.8] The body is extended [...] paint on the outside: the process of mummification as practiced in the Fifth Dynasty, from *EB*'s article "Mummy" (15:954).

1031 por el dibujo sabe? ... Quiere ver el dibujo [788.1]: "for the picture you know? ... he wants to look at the picture."

1032 Duro [788.30] duro: short for *peso duro* ("hard peso"), that is, a silver dollar.

1033 Dios de lo pague señor s.S.222 [789.11]: "May God repay you sir" (cf. 166.17).

1034 se olvida [790.17]: "you forgot."

1035 Trotzdem wollen sie ihr einen neuen Kopf aufsetzen, aus Wachs [791.6] new head out of wax: as they did with Maria Goretti (16.12).

1036 quién es? [792.1]: "Who is it?"

1039 an das Wunder von Bolsena [794.40] the miracle at Bolsena: "According to the Church," writes Marsh, "the [fourteenth-century] miracle of Bolsena was performed to convince a skeptical priest, and though him his doubting brethren, of the reality of the transformation of the sacred elements. When he cut the consecrated wafer, blood flowed from the bread and stained the napkin on which it lay. The napkin, or *corporale*, with its yet visible stains of the divine blood, is alleged to be still preserved in the Cathedral of Orvieto, in which diocese Bolsena lies" (*MMSM* 49).

1040 Stephan Asche [795.39]: ash (Ger.: *Asche*) recalls the phoenix myth; see notes to 390.1, 700.3, 774.3.

1041 Dies irae [...] in favilla s. S. 436 [796.37]: see 322.29ff.

1042 *Francisco alegre, olé!* [797.23]: unidentified.

[797.36] feeling chilly and grown old: the last line of Browning's "A Toccata of Galuppi's" (see 193.12).

[798.2] as the poet wrote, the natural in woman closely is allied to art: Gaddis thinks this may be in Goethe's *Faust* (WG/SM).

[798.27] de couloir: Fr. "of the hallway."

1045 Karneval [...] *Carne vale* [800.8] Carnival [...] carne vale: the Latin *carne vale* ("flesh, farewell") was a folk etymology of "carnival" (see 428.2).

Ave carne! ... Salve! ... macte virtute esto! [800.8]: Lat.: "Hail flesh! ... Greetings! ... good work [bravo]!"

Descartes [800.10] Descartes [...] Larvatus prodeo [...] he kept a Salamander: cf. 96.21–23, where "he advanced masked" derives from "Larvatus prodeo." Maritain explains: "In the juvenilia of Descartes we find the phrase *Larvatus prodeo*. 'Like an actor wearing a mask, I come forward, masked, on the stage of the world.' [...] It will be for the *masked philosopher* to unmask the sciences and to make their continuity and their unity appear with their beauty" (*The Dream of Descartes*, 41, 92 n.25). The phrase also refers to the precautions Descartes took not to offend the authorities with his new philosophical systems.

copulo, ergo sum [800.12]: Descartes's *cogito, ergo sum* altered to "I copulate, therefore I am."

1045 Carne, O te felicem! [800.12]: "O, you happy flesh!"

Stesichorus [800.15]: (ca. 640–555 B.C.), Greek lyric poet. He wrote that Helen of Troy was a phantom created by Hera to instigate the Trojan War, while the real Helen remained in Egypt during the conflict; this is the story Euripides used in his *Helen*. Plato relates the legend that Stesichorus was blinded by Helen herself – by then a goddess – for this "slander." The anecdote is also related in Irenaeus's *Against Heresies* (1.23), where Simon Magus's prostitute-consort is said to be Helen's avatar.

1046 Jesús del Gran Poder [800.27]: "Jesus of the Great Power."

1047 Bin zwischen die Fässer gerutscht [801.22] sliding down between the casks: cf. Faust riding a wine cask in Goethe's "Auerbach's Tavern" episode.

Witz von den fünf Jones-Brüdern [...] Los cinco-jones [802.1] five Jones brothers [...] Los cinco-jones: the joke is a pun: *Los cinco Jones* looks and sounds like *los sin cojones* ("Those without balls").

1048 cien iguales me quedan [802.28]: "I have a hundred of the same left."

juerga [802.41]: a drinking party.

1049 Pastora [802.44]: Sp. "shepherdess." Originally, Gaddis intended Wyatt to have a daughter by Pastora, and in the illegitimate daughter to be "at last redeemed through love" (Gaddis's notes, quoted in Koenig's "'Splinters of the Yew Tree,'" 36). Although there are hints about a child later (and see 897.16ff. and 900.3–6), Gaddis decided that such a redemption would be dishonest and facile.

Krishna hat seinerzeit sechzehntausend Jungfrauen verführt [803.24] Krishna seduced sixteen thousand maidens: an anecdote first recorded in the *Bhagavata Purana* and repeated elsewhere in Indian literature and art.

Sie halten den Pfad zum Himmel immer schön schmutzig s. S. 42 [803.37] They let the path stay dirty: see 28.44.

1050 Déjame! [...] déjale! [804.3]: "Leave me! [...] Leave!"

Hoy los nobios se van a casar [804.6]: "Today the sweethearts [should be *novios*] are going to get married" – the first line of "La Tani" (see 771.27); line 12 below is the chorus.

no sale la cuenta porque falta un churumbel s. S. 1061 [804.12]: see 813.11–16 below.

me quieres? [...] yo te quiero y tu no me queires [804.17]: "Do you love me? [...] I love you but you don't love me."

1050 vámonos [804.23]: "Let's go."

vida! ... Cielo! ... No termina ... mi vida! ... vamos hacer un niño [804.24]: "Life! ... Heaven! ... don't stop ... my life! ... Let's make a baby!"

me quieres? ... Díme lo, aunque no es verdad! [804.34]: "Do you love me? ... Tell me so, even if it's not true!" Cf. Esther's plea at 117.41–42.

1051 vaya Usted con Diós s.S.1070 [805.8]: Good-bye; but see 821.38ff.

1052 *La Zarza Mora* [805.39]: unidentified (*zarzamora* is Spanish for "blackberry").

1057 Point d'argent, point de Suisse [810.27]: Fr.: "No money, no Swiss [soldiers]" – from Racine's *Les Plaideurs* (*ODQ*).

1058 aber die jüngste [...] Sonne selber s.S.367 [810.31]: see 273.14ff.

Allí se mueren [811.3] Allí se mueren [...] allí se mueren: "Then they die. [...] Not in winter, but when the leaves return to the trees, then they die" (see 813.19, .23–24).

1064 ein Leben auf See ist das beste Äquivalent für den Selbstmord [815.40] Somebody's said that going to sea is the best substitute for suicide: so says Ishmael in the first chapter of Melville's *Moby-Dick*.

[816.20] Herr von Falkenberg: see 770.30.

1067 un extranjero [...] un falsificador [818.39]: "A foreigner, see, a North American, you know ..." "Why?" [asked in Italian] "Sure, look, a North American ..." "Why?" [...] "Yes sir, a counterfeiter, get me? A North American, you know, a counterfeiter."

1069 Calderóns *La Vida es Sueño* [820.37]: Calderón's *La Vida es Sueño* [...] "El delito mayor del hombre es haber nacido": *Life Is a Dream*, a tragicomedy of ethics and intrigue by Spanish dramatist Pedro Calderón de la Barca (1600–81), concerns the testing of heir-apparent Sigismundo for his suitability as King Basil's successor. Sigismundo was imprisoned at birth because the stars predicted his tyranny and cruelty, which he indeed fulfilled when allowed out of his cell. After this he was imprisoned again and was led to believe that his short-lived freedom was only a dream – hence the play's title. When released from his cell a second time, he is just and noble. The quoted line, used by Wyatt earlier (393.3–4), is from Sigismundo's first speech.

Wenn es stimmt, daß nicht einmal die Götter ihre Geschenke zurücknehmen können s.S.453 [820.44] even the gods themselves, can't recall their gifts: see 335.15.

[821.1] Quiere comer?: "Do you want to eat?" (from 771.39).

1069 **Dem Reisenden wurde immer Obdach geboten** [821.4] shelter to travelers [...] a god in disguise: *Faust II* (ll. 11043–142) adapts Ovid's tale of the aged couple Philemon and Baucis, the only couple who offered shelter to Jupiter and Mercury when they traveled in disguise.

Die ganze Familie beim Nachtmahl s.S. 357 [821.5] The whole family there, eating, the whole ... all the family: Wyatt recalls his underlined passage from Thoreau (see 265.2–4).

1070 **los turistas, sí ... pero los marecones** [822.10]: "The tourists, yes ... but the queers."

1071 **sereno** [822.30]: night porter.

1072 **Luna, die Alte mit der Worfschaufel** [823.33] the hag of the moon, the dark winnower: cf. Graves's suggestion "that the [White] Goddess was once worshipped at Moeltre [in Wales] in her triple capacity of white raiser, red reaper and dark winnower of grain" (*WG* 52–53).

III.4

1073 **Sonn' und Mond, die Zweifel hätten** [...] **Blake** [824.epigraph] If the sun [...] Blake: from his poem "Augeries of Experience," as quoted by *ODQ*:
He who doubts from what he sees
Will ne'er believe, do what you please.
If the Sun and Moon should doubt,
They'd immediately go out.
To be in a passion you good may do,
But no good if a passion is in you.

Blessed Mary went a-walking s.S. 1008 [824.1]: see 768.11.

Splitter vom Kreuze Christi [825.11] a shred of the True Cross [...] tears of the Virgin: the fraudulence and popularity of these relics in the Middle Ages are discussed by Mackay (*EPD* 696–97).

Fußnägel von irgendwelchen obskuren Kirchenmännern [825.13] toenail parings of some venerable ecclesiastic: "The unscrupulous ecclesiastics of the Holy Land carried on a flourishing business in selling parings from their own toe nails, which they represented to the pilgrims who annually visited Palestine as coming from the nails of dead saints" (*DDD* 301).

1075 **Stanley starrte dem Machwerk hinterher, dieser Aufforderung zur Todsünde** s.S. 1079 [826.8] a book [...] that invitation to mortal sin: identified later (829.14) as Milton's *Paradise Lost*.

für manche Fische ist das Meer ein großer, großer Himmel. s.S. 112 [826.14] For some fishes the sea is a big sky: a recurring image in Fort's *Book of the Damned* (81.10).

1076 Dogma von der leiblichen Aufnahme Mariens [...] **Eva aus** *Onkel Toms Hütte* s. S. 1185 u. 1198 [826.35] Assumption of the Virgin [...] Little Eva: see 913.30 and 922.44.

Heiligen Simeon Stylites [826.38] Saint Simeon Stylites [...] – Eat what God has given you: (390–459); Stylites means "raised on a pillar," and it was on a three-foot-wide platform on a pillar sixty-six feet high that he spent the last thirty-seven years of his life practicing extreme austerities. Gaddis's details are from Haggard (*DDD* 271):

St. Simeon Stylites furnishes a most remarkable picture of the desert anchorite. He bound a rope around his body so tightly that it became imbedded in the flesh, which putrefied around it. Worms found their way into the corrupt flesh of ulcers that covered his leg. For a year during which he stood on one foot he had an associate by his side who picked up the worms which fell from his body to replace them in the sores, the saint saying to the worms, "Eat what God has given you." At his death he was pronounced to be the highest model of a Christian saint and an example for the imitation of other anchorites.

Heiligen Maria von Ägypten [826.41] Saint Mary of Egypt: again from Haggard (*DDD* 271–72):

The life of one of the anchorites of the desert, St. Mary of Egypt, throws light on the attitude of the early Christians toward prostitutes. The prostitute could atone for her past sins and become a Christian; Christ had forgiven Magdalene. Egyptian Mary was a prostitute, but she became penitent. She confessed to Zosimus that she had practiced her profession for seventeen years at Alexandria. Once converted, she took a boat for Jerusalem and paid her passage by exercising her calling on board. She expiated her sins by a life of penance in the woods. For forty-seven years she wandered, black with filth and covered only with her white hair; but she spoke to no man. To such acts of piety does perversion of sex lead.

Ana Raguza [827.2]: in a discussion of fake mystics, Summers writes: "At Seville on 18th May, 1692, Ana Raguza, a Sicilian, was sentenced to seclusion in an enclosed convent, and two years exile. This is very lenient treatment since she denied the efficacy of Masses and Fasting. Moreover she termed herself the Bride of Christ, declared that she could detect sinners by the sense of smell, and prated of her visions and revelations" (*PPM* 205).

der rechte Fuß der Heiligen Teresa [827.4] right foot of Santa Teresa de Jesús: location noted in *PPM* (192; the Spanish form of her name is taken from a book title that appears in the same paragraph).

der Eiter des Heiligen Johannes vom Kreuz [827.6] pus of Saint John of the Cross: "The pus of St. John of the Cross and of the Blessed Didée [367.36] gave forth a strong scent of Madonna lilies" (*PPM* 175).

1077 mit dem bekannten *Imprimatur* und *Nihil obstat* darauf [827.18] *Nihil obstat* and *Imprimatur*: official declarations that a Catholic book is free of doctrinal or moral error. The statement usually appears on the copyright page.

Ein Tag mit dem Papst s. S. 729 [827.19] *A Day With the Pope* [...] the Court of San Damaso: featured on pp. 26–27 of Doyle's book (see 546.22).

1078 *Der Vatikan im Heiligen Jahr* [828.30] *The Vatican and Holy Year*: a 1950 study of the history of the Holy Year by Stephen Fenichell and Philip Andrews. The slim book is noted for its many fine photographs.

die Augustinische Doktrin [828.37] Augustinian doctrine [...] man from his power: cf.: "In Irenaeus emerges the strange doctrine that the death of Christ was a ransom paid to the devil" (*EB* 7:284).

Margaret Shepherds *Aus meinem Klosterleben* [828.44] Margaret Shepherd's *My Life in a Convent*: published about 1892 when Shepherd was in her forties; probably an "exposé" of Catholic practices in the same vein as those that follow.

1079 Rosamond Culbertson [829.6] the tale of Rosamond Culbertson: *Rosamond; or, A narrative of the captivity and sufferings of an American female under the popish priests, in the island of Cuba, with a full disclosure of their manners and customs, written by herself* (1836). She claims she was for five years the mistress of a Catholic priest.

Rebecca Reeds *Sechs Monate hinter Klostermauern* [829.7] Rebecca Reed's *Six Months in a Convent*: subtitled *The Narrative of Rebecca Theresa Reed, who was under the influence of the Roman Catholics about two years, and an inmate of the Ursuline convent on Mount Benedict, Charlestown, Mass., nearly six months, in the years 1831–32* (1835).

1082 *Jungfrau und Märtyrerin in heutiger Zeit* [831.35] *A Modern Virgin Martyr: A Modern Virgin Martyr: Saint Maria Goretti*, by Alexander Gits, S.J. (London: Catholic Truth Society, 1949), a fifteen-page pamphlet, presumably the source of the quotations at 828.32–33 and 842.25–26.

1087 Semper aliquid haeret s. S. 454 [836.27]: see 336.32.

1089 das Misereatur [838.17] misereatur: the Absolution (from its opening words, "May [God] have mercy"), in which a priest or bishop absolves a penitent from potential damnation.

Sieben ... Glasen [838.19] ship's bells and seven might be any hour: seven bells indicate 3:30, 7:30, or, as here, 11:30.

1090 Per istam [...] Deliquisti per manus [838.24]: from the Catholic rite of Extreme Unction, in which the parts of a dying person's body are anointed: "By this unction, and by his most holy sympathy [...] God forgives you [...]

Whatever [sins] you committed with your eyes [...] Committed with your ears [...] Committed with your hands."

[839.10] sciamachy: fighting with a shadow.

[841.20] Angelic Salutation: that is, the Hail Mary (Luke 1:28).

1096 der Eremit Paulus [843.26] hermit Paul: "The Christian practice of repeating prayers is traceable to early times: Sozomen mentions (*H.E.* v. 29) the hermit Paul of the 4th century who threw away a pebble as he recited each of his 300 daily prayers" (*EB* 19:551).

die Gebeine der von Herodes gemordeten Kinder [844.4] Holy Innocents: male children murdered by Herod's decree (Matt. 2:16). No documents, Jewish or otherwise, record this alleged massacre.

Marquise de Brinvilliers [844.8] Marchioness of Brinvilliers [...] her ashes sought as a preservative against witchcraft: Marie Madeline, marquise de Brinvilliers (1630?–76). "She was convicted of poisoning several persons," Mackay explains, "and sentenced to be burned in the Place de Grève, and to have her ashes scattered to the winds. On the day of her execution, the populace, struck by her gracefulness and beauty, inveighed against the severity of her sentence. Their pity soon increased to admiration, and, ere evening, she was considered a saint. Her ashes were industriously collected; even the charred wood, which had aided to consume her, was eagerly purchased by the populace. Her ashes were thought to preserve from witchcraft" (*EPD* 699).

1097 Ma signorino, che ... [844.25]: It.: "But sir, what ..."

1099 die Allmutter, die letzte Gespielin [845.37] the mother, last lover: cf. Swinburne's "The Triumph of Time": "I will go back to the great sweet mother, / Mother and lover of men, the sea" (*ODQ*).

O Christ, the plough [...] the laughter, of holy white birds [846.11]: from English poet John Masefield's (1878–1967) long narrative poem *The Everlasting Mercy* (1911), about a drunk named Saul Kane who at a revival meeting tells of his vision of Christ and subsequent conversions. The quoted lines are from *ODQ*.

Mann in den besten Jahren s.S.1113 [846.18] a man who [...] might have been described as of comfortable middle age: see 857.20.

1100 das Logo für eine Lebensversicherung [846.24] broken-down bump doesn't look like a life-insurance ad: the Rock of Gibraltar, symbol of the Prudential Life Insurance Company.

Purdue Victory s.S.8 [847.9]: see 4.10.

1101 John Mansfield [847.24]: that is, Masefield.

1101 Fahrt zu, fahrt zu, fahrt immer nur zu [847.27] Sail on! [...] sail on!: from Joaquin Miller's (1841–1913) once-popular poem "Columbus."

1102 Unterdessen führt Columbus zwei Logbücher [847.28] Columbus [...] is keeping two sets of logs: these details, though somewhat garbled, are from *EB*'s account of Columbus's voyage (6:80).

Und wissen Sie, was Columbus dann in Amerika entdeckt hat? Die Syphilis. [848.3] Columbus discovered [...] Syphilis: Haggard agrees with other historians that this does seem likely: see *DDD* 235–39.

1103 *Jealousy* [849.6]: originally a Danish instrumental by Jacob Gade entitled "Jalousie, a Tango Tzigane." The 1938 Boston Pops recording was one of the first records of light music to reach one million sales (as it had by 1952).

1104 coraggio [849.39]: It.: "courage, heart."

1105 der Bischof war da und zwölf Priester [...] die Kerzen hingeworfen s.S.1176 u.1189 [850.34] high altar with a bishop and twelve priests [...] threw their candles down: from the ritual of anathema (excommunication), as described in the *Pontificale Romanum,* as related in *EB* (1:879–80, which furnishes the Latin used at 907.1–4 and 916.40–42).

1107 der Heilige Hilarion [851.41] Saint Hilarion: "The extent to which faith in faith cures may go is shown by the fact that St. Hilarion, of the fourth century, is said to have courageously confronted and relieved a possessed camel" (*DDD* 284).

Ich exorziere dich s.S.268 [852.18] "I exorcise thee [...] Let us pray": from the Catholic rite of exorcism as recorded in *MM* 183; cf. 200.22 ff.

1108 Selige Catharina von Racconigi, die Heilige Veronica Giuliani oder wie die Heilige Lutgarde von Tongres s.S.843 [853.7] Blessed Catherine Racconigi [...] Saint Veronica Giuliani [...] Saint Lutgarde of Tongres: see 634.14–15.

Selige Stefana Quinzani [853.9] Blessed Stefana Quinzani: "The Dominicaness, Blessed Stefana Quinzani of Soncino (near Bergamo), who lived 1457–1530, on every Friday experienced the agony of the sweat of blood in Gethsemane and the pains of the Crown of Thorns which was often plainly seen encircling her head" (*PPM* 154).

die arme Clara von Rovereto [853.11] that Poor Clare of Rovereto: "Joanna Maria della Croce (1603–1673), a Poor Clare of Rovereto (Italian Tyrol), received the Four Wounds and the Crown of Thorns, which latter she used to conceal beneath her veil" (*PPM* 154). The Poor Clares are a religious order, founded by Saint Francis of Assisi and Saint Clare in 1212.

1110 Pater noster [...] Qui tollis peccata mundi s.S.1008 u. 855 [854.37]: see 768.25 and 643.39.

1111 **Er hatte Neapel gesehen** [855.22] He had seen Naples: the old Italian saying "see Naples and die" implied that nothing more beautiful than Naples could be seen; but the proverb was often literally true because Naples was once a center of typhoid and cholera.

III.5

1112 **So lauf ihr nur entgegen [...] Das Zweite Buch der Könige 4,26** [856.epigraph] Run now [...] II Kings 4:26: from the story of the prophet Elisha and the Shunammite woman. In return for her hospitality, he had granted the barren woman a son, who later dies. Going to Elisha to report his death, she overtakes him on the road. Elisha sends his servant to ask if all is well, but she answers falsely (4:26), only later confessing the true situation to Elisha, who then returns to her home and restores the boy to life. The episode has been interpreted as a prophecy of Christ's resurrection. (In light of Gaddis's acquaintance with Robert Graves, the choice of epigraph may owe something to the latter's novelistic treatment *My Head! My Head!*, "Being the History of Elisha and the Shunammite Woman; with the History of Moses as Elisha related it, and her Questions put to him" [1925]; there, Elisha sacrifices his own life to bring the child back to life.)

hinterließ einen Himmel wie eine Leiche [856.1] Day [...] a treated corpse: cf. the opening of Eliot's "Love Song of J. Alfred Prufrock": "Let us go then, you and I, / When the evening is spread out against the sky / Like a patient etherised upon a table."

1113 **Er war ein Mann in den besten Jahren** [857.20] He was a comfortable man [...] referred to by his publishers as distinguished: based to some extant on successful Scottish novelist A. J. Cronin (1896–1981), whose article "What I Learned at La Grande Chartreuse" (*Reader's Digest*, February 1953, 73–77) is quoted and parodied throughout this chapter (858.29–41, 863.40–44, 889.1–890.28). The editorial headnote to the pious essay reads "A distinguished novelist visits the famous monastery of the Carthusian monks."

1114 **ein etwas düsteres Bild seiner Gastgeberin** [858.6] his hostess [...] Moorish ascendancy: the Convento de los Jerónimos (Gaddis's Real Monasterio) contained "the 'Virgen de Guadalupe,', a figure of the Madonna said to have been carved by St. Luke. It was presented by Pope Gregory the Great to Archbp. Leander of Seville, was hidden away during the Moorish period, and found again at Guadalupe by a shepherd in 1330" (Baedeker 461).

Boccaccio [858.17]: Giovanni Boccaccio (1313–75), Italian writer, best known for his story cycle *The Decameron*, the more lascivious episodes of which have fired the imaginations of many illustrators.

1115 Fr. Eulalio s.S.17 [859.5]: cf. 10.13.

Somos españoles [859.8] Somos españoles [...] en el mundo [...] José Antonio: "We are Spaniards [...] which is one of the few serious things to be in the world" – José Antonio Machado (1875–1939), Spanish poet, a member of the group of writers called the "generation of '98."

1116 *Como Ganar Amigos y Vencer Todos los Otros* [859.29]: Carnegie's *HWF;* see 862.35 for a comic mistranslation.

Se puede? [859.44]: "May one?"

1118 *Se ruega* [...] *cristiana* [861.24]: "It is requested, therefore, of our guests the strictest moral behavior in all their acts and conversation. For the ladies it is recommended that their attire be in accordance with Christian modesty."

Jungfrau von Rimini [861.32] Virgin of Rimini: one of Marsh's objects of scorn:

A few years ago, the Virgin of Rimini, which represents a numerous class, the automatic or pantomimic Madonnas, was in high repute; but the profane hands of the Piedmontese civil and military authorities have detected and exposed the springs, cords, pulleys, and other contrivances by which so many sacred pictures and statues were made to roll the eyes, to shed tears, and make puppet-like gestures, that they have fallen rather into discredit. The Virgin of Rimini is a picture of some merit, given by the family of the artist to a church at Rimini in 1810. It manifested no signs of life until 1850, when it was observed by three ladies to roll its eyes upward until the pupil disappeared beneath the upper eyelid, nothing but the white remaining visible. This graceful and expressive movement was repeated during the following days, and after some weeks' practice the image acquired the valuable additional accomplishments of turning the eye-balls laterally, and even rolling them in different directions at the same time. The prodigy excited great attention, the bishop took the matter in hand, and it was swiftly laid before the pope himself, by whose orders an ecclesiastical commission was organized to inquire into the genuineness of the miracle. [...] The pope authorized the coronation of the image in his name, and bestowed upon all who should visit the Church on the day of coronation, or within fifteen days afterward, and perform the required services, plenary indulgence and remission of all sins, transferable, *per modum suffragii,* to any of their friends in purgatory. (*MMSM* 150–51)

daß er es in diesem Punkt den Griechen aus dem Korintherbrief nachtat [861.37] having come, like a vulgar Greek, seeking a sign: perhaps an allusion to the same text "Dick" had used earlier (718.13): "For the Jews require a sign, and the Greeks seek after wisdom: But we preach Christ crucified, unto the Jews a stumblingblock, and unto Greeks foolishness" (1 Cor. 1:22–23).

1119 Fr. Manomuerta s.S.18 [862.2]: cf. 11.2.

[862.12] chasubles worked with thread of gold [...] the gothic cloister: compare Baedeker's description: he notes that the Convento de los Jerónimos was one of the richest monasteries in Spain. The building, in the plaza, resembles a castle. Adjoining the vestibule are the *Sagrario,* with the votive chains of

Christians freed from slavery, and the *Chapel,* containing the 'Virgen de Guadalupe' [...]. The Gothic *Church* is very imposing, though the effect is somewhat marred by the over-massive coro. The latter has a superb reja by *Francisco de Salamanca* and *Juan de Avila* (1520). The Renaissance retablo in the capilla mayor is by *Juan Gómez de Mora* [...]. The tombs of *Henry IV. of Castile* and *Constable Alonso Velasco* are also interesting. – The beautiful *Sacristía* contains eight good pictures (scenes from the life of St. Jerome [...]) by *Zurbarán.* – There are two *Cloisters,* one in the Gothic style, the other, with its charming well-house, in the Moorish style. (461)

1119 Zurbarán [862.17]: Francisco de Zurbarán (1598–1664), Spanish artist who executed paintings for churches and monasteries in southwest Spain as well as the New World; known for his austere depiction of saints' lives. Baedeker devotes half a page to his work (lxxxiii).

1121 Unter der sengenden Sonne der Sierra de G*** [863.40] Sierra de G — [...] bridle path [...] Logrosán: a small village near the Sierra de Guadalupe; Baedeker (461) notes the bridle path that leads from it to the town of Guadalupe, where the monastery is located.

1125 Das Gemälde zeigte einen Mann in geistlichem Gewand [867.3] painting showed [...] in midair: later identified as a portrait of Saint Dominic by Navarrete (see next note).

1128 Navarette, Juan Fernández [869.43] Navarrete ... Juan Fernández [...] He learned from Titian: (1526–79), called "El Mudo" (The Mute): Spanish artist, court painter to Philip II. Baedeker notes "after the king had commissioned him to paint the Apostles (in the church) and other extensive works at the *Escorial,* he remodelled his style by a study of the paintings by Titian he saw there, and showed that he understood the grand old master better than many of his immediate pupils" (lxxix).

1130 Der Heilige Dominik [...] *Ganssanios Vita Dominici Ordiis Praedicatorum Fundatoris* [871.18] Saint Dominic [...] Ganssenio's *Vita* [...] ejusque efficacia: "Our Lady Herself revealed the Rosary to St. Dominic, who may truly be said to be the Author of this Devotion, and a possessed person (however unwillingly) was compelled on one occasion to confess that all who are constant in their love of the Rosary will receive the reward of Eternal life" (*PPM* 39). This statement carries the following citation: "*Vita S. P. Dominici Ordinis Praedicatorum Fundatoris,* Auctore R. P. E. Nicholas Ganssenio ... Antverpiae M.D.C. XXII. Liber I. Cap V. *De auctore Sanctissimi Rosarii, ejusque efficacia,* pp. 31–40" (*PPM* 51 n.105). The detail that follows about enclosing nuns is also from *PPM* (34).

[872.8] El Greco's: his portrait of Saint Dominic is reproduced in *EB*'s article on El Greco (22:opposite p. 70).

1131 *Die Ausgießung des Heiligen Geistes* [...] Auch er hat von Tizian gelernt [872.16] *Descent of the Holy Spirit* [...] He studied with Titian too: an Annunciation. Baedeker notes that he was a pupil of Titian (lxxix).

1132 Jede Kunst braucht den geschlossenen Raum [872.25] "all art requires a closed space": source unknown.

Homunkulus s. S. 7 u. 353 [872.26] Homunculus: see I.1 epigraph and 262.17–18.

1133 Valdés Leal s. S. 515 [873.21]: see 381.5.

1135 Erinnern Sie sich an den Satz Ciceros in den *Paradoxa*? s. S. 168 [875.22] Cicero, in the *Paradoxa*: see 124.6.

1136 Casa con dos puertas, mala es guardar [875.41]: "A house with two doors is difficult to guard," a Spanish proverb.

1137 wie bei Sigismundo in der Zelle [876.18] Sigismundo [...] *La Vida es Sueño*: in act 2 of Calderón's play (see 820.37), Sigismundo throws an impudent servant off the balcony into the sea – the play is set in an ahistorical Poland, indifferent to its actual geography – after which he laments "Vive Dios, que pudo ser!" ("I'd see it literally as 'Live, God, that I may be' [WG/SM]).

mit Lilien, die zu Flammen werden [876.38] she comes to him carrying lilies: Alessandro Serenelli, Saint Maria Goretti's murderer (see 16.12), was sent to prison for his crime and for many years was a difficult, unrepentant prisoner. Then he had a dream or vision in which Maria gathered flowers and offered them to him. He became repentant and a model prisoner and was released after twenty-seven years in prison and performed penance in a Capuchin monastery.

vor zweitausend Jahren lag die Lebenserwartung kaum über dreiunddreißig [876.43] two thousand years ago, thirty-three was old, and time to die: cf. 229.12, and see Frazer for the ancient practice of putting a king to death at the height of his powers (*GB* 265).

Verflucht die Jugend, die dem Alter unterlegen [876.44] "A curse on youth, that age must overcome [...] could they be forever enchained!": the Buddha's decision to retire from the world and formulate his philosophy was confirmed, writes Saltus, after the following episode: "On the high-roads about Kapilavastu he encountered a man bent double with age, another stricken by fever, and lastly a corpse. 'A curse,' he cried, 'on youth that age must overcome; a curse on health that illness destroys; a curse on life which death interrupts! Age, illness, death, could they but be forever enchained!'" (*AN* 15–16). Saltus goes on to discount this legend.

1138 **daß auch Buddha nach einer unbefleckten Empfängnis geboren wurde** [877.2] Buddha's immaculate conception, and dead of an indigestion of pork: "The accounts of his life are contained in the Lalita Vistâra, a collection of fabulous episodes in which the supernatural joins hands with the matter-of-fact. It is said, for instance, that he as born of an immaculate conception, and died of an indigestion of pork" (*AN* 14).

J'ai le Cafard [877.15]: Fr: "I've got the blues," but "cafard I associate with something [...] nearer total despair" (WG/SM).

Ghoum [877.20]: a native policeman; "with ghoum I associate elements of sadism, depravity" (WG/SM).

Et toi, divine Mort [877.22] "Et toi, divine Mort [...] Leconte de Lisle [...] la vie a troublé": Charles Marie René Leconte de Lisle (1818–94), French poet. Quoted here is the first stanza of his poem "Dies irae" (from *Poëmes antiques*, 1852), which, like *R* itself, concerns alienation, suffering, the loss of God, and nostalgia:
Et toi, divine Mort, où tout rentre et s'efface,
Accueille tes enfants dans ton sein étoilé;
Affranchis-nous du temps, du nombre et de l'espace,
Et rends-nous le repos que la vie a troublé!
("And you, divine death, where all return and obliterate themselves, / Welcome your children into your starry breast; / Free us from time, from number and space / And give us the repose that life has disturbed!") These lines are quoted at the beginning of Saltus's *AN* as a motto, and Leconte de Lisle is the subject of his final chapter, "A Poet's Verdict."

1139 **Ouled-Naïl** [877.43]: an Afro-Arab tribe noted for its sensuous exotic dancers.

Défense de raser [878.3] "Défense de raser," [...] "les médicastres français e'entendent": Fr. "Don't shave, [...] the French medicasters (quacks) are in the know."

[878.32] Sir-reverence: an Elizabethan corruption of "save your reverence," used before saying anything indecorous.

1140 **stellte sich heraus, daß ein großes Gesicht auf seinen Hintern tätowiert war** [879.5] a face tattooed on his fundament! There's homage for a whole coven: at a key point in a witches' sabbath, the devil's posterior (or a facemask attached thereon) was kissed, a parody of the pax of the Mass. This practice is noted by Mackay (*EPD* 470).

1141 **Rubens** [879.19] Rubins: Peter Paul Rubens (1577–1640), Dutch painter, the most important artist in northern Europe in his time.

1141 un escritor muy distinguido, muy culto [879.37]: "a very distinguished writer, very cultivated."

1143 an dem Überfall mindestens zur Hälfte mit schuld [...] zur falschen Zeit am falschen Ort [...] von Dante [881.20] the victim abets the violence just by being there [...] From Dante: untraced, but the statement is in keeping with Schopenhauer's views.

1144 *Transcendente Spekulation* s. S. 143 [881.32] *Transcendent Speculations*: see 105.19.

Mamie [881.41]: if Rev. "Dick" is named after Dick Nixon, this ridiculous woman is probably named after President Eisenhower's wife.

cuando tiene las Fallas en Valencia? [882.8]: "When do you hold the Fallas in Valencia?" (the double *l* in Spanish has a *y* sound; otherwise "Fallas" would sound like "phallus"). Baedeker doesn't mention the Fallas, a Valencian word for "bonfires."

Granada [...] the Hospital de San Juan de Dios [882.18]: see Baedeker 345.

1145 Pietà [882.43]: a Pietà is not an artist but a subject: "the Virgin mourning over Her son" (127.13–14).

[884.38] merkins: that is, Americans, but cf. 392.20.

1148 Gebetsstock der Zuñi-Indianer s. S. 64 [885.3] Zuñi prayer stick: see 45.14.

[885.41] extreme unction [...] renounce matrimonial relations: from the concluding paragraph of "Extreme Unction" in *EB*: "It was a popular opinion in the middle ages that extreme unction extinguishes all ties and links with this world, so that he who has received it must, if he recovers, renounce the eating of flesh and matrimonial relations. Such opinions, combated by bishops and councils, were due to the influence of the *consolamentum* of the Cathars" (9:3; see 532.5 for Catharism).

1149 La comedia está muy bien [886.10]: she means *comida*, "meal."

1150 in den Farben der H. A. C. s. S. 658 [886.25] H.A.C.: Honourable Artillery Company (80.38); Sinisterra too owns an H.A.C. tie (493.37).

[887.25] "The world is too muhvh with us [...] we lay wasre ...": Wordsworth's famous sonnet begins: "The world is too much with us; late and soon / Getting and spending, we lay waste our powers." The Christian Ludy does not seem to realize that the poem extols the affinity with nature last enjoyed by the pagans.

1151 Kinderkreuzzug [887.36] Children's Crusade: the ill-fated crusade of 1212 in which twenty thousand children perished.

1152 Blautöne [...] von deren Verwendung Leonardo stets abgeraten hatte [888.42] blue tones which Leonardo observed [...] and warned: "Somewhere in his treatises Leonardo describes and explains the blue middle tones which he (like the early Italian masters and Van der Weyden, Bosch, etc.) had observed in nature, but warns against painting this 'optical illusion'" – from H. Ruhemann's article "Discoveries beneath the Paint of Masters" (*Art News* 50.10 [February 1952]: 34), which Koenig notes Gaddis read ("'Splinters from the Yew Tree,'" 76).

[889.42] of wars and rumors of wars: from Matt. 24:6.

[889.43] the service of both God and Mammon: from Matt. 6:24.

[892.2] *Eclogues*: another name for Vergil's *Bucolics* (see 28.22).

1157 George Borrow [892.11] George Borrow [...] the most vivid interview with desolation: (1803–81), English traveler, philologist, and writer, best known for his autobiographical novels on Gypsy life (*Lavengro, The Romany Rye*). He was an agent for the Bible Society in Spain and Russia, and his experiences in the former are recounted in *The Bible in Spain* (1843), to which the present allusion refers. En route from Portugal to Spain, Borrow comes upon a madman among some ruins and comments: "But the maniac, on his stone, in the rear of the wind-beaten ruin overlooking the blasted heath, above which scowled the leaden heaven, presented such a picture of gloom and misery as I believe neither painter nor poet ever conceived in the saddest of their musings" (66). Gaddis "mentioned Borrow once to Robt Graves who dismissed him as 'the biggest liar who ever lived'" (WG/SM).

1158 Jetzt ist die Zeit, da die Plejaden aufgehen s.S. 11 [892.36] The Pleiades are rising: see 6.12; the rising of the Pleiades in May was, of course, an auspicious occasion.

Könige sollten nicht sterben, sondern entschwinden [892.43] "Kings should disdain to die, but only disappear": writing of the death of Charles II, minor English poet Thomas Flatman (1637–88) was surprised that a monarch simply dies as any commoner would, and he wrote the quoted line, cited in a footnote in De Quincey's *Confessions of an English Opium-Eater* (see epigraph to II.1).

Ich war einmal König [893.1] "I was that king [...] have vanished away": Lethaby (*AMM* 145–46) records "the story told by the Buddha to Ananda of 'The Great King of Glory'," in which the Buddha describes the splendor of his royal capital of Kasavati; he concludes his description with the passage quoted here (which is in turn quoted from vol. 11 of the *Sacred Books of the East*, ed. Rhys Davids).

1160 Geh dorthin, wo man dich sucht [894.24] Go where you're wanted: cf. Housman: "'Oh, go where you are wanted, for you are not wanted here.' / And that was all the farewell when I parted from my dear" (*A Shropshire Lad*, no. 34, quoted in *ODQ*).

denn wie das Herz, so hatte auch die Hand ihre eigenen Gründe [894.33] hands which like the heart, knew their own reasons: from Pascal's *Penseés*: "The heart has its reasons which reason knows nothing of" (*ODQ*).

1161 immer vor Kap Horn, die Deutschen haben die Geschichte ganz schön aufgemotzt [895.7] sailing off the Cape forever, the Germans dressed that up [...] with a woman: adding to the basic legend of the Flying Dutchman (see 770.30), Wagner drew upon Heinrich Heine's amusing story "From the Memoirs of Herr von Schnabelewopski" (1831) to equate salvation with a woman's constancy.

1162 Leptis Magna s. S. 431 [895.38]: see 319.44.

der Tempel der Hera, Lilien blühten aus ihrer Milch [895.42] Hera, and the lilies sprung from her milk: source unknown (not in Frazer or Graves).

ein alter Mann auf einer Folterbank s. S. 103 [896.2] detailed figure [...] being flayed: see 74.30 ff.; it will be remembered that Wyatt cut this detail from Brown's painting.

1164 ganze Familie beim Nachtmahl s. S. 357 u. 1069 [897.10] all the family at dinner: from Thoreau; see 265.2–4, 821.5–6.

wer hätte gedacht, daß der alte Mann noch so viel Blut in sich hätte [897.28] who would have thought the old man to have had so much blood in him: from *Macbeth* 5.1.43.

Und die Freier? Ach Gott, wer wollte sie umbringen [898.2] not slaying the suitors [...] Penelope spinning a web: from Homer's *Odyssey*.

1165 Wenn die Götter schon ihre Geschenke nicht zurücknehmen können s. S. 453 u. 1069 [898.24] if the gods themselves cannot recall their gifts: see 335.15, and cf. 820.44. (Pages 820–21 and 897–98 share a number of details, it will be noticed.)

1166 nach Biskra oder Nalut [898.40] Biskra [...] Nalut: small towns in Algeria and Libya, respectively.

könnte sein, ich hegte und pflegte dich gewiß zu Tod s. S. 519 [899.9] yet should I kill thee? with much cherishing?: from *Romeo and Juliet;* see 383.29.

Varé tava soskei me puchelas s. S. 343 [899.13]: see 255.24 ff.

1167 Der Bischof von Hippo, ein ehemaliger Manichäer [899.25] ex-Manichee bishop of Hippo [...] Dilige et quod vis fac [...] Love, and do what you want to: from Saint

Augustine's *On the First Letter of John* (*ODQ*, where it is translated "Love and do what you will"), meaning esteem (charity, respect) should motivate all actions.

[900.11] to live deliberately: from Thoreau's *Walden:* "I went to the woods because I wished to live deliberately, to front only the essential facts of life, and see if I could not learn what it had to teach, and not, when I came to die, discover that I had not lived" (chap. 2).

[900.22] The old man, ringing me on: cf. 481.19. Marlowe's *Doctor Faustus* ends with an "Old Man" attempting to save Faustus's soul. Jung notes the role the old man archetype plays in the process of individuation (*IP* 127).

Epilogue

1169 Aux Clients [...] rue de l'Aqueduct, Oran [901.epigraph]: Fr.: "To Clients Recognized as sick, MONEY will not be refunded." Oran is a seaport city in Algeria.

1170 aus dem Fuhrpark von Papst Benedikt XV. [901.23] ascent of Benedict XV: died 1922.

Einem hervorragenden spanischen Kopf zufolge [...] höchstens der Triumph über den Raum [901.24] as an eminent Spaniard supplies [...] his vital time is limited: to his statement "It was a question of honour for man to triumph over cosmic space and time," Ortega appends this footnote: "It is precisely because man's vital time is limited, precisely because he is mortal, that he needs to triumph over distance and delay. For an immortal being, the motorcar would have no meaning" (*RM* 39, n.1; WG/SM).

Triumph der Judith [...] Donatello [...] Salome [902.12] Judith over Holofernes [...] Donatello [...] his Salome: the Italian sculptor executed a *Judith and Holofernes* (cf. 74.32), but he lived in the fifteenth century, not the nineteenth. Later, Mrs. Deigh calls the Victorian sculpture "his famous David" (925.35).

1171 ein Splitter vom Wahren Kreuz [...] Paulinus s. S. 329 [903.16] True Cross [...] Paulinus: see 245.31 and 719.10.

1172 Hadrian [903.28]: perhaps named after *Hadrian the Seventh,* the 1905 novel by Baron Corvo (Frederick Rolfe [1860–1913], whom Gaddis says he read while working on *R*).

Verkündigung von Tintoretto [903.36] *Annunciation* by Tintoretto: Jacopo Robusti, called Tintoretto (1518–94), Venetian artist; he painted many Annunciations.

1173 Marienerscheinung s. S. 1206 [904.29] an apparition of the Virgin: see 917.1 ff.

1175 Laokoongruppe [905.37] Laocoön: one of the most famous sculptures of the Classical era, now in the Vatican.

1175 *Le cinque fonti sanguinose* s. S. 1226 [906.4]: It.: The Five Bloodstained Fountains (unidentified; a French version appears at 944.28).

San Clemente? [...] Prior Mullooly [...] den Dominikanern gehört [906.6] San Clemente! [...] Prior Mullooly [...] it's all owned by Dominicans: cf. pp. 37–38. In 1857 Father Joseph Mullooly, then Prior of San Clemente, began excavations beneath the basilica and uncovered both the fourth-century basilica underneath (which incorporates a room previously used for the worship of Mithra) and, lower still, the remains of a first-century building. See his *St. Clement Pope and Martyr and His Basilica in Rome* (2d ed., 1873). But since Fr. Mullooly died in 1880, it is impossible for Mrs. Deigh to have known him. The basilica has been in the hands of the Irish Dominicans since the end of the seventeenth century – and was still in 1984 when Gaddis visited the Mithræum for the first time.

1176 E. M. Forsters *Engel und Narren* [906.26] Forster's *Where Angels Fear to Tread*: Forster's 1905 novel concerns the effect of Italy's culture and atmosphere on some provincial English personalities and a scandal that ensues.

et eum a societate [...] et excommunicatum [907.1]: from the rite of excommunication (the Latin is given in *EB*'s article "Anathema" [1:879–80], and an English translation in its "Bell, Book and Candle" [3:376]): "[We separate him, together with his accomplices and abettors, from the precious body and blood of the Lord] and from the society of all Christians; we exclude him from our holy mother the Church in heaven and on earth; we declare him excommunicate [and anathema]" – continued at 916.40.

1178 Schaufensterdekoration mit lauter Wagner-Motiven s. S. 263 [907.44] Nibelungs [...] Wagnerian panorama: see 196.16.

arca musarithmica s. S. 1202 [908.11]: see 926.22.

1179 I H S s. S. 1202 [908.38]: see 926.38.

Das Lendentuch des Heiligen Stephan [909.4] Saint Stephen: see 27.25; Foxe gives this account of his martyrdom: "His death was occasioned by the faithful manner in which he preached the Gospel to the betrayers and murderers of Christ. To such a degree of madness were they excited, that they cast him out of the city and stoned him to death. The time when he suffered is generally supposed to have been at the passover which succeeded to that of our Lord's crucifixion, and to the era of his ascension, in the following spring" (*BM 2*).

1180 *Ein Zimmer mit Aussicht* [910.7] *A Room with a View*: another Forster novel (1908), also partly set in Italy, concerning the experiences of a young upper-middle-class Englishwoman.

1181 **Heilige Joseph von Copertino** s.S.72 [910.41] Saint Joseph of Copertino: see 51.18.

1182 **Chez** [911.3]: Fr.: "at the home (place) of."

Thomas Becket [911.19] Thomas à Becket: (1118?–70), English prelate and archbishop of Canterbury; the circumstances of his murder by Henry II's knights are dramatized in Eliot's *Murder in the Cathedral* (1935).

1184 *Lilies without, roses within* [912.25] a lance tipped with golden fire [...] "Lilies without, roses within": some of these details are from *PPM*, but the quotation is from Marvell's poem "Nymph Complaining for the Death of Her Fawn" (*ODQ*).

Caravaggio [912.29]: Italian painter (1569–1609) who introduced a harsh realism into biblical subjects.

1185 **Moses im Koran der Zauberei bezichtigt** s.S.78 [913.10] Moses is accused of witchcraft in the Koran: see 55.40.

1186 **Stadt mit dem Rosengarten** s.S.1080 [914.4] rose garden: the one into which Saint Francis threw himself in Assisi; see 830.18ff.

1189 **toleratus** [...] **vitandus** [916.17] toleratus [...] vitandus [...] to take part in the Mass: from *EB*'s "Anathema" (1:879–80).

1190 **et anathematizatum** [...] **aeternum indicamus** [916.40]: continued from 907.1–4: "we declare him [excommunicate] and anathema; we judge him damned, with the Devil and his angels and all the reprobate, to eternal fire [until he shall recover himself from the toils of the Devil and return to amendment and to penitence]" (*EB* 3:376).

Amerikaner suchen auf dem Berg Ararat nach Überresten der Arche Noah [916.43] Mount Ararat [...] Noah's Ark: in 1951, American historian and missionary Aaron Smith spent twelve days with forty companions fruitlessly searching for Noah's Ark on the ice cap of Ararat.

Eine amerikanische Zeitung [917.1] American picture magazine [...] sun's antics over Portugal: a reference to the miracle of Fátima (1917), where three children's vision of the Virgin Mary was climaxed by the sun's dancing in the sky. There is an article in the 5 November 1951 issue of *Life* on Fátima, in which Cardinal Tedeschini is quoted (and pictured) on the papal vision reported earlier in the *Osservatore Romano* (see 414.22ff.), but the article does not feature the photograph referred to in the novel. We are meant to remember that as a girl – perhaps about 1917 – Mrs. Deigh "one day, floating naked on her back in the blue waters off Portugal, [...] was discovered by some peasant children who took her for an apparition of the Virgin" (904.27–29).

1192 **Firbank** s.S.1200 [918.34]: see 925.1.

1192 Fenn és ... [918.40]: Hungarian: "Above and ..."; *Fenn és lenn* (Above and Below) is a novel by Francis Herczeg mentioned in the article on Hungarian literature in *EB* (11:896).

1193 Wenn wir auch nur eine einzige Minute hätten den Mund halten können, eine einzige Minute des Schweigens s.S.1213 [919.2] "If we had stopped [...] a minute of silence": see 935.13.

Keats ist auch dort begraben, oder war es Shelley [919.12] Keats is buried, or is it Shelley: Keats died in Rome and is buried in a Protestant cemetery there; Shelley's corpse was burned on the beach at Viareggio.

1195 *A Véres költö* s.S. 860 [921.5]: see 648.32.

1196 unter dem Schirm des Heiligen Peter s.S. 866 [921.21] Saint Peter's Umbrella: see 652.39.

mir doch egal, ob Johanna von Orleans eine Hexe war [921.30] Joan of Arc was a witch: Joan was tried by the French ecclesiastical courts on twelve charges of sorcery, among other things. She is regarded as a witch in Shakespeare's *Henry IV*, a reflection of English sentiments at that time.

daß die Franziskaner für genau die Eigenschaften kanonisiert wurden, für die man die Waldenser noch verbrannt hat [921.32] Franciscans were canonized for the very things the Waldensians were burned alive for: Waldensians (after Peter Waldo of Lyons) threw off the authority of the pope, bishops, and clergy, appointed lay teachers (including women), and rejected infant baptism and many other rites; as a result they were persecuted by the church. The twelfth-century Waldensians anticipated the thirteenth-century Franciscans in returning to a more basic, primitive form of Christianity and in attacking the wealth and pomp of the medieval church.

1198 Dogma [...] über die leibliche Aufnahme Mariens in den Himmel [922.44] the most recent dogma, that of the Assumption: the popular belief that the Virgin Mary was bodily assumed into heaven upon her death was proclaimed dogma by Pius XII on 1 November 1950.

Maria [...] Elisabeth [923.32] Mary [...] Elizabeth: Mary was the daughter of Anne, not Elizabeth; the latter was John the Baptist's mother.

1199 der Heilige Antonius von Padua [923.36] Saint Anthony of Padua: (1195–1231), Portuguese-born Italian preacher and wonder-worker.

Heilige Johannes hat gesagt [...] wo da ist keine Liebe s.S. 603 [923.39] Saint John of the Cross [...] Where there is no love: see 451.35.

1200 *Exzentrizitäten des Kardinals Pirelli* [925.1] *Eccentricities of Cardinal Pirelli*: English writer Ronald Firbank's (1886–1926) last novel, *Concerning the Eccentricities of Cardinal Pirelli* (1926), concerns an eccentric cardinal in Spain who baptizes dogs and finally meets his death while chasing a choirboy around the altar of an empty church. It was reprinted in 1949 as one of *Five Novels* during what was briefly a Firbank "revival."

1200 *Justine* s. S. 246 [925.2]: see 183.40.

[925.28] coign of vantage: a convenient corner, from *Macbeth* (*ODQ*).

Herkules **von della Robbia** [926.30] *Hercules,* by della Robbia: Luca della Robbia (1400–82), Italian sculptor, along with Donatello one of the great innovators of the fifteenth century.

Impubis Hadrianus Semper [926.38]: "May Hadrian Be Forever Pure." The Latin abbreviation I.H.S. derives from a Greek abbreviation of the name of Jesus and is usually interpreted *In Hoc Signo – Vinces* ("In This Sign – Conquer") or *Jesus Hominium Salvator* ("Jesus, Savior of Man").

1205 **Sankt Raphael [...] Sankt Auriel** [928.36] Saint Raphael [...] Saint Auriel: these angels preside over the east, west, south, and north, respectively.

1206 **FIAT** s. S. 1105 [930.8]: Lat.: "So be it": the final word in an excommunication ceremony, followed by an amen. Cf. 850.37.

1213 **Packend, sensibel und lebensnah** [935.13] "Deft, moving, genuine [...] the *Confessions*": Anselm's joining a silent order and writing his confessions seem modeled on the career of Thomas Merton (1915–68), whose autobiographical *Seven Storey Mountain* (1948) was similarly compared to the *Confessions* of Saint Augustine.

1215 *rekognoszierten,* **daß sie beide das gleiche Buch dabei hatten** [936.38] a thick book [...] no necktie: the description is of the first edition of R. Martin Dworkin's photograph of Gaddis "sans gêne with a cigarette, sang-froid with no necktie" appeared in both the *Time* and *Newsweek* reviews.

1216 *Der Idiot* [937.30] *The Idiot* [...] Goodbye!'": Dostoevski's 1869 novel concerns Prince Myshkin, an epileptic and a good, guileless man. The lives of a number of singular characters become involved with his, and although they all admire Myshkin's personal qualities, they consider him, for all practical purposes, an "idiot." Ippolit, a tortured consumptive who fails in his attempt to commit suicide, asks, "Did you imagine that I did not foresee all this hatred!" shortly before the attempt when he receives a negative reaction to a long confession he has just read (3.7). The quotation about Europe is from the last page of the novel and is spoken by Lizaveta Prokofyevna, the eccentric matriarch of the novel. The final exchange is again between Ippolit and Myshkin and concludes 4.5; Ippolit has asked, "What do you think would be the best way for me to die?" and Myshkin answers as quoted. The translation used is Constance Garnett's.

1217 **der alternde George Washington** s. S. 88 [938.11] George Washington [...] about the time he said farewell to his troops: 1783; see 63.2.

Partisan Review [938.14]: progressive American literary magazine founded in 1934; Gaddis's editor Catharine Carver was managing editor at the time *R* was published.

Mochten andre Städte, die Lust gewähren, sätt'gen [938.16] Other cities might cloy the appetites they fed [...] a morsel for a monarch: two passages from Shakespeare's *Antony and Cleopatra* are parodied here; first, Enobarbus's famous description of the queen (used earlier at 63.17):

Age cannot wither her, nor custom stale
Her infinite variety. Other women cloy
The appetites they feed, but she makes hungry
Where most she satisfies. For vilest things
Become themselves in her, that the holy priests
Bless her when she is riggish. (2.2.240–45)

And second, Cleopatra's musings on the absent Antony:

He's speaking now,
Or murmuring, "Where's my serpent of old Nile?"
For so he calls me. Now I feed myself
With most delicious poison. Think on me,
That am with Phoebus' amorous pinches black
And wrinkled deep in time? Broad-fronted Caesar,
When thou wast here above the ground I was
A morsel for a monarch ... (1.5.24–31)

ciné cochon? deux femmes s. S. 92 [938.20]: see 66.11.

1218 **der erste Bischof der Stadt** s. S. 93 [938.24] the first bishop: Saint Denis (see 67.8).

das Kunststück aus geschärfter weiblicher Feder [938.26] a comment [...] in a woman's pen: commenting on Saint Denis's two-league march with head in hand, Madame du Deffand (1697–1780) wrote to d'Alembert: "The distance is nothing; it is only the first step that is difficult" (*ODQ*).

vous m'emmenez s. S. 105 [938.33]: "Take me with you?" (cf. 75.43).

Frischfleisch für einen König, nichts anderes war die ehemalige Lutetia [938.36] Lutetia succumbed after a struggle: Julius Caesar defeated Vercingetorix at Alésia in 52 B. C. and appointed Paris the meeting place for the deputies of Gaul.

In ihren [...] blumengeschmückten Gewändern [938.41] flowered robes [...] courtesans throughout the ages: from Haggard (*DDD* 266):

Among the Greeks the law designated flowered robes as the costume of the courtesans, but was modified to prevent them from wearing scarlet or purple or jewels. It was the fashion among the courtesans to dye their hair blond or use flaxen wigs. At a late period in Greek history this fashion was followed by women who were not courtesans. All through the ages fashions have originated with courtesans. In Rome it is said that prostitutes could be distinguished from virtuous matrons only by the superior elegance of their dress and the swarm of admirers who surrounded them.

1218 Die Edelhure führte auf einmal einen angesehenen Salon [939.3] like the better class of whores in ancient Greece, a trained entertainer: "The better class of these women were trained entertainers" (*DDD* 267).

Nicht anders also als im Athen des Sokrates oder Perikles [939.5] Socrates [...] Pericles [...] clasp Aspasia to his breast and weep": also from Haggard (*DDD* 267):

Socrates had no compunction in visiting Aspasia who had migrated from Milesia and established a house of prostitution in Athens. He even gave her sound philosophical advice for running her establishment. Subsequently Aspasia exercised such an influence over Pericles that he divorced his wife. He was accused of allowing Aspasia to govern Athens through her influence over him. Popular feeling rose high against her. The power of Pericles declined. Aspasia was accused of impiety and tried. Pericles appeared as her advocate, but in court his eloquence failed him; he could only clasp Aspasia to his breast and weep. She was acquitted, deserted Pericles, and married a wealthy grain merchant.

1219 Daß auch die Syphilis dazugehörte [939.13] English, Italians, and even Turks [...] from conversing with the rest of the world": from Haggard's discussion of syphilis:

The Europeans, faced with a new disease, were hard pressed for a name. Each country blamed some other and named the disease accordingly. The Spaniards called it the disease of Española; the Italians called it the French disease; the French called it the Italian disease; the English credited it to the French; the Russians named it the Polish disease; for the Turks it was the French disease; and for the Indians and Japanese the Portuguese disease. France for some reason bore most of the onus. [...] In 1497, by act of the parliament of Paris, all persons infected with the new disease were prohibited, "under pain of death, from conversing with the rest of the world." The diseased persons who lived in the city were isolated in the suburbs of St.-Germain.

Red River Valley [939.25]: traditional American folk song.

enkonnü, verstehst du s. S. 89 [939.36] ankonoo [...] poorbwar: see 64.8.

1220 Beethovens Duo für Viola und Cello [940.19] Beethoven's duet for viola and cello: 1796 composition in E-flat major.

Pissarro s. S. 760 [940.25]: Camille Pissarro (1830–1903), French Impressionist painter. Cf. 569.14.

La Macule s. S. 97 [940.27]: see 70.14.

1221 George Sank [940.44]: that is, the Georges Cinq, an elegant luxury hotel.

Nachtgewächs [941.6] *Nightwood*: Djuna Barnes's (see 188.28) best-known novel (1936), dealing with a romantic lesbian triangle.

1221 **Mozart hat sogar von sich selber geklaut** [941.11] Mozart [...] wind instruments in the dinner scene with Leporello: Leporello is the servant of Don Giovanni in Mozart's opera of the same name. The last scene opens with the don dining and joking with his servant while his private orchestra plays various tunes, one of which is the "Non più andrai" from Mozart's own *Marriage of Figaro*.

1222 **Marecones** [...] **Marecones y nada mas** [941.24]: Sp.: "Queers. [...] Queers and nothing more" (cf. 65.34). Here, as at 822.10, the word should be spelled *maricones*.

[941.25] Wie Eulen nach Athen bringen: Ger.: "Taking owls to Athens" – see 754.14–15.

1223 *On est prié* [...] *se supporter* [942.29]: Fr.: "It is requested that the window not be opened because the front of the hotel depends on it for support."

1224 **Boeuf à la sale anglaise** [943.1] boeuf à la sale anglaise [...] boeuf salé à l'anglaise: the first means "beef of the dirty Englishwoman," the second "English salted beef."

Monsieur Clot, Chef der Sureté Nationale [943.19] Commissionier Clot of the Sureté Nationale: unidentified, as is the source of his quotation below.

1225 **coll' arte** [...] **francese** [943.41]: It.: "with the well-known art (guile) of French treachery."

in einem Vorort namens Banlieu s. S. 92 [944.15] a suburb called Banlieu: see 66.6.

eine Stadt namens Condom [944.19] Condom: a town in southwestern France, from its Latin name Condomus.

1226 **die Prophezeiung des Malachi s. S. 51** [944.25] Malachi prophecy: see 35.36.

Glaubst du, Paris ist wirklich eine Messe wert [944.27] Paris is worth a Mass: Henri of Navarre, upon becoming Henri IV of France by converting to Catholicism, is reported to have justified his conversion with "Paris is well worth a Mass" (*ODQ*).

Les cinq fontaines ensanglantées s. S. 1175 [944.28]: see 906.4.

Nostradamus [944.28] Nostradamus predicts it will last until 3420: Michel de Nostre-Dame (1503–66), French astronomer, made many cryptic prophecies in his book *Centuries* (1555) that are open to numerous interpretations.

1227 *Emmerdant* [...] *Les americains, alors* [945.9] emmerdant ... – les americains, alors: Fr.: "shitty ... – Americans, then."

[945.10] sleep out this great gap of time: from *Antony and Cleopatra* (1.5.4).

1227 kannst du lieben? -Ja, gnäd'ge Fürstin. [...] was Venus tat mit Mars [945.11] Hast thou affections? [...] what Venus did with Mars: *Antony and Cleopatra*, 1.5.12–18. Cleopatra has asked her eunuch Mardian if he still has sexual impulses. The ellipsis omits Mardian's comment: "for I can do nothing / But what indeed is honest to be done."

viel Zeitvertreib für dem Wurm [945.20] joy of the worm: the rustic who brings Cleopatra the fatal asp departs with: "I wish you joy o' the worm" (5.2.281).

et toute nue ... quelle envahisseuse! [945.20]: Fr. "And completely nude ... what an invader! [fem.]"

1229 Porträt im Kerzenschein [946.33] "Study by Candlelight" by Vincent van Gogh: the authenticity of this painting, an alleged self-portrait, was "the subject of the great art controversy of the year" in 1949; see "Is It, or Isn't It Van Gogh? Reasons Con & Pro," *Art Digest*, 15 December 1949, 15, 26. The "Hollywood movie producer" is identified as William Goetz, executive producer of Universal Pictures.

verbrannte öffentlich zwei Bibeln, weil dort das Wort »Jungfrau« durch »junge Frau« ersetzt worden war [947.17] a new revised version [...] substituted the words *young woman* for *virgin*: when the Revised Standard Version of the Bible was published in 1952, its more accurate translation aroused the ire of many fundamentalists. An often-quoted example was the rendering of the famous prophecy of Christ in Isa. 7:14: "Therefore the Lord himself shall give you a sign; Behold, a virgin shall conceive, and bear a son, and shall call his name Immanuel," in which *virgin* was more correctly rendered in the RSV as "a young woman."

1230 Napok óta nem aludt [...] kényszerüsegükben [948.3]: Hungarian: "He hasn't slept for days." "For weeks." "Seconal, Luminal, Somnadex, we've tried everything. Even American drugs in our desperation." (Green reveals "actually the hungarian phrases in *the recognitions* were picked up by asking a few questions in the bar of a hungarian restaurant" [55, n.]; see Gaddis's own account in his *Paris Review* interview).

1231 Nincsen oka [948.27]: "No reason."

Gold macht man am besten aus Gold s. S. 914 [949.1] "Thank God there was the gold to forge": so said Wyatt at 693.32–33.

1232 Aetas parentum pejor avis tulit nos nequiores [949.4]: from Horace's *Odes* (3.6):
Aetas parentum pejor avis tulit
nos nequiores, mox daturos
progeniem vitiosiorem.
("Our fathers, viler than our grandfathers, begot us who are even viler, and we shall bring forth a progeny more degenerate still.") Ortega uses

this quotation to illustrate the "decay and loss of pulse" in the Roman Empire (*RM* 30 and n.1).

1232 Nincsen oka nem aludni [949.19]: "There's no reason for him not to sleep."

Nézzen rá, nézzen a szemére [949.24]: "Look at him, look at his eyes."

indulgeat tibi Dominus [949.25]: "God forgives you" – from Extreme Unction (see 838.24ff.).

Aut castus [...] et pereat! [949.26]: "Aut castus sit aut pereat" means "Be pure or perish"; "et pereat" means "and perish." Source unknown.

deliquisti per oculos [...] Quidquid deliquisti per manus [949.31]: from Extreme Unction: "committed with your eyes [...] Whatever you committed with your hands" – an appropriate note for him to end on: Valentine's preoccupation with hands runs through the novel.

1235 Zauberei, kommt das jetzt von *male de fide sentiendo* [951.39] Sorcery [...] matters of faith?: cf. the following passage in *MM* (20): "Moreover, witchcraft differs from all other harmful and mysterious arts in this point, that of all superstition it is essentially the vilest, the most evil and the worst, wherefore it derives its name from doing evil, and from blaspheming the true faith. (*Maleficae dictae a Maleficiendo, seu a male de fide sentiendo.*)"

1241 prego [...] capisce [956.10]: "Please, pay attention, don't use too much bass, and low notes. The church is so old that the vibrations, you see, could be very dangerous. Please, no bass ... and no strange combinations of notes, you understand."

diabolus in musica [956.23] the devil's interval: the tritone, the interval of the augmented fourth (e.g., c-f#). Its use was prohibited by early theorists.

eher wie der Jubelschrei der Erlösung [956.25] Everything moved, and even falling, soared in atonement: Koenig ("Recognizing Gaddis' *Recognitions*" 71) suggests this echoes the final lines of Rilke's *Duino Elegies*:

And we, who have always thought
Of happiness climbing, would feel
the emotion that almost startles
when happiness falls.

Abbreviated Sources and References

A&H: Bernard Berenson, *Aesthetics and History in the Visual Arts* (New York: Pantheon, 1948). One of Gaddis's sources for art theory.

AMM: William Richard Lethaby, *Architecture, Mysticism and Myth,* 2d ed. (1892; rpt. New York: George Braziller, 1975). An unusual survey of the mystical symbolism associated with various forms of architecture.

AN: Edgar Saltus, *The Anatomy of Negation* (1886; rpt. New York: Brentano's, 1925). A humanistic survey of atheism "from Kapila to Leconte de Lisle." (See note to 311.24 for Gaddis's use of this particular edition.)

ANT: The Apocryphal New Testament, ed. and trans. Montague Rhodes James (Oxford: Clarendon Press, 1924). See 23.26.

Baedeker: Karl Baedeker, *Spain and Portugal: Handbook for Travellers.* 4th ed. (Leipzig: Karl Baedeker, 1913). Both Frank Sinisterra (500.1) and Ludy (861.16) use this edition, as did Gaddis when in Spain in the late 1940s.

BM: Fox's Book of Martyrs: A History of the Lives, Sufferings and Triumphant Deaths of the Early Christian and the Protestant Martyrs, ed. William Byron Forbush (New York: Holt, Rinehart and Winston, 1926). See 26.28. It is this (or a similar) one-volume abridgement and updating that Gaddis used, not the unabridged edition in eight volumes. (Although this edition spells the author's name Fox, I shall use the more common Foxe, as does Gaddis.)

BS: George Borrow, *The Bible in Spain* (1843; London: Dent/Everyman's Library, 1961). An entertaining account of Borrow's experiences as an agent for the Bible Society in Spain in the 1830s. See 892.11.

CCP: Laurence Dwight Smith, *Counterfeiting: Crime against the People* (New York: Norton, 1944). Gaddis's major source for counterfeiting and the technical details of Frank Sinisterra's "art."

DDD: Howard W. Haggard, *Devils, Drugs, and Doctors: The Story of the Science of Healing from Medicine-Man to Doctor* (New York: Harper and Row, 1929). An account of the obstacles ignorance and religion have placed in the path of medical advancement.

DS: Denis de Rougemont, *The Devil's Share,* trans. Haakon Chevalier (New York: Pantheon, 1944). The influence of the devil on modern life and thought. "It is no more than an attempt to interpret certain shortcomings of our time by referring them to the activity of the only being to whom these can give cause for rejoicing" (4).

EB: *Encyclopædia Britannica,* 14th ed. (1929). Rev. Gwyon owns this edition (the Town Carpenter borrows volume 18 to read up on Prester John), and Gaddis drew upon it for a variety of details.

EPD: Charles Mackay, *Extraordinary Popular Delusions and the Madness of Crowds* (1841, 2d ed. 1852; rpt. New York: Farrar, Straus and Cudahy, 1932). Gaddis borrowed only a handful of details from this compendium of human folly, most from the chapter "The Alchymists" (98–256), whom Mackay considered self-deluded idealists at best.

Faust: Johann Wolfgang von Goethe, *Faust: A Tragedy,* Norton Critical Edition, trans. Walter Arndt, ed. Cyrus Hamlin (New York: Norton, 1976). Obviously not the edition used by Gaddis, whichever that might have been (perhaps the Bayard Taylor translation), but convenient for purposes of reference.

FRR: Jessie L. Weston, *From Ritual to Romance* (Cambridge Univ. Press, 1920; rpt. New York: Doubleday Anchor, 1957). A study of Grail symbolism; strongly influenced by Frazer's *Golden Bough* (below), it in turn strongly influenced T. S. Eliot's *The Waste Land.*

GAF: Riccardo Nobili, *The Gentle Art of Faking* (London: Seeley, Service, 1922). As the subtitle reveals, *A History of the Methods of Producing Imitations & Spurious Works of Art from the Earliest Times up to the Present Day.* (Both this book and Eudel's *Trucs et Truqueurs* – which supplies the epigraph to I.2 – are named in *EB*'s short bibliography on the "Detection of Fraud" [17:65].)

GB: Sir James George Frazer, *The Golden Bough: A Study in Magic and Religion,* abridged ed. (New York: Macmillan, 1922). An early, monumental study in comparative mythology.

HWF: Dale Carnegie, *How to Win Friends and Influence People* (New York: Pocket Books, 1940). The best-selling "synthesis of Christly conduct and Cartesian method to Machiavellian ends" (498:34–35). Cited by part and chapter.

Inferno: Dante Alighieri, *The Divine Comedy,* trans. John Ciardi (New York: Norton, 1977). Again, not the translation used by Gaddis, but convenient for reference.

IP: Carl G. Jung, *The Integration of the Personality,* trans. Stanley M. Dell (New York: Farrar & Rinehart, 1939). A description of the process of "individuation" by way of dream analysis and alchemical symbolism. Gaddis's principal source for alchemy.

LEP: Diogenes Laërtius, *Lives and Opinions of Eminent Philosophers.* See 81.7. Gaddis's source for anecdotal material on Greek philosophers. Cited by book number.

LWW: Denis de Rougemont, *Love in the Western World,* trans. Montgomery Belgion (New York: Harcourt, Brace, 1940). A "kind of outline-history of the cult of passion" and its conflict with marriage.

M: W. J. Phythian-Adams, *Mithraism* (London: Constable, 1915). This slight (95 pp.) study served as Gaddis's major source on the religion.

M&R: Andrew Lang, *Magic and Religion* (New York: Longmans, Green, 1901). A study in anthropology and comparative religion, much of which is devoted to refuting various theses put forth in the second edition of Frazer's *GB* (blithely ignored by Frazer in his third edition).

MM: Heinrich Kramer and James Sprenger, *The Malleus Maleficarum,* trans. and ed. Rev. Montague Summers (London: John Rodker, 1928). See 49.14.

MMM: Frederick Cornwallis Conybeare, *Magic, Myth and Morals: A Study of Christian Origins* (1909; I have used a modern reprint of the second, slightly revised edition of 1910, blandly retitled *The Origins of Christianity* [Evanston: University Books, 1958]). A study of the Gospels and the pagan atmosphere in which they were written, and a demonstration that Christianity owes more to the "hallucinations and transcendental fancies" of Paul than to the teachings of Jesus.

MMSM: George P. Marsh, *Mediæval and Modern Saints and Miracles* (1876; rpt. New York: Harper and Row, 1969). A semischolarly "exposé" of Catholic superstition with a strong anti-Jesuit bias. Gaddis drew upon it for details of Jesuit activity in France (I.2) as well as for some of the broader targets of Catholic ridicule. Gaddis's tongue-in-cheek relation of saints' lives and religious marvels is similar to Marsh's treatment.

ODQ: *The Oxford Dictionary of Quotations,* 1st ed., 6th impression (London: Oxford University Press, 1949). Gaddis owned this particular impression, given to him by Ormonde de Kay in Paris, 1950.

PC: Ruth Benedict, *Patterns of Culture* (Boston: Houghton Mifflin, 1934). A popular and well-regarded introduction to anthropology, the source for Rev. Gwyon's remarks on Native American beliefs.

PH: *The Pilgrim Hymnal* (Boston: Pilgrim Press, 1931). Cited by hymn number. Many of *R*'s Old Testament references can be found in the "Responsive Readings" section that follows the hymns.

PPM: Montague Summers, *The Physical Phenomena of Mysticism* (New York: Barnes and Noble, 1950). A scholarly (and orthodox, though lacking the imprimatur) but uncritical review of stigmatics and other curiosities of Catholic mysticism.

R: William Gaddis, *The Recognitions* (1955; rpt. New York: Penguin, 1993). Gaddis made about sixty corrections for the 1962 Meridian edition of *R*, and made another dozen or so for the 1985 Penguin edition, of which the 1993 edition is a reprint, with the addition of an introduction by William H. Gass, "Suggestions for Further Reading," and a dedication.

RM: José Ortega y Gasset, *The Revolt of the Masses*, trans. anon. (1932; rpt. New York: Norton, 1957). A call for the benevolent rule of an intellectual elite to counter the effects of the masses on art and government.

SL: William Tyler Olcott, *Star Lore of All Ages* (New York: Putnam's, 1911). Subtitled: *A Collection of Myths, Legends, and Facts concerning the Constellations of the Northern Hemisphere.* Gaddis used only the sections dealing with Sirius, Orion, Argo Navis, and the Pleiades.

S&W: Jules Michelet, *Satanism and Witchcraft: A Study in Medieval Superstition*, trans. A. R. Allinson (New York: Citadel, 1939). A translation of the French historian's classic *La Sorcière* and Gaddis's source for details on the Black Mass (see 372.31) and the titles of older studies of witchcraft.

VEF: Sir Martin Conway, *The Van Eycks and Their Followers* (New York: Dutton, 1921). With Huizinga's *WMA* (below), Gaddis's major source on the Van Eycks (Conway firmly believes in Hubert's existence: see his long footnote on p. 51) and other Flemish painters. *VEF* is listed in *EB*'s short bibliography on Van Eyck.

WG: Robert Graves, *The White Goddess: A Historical Grammar of Poetic Myth* (New York: Creative Age Press, 1948). A wide-ranging study of mythology, tree symbolism, and Celtic poetry.

WMA: J[ohan] Huizinga, *The Waning of the Middle Ages: A Study of the Forms of Life, Thought and Arts in France and the Netherlands in the 14th and 15th Centuries*, trans. F. Hopman (London: Edward Arnold, 1924). A highly regarded study of the religious and historical environment in which the brothers Van Eyck and their contemporaries worked; often cited in *LWW*.

WG/SM designates communications made to me by Gaddis over the years, especially a four-page letter dated 12 June 1983 in which he addressed a number of specific points in the first edition of this book. Other minor sources are cited in the body of the annotations; other Gaddis critics I cite are listed below.

All biblical references are to the Authorized (King James) Version, and all Shakespearean quotations are from G. B. Harrison's edition of *The Complete Works* (New York: Harcourt, Brace and World, 1968).

Secondary Works Cited

Abádi-Nagy, Zoltán. "The Art of Fiction CI: William Gaddis." *Paris Review* 105 (Winter 1987): 55–89.

Banning, Charles Leslie. "The Time of Our Time: William Gaddis, John Hawkes and Thomas Pynchon." Ph.D. diss., State University of New York at Buffalo, 1977.

Benstock, Bernard. "On William Gaddis: In Recognition of James Joyce." *Wisconsin Studies in Contemporary Literature* 6 (Summer 1965): 177–89.

Brownson, Robert Charles. "Techniques of Reference, Allusion, and Quotation in Thomas Mann's *Doktor Faustus* and William Gaddis's *The Recognitions*." Ph.D. diss., University of Colorado, 1976. Dr. Brownson also contributed a number of details during an interview on 24 February 1980.

Eckley, Grace. "Exorcising the Demon Forgery, or the Forging of Pure Gold in Gaddis's *Recognitions*." In *Literature and the Occult*. Ed. Luanne Frank. Arlington: University of Texas, 1977. 125–36.

Gaddis, William. *JR*. New York: Knopf, 1975.

A Frolic of His Own. New York: Poseidon, 1994.

Green, Jack. *Fire the Bastards!* Normal, IL: Dalkey Archive Press, 1992.

Koenig, Peter William [now David]. "'Splinters from the Yew Tress': A Critical Study of William Gaddis' *The Recognitions*." Ph.D. diss., New York University, 1971.

"Recognizing Gaddis's *Recognitions*." *Contemporary Literature* 16.1 (Winter 1975): 61–72.

"The Writing of *The Recognitions*." In Kuehl and Moore (below), 20–31.

Kuehl, John, and Steven Moore, eds. *In Recognition of William Gaddis*. Syracuse: Syracuse Univ. Press, 1984.

Minkoff, Robert L. "Down, Then Out: A Reading of William Gaddis's *The Recognitions*." Ph.D. diss., Cornell University, 1976.

Moore, Steven. "Chronological Difficulties in the Novels of William Gaddis." *Critique* 22.1 (1980): 79–91.

Das Papier dieses Buches, einschließlich Überzug
und Vorsatz, besteht zu 100 Prozent aus Altpapier. Das Kapitalband
und das Leseband wurden aus ungefärbter und
ungebleichter Baumwolle gefertigt.